Studies in Natural Language Processing

Relational models of the lexicon
Representing knowledge in semantic networks

Studies in Natural Language Processing

Executive Editor: Aravind K. Joshi

Sponsored by the Association for Computational Linguistics

This series publishes monographs, texts, and edited volumes within the interdisciplinary field of computational linguistics. Sponsored by the Association for Computational Linguistics, the series represents the range of topics of concern to the scholars working in this increasingly important field, whether their background is in formal linguistics, psycholinguistics, cognitive psychology or artificial intelligence.

Also in this series:

Memory and context for language interpretation by Hiyan Alshawi

Planning English sentences by Douglas E. Appelt

Computational linguistics by Ralph Grishman

Language and spatial cognition by Annette Herskovits

Semantic interpretation and the resolution of ambiguity by Graeme Hirst

Text generation by Kathleen R. McKeown

Machine translation edited by Sergei Nirenburg

Systemic text generation as problem solving by Terry Patten

Machine translation systems edited by Jonathan Slocum

Relational models of the lexicon

Representing knowledge in semantic networks

Edited by
MARTHA WALTON EVENS
Department of Computer Science
Illinois Institute of Technology

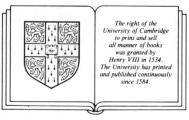

The right of the
University of Cambridge
to print and sell
all manner of books
was granted by
Henry VIII in 1534.
The University has printed
and published continuously
since 1584.

CAMBRIDGE UNIVERSITY PRESS

CAMBRIDGE

NEW YORK   NEW ROCHELLE

MELBOURNE   SYDNEY

Published by the Press Syndicate of the University of Cambridge
The Pitt Building, Trumpington Street, Cambridge CB2 1RP
32 East 57th Street, New York, NY 10022, USA
10 Stamford Road, Oakleigh, Melbourne 3166, Australia

First published 1988

Printed in Great Britain at the University Press, Cambridge.

British Library cataloguing in publication data

Relational models of the lexicon:
representing knowledge in semantic networks
– (Studies in natural language processing).
1. Lexicography
I. Evens, Martha Walton
413′.028

Library of Congress cataloguing in publication data

Relational model of the lexicon: representing knowledge in semantic
networks / edited by Martha Walton Evens.
    p.   cm. – (Studies in natural language processing)
1. Lexicology – Data processing   2. Semantics – Data processing.
I. Evens, Martha W.   II. Series.
P326.R44 1988
413′.028 – dc19   88-11883
CIP

ISBN 0 521 36300 4

US

To Leonard Evens

Contents

Acknowledgments

Preliminary versions of many of these papers were given at a Workshop on Relational Models held at Stanford University in conjunction with the 1984 International Conference on Computational Linguistics with financial and logistical support from the Association for Computational Linguistics. The workshop would never have happened without the help of Donald Walker and Martin Kay.

I learned about relational models from Oswald Werner and Raoul Smith at Northwestern University in company with Bonnie Litowitz, Madelyn Iris, and Judith Markowitz; all of them have contributed to this book in one way or another.

My own work on relational models would have been impossible without my colleagues, students, and friends at Illinois Institute of Technology: Thomas Ahlswede, Jeffrey Anderson, John Takao Collier, Michael Glass, Steven Gordon, Sharon King, Sun M. Li, Glenn Mayer, James Neises, Sumáli Pin-Ngern, Kay Rossi, Duc Bui Tran, and Yuemei Zhang.

Sumali Pin-Ngern, Yuemei Zhang, and Sarah Evens helped patiently in the physical preparation of the text. My husband, Leonard Evens, provided essential TEXpertise at all hours of the day and night. My own department and the Mathematics Department at Northwestern University let me use laser printers and copiers at extraordinary length.

Finally, I am grateful for material assistance in editing this volume from grant IST-85-10069 to Illinois Institute of Technology from the Information Science Division of the National Science Foundation.

1
Introduction

The lexicon has become a center of attention for those involved in all problems of language. Linguists have discovered that complete analyses of both syntax and semantics require a model of the lexicon. Anthropologists cannot describe a culture without talking about the vocabulary used by the participants in the activities of that culture. Psychologists examining the development and use of language have decided that the development and organization of the lexicon is an essential part of the picture. Computer scientists have discovered that large lexicons are a prerequisite for building computer systems that interact gracefully with human beings.

Linguists, who for a long time equated linguistics with syntax and viewed the lexicon as merely a convenient storage place for exceptions to syntactic rules, have finally discovered that much of the rest of the world is convinced that language resides in the lexicon and that the function of syntax is to provide a place to record lexical regularities. Two new theoretical approaches to language, Lexical Functional Grammar and Word Grammar, reflect this change and have helped to refocus attention on the lexicon.

Anthropologists are focusing on the problems of ethnography, which involves describing a cultural milieu in terms of its sublanguage. The first step is to build a lexicon for that sublanguage. In return, research in ethnography is providing us all with a methodology for eliciting lexical information from informants when written sources are not available or not complete.

Psychologists interested in the organization of memory are necessarily concerned with the organization of lexical and conceptual information, the ways in which we access this information, and the ways we use it to build cohesive discourse. They are also asking questions about the acquisition of lexical knowledge in human beings and the evolution of the ability to make definitions. Neural network research is providing more detailed models of lexical access and other natural language processes.

Computer scientists cannot build natural language processing systems large enough to handle real world problems without figuring out how to build larger and more detailed lexicons. The move from natural language front ends and text understanding systems to text generation, machine translation, and speech systems is making overwhelming demands for much more detailed lexical information about much larger vocabularies.

This book focuses on a collection of approaches to the lexicon that use relational semantics. Relational semantics is one of three major competing approaches to the study of meaning. The first approach views concepts as forming semantic fields or domains. This approach is essentially structural: a term is defined by its place in the field. Semantic fields have been useful in descriptive linguistics, but they do not provide a theoretical framework strong enough to use as a foundation for building lexicons for parsing and text generation.

The second approach includes componential and feature analyses. Here the focus is on those common features that enable items to form a domain and also on the different features that distinguish items in a domain from each other. Componential analysis works well for closely circumscribed domains like color terms, kinship terms, and personal pronouns, but it is of limited use when we are dealing with more complex lexical domains that contain words with overlapping meanings.

The third approach, the relational approach adopted in this book, accepts the existence of semantic domains, but attempts to make explicit the structural organization that is implicit in other models, and describes how the elements of a domain are related to each other. The links that connect the elements of the domain are called lexical or semantic relations. Relations between words are called *lexical relations*. Relations between concepts are called *conceptual* or *semantic relations*. Since words and concepts are inextricably intertwined the phrase *lexical semantic relations* is often used when it is unnecessary or impossible to make a distinction.

The most familiar lexical relations are *synonymy* and *antonymy*, which are often marked explicitly in dictionaries. Often *promise* and *pledge* are listed as synonyms of each other, while *hot* and *cold* are coded as antonyms. Many other lexical relations, such as *taxonomy, cause, child, part,* and *sequence*, appear implicitly in the dictionary, but are used more or less explicitly in discourse and in making inferences. For example, a *lion* is a (kind of) *mammal* (the concepts are taxonomically related); to *send* means to cause *to go*; a *cygnet* is a baby *swan*; a *petal* is part of a *flower*; and *Monday* is always followed by *Tuesday*. [See Evens et al. 1980 for more examples.] We can abbreviate this information with word-relation-word triplets as shown below. We can even picture these words as nodes in a network with relation names as labels on the arcs connecting them.

promise	SYN	pledge
hot	ANTI	cold
lion	TAX	mammal
to send	CAUSE	to go
cygnet	CHILD	swan
petal	PART	flower
Monday	SEQUENCE	Tuesday

This book attempts to include the best work in relational models from linguistics, anthropology, psychology, and computer science. The authors include not only university professors of anthopology, computer science, information science, linguistics, psychology, and Slavic languages and literatures, but also real-world experts on database interfaces and machine translation – and one whose job is making trucks talk to their drivers.

While the authors of the papers in this volume have all chosen to use relational models, they disagree on almost every other aspect of the care and feeding of the lexicon. The psychologists, naturally, are concerned to establish the psychological reality of relations, whereas most computer scientists think that psychological reality is irrelevant; what counts is computational convenience. The anthropologist Werner considers lexical relations only as a reflection of underlying conceptual relations, while Mel'čuk, a linguist, rejects relations that are "too semantic" as not sufficiently precise. Some agree with John White that all semantic problems can and should be solved with relational models; others like John Sowa combine relations freely with other kinds of models. But the focus of the greatest disagreement is the number of relations posited. Werner claims that all knowledge can be expressed in terms of just three relations: Modification, Taxonomy, and Queuing or Sequencing. Mel'čuk has precisely fifty-three. Evens and Ahlswede use more than 100 relations for adjectives alone. Efforts to resolve these controversies have led to much new research and debate.

This book is divided into three parts. The first part examines alternative structures for the lexicon. The second part explores the place of relational models in the representation of knowledge for a variety of applications. The papers in the last part investigate the nature of relations themselves.

The papers in the first part concentrate on the structure of the lexicon. This is an absorbing research problem for linguists and cognitive psychologists. It is also a crucial practical problem for anyone trying to construct a natural language processing system. The first chapter describes Igor Mel'čuk's revolutionary ideas about dictionaries. In the second Nicoletta Calzolari talks about the structure of the lexical database for Italian that she has constructed at the University of Pisa. In the third chapter Tom Ahlswede describes methods for the organization and construction of a lexicon for a medical sublanguage. Part I ends with a more theoretical and philosophically oriented paper about conceptual structures and John Sowa's approach via canonical graphs.

The papers in Part II use relations in the representation of knowledge for a variety of applications. Werner uses just three relations, *modification*, *taxonomy*, and *queuing*, to represent the whole variety of cultural knowledge acquired by C-KAD, his cultural knowledge acquisition device. Then Grimes tells us how to develop a relational database to store a lexicon full of relational material. The next chapter by John White uses relations to structure a machine translation system. Edward Fox explains how to improve the performance of an information retrieval system with a relational thesaurus. Bruce Ballard's chapter rounds off Part II with a description of the relational knowledge structure used in his natural language front end.

In Part III we turn from a study of ways to use relations as tools to an exploration of the nature of relations themselves. Should they be considered as atomic and indivisible or is it useful to try to analyze them into yet smaller components? What about important properties of relations like reflexivity, symmetry, and transitivity? Judith Markowitz leads off this part with an examination of the role that relations play in category judgments. Then Madelyn Iris and her colleagues take a careful look at the part-whole relation and decide that it is really a family of four relations – a solution that explains several of the contradictions surrounding this relation. In the next chapter, Roger Chaffin and Douglas Herrmann take a totally orthogonal approach to these same problems and propose that relations are themselves composed of smaller psychological components called relation elements. Then William Frawley gives a philosophical close to the book in an examination of metascience that illuminates the roles that relations play in the organization of the scientific vocabulary.

This introduction discusses some of the issues that arise in building relational models of the lexicon. Next comes a review of current research in the development of relational lexicons and an explanation of the place of the papers in Part I within this stream of research. The following section discusses the applications of relational lexicons illustrated by the papers in Part II. The last section describes some current research into the nature of relations and the contributions made to this research by the papers in Part III.

Issues in the design of relational models

Lexical vs. semantic relations

Semantic relations connect concepts; lexical relations connect words. While most models use a combination of lexical and semantic relations, some people have chosen to work with just one kind. People building memory models naturally concentrate on semantic relations. People building lexicons with words and phrases as entries need lexical relations primarily. Oswald Werner (Chapter 6) is trying to build a language universal memory model. It is not surprising that his relations are semantic. John Sowa (Chapter 5) is building canonical graphs as a part of a comprehensive memory model; his relations are also primarily semantic. On the other hand Mel'čuk (Chapter 2) and Calzolari (Chapter 3) are both involved in lexicography. Naturally their models stress lexical relations, as do the lexical databases designed by Ahlswede (Chapter 4), Grimes (Chapter 7) and White (Chapter 8).

Psychological reality vs. computational convenience

Anthropologist, linguists, and psychologists are all concerned with establishing the psychological reality of their models. Traditionally, confirmation of psychological reality comes from native speaker intuitions or from informant behavior given a variety of tasks. But this kind of evidence for psychological reality may be difficult to judge. Language behavior is so complex that models of entirely different structure can account for the same language phenomena [Morton and Bekerian 1986].

Computer scientists are split into two camps: those who are deliberately trying to model human behavior and take the question of psychological reality seriously, and those who view human psychology only as a possible source of useful algorithms and relations as a convenient structure for organizing a lexicon or accessing individual words. Edward Fox [1980, Fox et al. 1988] is ready to include any relation that can be useful in information retrieval, without reference to its ontological status. Ahlswede and Evens (Chapter 4) also add relations as it becomes convenient. The taxonomy relation is divided into three separate relations, one for nouns, one for verbs, and one for adjectives, since the machine-readable dictionary that is the source of their data uses different definition patterns for different parts of speech and the inference process that makes use of the relational information also uses different axioms for objects and predicates. Other relations are also treated in this way.

Zholkovsky and Mel'čuk [1967/1970], in a design for a system to do automatic paraphrase, discuss the possibility of adding new relations as needed but now (Chapter 2) insist that there are precisely fifty-three and that they have them all neatly categorized and listed. A conviction of the need for psychological reality seems to have crept up on them over the years. They do allow for flexibility in other ways – their relations can be combined in a number of ways, for which they give only a few examples, and they provide for *non-standard lexical functions*, which are too specific or too limited in range to be granted full status as lexical functions, but which are available for use in applications.

Markowitz, on the other hand, has always been convinced of the importance of establishing psychological reality. The work described in Chapter 11 is based on a large number of extensive interviews of human informants. She has also performed a series of studies on the development of definitions in children based on experience as a participant-observer and on transcriptions of taped sessions.

Discovery procedures

The commitment to psychological reality affects the methodology used to establish relations very strongly. Those who believe in the psychological reality of relations are very properly concerned with discovery procedures for determining them; those who view relations as a convenient lexical access method are content to invent them as needed.

The anthropologists Casagrande and Hale [1967] collected 800 folk definitions from a single informant in a study of dialect differences between Pima and Papago, two Uto-Aztecan languages of the American Southwest. They later realized that they had a valuable source of data for a study of semantics and began to examine the internal organization of the definitions themselves. They classified the definitions into thirteen relation categories, using consistent syntactic cues for each category. For example, all examples categorized as *antonymy* are adjectives defined by phrases of the form "not ...." Thus, low is categorized as "not high." As native speakers of English they propose a fourteenth relation, the *constituent* relation, where "X is defined as being as constituent or part of Y," which did not appear in their data. They classify "*stinger*: it stands on the end of his [the scorpion's] tail" as a spatial relation and "*horns*: cows have horns" as *exemplification*; not as *part-whole*. This rigid methodological standard helped to establish the reality of relations in their data and to provide a basis for the use of relations in ethnography.

Although John White's focus is on the application of relational models to machine translation (Chapter 8), he discusses his methodology for establishing relationships at length and insists that rigor in the collection of data is essential to produce results that will satisfy users of his system.

Smith [1981] describes a methodology for finding relations in machine-readable dictionary definitions that has been used in a number of experiments by Ahlswede [1985a], Evens et al. [1985, 1987], and Markowitz et al.

[1986], among others. Smith made an extensive study of defining formulae, those phrases that appear in many different definitions like "of or relating to ..." or "the quality or state of being...." Smith showed that these defining formulae provide reliable clues to lexical semantic relations. Thus we can use phrase counts and KWIC indices of definition texts to discover relations. These same tools give a way to judge the relative importance or at least the relative frequency of particular relations. Smith [1985] discovered, for example, that *act* is the most frequent noun in definitions of nouns in W7 and *part* is the second most frequent.

Paradigmatic vs. syntagmatic relations

The distinction between *paradigmatic* and *syntagmatic relations* has been debated for a number of years. Syntagmatic relations connect words that co-occur frequently; they are sometimes called collocation relations. Paradigmatic relations relate words that express the same meaning (or some part of that meaning) in some other form. In linguistics paradigmatic relations can be viewed as an extension of the relationships between members of a verb paradigm. *Swim* is paradigmatically related to *swam, swum, swims, swimming, swimmer, swimmingly,* and *bathe*. It is syntagmatically related to *water, pool,* and *bathing cap. Star* is paradigmatically related to *starry* and *sun,* while it is syntagmatically related to *shine* and *moon.*

The terms *paradigmatic* and *syntagmatic* have also been used by psychologists to characterize responses in word association and definition tasks. Some examples of paradigmatic responses are: *duck – drake, send – go,* and *lion – mane.* Some syntagmatic responses are: *duck – swim, send – money,* and *lion – roar.*

We get information about paradigmatic and syntagmatic relationships in different ways. Paradigmatic information typically appears in standing or generic sentences, that is, sentences that are always true:

> Adult male lions have manes.
> A drake is a male duck.

Syntagmatic information, on the other hand, appears most often in occasional sentences, sentences that describe particular situations.

> The lion roared in fury at being caged.
> We saw a family of ducks swimming in the pond.

Some models, like Fahlman's NETL, emphasize paradigmatic relations; others lay much more stress on syntagmatic relations [Smith 1984].

New research on bilingualism and new approaches to machine-translation have brought forward a new kind of paradigmatic relation, the *transfer re-*

lation. Transfer relations relate a word or phrase in one language to a semantically equivalent word or phrase in another language. There are many situations when a whole phrase is necessary in one language to translate what is expressed by a single word in another. Thus, the psychologists and computer scientists involved with translation models tend to be enthusiastic supporters of Becker's [1975] arguments for the phrasal nature of the lexicon. White gives a number of examples of the use of transfer relations in Chapter 8 from his work on machine translation. He argues for building a relational network of terms for each language in the machine translation system and then connecting these networks wherever possible with transfer relations.

Lumpers vs. splitters

The greatest debate is between the lumpers and the splitters – between those whose relational models contain a small number of fairly general relations and those whose models have a large number of specific relations. Generally, models with a smaller number of relations have more concept-based semantic relations such as the models of Sowa (Chapter 5) and Werner (Chapter 6). Models with a larger number of relations tend to be populated by more surface-oriented lexical relations, as in the models developed by Calzolari (Chapter 3), Ahlswede (Chapter 4), Grimes (Chapter 7) and White (Chapter 8). Some lexically-oriented models have families of relations with the same core meaning; for example, one relation for expressing noun-taxonomy, another for verb-taxonomy, another for adjective-taxonomy, etc. There are at least two reasons for this proliferation of relations. Where relations are motivated by defining formulae, the fact that nouns, verbs and adjectives are defined differently suggests different relations for different parts of speech. Alternatively, where relations are used heavily in inference making, different parts of speech require different predicate calculus axioms. For example, if A and B are nouns and A ISA B, then we need an axiom that says that $A(x) \Rightarrow B(x)$. If, on the other hand, A and B are two transitive verbs and A ISA B, we need an axiom of the form $A(x,y) \Rightarrow B(x,y)$.

At first glance it may seem that the lumpers have all the psychological reality on their side; they can certainly claim a large chunk. But if we look again, remembering the large number of relations proposed by those eminent psychologists George Miller and Philip Johnson-Laird [1976], a second glance suggests that the lumpers are allied with the mentalist camp in psychology, while the splitters are closer to the behaviorist side. Certainly, the easiest way to garner a large collection of relations is to treat each different syntactic strategy as signalling a separate relation.

Werner's system of only three relations (supplemented by the logical operators AND, OR, and NOT) is the smallest we are aware of (Chapter 6). Mel'čuk and Zholkovsky (Chapter 2) have exactly 53. Evens lists more than twice as many in an analysis of W7 [1981]. But Raoul Smith can definitely top that. In an analysis of adjectives defined in W7 with the formula "relating to," he identified twenty-three different adjective relations (corresponding to different adjective suffixes) [1981]. The effects of making choices among these alternatives are best seen in the designs for lexicon building described in the next section.

Constructing a relational lexicon

The process of actually building a lexicon raises not only the kinds of theoretical issues discussed in the previous section, but many immediate practical questions. The papers in the first part concentrate on the structure of the lexicon. This is an absorbing research problem for linguists and cognitive psychologists. It is also a crucial practical problem for anyone trying to construct a natural language processing system.

Computer technology has become so pervasive that almost everyone who constructs a lexicon today will use a computer as a tool, even when the goal is a printed book. This technological change implies that scholars working on lexical problems, whether they are anthropologists, commercial lexicographers, linguists, psychologists, or computer scientists are facing a common problem. Essentially all of us are, of necessity, in the process of constructing lexical databases. Two fundamental questions must be answered by everyone who starts out to construct a lexical database: What are your goals, that is, what is the database going to be used for? And where is the data going to come from?

The uses of lexical databases

What advantages does a lexical database on a computer give us that cannot be found in a print dictionary? If we look at the ordinary person who uses the computer only for word-processing, at first the benefits appear to be rather slight, seemingly limited to the convenience of having spelling correction, definitions, and hyphenation available online [Mark Fox et al. 1980]. With the addition of lexical relationships, however, the lexical database also becomes a thesaurus; thus word lookup is also available online.

Martin Kay [1983] has proposed a dictionary server as part of his plans for the dictionary of the future. Kay is talking about making available online whatever the dictionary user asks for – spelling, pronunciation, hyphenation, regular and irregular grammatical forms, idioms, relations and related words. The dictionary server may need a facility for synthesizing definitions; Evens et al. [1985] suggest ways of generating definitions using defining formulae.

The advantages for an advanced learner of English trying to write essays and business letters are more obvious. The new advanced learner's dictionaries have made some information explicit for the first time. They have been an important force in the construction of lexical databases. They are not, however, easy to use. It is necessary to search backwards and forwards for material, to memorize the symbols that designate fifty or one hundred verb patterns or to look them up every time you search for a new word. A lexical database can find the verb pattern information, present it in human-readable form and provide appropriate examples.

The kind of explicit information needed by advanced learners is precisely the kind of information needed by natural language processing programs. Information retrieval systems need relational thesauri to add index terms to queries. Natural language front ends and text understanding programs need verb pattern information and verb forms for parsing. Text generation systems need even more lexical data to generate coherent text [Collier et al. 1988]. Machine translation systems need lexical databases for both languages and a set of transfer relations to record bilingual correspondences.

There are already fairly good speech synthesis systems that can read text aloud [Church 1985]. But if such a system is to be able to handle a large range of text it needs a large lexicon with phonetic information.

Lexicographers need lexical databases both as a tool and a source for information in dictionary building.

Research psychologists need lexical information of at least two different kinds. People who are setting up word recognition experiments need collections of words that satisfy particular phonetic or syntactic criteria for subjects to recognize and combine in a variety of different tasks [Schreuder 1986]. Psychologists are also interested in definition material as a subject for study in itself to determine defining strategies and to infer memory models.

A lexical database encapsulates a great deal of information about the culture that created it. Anthropologists can find semantic fields and other ethnographic information organized for retrieval in a lexical database. Furthermore, a lexical database is an essential tool for making models of informants [Werner 1978].

Linguists need lexical databases to support the development of grammars both at the sentence and discourse level. But the most obvious use for lexical information is in the study of semantics by linguists and philosophers. John Olney [1968] made the first machine-readable dictionary by keypunching *Webster's Seventh Collegiate Dictionary* with a series of philosophical studies in mind. William Frawley (Chapter 14) is using a lexical database to study the philosophy of science – he finds lexical gaps and uses them to track scientific revolutions.

Sources of lexical data

The major sources of data are machine readable text, machine readable dictionaries, and human informants. If it is feasible to arrange for the human informants to use an interactive computer program then horrible problems of data transcription and data entry can be avoided or at least controlled. Unfortunately the most interesting informants, jungle story tellers, aphasic adults, and young children, cannot use such programs.

People from other fields who have seen the movie *2001* often think that their computer scientist colleagues ought to provide software/hardware combinations that can understand recorded speech. Unfortunately it seems likely that the research problems involved in making these facilities available will not be solved even by that date, now only thirteen years in the future.

The repository of text in the Oxford Text Archives has provided help for hundreds of researchers. There is now a serious effort to provide such an archive in the Western Hemisphere under the auspices of AITRC. In the meantime there is a growing body of machine-readable lexical data available as the result of a number of research projects. The problem is that each of these reflects the theoretical biases of its maker and may need significant translation to put it into a usable form.

Mel'čuk and his colleagues

The most revolutionary proposals for the design of the lexicon have come from the famous Soviet linguist, Igor Mel'čuk. He invented lexical functions (his name for lexical relations) twenty-five years ago when caught out in a rainstorm in the Russian countryside. He started to wonder about the fact that we say "heavy rain" but "bright lightning" and the first function (*Magn*) was born. He began to develop this idea systematically and came up with many more functions. He is responsible for the concept of the Explanatory Combinatorial Dictionary (formerly the Explanatory-Combinatory Dictionary, but always referred to as the ECD). The ECD is intended to give a detailed description of what it is that the native speaker knows about everyday vocabulary, a description so detailed that it gives non-native speakers enough information to write correct sentences. The ECD is termed *Explanatory* because it explains all forms and uses of the word and it is called *Combinatorial* because it tells how this word combines with other words in the language. Lexical-semantic relations, or lexical functions, as Mel'čuk calls them, are an important part of the entries in the ECD.

When the concept of the ECD first appeared in English in 1970 [Apresyan et al. 1970], it seemed to many linguists like an impossible dream, but Mel'čuk and his students had already begun work on it. When he left Russia for the University of Montreal, a 1200 page manuscript of an ECD for Russian with 2000 entries was smuggled out in an American diplomatic pouch. The Russian ECD was published in Vienna in 1984; a revised and translated version of the introduction appears as Chapter 2 of this volume. Mel'čuk and his colleagues in Montreal have also published two volumes of a French ECD [1984, 1988].

Moving from dictionary to lexical database in England

Although Mel'čuk, and indeed most linguists outside England, were unaware of it, the development of a remarkable series of dictionaries for the advanced learner was already underway in that country. It all began with A. S. Hornby, who edited the first edition of the *Oxford Advanced Learner's Dictionary of Current English* in 1948. He went on thinking of more useful information for non-native speakers and writers of English for a whole series of new editions. It was Hornby who thought of adding verb complement patterns to verb entries (eventually fifty of them describing all possible arguments of the verb). Full explanations of affixes are included along with irregular verb forms and plurals. Thousands of phrases and idioms appear, occasionally as main entries, but more often within other entries. Illustrative examples appear everywhere [Hornby 1980].

The Oxford University Press effort was such a success that one of their chief competitors in reference book publishing, Longman, hired Paul Procter [1978] to put together an advanced learner's dictionary for them, *The Longman Dictionary of Contemporary English* (LDOCE). A major innovation was the use of a controlled vocabulary of four thousand words. Along with an extensive set of verb patterns of its own, LDOCE lists adjective categories and gives semantic fields for all content words. Much of the editing was computerized, including programs to check the use of the controlled vocabulary and to control circularity in definitions. Procter was able to persuade Longman to make the dictionary tape available to researchers in linguistics in return for a carefully worded contract restricting use to research projects and a moderate sum of money. This generous program is now under the guidance of Della Summers, a well-known lexicographer. It has contributed significantly to the spurt of research work on the lexicon that has grown over the last ten years. The work of Michiels and Noel [1982, 1983] is based on the Longman source. More recently, Branimir Boguraev

1987, Boguraev et al. 1987] has developed a lexical database using data from LDOCE to support a large parser.

The ultimate in cooperation between academic research on language and the commercial lexicographer is the COBUILD Project, a joint enterprise of the University of Birmingham and Collins Publishers. Beginning in 1980 they set out to build a huge corpus of 7.3 million words with a reserve corpus of 13 million words. (The total of twenty million words is twenty times the size of the pioneering Kučera and Francis corpus [1967].) The corpus includes the first 70,000 words of 214 books plus selections from newspapers, magazines, and journals, and also transcripts of spoken language, mainly from radio interviews. The emphasis is on modern English (the source texts have all been written since 1960); the majority of the source texts are British, but the project deliberately included American, Australian, Indian, and South African English. A concordance was made of the whole corpus and every item is tagged with information about its source so that it is possible to pick examples for any dialect or register or sublanguage included in the corpus. The corpus has been used for a number of academic research projects, but the people on the Collins side have spent even more time and effort on constructing a huge lexical database from the corpus. A large number of programs to extract information from the corpus, construct database entries, and access database information have been built to support the lexicographers. Under the editorial direction of Patrick Hanks, Collins has already compiled and published an advanced learner's dictionary, the *COBUILD English Language Dictionary* [Sinclair 1987a]. This is planned to be the first in a series of bilingual and monolingual dictionaries to be derived from the database. The design, the organization, and the implementation of the COBUILD Project is described in a book edited by J. M. Sinclair [1987b].

These landmark efforts in lexical computing so stirred John Simpson and his staff working on the *Oxford English Dictionary* (OED) that they decided to build the new version of the OED using a lexical database. With the cooperation of the British branch of IBM and the University of Waterloo, they have built a huge database and a large collection of editorial tools. The New OED is now available on CD-Rom complete with retrieval tools and can now be addressed as a database by anyone with a large PC equipped with a CD-Rom reader. The plan is to maintain the dictionary and make it available in both print and electronic form indefinitely [Simpson 1985].

The Italian lexical database and other European developments

The most complete lexical database in the world is not English but Italian. It was built by Nicoletta Calzolari at the University of Pisa [Calzolari 1982, 1983a,b,c, 1984]. Working at first mainly by hand she has put together a lexical database for Italian with 106,000 word stems and 186,000 definitions. She has now developed a powerful set of tools both for constructing entries and for extracting information. Associated with each entry is a list of relation-word pairs. These impose on the database a relational network structure, through which every word in a given semantic field can be accessed from every other word in that field. By taking advantage of this relational structure and the web of information about derivation morphology already built into the database, it is now possible to add much information to the lexical database automatically, with merely an editorial check for correctness. The resulting database is a combination of a dictionary and a thesaurus provided with a variety of tools to support queries by linguists studying Italian and by computer programs working on all kinds of natural language processing tasks. Her paper in this volume (Chapter 3) describes the lexical relations that she uses and the organization of the relational network.

The work at Pisa has inspired work on lexical databases at a number of sites in Europe. One notable effort is the CELEX project, which is building lexical databases for English and for Dutch using the Oracle database management system.

Experiments in the United States

Modern developments in American lexicography began with Philip Gove's editorship of *Webster's Third New International*. When John Olney [1968] visited a number of American dictionary publishers trying to decide which one he wanted to work with, he chose the G&C Merriam Company family of dictionaries because of their large collection of citations and their systematic approach to compiling definitions. With a grant from the National Science Foundation he organized the production of a machine-readable form of the *Webster's Seventh Collegiate Dictionary* (a condensed version of the *Third International*) and the *Merriam-Webster Pocket Dictionary*. Olney's own goal was a number of philosophical studies of language [Olney et al. 1977], but much further work has been done on these tapes through the generosity of Olney and the Merriam Company in allowing others to use these materials.

While Philip Gove was compiling dictionaries for the G&C Merriam Company in Springfield, Massachusetts, Henry Kučera and Nelson Francis, not far away at Brown University, were planning to develop the largest possible corpus of contemporary English. They put together a million words of running text, choosing two thousand words each from a wide variety of recent sources including books, newspapers, and journals [Kučera and Francis 1967]. They made a concordance of every word in the text and eventually added grammatical tags. This corpus has provided valuable data about the language for all kinds of natural language processing projects ever since, in spite of its age.

More recently Kučera has collaborated with Howard Webber in the compilation of the new *Random House Dictionary* published by Houghton Mifflin. This effort was heavily supported by computers and Houghton Mifflin offers online access to the computerized version of the dictionary.

Raoul Smith, a student of Kučera and Francis at Brown, was one of the first to use Olney's tapes for extensive research. He made an intensive study of relations in adjective definitions in W7 [1981], while he was a Professor of Linguistics at Northwestern University. He left Northwestern for the GTE Research Laboratory in Waltham to apply relational models in the building of practical natural language interface systems. He left GTE to start the graduate program in Computer Science at Northeastern University. Now that he is a Professor of Computer Science there he has taken up his lexical research again. His [1985] paper on semantic primes derived from definitions in W7 has been particularly influential.

Robert F. Simmons of the University of Texas had already used relational models in a series of natural language systems for question-answering and text generation, when Robert Amsler persuaded him to start work on an analysis of the Merriam dictionary tapes [Simmons and Amsler 1975]. Amsler developed extensive taxonomies of nouns and verbs in the *Merriam-Webster Pocket Dictionary* [1980, 1981]. He has gone on to provide this field with an agenda and a new name, "computational lexicology" [1982]. A series of experiments with dictionaries, almanacs, and encyclopedias at SRI and at Bell Communications Research have paved the way for new ways of organizing reference information and for electronic access to reference books of all kinds [1984, 1987].

Thomas Ahlswede started out to be a printer but a life-long love of linguistics and a passion for computers led him to graduate school where he found Martha Evens (who had learned about relational models from Raoul Smith and Oswald Werner) struggling with a project to extract information for a thesaurus for an information retrieval system from a machine-readable dictionary. His master's thesis describes an experiment using Sager's [1981] Linguistic String Parser to parse adjective definitions from *Webster's Seventh Collegiate Dictionary* (W7) and extract information for a relational thesaurus [Ahlswede 1985a]. During the last few years he has published a stream of papers with Evens on the automatic extraction of syntactic and semantic information from W7 and the development of tools for automatic lexicon construction [1985b; Ahlswede and Evens 1988; Ahlswede et al. 1986], all of this while working for R. R. Donnelley & Sons, the world's most automated printing house. This work has recently resulted in a large grammar for W7 definitions, a large lexical database, and a Ph.D.

in Computer Science from Illinois Institute of Technology [1988]. Chapter 4 describes the application of some of these techniques to the building of a lexicon for an expert system.

During the last five years a group at IBM headed by Roy Byrd has done extensive research with both the W7 and the LDOCE tapes from which they also developed a lexical database [Chodorow et al. 1985].

BBN and ISI, two contract research corporations, based at opposite sides of the country, have cooperated to build a large lexicon containing enough explicit information so that lexicons can be derived from it to support several different parsing strategies, including an ATN parser at BBN and a systemic parser at ISI [Cumming 1986, Cumming and Albano 1986]. Another cooperative effort is going on at CSLI to build a lexicon to support several different kinds of parsers being constructed as part of research into new theories of grammar such as GPSG and LFG.

Canonical graphs

For a more theoretical approach to the problems of lexicon construction we turn to the work of John Sowa. Philosophers have always been concerned with the problem of meaning and the representation of knowledge. John Sowa tells us that Aristotle and Leibniz are the heroes of the first six chapters of his book on *Conceptual Structures*. "Aristotle was the founder of cognitive science," he says, and "Leibniz was the first proponent of artificial intelligence" [1984, p. vii]. Sowa has a background in philosophy but he teaches and does research in Artificial Intelligence and Computational Linguistics at the IBM Systems Research Institute.

Canonical graphs are similar to the case frames of case grammar, but they are generalized to handle all parts of speech, not just verbs. They are used to represent patterns of lexical relationships between concepts. The "combinatorial" information, as Mel'čuk would call it, is described in terms of a graph that can be entered and traversed from any node. Sowa's theory includes formal rules for manipulating the graphs both in parsing and in generation. His experiments in text generation [Sowa 1983] and parsing [Sowa and Way 1986] using these graphs have been widely discussed.

Applications of relational models of the lexicon

Applications fall into two fundamental categories: computer implementations of relational models constructed by anthropologists, linguists, and psychologists in order to investigate the implications of their theories or simply to store and manipulate data effectively; and lexicons and knowledge bases built by computer scientists, borrowing ideas from everywhere, for information retrieval, natural language interfaces, or other natural language processing projects. The papers in Part II describe a variety of applications of both types.

The branch of anthropology called ethnography, which concentrates particularly on the description of a culture in terms of its vocabulary, has made relational models more interesting to anthropologists. Relationships between lexical items are crucial to ethnographers. Anthropologists are also interested in text organization and differences and similarities between cohesive strategies in various cultures.

Frake [1964] used relations to analyze the results of a set of questions used for eliciting folk knowledge:

?k	–	What kind of X is it?
?w	–	What is X (a kind of)?
?u	–	What is X used for?
?i	–	What is the ingredient of X?
?p	–	What (separable/separated) part of X is it?
?s	–	What does X come from?

He proposed a model consisting of five bi-directional relations, derived from paired questions:

?k/?w	species-genus
?k/?u	species-use
?i /?u	ingredient-use
?p/?s	part-source
?u/?s	use-source

Williams [1966] organized a large semantic network with relations KIND, PART, and NAME to describe Japanese food, plant, season, and weather categories.

Casagrande and Hale [1967] collected 800 informal definitions in a study of dialect variation and categorized the definitions in terms of thirteen relations. In order of frequency the relations they found are: *attributive, contingency, function, spatial, operational, comparison, exemplification, class inclusion, synonymy, antonymy, provenience, grading,* and *circularity.*

Oswald Werner's work in ethnography began with the *Anatomical Atlas of the Navajo*, in wide use by the U. S. Public Health Service [1969/1981]. It is organized in terms of the part-whole relation and the taxonomy relation. Werner is a Professor of Anthropology at Northwestern, a former department chairman, and has also run their field school in the Southwest, while publishing a steady stream of papers in ethnography and writing a handbook for ethnographers.

In the process of carrying out a number of computer-aided experiments in the construction of a synthetic informant, he has decided that the ideal set of primitive relations consists of just three: M(*modification*), T(*taxonomy*), and Q(*queuing*). Other relations, he argues, can be analyzed in terms of these three. Synonymy between two terms *a* and *b* he describes as the limiting case of taxonomy, that is, the case where *a* T *b* and *b* T *a*. The part-whole relation he analyzes in terms of taxonomy: "A thumb is a kind of hand-part." Werner's queuing relation relates not only terms in generic lists like Monday and Tuesday or January and February, but consecutive portions of plans and narratives.

His paper in this volume, "How to Teach a Network," discusses the design of a learning device that can acquire new information and add it to a semantic network structured by his M, T, and Q relations. He proposes a minimal set of "built in" features needed to construct an ethnographic expert system learning about a new culture.

While Werner began with relational models of the lexicon and then later applied some of the same strategies to texts, the Cornell anthropologist Joseph Grimes has moved in the opposite direction. He is probably best known for his work on narrative structures in different cultures. His [1975] book, *The Thread of Discourse*, has provided a model for the study of narrative texts in English. He and his student Bonnie Meyer have developed a methodology for analyzing expository text in terms of textual relations as well. While he first used relational models at the text level, he is now applying these strategies to a comparative study of the lexicons of several American languages. He has also developed software to store his relational model of lexical data in a relational data base.

Grimes begins Chapter 7 by explaining how the power of the computer to represent knowledge in new ways has affected our understanding of lexical knowledge. "The attempt to understand the nature of the lexicon," he says, "is sometimes obscured by commercial limitations placed on the publication of dictionaries, which present certain information drawn from the lexicon in a stylized way. Now that information storage techniques allow us access to gigabytes, we are free to visualize just what information needs to be in the lexicon." He gives specifications for the representation of lexical knowledge in a relational database. This database was designed for a comparative study of the lexicons of several American languages, but his techniques would work equally well for organizing and storing other kinds of lexical knowledge. This chapter shows a powerful grasp of techniques in ethnography, linguistics, and computer science, which make it valuable reading for anyone who is trying to build a lexical database.

The last twenty years have seen the development of a number of relational models in linguistics. Fillmore [1971] set up a system of case relations to handle semantic problems that were not accounted for in transformational grammar. Fillmore's changes resulted in a verb-first or verb-favored deep structure and a model of the lexicon in which the verb entries include information about which cases can or must appear.

Chafe [1970] has further elaborated this approach, setting up separate systems for three different types of verbs – action, state, and process. Zholkovsky and Mel'čuk [1967/1970], before the adventures in lexicography described above, elaborated their collection of lexical functions in the process of designing a system for automatic paraphrase.

Lyons [1963] has extensive discussion of synonymy in which he puts forward an elaborate five-step methodology for mutual substitutability. In a later book [1968] he gives a careful discrimination of different kinds of antonymy and their logical implications. In his two volume work on semantics [1977], he comments on some of the problems of the part-whole relation and suggests that it may be not a single relation but a collection of relations. This last comment provoked some of us to the research that is described in Chapter 12.

Palmer [1976] played a significant role in popularizing relational models with his discussion of relations in what was designed to be an introductory book in semantics. He gives a cogent argument for dividing synonymy into five separate relations [1976:60-64]. The first is a kind of dialect transfer relation; it accounts for situations when words for the same concept originate in different dialects, e.g., *fall* and *autumn*. The second accounts for synonyms appropriate for different registers or roles; his examples are *a nasty smell, an obnoxious effluvium,* and *an 'orrible stink*. The third relates words that have the same cognitive meaning but different connotations, such as *thrifty* and *stingy*. The fourth kind of synonymy relates choices that collocationally determined; *butter is rancid* but *eggs are addled*. The fifth and last relates partial synonyms such as *promise* and *pledge*.

Some of these ideas spread rapidly from linguistics to psychology. Quillian [1968] developed a relational model of the lexicon as part of his thesis work with Marvin Minsky at MIT. Quillian was the first to recognize the need for a type-token relation connecting token nodes representing words used in definitions to the type node representing the concept. This led to a more fully developed model of the knowledge needed to use language [1969]. Collins and Quillian working together built a psychological model of memory [1972]. In their model concepts can overlap as in Venn diagrams; one consequence of their process of making inferences is that two concepts can be compared and found contradictory or similar, allowing for analogy and metaphor. Black, also working with Minsky over the same time frame, developed a relational model for logical deduction [1968]. Rumelhart, Lindsay, and Norman [1972] also developed a relational model of long term memory that includes narrative and episodic information. Kintsch [1974] has used relations to represent propositional information in memory. Perhaps the most complete relational model of memory was developed by George Miller and Philip Johnson-Laird in their book on *Language and Perception* [1976].

Computer scientists were quick to apply these models to problems in natural language processing. Bertram Raphael [1968] used a relational calculus as the basis of one of the first question answering systems, also developed as part of a thesis at MIT with Minsky. Robert Simmons [1973, Simmons and Slocum 1972] used a relational network as a basis for both question answering and text generation. Gary Hendrix, a student of Simmons at the University of Texas, developed partitioned networks and a more complete collection of relations to represent the knowledge base for a large experiment in speech understanding at SRI International [1975].

John White started out as an anthropologist at the University of Texas at Austin. There he met Robert Amsler, who was working with Simmons at the tremendous task of parsing the definitions in the *Merriam Webster Pocket Dictionary* and trying to organize the word senses into a taxonomic network. Amsler persuaded White to tackle the problem of disambiguating the word senses in the definitions using the emerging methods of ethnography [Amsler and White 1979]. When this research was complete he started to work on the machine translation project also based at the Linguistic Research Center at the University of Texas [1983]. The research described in Chapter 8 was completed while he was director of the Siemens Corporation METAL machine translation project.

The Siemens Corporation is developing a machine translation system that will translate a document from any one of nine European languages to any other of the nine languages. White tells us about his efforts to develop a large relationally structured multi-lingual terminology bank to handle the translation of technical terms. His approach uses ethnographic techniques from anthropology and the linguistic notion of collocation. While some disambiguation is performed by hand, much of the data is extracted automatically from a machine-readable dictionary. When Siemens moved the project out of Texas, White went to work for Martin Marietta.

Computer scientists trying to do new kinds of language processing must build lexicons to support tasks like question answering, automatic paraphrase, machine translation, and text generation. Small-scale experiments in these areas have succeeded. The problem of designing and creating a lexicon containing all the syntactic and semantic information to support natural language processing over a broad range of subject matter is a center of concern for the community and the focus of many of the papers in this collection. Research in information retrieval is leading the way; Fox and Evens are trying to build a large-scale relational thesaurus for information retrieval [Wang et al. 1985; Evens et al. 1985; Fox et al. 1988].

Edward Fox learned about relational models at Cornell while working with Gerard Salton, the father of information retrieval in the United States. Zholkovsky, Mel'čuk's collaborator in the design of the ECD, was then head of Slavic Studies there and Mel'čuk visited Cornell often from his headquarters at the University of Montreal. Fox has used relational models in a series of experiments in information retrieval (Chapter 9). The context of these experiments is a collection of documents with users searching for information on particular subjects. The information retrieval system already contains lists of words and phrases occurring in the documents. Once the query has been typed in, the information retrieval system matches the words and phrases in the query with the words and phrases in the documents and picks out those documents that give the best match.

Fox [1980] has done an experiment in which thirty-five natural language questions were enriched by adding terms from a relational thesaurus. The system did a significantly better job in retrieving the relevant documents from a collection of 1460 papers in information science using the enriched queries than it did with the original questions.

The success of this semantic approach has potentially important consequences for information retrieval. But to apply this research to a large scale information retrieval system requires the development of a relational thesaurus involving a huge vocabulary. Fox is now at Virginia Polytechnic Institute after a year of teaching in Nigeria and he has started working on methods for deriving a thesaurus from a machine-readable dictionary [Fox et al. 1988].

Relational models seem especially natural in question-answering applications. Thus they seemed like a reasonable approach to Bruce Ballard (Chapter 10) as he tried to solve an engineering problem. He had developed a simple but elegant natural language interface. Then he decided to make that interface retargetable – make it easy to transport to new application domains. When he started to characterize the domain knowledge necessary for a particular interface, he discovered that it fell naturally into a taxonomic hierarchy. It was not until he had reinvented much of this theory for himself that he discovered the literature on relational models. The development of a large taxonomically organized lexicon would make it much easier to retarget his interface.

In previous work Bruce Ballard developed a natural language interface for office databases called the Layered Domain Class (LDC) system [1982, 1984, 1986]. Chapter 10 is directed at the problem of enabling users to transfer this interface to new databases. The additional lexical entries needed for the new database are elicited from the user by a menu-driven program that then organizes this information in the special relational network used by LDC.

Ballard earned his Ph.D. at Duke with the computational linguist, Alan
Biermann, whose work with voice interfaces to software systems is particularly well-known. After teaching for two years at the Ohio State University,
he returned to Duke and began his work on interfaces. His paper in this
volume describes his use of taxonomy in making retargetable interfaces.
He is currently continuing this research at the AT&T Bell Laboratories at
Murray Hill.

The nature of relations

In this section we turn to the question of the nature of lexical semantic
relations themselves. The possible range of answers depends on whether
the relations in question are relations between concepts ("purely semantic")
or relations between words ("purely lexical") or somewhere in between.

Anthropologists, psychologists, and linguists have all been concerned
about the fundamental nature of the tools that they have employed in
model-building. Among anthropologists Werner, in particular, has been
concerned to establish the universal nature of his system of relations, which
consists of Modification – Taxonomy – Queuing (MTQ) and certain Boolean
relations from the propositional calculus. He has used this system in the
analysis of texts in languages as far apart as Navajo, English, Hungarian,
and Rapa Nui (Easter Island) and his students have used these relations
to study texts from a number of African languages as well [Werner and
Schoepfle 1987].

Riegel [1970] was one of the first psychologists to use relational models
to describe the organization of memory. He was revolutionary in another
way as well; he looked at language and memory not in children or college
students but in mature adults. He also studied the dissolution of language
in the aging and in aphasics. Riegel divided relations into two fundamental
categories depending on their "nature." *Logical relations* are derived by abstraction from the words themselves. Some examples of logical relations are
superordination (as in *table-furniture*) and coordination (as in *table-chair*).
Infralogical relations or physical relations are based on the denoted objects,
events, or qualities, and are a product of abstracting physical features from
items. Some examples of Riegel's infralogical relations are: parts (as in
table-leg, locations (as in *zebra-Africa*), and substance (as in *table-wood*).

Mel'čuk seems to make the same distinction, at least tacitly, with a distinct preference for the logical as opposed to the infra-logical. When asked
why he does not include the part-whole relation among his collection of
lexical functions, he explained [personal communication] that part-whole is
"too semantic" and "too vague."

Intension/extension

The perception of the nature of relations depends on whether the terms they relate are viewed intensionally or extensionally. The extension of a term is the set of things it names. The anthropologist Paul Kay [1971] treats the nodes of a taxonomic tree as collections of objects. In contrast, the intension of a term is the set of attributes it involves. From the intensional point of view which Werner and Topper [1976] take as primary, taxonomy relates sets of attributes, not sets of objects.

When A dominates B in a taxonomy, the extension of A, that is, the set of things named A, includes the extension of B. For example, the set of all dogs contains the set of all beagles. As Lyons [1968] has noted, inclusion points in the opposite direction for intension; the intension of B includes the intension of A. The intension of the term *beagle* contains all the attributes of the intension of *dog* and a good many more.

Effects of the nature of the objects in the model

We have been assuming that the relational models in question and the relations that inhabit these models involve single words and concepts. But relational models are now being used increasingly often to represent larger lexical and conceptual objects; sometimes these objects require a very different set of relations from those we have looked at so far.

Often lexical items are not just "single words," items which appear in text as strings of alphabetic characters bounded by spaces and punctuation marks. Becker [1975] has made a strong case for the phrasal lexicon, with the argument that when we produce language we seem to use much larger units, sometimes even whole preformed sentences. Professional lexicographers seem to agree; more than ten percent of the entries in W7 are headed by multi-word expressions. People who work on machine translation are also already convinced that they need to store many idiomatic phrases. Admission of multi-word lexical items to a relational lexicon is likely to require a richer stock of relations to describe the organizational structure of the lexicon.

It is when the underlying concepts are enlarged to include narratives and expository arguments that we are likely to find a multitude of new relations. Rumelhart, Lindsay, and Norman [1972] constructed relational memory maps of narratives, using story grammars that include relations such as "setting," "event," and "reaction." Bonnie Meyer, a student of Joseph Grimes at Cornell, has used relational models to describe the organization of expository prose [1975, 1985], with a set of rhetorical relations that include "explanation," "evidence," and "analogy." Perhaps the most complete relational model is contained in Miller and Johnson-Laird's book on *Language and Perception* [1976], which attempts to give a relational basis for the organization in memory of lexical, narrative, and expository information.

Properties of lexical semantic relations

If we view relations for the moment as mathematical objects, as sets made up of pairs of words or concepts, then we can exploit certain mathematical properties of these relations. Scholars differ about whether this kind of formalism is appropriate or useful in the midst of an essentially semantic enterprise. Even those who are enthusiastic about formal logical approaches argue about whether we should be sticking to an essentially relational calculus or seeking a way to combine relational operations with the predicate calculus. Raphael's [1968] question-answering system, SIR, was based entirely on a special purpose relational calculus, but Werner (Chapter 6) combines the relational and the propositional calculi.

Let us look briefly at some of the advantages to be gained from considering some of the more obvious mathematical properties of relations. Do they have inverses? Are they reflexive, symmetric, transitive? Are they one-to-one? To be more precise:

— The relation S is the *inverse* of the relation R if whenever xRy we know immediately that ySx. Consider the CHILD relation for which we have examples: puppy CHILD dog, kitten CHILD cat, lamb CHILD sheep, cygnet CHILD swan, and acorn CHILD oak.

puppy	CHILD	dog
kitten	CHILD	cat
lamb	CHILD	sheep
cub	CHILD	lion
cygnet	CHILD	swan
acorn	CHILD	oak

— The inverse of the child relation is the parent relation and just by reversing the examples given above, we get:

dog	PARENT	puppy
cat	PARENT	kitten
sheep	PARENT	lamb
lion	PARENT	cub
swan	PARENT	cygnet
oak	PARENT	acorn

— The relation R is said to be *reflexive* if and only if every item in its domain of definition is related to itself, that is, xRx for every x ∈ D. Thus the part-whole relation can be considered to be reflexive, since everything is a part of itself.

— The relation R is said to be *symmetric* if and only if whenever x is related to y, you can be sure that y is also related to x, that is if xRy always implies that yRx. The synonymy relation behaves this way. If we know that pledge is a synonym of promise, then we also know that promise is a synonym of pledge. Symmetric relations are their own inverses, which gives us a strong motive for keeping track of the symmetry property.

— The relation R is said to be *transitive* if and only if, whenever we know that xRy and yRz, we also know that xRz. The taxonomy or ISA relation is certainly transitive. If we know that a lion is a kind of mammal and a mammal is a kind of vertebrate, then we know that a lion is a kind of vertebrate.

— The relation R is said to be *one-to-one* if and only if, whenever xRy and zRy, we know that x and z must be the same, and also, if xRy and xRz, we know that y and z must be the same.

The one-to-one property was used by Bertram Raphael [1968] in his SIR (Semantic Information Retrieval) program. This property, which he called the *unique linkage property*, allowed him to make inferences of the variety: "If x is just-to-the-left-of y and z is not the same as x, then z is not just-to-the-left-of y."

But it is the transitivity property that has been most heavily used in inference-making. Fahlman's NETL system [1979] used the transitivity of the ISA relation and the transitivity of the part-whole relation (in geographical applications) as its major deductive strategies.

The *inheritance of attributes*, a major principle in many artificial intelligence systems, derives from the transitivity of the taxonomy (ISA) relation. If we know that a beagle is a kind of dog and a dog is a kind of mammal, then the standard attributes of dogs and mammals can immediately be attributed to beagles. Why? It is the transitivity of taxonomy that tells us that beagles are mammals. Frame systems are often organized as hierarchies in order to make use of this property.

Ways that relations interact

Some systems use not only properties of relations in inference-making, but information about interactions between relations. Raphael [1968] used such interactions extensively. There is a very useful interaction between the part-whole relation and taxonomy.

- If for all x, y, and z, x ISA y and z PART y, then z PART x.

For example, if we know that all dogs are mammals and that all mammals have hair then we can conclude that all dogs have hair.

The relations just-to-the-left-of and just-to-the-right-of are inverses of each other. Therefore,

- A is just-to-the-right-of B if and only if B is just-to-the-left-of A.

So if a system is told that the lamp is just to the left of the sofa it can conclude that the sofa is just to the right of the lamp.

The individual-set and taxonomy relations interact also.

— If x is in the set y and y ISA z then x is in the set z.

For example, if we know that Sheila is a beagle and that a beagle is a kind of dog, then we can conclude immediately that Sheila is a dog. Some people, Werner among them, do not distinguish between the individual-set relation and the taxonomy relations. For these, the above is just another example of the transitivity of the taxonomy relation. Category membership, in fact, has led to a lot of arguments between linguists, psychologists, and philosophers.

Category membership

The question of category definition has long been recognized as a crucial problem in semantics. Research has shown that categories like *animal* do not have rigid membership criteria but a continuum of grades of membership. Zadeh [1965] developed fuzzy set theory to model judgments about degrees of membership. Rosch [1978] developed a feature-based theory of prototypes to describe the same phenomenon. Judith Markowitz has used a relational approach to develop a model of the way categories are defined and how they are used to make membership judgments.

Chapter 11 describes a set of experiments that Markowitz designed to elucidate the structure of concepts underlying common categories, such as birds and furniture. She interviewed a number of adult subjects, questioned them about category membership and asked them to perform a ranking task. She then analyzed her subjects' responses in terms of the lexical-semantic relations, synonymy, taxonomy, antonymy, modification, function, part-whole, and agent. The results demonstrate that specific relations or factors are significant for entire classes of categories. Specific lexical semantic relations are important within and across categories and others are not. Her results also provide important insights into why certain category members are better exemplars. She winds up with a most attractive hypothesis about the conceptual structure of categories and the way in which typicality is characterized based on a relational foundation.

Markowitz earned a Ph.D. in Linguistics at Northwestern University and also a certificate in speech therapy. She did extensive work with aphasic patients at a Chicago hospital, most of them stroke victims. She then became a professional folksinger and a linguistic consultant to local advertising agencies (which needed help in finding and evaluating names for products). An M.S. in Computer Science led to a position at Navistar International Transportation Corp., where she is now head of an artificial intelligence project. In addition to the work on the structure of the adult lexicon described in Chapter 11, she has collaborated with Rae Moses of Northwestern University and others on several studies of lexical organization in elementary school children [Markowitz and Moses 1981; Markowitz 1982; Markowitz and Franz 1988]. She has also coauthored a book on lexical semantic relations [Evens et al. 1980] and a number of studies of definitions based on machine readable dictionary tapes [Markowitz et al. 1986].

Slicing relations vertically and horizontally

Several prominent linguists have discussed the nature of relations also, most notably Lyons [1977] and Cruse [1979, 1986]. Both Lyons and Cruse addressed some of the problems posed by the part-whole relation. One problem is that it is sometimes transitive and sometimes not. There is also wide disagreement about whether it should be considered as a logical primitive. The well-known philosopher and logician Tarski [1937] treated it as a primitive and provided it with a set of axioms (including transitivity). Mel'čuk, however, does not list it among his lexical functions, as we mentioned above. In spite of these dilemmas, most students of relations, except for Lyons, have taken it for granted that there is a single relation that can be called the "part-whole relation."

The papers by Iris, Litowitz, and Evens (Chapter 12) and Chaffin and Herrmann (Chapter 13) both address these problems and both chapters develop theories that divide up the part-whole relation into separate pieces. But beyond this point they take orthogonal approaches and they disagree completely about their resulting models. Iris and her colleagues have identified four different aspects of the part-whole relation and developed models to describe the meaning of each. In a sense they have made vertical slices through the part-whole relation to come up with four separate relations, each embodying a different aspect of the part concept.

Chaffin and Herrmann take an orthogonal approach - their slices are horizontal instead of vertical. They analyze relations in terms of atomic properties or features. Each familiar relation is defined as a constellation of relational features or properties. Chaffin argues that his analytic theory of relations can explain why some relations are ambiguous and why people can identify systematic similarities between relations. This strikingly original approach has the potential of changing our fundamental concepts about relations. It opens up many new lines of research into the nature of relations.

These two papers not only attack the analysis of relations from opposite directions, they come to different conclusions about several important issues, such as the transitivity of the part-whole relation. This may be partly because they have such different methodological approaches. Chaffin and Herrmann are cognitive psychologists working with test results from experiments using a number of different sorting tasks and discrimination tasks. Iris is an anthropologist working from dictionary data in collaboration with a linguist and a computer scientist.

Despite the differences between these two papers, there is a deep continuity between them as well. Iris et al. point out the inconsistencies in what has traditionally been considered a single relation, identifying a few similar but not identical relations - a "family." For Chaffin and Herrmann the existence of a family of relations is a given and they are concerned with its implications. if some relations are more alike than others, if some relations share properties not shared by others, then it can be argued that these properties constitute the internal structure of relations, or perhaps that relations can be characterized by their properties, somewhat in the manner of fundamental particles in physics. For Chaffin and Herrmann, then, the relation elements are entities with some reality and interest apart from the relations they characterize; for Iris et al. relations remain primary and their properties are of little interest viewed in isolation.

Madelyn Iris, a student of Oswald Werner, has used relational models in the study of child language both among the Navajo and in Israel, and also in an examination of the development of defining strategies in speakers of English [Iris et al. 1988]. More recently she has been involved with the Erikson Institute in making ethnographic studies and evaluations of several public service agencies in the Chicago area.

Bonnie Litowitz [1977], the former dean of the Erikson Institute, now back at Northwestern University, has studied the acquisition of concepts and defining strategies in children using relational models. She is a co-author of Iris' paper on the part-whole relation.

When Chapter 13 was written, Roger Chaffin was working for the Educational Testing Service, on leave from his regular position at Trenton. His research has been enriched by his experiences there looking at how analogy questions are invented and solved. He has written a number of papers about relations with his colleague, Douglas Herrmann, Professor of Psychology at Hamilton College [1984, 1987, 1988].

From relations to scientific revolutions

William Frawley is a spokesman for a school of the philosophy of science that believes that a study of the lexicon of a particular science is the best way to discover its conceptual structures. The same conviction was part of the motivation that drove the philosopher John Olney to produce the machine readable version of *Webster's Seventh Collegiate Dictionary* and to analyze the structure of its vocabulary. Frawley discovered relational models as a student of Raoul Smith at Northwestern University. He is now a Professor of Linguistics at the University of Delaware.

Frawley argues that the conceptual structure of the sciences is revealed by the structure of their lexicons. Using a relational model he analyzes the clustering of concepts and relations in particular scientific disciplines, such as the predominance of *part/whole* in biology. His analysis reveals the existence of lexical gaps, which, he suggests, are loci for semantic and conceptual innovations in the sciences. This analysis leads him to propose the use of relations as a meta-language in a descriptive philosophy of science [Frawley 1981, 1987].

The system of relations he uses for this study is Mel'čuk's set of lexical functions. Thus the last chapter of this book returns at least partly to the theme of the first with a discussion of the relations of the ECD – but with a very different focus.

Summary

The papers in this volume describe attempts to solve problems in lexicography in these various disciplines by means of relational models. These models are used in the design of the lexical entry for multilingual and monolingual dictionaries, in the analysis of language at the level of individual words, sentences, and full-scale texts, in the study of cultures western and exotic.

Relational models have proved to be easy to use and adaptable to a large number of different purposes in several different fields. The purpose of this book is to illustrate some of the successes and some of the problems, with the conviction that still others can use relational systems to their advantage, and with the hope that we can all learn from each others' insights and avoid each others' mistakes.

Even though the authors of these chapters come from diverse fields with very different goals, they express a common theoretical perspective: the belief that semantic problems cannot be solved until we have a sound basis for lexical semantics and the conviction that relational models can capture an essential component of meaning. Individually they enhance our understanding of the representation of knowledge. Together they demonstrate the power of relational models of the lexicon.

References

Ahlswede, Thomas. 1985a. A Linguistic String Grammar of Adjective Definitions. In S. Williams, ed., *Humans and Machines: The Interface Through Language*, Ablex, Norwood, New Jersey, 101-127.

Ahlswede, Thomas. 1985b. A Tool Kit for Lexicon Building. *Proceedings of 23rd Annual ACL*, Chicago, 268-275.

Ahlswede, Thomas. 1988. *Syntactic and Semantic Analysis of Definitions in a Machine-Readable Dictionary.* Ph.D. thesis, Department of Computer Science, Illinois Institute of Technology.

Ahlswede, Thomas, Evens, Martha, Markowitz, Judith, and Rossi, Kay. 1986. Building a Lexical Database by Parsing Webster's Seventh Collegiate Dictionary. *Advances in Lexicology.* University of Waterloo, Centre for the New OED, 65-78.

Ahlswede, Thomas, and Evens, Martha. 1988. Generating a Relational Lexicon from a Machine-Readable Dictionary. *International Journal of Lexicography,* special issue edited by William Frawley and Raoul Smith.

Amsler, Robert A. 1980. *The Structure of the Merriam-Webster Pocket Dictionary.* PhD Thesis, Austin: University of Texas.

Amsler, Robert A. 1981. A Taxonomy for English Nouns and Verbs. *Proceedings of the 19th Annual Meeting of the ACL,* Stanford, CA, June, 133-138.

Amsler, Robert A. 1982. Computational Lexicology: A Research Program. *Proceedings of the National Computer Conference,* Houston, May, AFIPS, 657-663.

Amsler, Robert A. 1984. Machine-Readable Dictionaries. In Williams, Martha E., ed., *Annual Review of Information Science and Technology,* ASIS, 161-209.

Amsler, Robert A. 1987. How Do I Turn This Book On? Preparing Text for Access as a Computational Medium. In *The Uses of Large Text Databases.* Waterloo: the University of Waterloo Centre for the New Oxford English Dictionary, 75-88.

Amsler, Robert, and White, John. 1979. *Development of a Computational Methodology for Deriving Natural Language Semantic Structures via Analysis of Machine-Readable Dictionaries.* NSF Technical Report MCS77-01315.

Apresyan, Yuri, Mel'čuk, Igor, and Žolkovsky, Alexander. 1970. Semantics and Lexicography: Towards a New Type of Unilingual Dictionary. In Ferenc Kiefer, ed., *Studies in Syntax and Semantics,* Dordrecht Holland: Reidel, 1-33.

Ballard, Bruce. 1982. A "Domain Class" Approach to Transportable Natural Language Processing. *Cognition and Brain Theory,* 5, 3, 269-287.

Ballard, Bruce. 1984. The Syntax and Semantics of User-Defined Modifiers in a Transportable Natural Language Processor. *COLING84* Stanford University, July, 52-56.

Ballard, Bruce. 1986. User Specification of Syntactic Case Frames in TELI, A Transportable, User-Customized Natural Language Processor. *COLING86*, University of Bonn, August, 454-460.

Becker, Joseph. 1975. The Phrasal Lexicon. In Roger Schank and Bonnie Nash-Webber, eds., *Theoretical Issues in Natural Language Processing*, Association for Computational Linguistics, 38-41.

Black, Fischer. 1968. A Deductive Question-Answering System. In M. Minsky, ed., *Semantic Information Processing*. Cambridge, MA: MIT Press, 354-402.

Boguraev, Branimir, 1987. Experiences with a Machine-Readable Dictionary. *The Uses of Large Text Databases: Proceedings of the Third Annual Conference of the UW Centre for the New OED*. Waterloo: University of Waterloo Centre for the New Oxford English Dictionary, November, 37-50.

Boguraev, Branimir, Briscoe, Ted, Carroll, John, Carter, David, and Grover, Claire. 1987. The Derivation of a Grammatically Indexed Lexicon from the Longman Dictionary of Contemporary English. *Proceedings of the 25th Annual Meeting of the ACL*, Stanford, CA, July, 193-200.

Calzolari, Nicoletta. 1982. Towards the Organization of Lexical Definitions on a Data Base Structure. *COLING82*, Prague: Charles University, 61-64.

Calzolari, Nicoletta. 1983a. Semantic Links and the Dictionary. *Proceedings of the Sixth International Conference on Computers and the Humanities*, Raleigh, North Carolina, 47-50.

Calzolari, Nicoletta. 1983b. Lexical Definitions in a Computerized Dictionary. *Computers and Artificial Intelligence*, **II**, 3, 225-233.

Calzolari, Nicoletta. 1983c. On the Treatment of Derivatives in a Lexical Database. *Linguistica Computazionale*, **III**, Supplement, 103-113.

Calzolari, Nicoletta. 1984. Detecting Patterns in a Lexical Data Base. *Coling84*, Stanford University, Association for Computational Linguistics, 170-173.

Casagrande, Joseph, and Hale, Kenneth. 1967. Semantic Relations in Papago Folk Definitions. In Dell Hymes and W. E. Bittle, eds., *Studies in Southwestern Ethnolinguistics*. The Hague: Mouton, 165-196.

Chafe, Wallace. 1970. *Meaning and the Structure of Language*. Chicago: Chicago University Press.

Chaffin, R. and Herrmann, D. J. 1984. The Similarity and Diversity of Semantic Relations. *Memory and Cognition*, **12**, 134-141.

Chaffin, Roger, and Herrmann, Douglas J. 1987. Relation Element Theory: A New Account of the Representation and Processing of Semantic Relations. In D. Gorfein and R. Hoffman, eds., *Learning and Memory: The Ebbinghaus Centennial Conference.* Hillsdale, NJ: Erlbaum, 1986.

Chaffin, Roger, and Herrmann, Douglas J. 1988. Effects of Relation Similarity on Part-Whole Decisions. *Journal of General Psychology,* **115**, 131-139.

Chodorow, Martin, Byrd, Roy, and Heidorn, George. 1985. Extracting Semantic Hierarchies from a Large On-line Dictionary. *Proceedings of the 23rd Annual Meeting of the ACL,* Chicago, June, 299-304.

Church, Kenneth. 1985. Stress Assignment in Letter to Sound Rules for Speech Synthesis. *Proceedings of the 23rd Annual Meeting of the ACL,* Chicago, June, 268-276.

Collier, J., Evens, M., Hier, D., Li, P-Y. 1988. Generating Case Reports for a Medical Expert System, to appear in the *International Journal of Expert Systems.*

Collins, Alan, and Quillian, M. Ross. 1972. How to Make a Language User. In E. Tulving and W. Donaldson, eds., *Organization of Memory.* New York: Academic Press, 310-354.

Cruse, D.A. 1979. On the Transitivity of the Part-Whole Relation. *Journal of Linguistics,* **15**, 29-38.

Cruse, D.A. 1986. *Lexical Semantics.* Cambridge: Cambridge University Press.

Cumming, Susanna. 1986. Design of a Master Lexicon. USC/ISI. Report to the National Science Foundation. In xerograph.

Cumming, Susanna, and Albano, R. 1986. A Guide to Lexical Acquisition in the JANUS System. USC/ISI. Report to the National Science Foundation. In xerograph.

Evens, Martha. 1981. Structuring the Lexicon and the Thesaurus with Lexical-Semantic Relations. Final report to the National Science Foundation on grant IST-79-18467. In xerograph.

Evens, Martha, Litowitz, Bonnie, Markowitz, Judith, Smith, Raoul, and Werner, Oswald. 1980. *Lexical-Semantic Relations: A Comparative Survey.* Edmonton, Alberta: Linguistic Research, Inc.

Evens, Martha, Vandendorpe, James, and Wang, Yih-Chen. 1985. Lexical-Semantic Relations in Information Retrieval. In S. Williams, ed., *Humans and Machines.* Norwood, NJ: Ablex, 73-100.

Evens, Martha, Markowitz, Judith, Ahlswede, Thomas, and Rossi, Kay. 1987. Digging in the Dictionary: Building a Relational Lexicon to Support Natural Language Processing Applications. *Issues and Developments in English and Applied Linguistics,* **2**, 33-44.

Fahlman, Scott. 1979. *NETL: A System for Representing and Using Real-World Knowledge.* Cambridge, MA: MIT Press.

Fillmore, Charles J. 1971. Types of Lexical Information. In D. Steinberg and L. Jakobovits, eds., *Semantics: an Interdisciplinary Reader,* Cambridge: Cambridge University Press, 370-392.

Fox, Edward A. 1980. Lexical Relations: Enhancing Effectiveness of Information Retrieval Systems. *ACM SIGIR Forum,* **15**, 3, 5-36, Winter 1980.

Fox, Edward, Nutter, Terry, Ahlswede, Thomas, Evens, Martha, and Markowitz, Judith. 1988. Building a Large Thesaurus for Information Retrieval. *Proc. ACL Conf. in Applied Natural Language Processing,* Austin, February, 101-108.

Fox, Mark S., Bebel, D. J., and Parker, Alice C. 1980. The Automated Dictionary. *Computer,* July, 35-48.

Frake, C. 1964. Notes and Queries in Anthropology. *American Anthropologist,* **66**, 132-145.

Frawley, William. 1981. Lexicography and the Philosophy of Science. *Dictionaries,* **3**, 18-27.

Frawley, William. 1987. *Text and Epistemology.* Norwood, NJ: Ablex.

Grimes, Joseph. 1975. *The Thread of Discourse.* The Hague: Mouton.

Hendrix, Gary G., 1975. Expanding the Utility of Semantic Networks through Partitioning. *Proc. IJCAI,* 4, 115-121.

Hornby, A. S. 1980. *Oxford Advanced Learner's Dictionary of Current English* (Eleventh edition). Oxford: Oxford University Press.

Iris, Madelyn, Litowitz, Bonnie, and Evens, Martha. 1988. Moving Toward Literacy by Making Definitions, to appear in the *International Journal of Lexicography,* Fall, 1988, special issue edited by W. Frawley and R. Smith.

Kay, Martin. 1983. The Dictionary of the Future and the Future of the Dictionary. *Linguistica Computazionale,* **III**, 161-174.

Kay, Paul. 1971. Taxonomy and Semantic Contrast. *Language,* **47**, 4, 866-887.

Kintsch, Walter. 1974. *The Representation of Meaning in Memory.* Hillsdale, NJ: Erlbaum.

Kučera, Henry and W. Nelson Francis, 1967. *Computational Analysis of Present-Day American English.* Providence: Brown University Press.

Litowitz, Bonnie. 1977. Learning to make definitions. *Journal of Child Language,* **4**, 289-304.

Lyons, John. 1963. *Structural Semantics.* Oxford: Basil Blackwell.

Lyons, John. 1968. *Introduction to Theoretical Linguistics.* Cambridge: Cambridge University Press.

Lyons, John. 1977. *Semantics*. Cambridge: Cambridge University Press.

Markowitz, Judith. 1977. *A Look at Fuzzy Categories*. Unpublished doctoral dissertation, Department of Linguistics, Northwestern University.

Markowitz, Judith. 1982. The Child as Lexicographer of Terms of the Classroom Culture. Paper presented at the 27th Annual Convention of the International Reading Assoc. (ERIC Document Reproduction Service Number ED 217 381).

Markowitz, Judith, and Moses, Rae. 1981. What is Rugtime? Linguistic Variation among First Graders. In C. S. Masek, R. A. Hendrick, and M. F. Miller, eds., *Papers from the Parasession on Language and Behavior of the Chicago Linguistics Society*. Chicago: Chicago Linguistic Society, 156-164.

Markowitz, Judith, Ahlswede, Thomas, and Evens, Martha. 1986. Semantically Significant Patterns in Dictionary Definitions. *Proc. 24th Annual Meeting of the ACL*, New York City, June, 112-119.

Markowitz, Judith, and Franz, Susan. 1988. The Development of Defining Style. *International Journal of Lexicography*, Fall, 1988.

Mel'čuk, I. A., Arbatchewsky-Jumarie, N., Elnitsky, L., Iordanskaja, L., and Lessard, A. 1984. *Dictionnaire explicatif et combinatoire du français contemporain. Recherches lexico-sémantiques. I.* Montreal: University of Montreal Press.

Mel'čuk, I. A., Arbatchewsky-Jumarie, N., Dagenais, L., Elnitsky, L., Iordanskaja, L., Lefebvre, M-N., and Mantha, S. 1988. *Dictionnaire explicatif et combinatoire du français contemporain. Recherches lexico-sémantiques. II.* Montreal: the University of Montreal Press.

Mel'čuk, Igor, and Zholkovsky, Alexander. 1984. *Explanatory Combinatorial Dictionary of Modern Russian. Semantico-syntactic Studies of Russian Vocabulary*. Vienna: Wiener Slawatischer Almanach.

Meyer, Bonnie. 1975. *The Organization of Prose and its Effects on Memory*. New York: American Elsevier North Holland.

Meyer, Bonnie. 1985. Prose Analysis: Purposes, Procedures, and Problems. In B. Britton and J. Black, eds. *Understanding Expository Text*. Hillsdale, NJ: Erlbaum.

Michiels, Archibal, and Noel, Jacques. 1982. Approaches to Thesaurus Production. *COLING82*, Amsterdam: North Holland, 227-232.

Michiels, Archibal, and Noel, Jacques. 1983. Automatic Analysis of Texts. Paper presented at the 1983 Workshop on Machine Readable Dictionaries, SRI International, April,1983.

Miller, George, and Johnson-Laird, Philip. 1976. *Language and Perception*. Cambridge: Cambridge University Press.

Morton, John, and Bekerian, Debra. 1986. Three Ways of Looking at Memory. In N.E. Sharkey, ed., *Advances in Cognitive Science I.* London: Ellis Horwood, 43-71.

Olney, John. 1968. To All Those Interested in the Merriam-Webster Transcripts and the Data Derived from Them. Systems Development Corporation L-13579, Santa Monica, CA.

Olney, John, Schonfeld, J., and Van Lam, 1977. Computer Processing of the Etymologies in a Standard Dictionary: Preliminary Results. *Cahiers de Lexicologie*, **31**, 3-62.

Palmer, F. R. 1976. *Semantics: A New Outline.* Cambridge: Cambridge University Press.

Procter, Paul. 1978. *Longman Dictionary of Contemporary English.* Harlow, Essex: Longman.

Quillian, M. Ross. 1968. Semantic Memory. In M. Minsky, ed., *Semantic Information Processing*, Cambridge, MA: MIT Press, 227-270.

Quillian, M. Ross. 1969. The Teachable Language Comprehender. *CACM*, **12**, 8, 459-476.

Raphael, Bertram. 1968. SIR, A Computer Program for Semantic Information Retrieval. In M. Minsky, ed., *Semantic Information Processing*, Cambridge, MA: MIT Press, 33-145.

Riegel, Klaus. 1970. The Language Acquisition Process: a Reinterpretation of Related Research Findings. In L.R. Goulet and P.B. Baltes, eds., *Theory and Research in Life-Span Developmental Psychology.* New York: Academic Press, 357-399.

Rosch, Eleanor. 1978. Principles of Categorization. In E. Rosch and B. Lloyd, eds., *Cognition and Categorization.* Hillsdale, New Jersey: Lawrence Erlbaum Associates, Inc., 111-144.

Rumelhart, David, Lindsay, Peter, and Norman, Donald. 1972. A Process Model for Long-Term Memory. In E. Tulving and W. Donaldson, eds., *Organization of Memory*, New York: Academic Press, 198-248.

Sager, Naomi. 1981. *Natural Language Information Processing.* Reading, MA: Addison-Wesley.

Schreuder, Robert. 1986. Using Lexical Databases in Psycholinguistic Research. Paper presented at the Grosseto Workshop, June.

Simmons, Robert F. 1973. Semantic Networks: Their Computation and Use for Understanding English Sentences. In Roger Schank and Kenneth Colby, eds., *Computer Models of Thought and Language*, San Francisco: W. H. Freeman, 63-113.

Simmons, Robert F., and Amsler, Robert A. 1975. Modeling Dictionary Data. In Ralph Grishman, ed., *Directions in Artificial Intelligence, Natural Language Processing*, Courant Institute Report #7, New York University, 1-26.

Simmons, Robert and Slocum, Jonathan. 1972. Generating English Discourse from Semantic Networks. *CACM*, **15**, 10, 891-905.

Simpson, John. 1985. The New OED Project. *Information in Data: Proceedings of the First Conference of the UW Centre for the New OED*. Waterloo: University of Waterloo Centre for the New Oxford English Dictionary, 1-6.

Sinclair, John M., ed. 1987a. *The Collins COBUILD English Language Dictionary*. London: Collins.

Sinclair, John M., ed. 1987b. *Looking Up: An Account of the COBUILD Project in Lexical Computing*. London: Collins.

Smith, Raoul N. 1981. On Defining Adjectives, Part III. *Dictionaries: Journal of the Dictionary Society of North America*, **3**, 28-38.

Smith, Raoul N. 1984. Collocational Relations. Presented at the Workshop on Relational Models, Coling '84, Stanford University, July, 1984.

Smith, Raoul N. 1985. Conceptual Primitives in the English Lexicon. *Papers in Linguistics*, **18**, 99-137.

Sowa, John F. 1983. Generating language from conceptual graphs. *Computers and Mathematics with Applications*, **9**, 1, 29-43.

Sowa, John F. 1984. *Conceptual Structures: Information Processing in Mind and Machine*. Reading, MA: Addison-Wesley.

Sowa, John F., and Eileen C. Way. 1986. Implementing a semantic interpreter using conceptual graphs. *IBM Journal of Research & Development*, **30**.

Tarski, Alfred. 1937. An Alternative System for P and T. Appendix E in J. H. Woodger, *The Axiomatic Method in Biology*. Cambridge: Cambridge University Press.

Wang, Yih-Chen, Vandendorpe, James, Evens, Martha. 1985. Relational Thesauri in Information Retrieval. *JASIS*, **36**, 1, 15-27.

Webster's Seventh New Collegiate Dictionary. 1967. Springfield, MA: G&C Merriam Company.

Werner, Oswald, 1978. The Synthetic Informant Model: the Simulation of Large Lexical/Semantic Fields. In M. Loflin and J. Silverberg, eds., *Discourse and Difference in Cognitive Anthropology*. The Hague: Mouton, 45-83.

Werner, Oswald, Austin, Martha, and Begishe, Kenneth. 1969/1981. *The Anatomical Atlas of the Navajo*. Department of Anthropology, Northwestern University and the U. S. Public Health Service.

Werner, Oswald, and Schoepfle, G. Mark. 1987. *Systematic Fieldwork.* Newbury Park, CA: Sage Publications.

Werner, Oswald, and Topper, Martin. 1976. On the Theoretical Unity of Ethnoscience Lexicography and Ethnoscience Ethnographics. In Clea Rameh, ed., *Semantics, Theory and Applications, Proceedings of the Georgetown Round Table on Language and Linguistics,* 111-143.

White, John S. 1983. An Ethnosemantic Approach to a Dictionary Taxonomy. Paper presented at the 1983 Workshop on Machine Readable Dictionaries, SRI International, April, 1983.

Williams, Gerald. 1966. Linguistic Reflections of Cultural Systems. *Anthropological Linguistics,* **8**, 8, 13-21.

Zadeh, Lotfi. 1965. Fuzzy Sets. *Information and Control,* **8**, 338-353.

Zholkovsky, Alexander, and Mel'čuk, Igor. 1967/1970. Semantic Synthesis. *Systems Theory Research,* **19**, 170-243. A translation of: O semantičeskom sinteze. *Problemy kibernetiki,* **19**, 177-238.

Part I:
The structure of the lexicon

2

The explanatory combinatorial dictionary*

IGOR MEL'ČUK
DEPARTMENT OF LINGUISTICS
UNIVERSITY OF MONTREAL
MONTREAL, CANADA H3C 3J7

ALEXANDER ZHOLKOVSKY
DEPARTMENT OF SLAVIC LANGUAGES AND LITERATURES
UNIVERSITY OF SOUTHERN CALIFORNIA
LOS ANGELES, CA

Abstract

More than twenty years ago Igor Mel'čuk and his colleagues, Alexander Zholkovsky and Yuri Apresyan, proposed a new kind of dictionary, an Explanatory Combinatorial Dictionary, designed to contain such explicit information about the words of a language that, for instance, it could enable language learners to write perfect texts (of course, if supplied with an ideal grammar). This kind of detailed and explicit information is just what a computer needs for automatic paraphrase, parsing, text generation, and machine translation. Entries include morphology, syntactic markings, style labels, definitions in logical form, the government pattern and all the restrictions on that pattern, examples, and especially the Lexical Functions

*Translated by Sally B. Hankwitz, Department of Slavic Languages and Literatures, State University of New York at Albany, Albany, New York, U.S.A.

that describe all the collocations the word takes part in and its relationship to other words in its semantic field. This chapter is a (slightly revised) translation of the introduction to the Explanatory Combinatorial Dictionary of Russian, finally published four years ago in Vienna, after many years of arduous labor [Mel'čuk and Zholkovsky 1984]. It explicates the theory behind the dictionary and describes the details of its organization.

> And indeed, every sufficiently complex word must actually become the subject of a scientific monograph; therefore it is hard to expect in the near future the completion of a good dictionary.
> Lev V. Ščerba, *An Outline of a General Lexicographic Theory* [1940]

Introduction

An Explanatory Combinatorial Dictionary (ECD) is an essential component of any full-fledged linguistic description within the Meaning-Text Model (MTM) Theory. This theory describes a natural language as a kind of logical device which associates with any given meaning M the set of all the texts in this language which are expressions of M (and which are consequently synonymous with one another), and with any text T, the set of all the meanings which are expressed by T (and which are, so to speak, homonymous with one another). For further information on the MTM theory see Zholkovskii and Mel'chuk 1967; Mel'čuk and Žolkovskij 1970; Mel'čuk 1973, 1974, 1978, 1981, 1988a: 43-101; Apresjan 1974, 1980.

The following four linguistic levels of representation are distinguished in the Meaning-Text Model: the semantic, the syntactic (with deep and surface sublevels), the morphological (also with deep and surface sublevels), and the phonetic or orthographic (with the same subdivisions). Establishing correspondences between meanings and texts is conceived of as a multi-stage process: 'translating' a given meaning, that is, a **SEMANTIC REPRESENTATION**, from one level to another, until one of the corresponding texts is reached (or vice versa: 'translating' a given text, that is a **PHONETIC REPRESENTATION**, from one level to another, until one of the corresponding meanings is reached). Thus if the Meaning-Text Model is to carry out this 'translation' from a given meaning to all the correct texts that express it and vice versa, then enormous amounts of specific information about the language in question are required. The most significant part of this information – namely, the information about all the essential properties of individual words – must be stored in a **DICTIONARY** of a new type. Ideally, such a dictionary should comprise, in a manner which is both exhaustive and formalized, ALL of the semantic and combinatorial relationships of a given word to other words. This is what the ECD undertakes. (For a better understanding of the proposed dictionary, familiarity with at least some of the following special lexicographic works is important: [Zholkovskij and Mel'chuk 1967; Apresjan, Žolkovskij and Mel'čuk 1968; Apresyan, Mel'čuk and Žolkovsky 1970, 1973; Iordanskaja 1973, 1979; Mel'čuk, Iordanskaja and Arbatchewsky-Jumarie 1981; Mel'čuk et al. 1984, 1988]. A fragment of an ECD for Modern Standard Russian is now available [Mel'čuk and Zholkovsky 1984], which contains over 250 VOCABLES. It was compiled over a period of ten years by a small team in Moscow (all in all, some 20 people contributed directly to the work). Its dictionary entries are designed both to test and to demonstrate the apparatus devised for the description of any type of word within the framework of the Meaning-Text approach. This apparatus for lexical description purports to do justice to words both as paradigmatic units that occupy definite places in the network of relations obtaining in the lexicon of the language, and as syntagmatic units capable of being mutifariously and systematically related to other such units in a discourse.

In this chapter, we propose to characterize briefly certain salient features of the ECD and to explain its organization. Before we begin, however, the following point must be stressed: this presentation does not make any claim to completeness. It does not describe systematically the whole of the Meaning-Text Model, an understanding of which is essential for maximum ease and profitability when consulting the ECD. Nor does it explain many of the technical details (e.g., the use of parentheses, square and angle brackets, etc.). The works cited above should therefore be referred to extensively.

First of all, let us see how the ECD compares with existing dictionaries. Even though it is a dictionary of a basically new type, the ECD follows certain promising trends present in contemporary lexicography. Three of them, in our view, stand out as the most important:

[1] Until recently, the predominant type of monlingual dictionary was the comprehension dictionary, to which the user would refer on encountering an unfamiliar word or phrase in a text. In other words, such dictionaries were oriented toward making texts comprehensible (i.e., providing for the transition from a text to the meaning expressed by it). Using the well-known opposition between passive grammar (= text understanding) and active grammar (= text production) introduced by L. V. Ščerba, we could call these dictionaries passive.

Since the first quarter of this century, however, there has also been experimentation with active dictionaries, spurred on chiefly by the practical needs of foreign-language teaching. These dictionaries have been oriented towards assisting in the PRODUCTION of texts (i.e., providing for the transition from a meaning to the texts which express it). The objective of this type of dictionary is to give the user as complete a set as possible of the correct means for the linguistic expression of a desired idea. Clearly, the Meaning-Text Model and its indispensable component, the Explanatory Combinatorial Dictionary, also aim at achieving this objective. In this sense the ECD is A DICTIONARY OF THE ACTIVE TYPE. It differs, however, from other active dictionaries in that the linguistic means needed for the expression of a given idea are selected for inclusion in the ECD according to explicitly formulated uniform principles, those means being given a formalized description in special artificial languages (such as the lexical functions employed for the description of restrictions on lexical co-occurrence).

At the same time, the fact that in the ECD expressions of a natural language are explicitly associated with corresponding expressions of a "deeper" formal language opens up the possibility of using the ECD not only in an active but also in a passive role, i.e., not only for the production but also for the understanding of texts. Thus the ECD is potentially a reversible dictionary.

[2] Until recently, the predominant type of monolingual dictionary was a specialized dictionary: the monolingual dictionary with word definitions (such as *The Oxford English Dictionary, Merriam-Webster's, The American Heritage Dictionary of the English Language*, etc.), the conceptual dictionary, the analogical dictionary, the phraseological dictionary, and so on. Such specialization is perfectly compatible with the concept of a passive dictionary. It does not agree well, however, with the aim of an active dictionary, which should attempt to systematize all synonymic means of expressing a given idea.

Let us look at a concrete example. Suppose we are dealing with the following meaning:

(1) 'The fact that the atmospheric air temperature became lower was the cause of the fact that the quantity of crops produced by cultivated lands became lower.'

(Note that (1) is not written in idiomatic English but in an artificial 'semantic' language designed to express the meaning in a thoroughly explicit way; English words and grammar are used solely for the reader's convenience.)

In Russian, meaning (1) can be expressed, for example, by sentence (2):

(2) *Poxolodanie vyzvalo sniženie urožaev* 'The cold wave caused a decrease in the harvest.'

It should be emphasized that in the above example and in what follows we are dealing with Russian, and not English, lexical material. We provide Russian examples with glosses which are as literal as possible since their only objective is to ensure an understanding of the Russian structure. They are not supposed to be written in idiomatic English.

In order to effect the transition from our artificial language as in sentence (1) into a natural language (in our case, Russian) as in sentence (2), it is necessary, first of all, to have command of the meanings of certain Russian lexical units: *poxolodanie* 'cold wave' ≅ 'lowering of the temperature of the atmospheric air'; *urožaj* 'harvest' ≅ ' (quantity of) crops produced by cultivated lands'; etc. This alone, however, is not sufficient, because the very same idea can be expressed in many other ways; cf., for example, (3) – (8):

(3) *Poxolodanie privelo k sniženiju urožaev* 'The cold wave led to a decrease in the harvest.'

(*Privesti k* 'lead to' is a synonym of the verb *vyzvat'* 'cause.')

(4) *Sniženie urožaev proisteklo iz-za poxolodanija* 'The decrease in the harvest stemmed from the cold wave.'

(5) *Urožai snizilis' iz-za poxolodanija* 'The harvest decreased on account of the cold wave.'

(*Snizit'sja* '(to) decrease' and *sniženie* '(a) decrease' in (4) and (5) are related by regular morphological derivation, while *vyzvat'* '(to) cause' and *iz-za* 'on account of' in (2), (4) and (5) stand in a deep-syntactic derivation relationship, *iz-za* being $\mathbf{Adv_2}$(*vyzvat'*); see below.)

(6) *Poxolodanie javilos' pričinoj sniženija urožaev* 'The cold wave was the cause of a decrease in the harvest.'

(7) *Sniženie urožaev javilos' rezul'tatom poxolodanija* 'The decrease in the harvest was the result of the cold wave.'

(*Pričina* 'cause' and *rezul'tat* 'result' are deep-syntactic (suppletive) derivatives of the verb *vyzvat'* 'cause,' namely, $\mathbf{S_1}$ and $\mathbf{S_{res}}$, respectively.)

(8) *Umen'šenie temperatury (vozduxa) vyzvalo sniženie urožaev* 'The lowering of the (air) temperature caused a decrease in the harvest.'

(*Umen'šenie* 'lowering' (e.g., of temperature) is a generic term for *poxolodanie* 'cold wave.')

It is also necessary to take into account the fact that not all of the near-synonyms *umen'šenie* 'lowering,' *padenie* 'fall,' *spad* 'drop,' *poniženie* 'decline,' *sniženie* 'decrease,' *sokraščenie* 'shrinking,' and other related words can be combined equally effectively with the words *temperatura* 'temperature' and *urožaj* 'harvest.' In Russian one can say *umen'šenie* <or *padenie*, or *spad*, or *poniženie*> *temperatury* 'lowering <fall, drop, decline> in temperature,' but not **sokraščenie temperatury* 'shrinking of temperature.' One can also say *umen'šenie* <*poniženie, sniženie, sokraščenie*> *urožaev* 'lowering <decline, decrease, shrinking> of the harvest,' but not *spad urožaev* 'drop of the harvest.' In addition, even semantically exact synonyms can differ in syntactic government. *Vyzvat' čto-l.* and *privesti k čemu-l.*, both meaning 'bring about something,' have different syntactic properties; in the sense given one cannot say **vyzvat' k čemu-l.* or **privesti čto-l.* In order to prevent the production of incorrect (albeit intelligible) sentences such as **Sokraščenie temperatury vyzvalo k spadu urožaev* 'The shrinking of the temperature brought about the drop of the harvest,' it is necessary to describe in a precise way the specific properties of each word: in particular, its lexico-semantic combinability (= co-occurrence relationships), and its syntactic government. Thus, an orientation toward the production of all synonymous texts which express the same content inevitably leads to the concept of a **GENERALIST** dictionary. As opposed to a specialized dictionary it must include: first, the definition of each word and of each set phrase; second, its synonyms, converses, antonyms, derivatives and other words or phrases related to it in meaning; and third, specifications of restrictions in its lexical co-occurrences and its syntactic government. The ECD is such a generalist dictionary; it combines (not eclectically, but according to the principles of an integrated linguistic theory) the functions of a defining, or explanatory, dictionary with those of phraseological, derivational, conceptual, analogical dictionaries, as well as dictionaries of synonyms, of syntactic patterns, etc.

[3] Until recently, traditional lexicography differentiated between two types of dictionaries – linguistic dictionaries, which describe meanings of words from the point of view of an unsophisticated native speaker; and what can be loosely called encyclopedic dictionaries (or better encyclopedias), which describe the corresponding objects, processes, facts, etc., taking a scientific approach. However, the development of linguistics, semiotics, logic and other related sciences has led to the realization that the correct use of words is determined to a significant degree by the way a language breaks down reality into distinct fragments and what typical linguistic representations are used to express these fragments. In consequence, some defining dictionaries began to provide minimal encyclopedic information for words where a cultural and factual-knowledge background is absolutely essential for them to be intelligently perceived and used.

Continuing this trend, the Explanatory Combinatorial Dictionary includes ELEMENTS OF ENCYCLOPEDIC INFORMATION in linguistic dictionary entries. However, unlike the other dictionaries, the ECD distinguishes these two types of information clearly, presenting them in different sections of the dictionary entry. In maintaining this basic division between linguistic information *per se* and encyclopedic material, the ECD is more consistent with traditional lexicography.

At the same time, the ECD possesses two important features that distinguish it from most existing dictionaries.

[4] The ECD is completely THEORY-ORIENTED. As stated above, it is conceived and implemented within the Meaning-Text Model theory, and the lexicographic method used is intimately tied to this general linguistic framework. The ECD does not aim to satisfy the specific needs of a well-defined class of prospective users; nor does it take into account their probable level of understanding of the corresponding language. It is designed primarily for scientific purposes (a fact which does not preclude its use for certain applied purposes, as described in the section on possible uses of the ECD) and tries to bridge the chasm between lexicography and theoretical linguistics by laying the basis for a fruitful interaction between both fields – an interaction which heretofore has been minimal. So an entry of the ECD is in fact a self-contained linguistic article on the corresponding Russian lexeme, and the published fragment of the ECD [Mel'čuk and Zholkovsky 1984] may actually be viewed as a collection of lexicographic papers all written within a unified linguistic theory.

[5] In accordance with its main orientation, the ECD purports to be as EXPLICIT and SYSTEMATIC as possible. In practice, this means at least two things. First, the ECD never relies on informal methods of communicating information about words (like examples or analogy) or on the native speaker's intuitive knowledge of his language. Everything that we feel must be communicated is communicated explicitly, using a uniform descriptive language for all entries. Such a degree of explicitness makes the ECD very complicated, but this is a price we find worth paying.

Second, the ECD bans logical circles – a weakness of many dictionaries – from its definitions and requires similar descriptions for semantically similar items. Thus, for example, all names of institutions or all names of movements must be described in exactly the same manner; all differences in the wording of the definitions or in the presentation of lexical collocations of semantically related words must be justified by actual linguistic differences.

To sum up: the Explanatory Combinatorial Dictionary is a monolingual dictionary featuring the following five important properties:

- it is ACTIVE (as opposed to passive);
- it is GENERALIST (as opposed to specialized);
- it includes much ENCYCLOPEDIC information (to the extent it is needed for the proper use of the words);
- it pursues THEORETICAL GOALS;
- it puts strong emphasis on providing EXPLICIT and SYSTEMATIC information in a formalized way.

Let us now proceed to a more detailed examination of the information about words that is presented in the ECD. We will deal with four topics:

1. Lexical stock represented in the ECD.
2. Types of relationships between words represented in the ECD.
3. Structure of an ECD entry.
4. Possible uses of the ECD.

Lexical stock represented in the ECD

Among the entries described in the published fragment of the Russian ECD, we have made a point of including words of diverse types, which represent, as far as possible, all vocabulary levels and which occur in any sort of text, including scientific and technical texts. Thus we present:

- Verbs of thinking, such as *sčıtat*[2] 'believe,' *ponimat'* 'understand,' *somnevat'sja* 'doubt.'
- Performative verbs, such as *predlagat'* 'propose,' *priglašat'* 'invite.'
- Verbs of emotion, such as *čuvstvovat'* 'feel,' *udivljat'sja* 'be surprised,' *gnevat'sja* 'be angry.'
- Verbs of physical impact, such as *rezat'* 'cut,' *žarit'* 'fry.'
- Verbs of information processing, such as *rassmatrivat'* 'examine,' *opisyvat'* 'describe,' *èksperimentirovat'* 'experiment.'
- Names of institutions, instruments, devices, means of transportation, etc.: *bol'nica* 'hospital,' *kinoteatr* 'movie theater'; *viselica* 'gallows,' *peč*[2] 'stove,' *očki* 'eyeglasses'; *sudno*[1] 'ship'; *sosud* 'vessel [container].'
- Names of measurable quantities, such as *skorost'* 'speed,' *vysota* 'height,' *temperatura* 'temperature.'
- Names of agents, such as *lyžnik* 'skier,' *passažir* 'passenger.'
- Names of abstract states, such as *pobeda* 'victory,' *poraženie* 'defeat.'
- Names of qualities, such as *bezgramotnost'* 'illiteracy,' *nadēžnost'* 'reliability.'
- Names of substances, such as *čaj* 'tea,' *kofe* 'coffee.'
- Names of physical objects, animals, body parts, etc.: *okno* 'window,' *doska* 'board'; *svin'ja* 'pig'; *serdce* 'heart.'
- Names of social institutions, such as *brak*[1] 'marriage,' and aspects of social interaction (*avtoritet* 'authority,' *agressija* 'aggression').
- And a number of other lexical types.

It is important to emphasize that the ECD describes not only separate lexemes but also set phrases with different degrees of idiomaticity: *administrativnyj vostorg* 'delight in bureaucratic regulations,' *učebnoe zavedenie* 'educational institution,' *kolot' glaza* '[to] throw something in someone's teeth,' *brosat' to v žar, to v xolod* '[to] feel hot and cold all over,' etc. All these are considered lexical items on the same footing as lexemes, and all the lexical items of Russian are described following the same rules.

The above list should suffice to show the range of Russian vocabulary covered by the ECD. While selecting words for our necessarily limited fragment of the ECD, we sought to fulfill the following four requirements:

(a) To represent a maximum number of semantic word types.

(b) To represent full words and phrases of all parts of speech. Our fragment of the ECD contains not only verbs and nouns, but also:

- adjectives such as *dosadnyj* 'annoying,' *gramotnyj* 'literate,' *strelkovyj* 'rifle-' and others;
- adverbs such as *zamuž* 'getting married (process),' *zamužem* 'married (state),' *naizust'* 'by heart,' and others;
- pronouns *ty* 'you (singular, familiar)' and *vy* 'you (plural or polite).'

Various syntactic classes of lexicalized phrases or phraseological collocations are represented by the ECD very much like individual words: noun phrases such as *učebnoe zavedenie* 'educational institution,' *administrativnyj vostorg*, lit. 'administrative ecstasy' [i.e., 'delight in bureaucratic regulations'], *dyrjavaja baška*, lit. 'pierced head' = 'forgetful, absent-minded person'; adverbial phrases such as *iz ljubvi k iskusstvu* 'for the love of it'; verb phrases such as *kolot' glaza* 'throw something in someone's teeth'; and so on.

(c) To represent as far as possible all of the senses of polysemous words: *cvet* [*travy*] 'color [of the grass]' – *cvet* [*moloděži*] 'flower [of youth]'; *okno* [*komnaty*] 'window [of a room]'– *okno* [*meždu zanjatijami*] 'break [in one's schedule, i.e., free time between two classes]'; *streljat'* [*iz ružja*] 'fire [a shotgun]' – *streljat'* [*sigarety*] 'bum [cigarettes].' Our attempt to give a detailed description of polysemy necessitates the inclusion of colloquial and even substandard lexical units; in our view, this is one of the ECD's strong points, since lexicographic description thus extends to another vocabulary level, characterized by a whole range of specific features.

(d) To represent whole semantic families, that is, sets of words with generic-specific and other similar relationships. Compare: *rezat'* 'cut' – *výrezat'* 'cut out' – *zarézat'* 'kill with a knife' – *prorézat'* 'cut through' – *razrézat'* 'cut open, slit'; *učebnoe zavedenie* 'educational institution' – *vuz* [= *vysšee učebnoe zavedenie*] 'higher educational institution' – *učit'sja* 'study'; *čajnik* 'teapot' – *čaj* 'tea' – *sosud* 'vessel [container]'; *zavtrak* 'breakfast' – *obed* 'dinner' – *užin* 'supper,' as well as *žarit'* 'fry' – *peč'*[1] 'bake' – *varit'* 'cook, boil'; *temperatura* 'temperature' – *termometr* 'thermometer'; *sčitat'*[2] 'believe' – *mne-*

nie 'opinion'; *bor'ba* 'struggle' – *pobeda* 'victory' – *poraženie* 'defeat'; *iskusstvo* 'art' – *kino* 'cinema'; and so forth.

The diversity of material dealt with in the ECD enables us to propose a universal standard structure for the dictionary itself and for the dictionary entries, which seems to meet all the demands concerning dictionary format and use. It should be borne in mind that since the lexical stock represented in Mel'čuk and Zholkovsky 1984 is so limited, there are perforce some references to items that do not appear in the published fragment. To put it differently, our lexical system is not closed.

Types of relationships between words represented in the ECD

The ECD allows for the representation of three basic types of relations between words.

– The first type is SEMANTIC (paradigmatic) relationships between words: e.g., synonymy, semantic proximity, etc. They are reflected in the definitions of related words: two fully synonymous words have identical definitions; two nearly-synonymous words have nearly identical definitions; and so on. The **DEFINITION** formulates one discrete sense of the entry word or entry phraseme in terms of specially selected elementary concepts (= word senses) and/or derived concepts, i.e., words, which are more basic in meaning than the word sense being defined and which are themselves defined quite independently of the entry word. Thus each word sense is semantically decomposed.

– The second type is SYNTACTIC (syntagmatic) relationships between the entry word, which is semantically a predicate, and other words or phrases, which may be syntactically dependent on it in a sentence and which are the expression of its semantic actants. These sentence elements are said to fill in the slots of the active syntactic valence of the entry word and are called its syntactic actants. The active syntactic valence is specified by means of a table called a **GOVERNMENT PATTERN**. The government pattern indicates three things: for each semantic actant of the entry word, the corresponding syntactic actant; the form which each syntactic actant takes on the surface; and which of the syntactic actants are incompatible (or, conversely, are inseparable, i.e., invariably used together), and under what conditions.

– The third type includes the LEXICAL (both paradigmatic and syntagmatic) relationships between the entry word and those other words which can either replace it in a text (under specific circumstances), or be joined to it in more or less fixed word combinations (also known as phraseological combinations). This involves what we term **LEXICAL FUNCTIONS**

(LF). A LF is a function in the mathematical sense representing a certain extremely general idea, such as 'very,' 'begin,' or 'implement,' or else a certain semantico-syntactical role. A lexical function **f** associates with a word W_0 called its argument, or **KEY WORD**, the set of words and phrases which express – contingent on W_0 – the meaning or role which corresponds to **f**. For example, the LF **Magn**, which can be glossed roughly as 'very,' in conjunction with the words *naprjaženie* 'voltage' or *temperatura* 'temperature' is expressed by the adjective *vysokij* 'high'; in conjunction with *vysota* 'height,' however, the same function is expressed by *značitel'nyj* 'considerable,' *bol'šoj* 'great,' and *ogromnyj* 'enormous'; and in conjunction with *vibracija* 'vibration,' by *sil'nyj* 'strong' and *intensivnyj* 'intense.' So we say *vysokoe naprjaženie* 'high voltage,' *vysokaja temperatura* 'high temperature,' *značitel'naja vysota* 'considerable height,' *bol'šaja vysota* 'great height,' *ogromnaja vysota* 'enormous height,' *sil'naja vibracija* 'strong vibration' and *intensivnaja vibracija* 'intense vibration,' but not **sil'noe naprjaženie, ogromnaja temperatura, intensivnaja vysota,* or **vysokaja vibracija*, etc. [See Mel'čuk 1982 for more details on Lexical Functions.]

Structure of an ECD entry

The basic unit of an explanatory/combinatory dictionary is a dictionary entry corresponding to a single **LEXEME** or a single **PHRASEME** – one word or one phraseme taken in one separate sense. A family of dictionary entries for lexemes which are sufficiently close in meaning and which share the same signans (i.e., an identical stem) is subsumed under one **VOCABLE**, which is identified in UPPER-CASE letters before all of the dictionary entries it covers, and in page headings as well. Different vocables which are the same graphically (= homonyms) are distinguished by numerical superscripts: BRAK[1] 'marriage' vs. BRAK[2] 'defective merchandise.'[1] The different lexemes within a single vocable are distinguished by special indices mentioned here in order of increasing semantic proximity:

Roman numerals differentiate lexemes whose definitions have a non-trivial common semantic component but whose semantic relationships are not sufficiently regular: e.g., VYSOTA I 'height or altitude [as a vertical measure],' VYSOTA II 'level [of prices, aspirations, pressure],' VYSOTA III 'pitch [of sound],' VYSOTA IV 'altitude [of the sun over the horizon],' VYSOTA V 'altitude [of a triangle].'

Arabic numerals indicate sufficiently regular semantic relationships among lexemes that share non-trivial semantic components, or regular polysemy: e.g., SPAT'[1] I.1 'sleep' vs. SPAT'[1] I.2 'be inert, as if sleeping.' The literal and the figurative meanings of *vspyxivat'* 'blaze up' – 'flare up' are distinguished in this way, as are *kipet'* 'boil' – 'seethe with,' *zastyt'* 'congeal' – 'become still (with fright, etc.)'; and the like.

Lower-case letters differentiate lexemes with slight semantic differences which are maximally regular: e.g., SKOROST' 1a 'rate of speed' – SKOROST' 1b 'great speed.' The same goes for *vysota* 'height' – 'great height,' *temperatura* 'temperature' – 'high temperature,' *kačestvo* 'quality' – 'excellent quality,' etc.

Within each of these three rubrics, the ordering of the lexemes (i.e., I,II, III,..., or 1,2,3,..., or a,b,...,) tends to follow a logical principle: if the definition of lexeme L' mentions lexeme L belonging to the same vocable, then L' must follow L. In other words, an 'including' definition always follows the 'included' one, so that within a vocable all interlexemic references with inclusion are made only backwards. For example, OPYTNYJ I.1 'experienced' and OPYTNYJ II 'experimental'; SVIN'JA 1a 'pig,' SVIN'JA 1b 'female pig,' and SVIN'JA 2 'a piglike, greedy or gross person'; and the like. In cases where this logical inclusion is absent, a number of other principles are observed (what is more concrete precedes what is more abstract; what is modern precedes what is archaic; current meanings precede rare ones). In short, we try to present the vocable as a highly structured unit rather than as an arbitrary sequence of entries. We also try to ensure, as far as possible, that semantically similar vocables have similar structures: related lexemes are ordered in an identical manner, etc. [See Mel'cuk et al. 1983, pp. 115-118, 1988b.]

Important warning: when they appear with items that do not have entries in Mel'čuk and Zholkovsky 1984, the lexeme-distinguishing indices are more or less arbitrary; they are used only to draw the reader's attention to the presence of a polysemous word.

It should be stressed once more that all full idioms are entered in the ECD separately. A **FULL IDIOM** is a phrase which cannot be constructed from its constituent words by general rules and such that no constituent word retains its full meaning; cf., *shoot the breeze* or *kick the bucket* in English. Full idioms are provided with dictionary entries as if they were single lexemes: see, for example, *iz ljubvi k iskusstvu* or *kolot' glaza* mentioned above. Thus the ECD does not distinguish between mono-lexemic and multi-lexemic units. In order to facilitate the retrieval of idioms (and for reference purposes), each idiom is also entered under each of its constituent full words: thus *iz ljubvi k iskusstvu* will be entered three times – as a separate entry, under LJUBOV', and under ISKUSSTVO.

A regular dictionary entry is divided into ten parts:

1. *Morphological information* about the entry lexeme (declension or conjugation type; gender of nouns; aspect of verbs; missing or irregular forms; etc.).

2. *Stylistic specification*, or usage label (specialized or technical; colloquial; substandard; archaic; etc.).

3. *A definition*, consisting of constants (elementary and derived concepts, or word senses of the language in question) and variables (X,Y,Z,...), the latter being present if the entry lexeme happens to be a predicate (in the semantic sense of the term). For instance, the word SKOROST' 1a 'speed' has the following definition:

'quantity II which characterizes the motion P of the body or wave X, the distance Y which X covers in a unit of time, or the value of this quantity.'

The constants, such as 'quantity II,' 'characterize,' 'motion,' 'body,' etc., carry the meaning proper. The corresponding lexemes are taken to be semantically simpler than the entry word, which, first of all, means that their own definitions do not require the concept of 'speed.'

The variables P, X and Y indicate the places for the arguments or semantic actants of the entry lexeme: the motion characterized by the given speed is P; the body or wave which is in motion is X; and the value of the quantity II is Y. The correspondence between the semantic actants of the entry lexeme and its syntactic actants is specified by the government pattern discussed below.

Following the definition are informal explanations or comments (preceded by the symbol N.B.) and so-called **CONNOTATIONS**, i.e., the semantic associations induced by the lexeme in the given language. For the lexeme VETER 'wind,' for example, the connotations are 'freedom,' 'quickness of movement,' 'changeability, capriciousness,' and 'frivolity, lack of seriousness.' [See Iordanskaja and Mel'čuk 1984.]

4. *Government Pattern* (GP). This is a table in which each column represents one semantic actant of the lexeme (marked by the corresponding variable), and each element in the column represents one of the possible surface realizations of the corresponding syntactic actant. For instance, the GP for the lexeme SKOROST' 1a 'speed' has the form:

I = P or I = X	II = Y
1. N_{gen} 2. A_{poss}	1. Num_{nom} N' [v 'per' N''_{acc}] 2. v 'of' Num_{acc} N' [v 'per' N''_{acc}] 3. Num_{nom} N 4. v 'of' Num_{acc} N 5. A 6. N_{gen}

The first deep-syntactic actant of the lexeme *skorost'* 'speed' fills the slot of the variable X or P in its definition (I = X or I = P, where X stands for the body, and P stands for the motion whose speed is described). The second deep-syntactic actant fills the slot of the variable Y (II = Y, Y being the value of the speed). The first deep-syntactic actant may be expressed either as a noun in the genitive case or as a possessive adjective (*skorost' samolëta* 'the speed of a plane' – *naša skorost'* 'our speed'). The second deep-syntactic actant has six surface realizations: (1) a complex noun phrase in the nominative consisting of two phrases: a noun phrase [Numeral in the nominative + Noun denoting unit distance] and a prepositional phrase [*v* 'per' + Noun denoting a unit of time], for instance, *skorost' desjat' kilometrov [v čas]* 'a speed of ten kilometers [per hour]'; for the other five realizations we shall restrict ourselves to examples: (2) *skorost' v desjat' kilometrov [v čas]* 'a speed of ten kilometers [per hour],' (3) *skorost' 40 uzlov* 'a speed of 40 knots,' (4) *skorost' v 40 uzlov* 'a speed [of] 40 knots,' (5) *kosmičeskaja [tysjačekilometrovaja] skorost'* 'cosmic [1000-kilometer] speed,' and (6) *skorost' sveta [zvuka]* 'speed of light [of sound].'

A preposition appearing in the GP is, as a rule, a semantically empty means of marking the syntactic relation between the entry lexeme and its syntactic actant; that is to say, it does not contribute its own meaning to that of the utterance: *skorost'* **v** *40 km/čas* 'a speed **of** 40 km per hour,' *somnevat'sja* **v** *ètom utverždenii* 'have doubts **about** the statement,' *nadejat'sja* **na** *udaču* 'count **on** luck,' *vystrel* **iz** *puški* 'a shot **from** a cannon.' However, if a preposition does, in fact, sustain a meaning of its own, and thus carries part of the meaning of the corresponding utterance, then this fact is indicated by a deep-syntactic arrow leaving it (in the GP); for example, because of the semantic contrast *streljat'* **v** *zajca* 'shoot at a hare' vs. *streljat'* **po** *zajcu* 'shoot at a hare which is moving, without taking precise aim,' we have in column two of the GP of the lexeme STRELJAT'[1] 1a 'shoot' two different elements containing deep-syntactic arrows: V $\xrightarrow{II}$ N$_{acc}$ and PO $\xrightarrow{II}$ N$_{dat}$ (the number II on the arrow stands for the 2nd deep-syntactic actant); this means that here the prepositions V and PO are meaningful.

5. *Restrictions on the government pattern.* These establish the conditions under which the deep- or surface-syntactic actants of the entry lexeme can co-occur and give all possible details relevant to the combinability of the lexeme in question with its syntactic actants. The notations used are:

$M_{1,2,3,...}$ – 1st, 2nd, 3rd,... deep-syntactic actant of the lexeme;
$D_{1,2,3,...}$ – surface realization of the 1st, 2nd, 3rd,... deep-syntactic actant [in most cases, this realization is the grammatical subject or

the 1st, 2nd,... complement[2] of the lexeme but it may also be an attributive or adverbial modifier];

$D_{i.j}$ – a specific means of marking the surface-syntactic element D_i [that is, i is the number of the column in the GP, and j is the number of the element in that column]; for example, in the GP cited for SKOROST' 1a the notation $D_{2.4}$ refers to the expression "v Num$_{acc}$ N."

In addition to the various restrictions on actant co-occurrence, this part of the dictionary entry presents all the rules which may be required for partial changes in the definition in connection with the use of a specific $D_{i.j}$: compare, for instance, the rules of this kind for the words VYSOTA I.1 'height,' VEJAT'[1] I.1 'blow (as of the wind),' and others.

A lexeme can have several alternative government patterns called **(SYNTACTIC) MODIFICATIONS.** Such GPs are given in the dictionary entry under the headings Mod 1, Mod 2, etc., and are provided with rules formulating the transformations necessary to pass from an expression containing one of the modifications to a synonymous expression containing another modification.

6. *Illustrations.* The GP and all the restrictions on it are illustrated by all possible combinations of the entry lexeme with its actants as well as by all the impossible combinations prohibited by those restrictions; every starred expression is followed by the number of the restriction it violates.

7. *Lexical Functions.* This part, characterizing the idiomatic, that is, language-specific substitutability and co-occurrence relations of the entry lexeme, makes up the major part of the dictionary entry. We will enumerate here the **STANDARD BASIC** LFs used in the ECD (in the order in which they appear in the dictionary entry):

Syn – synonym; **Syn$_\subset$**, **Syn$_\supset$**, and **Syn$_\cap$** stand for, respectively, synonyms with broader, narrower, and intersecting meanings. (The symbols $\subset$, $\supset$, and $\cap$ have the same meaning when used with **Conv**, **Anti** and other LFs.) Examples: **Syn**(*streljat'* 'shoot') = *palit'* 'fire'; **Syn$_\subset$**(*streljat'* 'shoot') = *obstrelivat'* 'fire upon; shell; machine-gun'; etc.

Conv$_{ij}$ – conversive, i.e., a lexical item with the same meaning as the key word W_0 but with the arguments i and j permuted: **Conv$_{21}$**(*vključat'* 'include') = *prinadležat'* 'belong [to a set]'; **Conv$_{231}$**(*mnenie* 'opinion') = *reputacija* 'reputation.'

Anti – antonym: **Anti**(*pobeda* 'victory') = *poraženie* 'defeat.'

Gener – generic concept such that '**Gener** + W_0' = 'W_0' (where W_0 is the key word or entry lexeme): **Gener**(*gaz* 'gas') = *veščestvo* 'substance' (cf., *gazoobraznoe veščestvo* 'gaseous substance' = *gaz* 'gas').

Figur – standard metaphor for W_0: **Figur**(*blokada* 'blockade') = *kol'co*, lit. 'ring' [*kol'co blokady* 'the grip of a blockade, a siege']; **Figur** (*tuman* 'fog') = *pelena* 'curtain' [*pelena tumana* 'curtain of fog'].

Dimin – diminutive: **Dimin**(*dom* 'house') = *domik* 'a small [and pleasant] house'; **Dimin**(*ozero* 'lake') = *ozerko* 'a small [and pleasant] lake.'

Augm – augmentative: **Augm**(*dom* 'house') = *domišče, domina* 'a huge house'; **Augm**(*ruka* 'hand') = *ručišča* 'a huge hand.'

S_0, A_0, Adv_0, V_0 – syntactic derivatives of W_0, that is, a noun [= substantive], an adjective, an adverb, and a verb, respectively, which have the same meaning as W_0: S_0(*streljat'* 'shoot') = *strel'ba* 'shooting'; A_0(*streljat'* 'shoot') = *strelkovyj* 'rifle- [attrib.].' S_i – standard name of the *i*-th participant in a given situation: S_1(*učit'* 'teach') = *učitel'* 'teacher'; S_2(*učit'* 'teach') = *učenik* 'pupil'; S_3(*učit'* 'teach') = *učebnyj predmet* 'subject [at school].'

$S_{instr}, S_{med}, S_{mod}, S_{loc}, S_{res}$ – standard name of an instrument, means, mode, location, or result pertaining to a given situation: S_{instr}(*streljat'* 'shoot') = *ognestrel'noe oružie* 'firearm'; S_{med}(*streljat'* 'shoot') = *boepripasy* 'ammunition'; S_{mod}(*rassmatrivat'* 'examine') = *vzgljad na čto-l.* 'a view of something,' *podxod k čemu-l.* 'approach to something'; S_{loc}(*sražat'sja* 'fight [as of two armies]') = *pole bitvy/boja* 'battlefield'; S_{res}(*učit'sja* 'learn') = *navyki* 'skills.'

Sing – 'one instance,' or 'one unit': **Sing**(*gorox* 'peas') = *gorošina* 'pea'; **Sing**(*celovat'* '[to] kiss') = *pocelovat'* 'give a kiss.'

Mult – 'aggregate': **Mult**(*korabl'* 'ship') = *flot* 'fleet'; **Mult**(*student* 'student') = *studenčestvo* 'student body.'

Cap – 'head': **Cap**(*universitet* 'university') = *rektor* 'president'; **Cap** (*fakul'tet* 'faculty') = *dekan* 'dean.'

Equip – 'staff' or 'crew': **Equip**(*teatr* 'theater') = *truppa* 'troupe'; so **Equip** (*bol'nica* 'hospital') = *personal* 'personnel'; **Equip**(*brak*[1] 'marriage') = *suprugi* 'spouses.'

Centr – 'center,' 'climax,' 'culmination': **Centr**(*les* 'forest') =*čašča* [*lesa*] 'the thick [of the forest]'; **Centr**(*slava* 'glory') = *veršina* [*slavy*] 'summit [of glory]'; **Centr**(*bor'ba* 'struggle')=*apogej* [*bor'by*] 'climax [of struggle].' **Centr** is current in combination with **Loc_{in}** [see below]: **Loc_{in}Centr** (*pustynja* 'desert')=*v serdce*[*pustyni*] 'in the heart [of the desert]'; while **Loc_{in}Centr**(*doroga* 'road') = *posredi* [*dorogi*] 'in the middle [of the road].'

A_i – standard property of the *i*-th participant in a given situation: A_1(*skorost'* 'speed') = *so* [*skorost'ju ...*] 'with a speed of,' *na skorosti* 'at a considerable speed' [compare *spusk s takoj skorost'ju* 'a descent at such a speed']; A_2(*streljat'* 'shoot') = *pod obstrelom* 'under fire.'

$Able_i$ – standard property of the *i*-th potential participant in a given situation ['such that it can ... easily'/'such that it can be ... easily']:

Able₁(*plakat'* 'cry') = *slezlivyj* 'tearful'; **Able₂**('doubt') = *somnitel'nyj* 'doubtful.'

Qualᵢ – typical property of the *i*-th participant in a given situation which is likely to entail his participation ['such that it is probable that he ...']. **Qual₁**(*serdit'sja* 'be angry') = *razdiažitel'nyi* 'irascible'; **Qual₂**(*packat'* 'get something dirty') = *belyi* 'white.'

Magn – 'very,' 'to a [very] high degree': **Magn**(*temperatura* 'temperature') = *vysokaja* 'high'; **Magn**(*rassmatrivat'* 'examine') = *vnimatel'no* 'attentively,' *pristal'no* 'fixedly, intently.'

Plus, Minus – respectively, 'more,' 'less' [or 'to a greater/lesser extent']; as a rule, used within compound functions.

Plusʳᵉᶠˡ, **Minus**ʳᵉᶠˡ – indicate that the comparison is made with a former state of the same object: **IncepPredPlus**ʳᵉᶠˡ(*temperatura* 'temperature') = *povyšat'sja* 'increase, rise' [for the LFs **Incep** and **Pred**, see below].

Ver – 'as it should be' [meeting intended requirements]: **Ver**(*udivlenie* 'surprise') = *nepoddel'noe* 'unfeigned'; **Ver**(*sosud* 'vessel' [container]) = *celyj* 'whole,' *germetičnyj* 'hermetic, leak-proof'; **Ver**(*pribor* 'instrument') = *točnyj* 'precise.'

Bon – 'good' [standard praise for *W₀*]: **Bon**(*rezat'* 'cut') = *akkuratno* 'neatly, cleanly'; **Bon**(*sudno¹* 'ship') = *komfortabel'noe* 'comfortable.'

Posᵢ – standard praise for one of the participants of the situation denoted by *W₀* [but not for the situation itself]: **Pos₂**(*recenzija* 'review') = *položitel'naja* 'positive' while **Bon** (*recenzija* 'review') = *xorošaja* 'good,' *zamečatel'naja* 'excellent,' ... , *blestjaščaja* 'brilliant'; however, *blestjaščaja recenzija* 'a brilliant[ly written] review' may well be *otricatel'naja* 'negative,' that is, **AntiPos₂**.

N.B. The LFs **Magn, Ver, Bon** and **Pos** are often combined with **Anti**. Thus, for instance, **Magn**(*temperatura* 'temperature') = *vysokaja* 'high,' and **AntiMagn**(*temperatura* 'temperature') = *nizkaja* 'low'; **Pos₂**(*mnenie* 'opinion') = *položitel'noe* 'positive,' and **AntiPos₂**(*mnenie* 'opinion') = *otricatel'noe* 'negative.'

Advᵢ – standard qualification of an action of the *i*-th participant in a given situation, expressed in adverbial form: **Adv₁**(*skorost'* 'speed') = *so skorost'ju ...*] 'at a speed of,' cf. *mčat'sja so skorost'ju 100 km v čas* 'tear along at a speed of 100 km an hour'; **Adv₂**(*somnevat'sja* 'doubt') = *vrjad li* 'hardly.' [*Ja somnevajus' v ego priezde,* 'I doubt his coming.' ≅ *ja polagaju, čto on vijad li priedet,* 'I think that he'll hardly come.']

Locᵢₙ, Locₐᵦ, Locₐd – preposition denoting standard localization in space relative to *W₀*: 'being there,' 'moving away' and 'moving toward,' respectively. Examples: **Locᵢₙ**(*vysota* 'height') = *na [vysote]* 'at [a height]'; **Locₐd**(*vysota* 'height') = *na [vysotu]* 'to [a height]'; **Locₐᵦ**(*vysota* 'height') = *s [vysoty]* 'from [a height].'

$\mathbf{Loc_{in}^{temp}}$ – preposition [analogous to $\mathbf{Loc}$] denoting temporal localization: $\mathbf{Loc_{in}^{temp}}$(*arest* 'arrest') = *pri* [*areste*] 'while being [arrested]'; for a more abstract example, $\mathbf{Loc_{in}^{temp}}$(*analiz* 'analysis') = *v xode* [*analiza*] 'in the course [of analysis].'

$\mathbf{Instr}$ – preposition meaning 'by means of': $\mathbf{Instr}$(*pistolet* 'pistol') = *iz* [*pistoleta*] 'with [a pistol]'; $\mathbf{Instr}$(*mašinka* 'typewriter') = *na* [*mašinke*] 'on [a typewriter].'

$\mathbf{Propt}$ – preposition meaning 'because of,' 'as the result of': $\mathbf{Propt}$ (*strax* 'fear') = *ot* [*straxa*], *so* [*straxu*] 'from [fear]'; $\mathbf{Propt}$(*ljubov'* 'love') = *iz* [*ljubvi k ...*] 'out of [one's love for ...]'; $\mathbf{Propt}$(*opyt I.1* 'experience') = *na* [*svoëm opyte*] 'from [one's own experience].'

$\mathbf{Copul}$ – copula: $\mathbf{Copul}$(*učitel'* 'teacher') = *byt', rabotat' učitelem* 'be, work as a teacher'; $\mathbf{Copul}$(*primer* 'example') = *byt', javljat'sja, služit'* [*primcrom*] 'be, represent, serve as [an example].'

$\mathbf{Pred}$ – verb meaning 'be ...,' i.e., combining $\mathbf{Copul}(W_0)$ with W_0. Thus $\mathbf{Pred}$ is merely a 'fused' expression of $\mathbf{Copul}(W_0) + W_0$ needed for the convenience of some synonymic transformations. For example, $\mathbf{Pred}$(*pjanica* 'drunkard') = *pjanstvovat'* 'drink,' $\mathbf{Pred}$(*rjadom* 'next to') = *sosedstvovat'* '[to] neighbor.'

The next three LFs are verbs, which are semantically empty in the context of the entry lexeme [= their key word] and which serve to link, on the syntactic level, the name of a participant of the situation denoted by W_0 to the name of the situation itself, i.e., to W_0. They play an important semantico-syntactic role and can be loosely called semi-auxiliaries.[3]

$\mathbf{Oper_i}$ – the role of the 1st deep actant (and of the grammatical subject) of the *Oper* verb is played by the *i*-th participant of the situation, while the 2nd deep actant (or the 1st surface complement) is represented by W_0 (other actants, if any, denote further participants of the situation): $\mathbf{Oper_1}$(*slëz* 'tears') = *lit', prolivat'* 'shed'; $\mathbf{Oper_1}$(*arest* 'arrest') = *proizvodit'* 'make [an arrest]'; $\mathbf{Oper_2}$(*arest* 'arrest') = *popadat'* [*pod arest*] 'fall [under arrest], *podvergat'sja* [*arestu*] 'undergo [arrest]'; $\mathbf{Oper_1}$(*soprotivienie* 'resistance') = *okazyvat'* 'show, put up'; $\mathbf{Oper_2}$(*soprotivlenie* 'resistance') = *vstrečat* 'meet,' *natalkivat'sja* [*na soprotivlenie*] 'run [into resistance].'

$\mathbf{Func_i}$ – the 1st deep actant (and the grammatical subject) of the *Func* verb is W_0 – the name of the situation, and the 2nd deep actant (or the 1st surface complement) is its *i*-th participant: $\mathbf{Func_1}$(*udivlenie* 'surprise, astonishment') = *oxvatyvat'* 'seize' (i.e., the person is overcome by surprise, astonishment); $\mathbf{Func_2}$(*temperatura* 'temperature') = *ravnjat'sja* 'be equal to'; $\mathbf{Func_1}$(*predloženie* 'proposal') = *isxodit'* [*ot kogo-l.*] 'be initiated by someone'; $\mathbf{Func_2}$(*predloženie* 'proposal') = *kasat'sja* [*čego-l.*] 'concern [something].' If $\mathbf{Func}$ has no complement at all, the subscript $_0$ is used: $\mathbf{Func_0}$(*dožd'* 'rain') = *idti*, lit. 'go.'

Labor$_{ij}$ – the 1st deep actant (and the grammatical subject) of the Labor verb is the *i*-th participant of the situation, while the 2nd deep actant is the *j*-th participant of the situation, and the 3rd deep actant (implemented by the 2nd surface complement) is W_0. Examples: **Labor$_{12}$**(*dopros* 'interrogation') = *podverget'* [*kogo-l. doprosu*] 'subject [someone to an interrogation]'; **Labor$_{32}$**(*arenda* 'lease') = *sdavat'* [*čto-l. v arendu*], lit. 'give [something on lease].'

Oper, Func, and Labor can be paired in converse relationships, that is, Oper$_1$ = Conv$_{21}$(Func$_1$); Labor$_{12}$ = Conv$_{132}$(Oper$_1$), and so on. These relationships can be diagrammed as follows. (The arrows represent semi-auxiliary verbs; an arrow's tail indicates the grammatical subject, while its head points towards the first complement.)

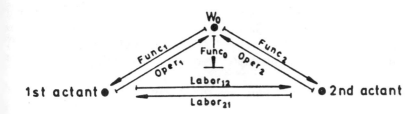

The same idea can also be represented in matrix form:

Surface-syntactic roles \ Semi-auxiliary verbs	Grammatical subject	1st complement	2nd complement
Oper$_{1/2}$	1st/2nd actant	W_0	—
Func$_{0/1/2/}$	W_0	none/1st/2nd actant	—
Labor$_{12/21}$	1st/2nd actant	2nd/1st actant	W_0

An illustration will be helpful. The diagram below represents the situation A changes B':

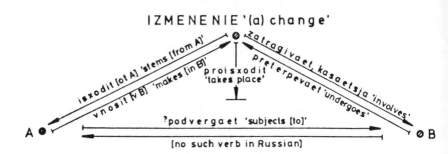

IZMENENIE '(a) change'

isxodit [ot A] 'stems [from A]'

vnosit [v B] 'makes [in B]'

proisxodit 'takes place'

zatragivaet, kasaetsja 'involves'

preterpevaet 'undergoes'

A ● ───────────────────────── ∅ B

?podvergaet 'subjects [to]'

[no such verb in Russian]

Now let us return to the survey of LFs.

Involv – verb linking a non-participant of a situation with the name of the given situation, which acts on him: $\mathbf{Conv_{21}Involv}$(*veter* 'wind') = *stojat'* [*na vetru*] 'stand [in the wind]'; $\mathbf{IncepInvolv}$(*metel'* 'snowstorm') = *zastigat'* 'catch'; $\mathbf{A_2Involv}$[*metel'* 'snowstorm'] = *v* [*meteli*] 'in [a snowstorm].'

The following three LFs represent the meanings of the so-called phase verbs:

Incep – 'begin';

Cont – 'continue';

Fin – 'end, cease.'

These verbs are connected by obvious semantic relationships:

$\mathbf{Fin}$(P) = $\mathbf{Incep}$(non P); $\mathbf{Cont}$(P) = non $\mathbf{Fin}$(P) = non $\mathbf{Incep}$(non P). Incep, Cont and Fin are used [at least in Russian] in combination with other LFs. Examples: $\mathbf{Oper_2}$(*vlast'* 'rule') = *naxodit'sja* [*pod vlast'ju ...*] 'be [under the rule of]'; $\mathbf{IncepOper_2}$(*vlast'* 'rule') = *popadat'* [*pod vlast* ...] 'fall [under the rule of]'; $\mathbf{FinOper_2}$(*vlast'* 'rule') = *vyxodit'* [*iz-pod vlasti...*] 'be no longer [under the rule of]'; $\mathbf{ContOper_1}$(*vlijanie* 'influence') = *soxranjat'* 'maintain'; $\mathbf{ContOper_2}$(*vlijanie* 'influence') = *ostavat'sja* [*pod vlijaniem ...*] 'remain [under the influence of]'; $\mathbf{ContFunc_0}$(*zapax* 'odor') = *deržat'sja* 'linger.'

Caus – 'cause,' 'do something so that a situation occurs'; Caus is often used in combination with other verbal Lexical Functions. For example, $\mathbf{CausOper_1}$(*mne nie* 'opinion') = *privodit'* [*kogo-l. k mneniju*] 'lead [someone to an opinion]'; $\mathbf{CausFunc_1}$(*nadežda* 'hope') = *vseljat', vdoxnut* [*nadeždu v kogo-l.*] 'raise [hope in someone], inspire [someone with hope]'; $\mathbf{CausOper_2}$(*obed* 'dinner') = *gotovit'* [*čto-l. k obedu*] 'prepare [something for dinner]'; $\mathbf{CausFunc_0}$(*obed* 'dinner') = *gotovit', strjapat'* [*obed*] 'make cook [the dinner].' The LF Caus naturally suggests the LFs Perm and Liqu:

Liqu(P) $\cong$ **Caus (non P), Perm(P)** $\cong$ **non Liqu(P)** $\cong$ **non Caus(non P)**. Both **Perm** and **Liqu** are normally used in combination with other verbal LFs.

Perm – 'permit,' 'allow': non **PermOper$_2$**(*kritika* 'criticism') = *ograždat'* [*kogo-l. ot kritiki*] 'protect [someone from criticism]'; similarly, **Perm-Oper$_2$**(*èkzamen* 'exam') = *dopuskat'* [*kogo-l. k èkzamenu*] 'allow [someone to take an exam].'

Liqu – 'liquidate,' 'do something so that a situation does not occur or stops occurring': **LiquFunc$_0$**(*negramotnost'* 'illiteracy') = *pokončit'* [*s negramotnost'ju*] 'wipe out [illiteracy]'; **Liqu$_1$Func$_0$**(*kostër* 'campfire') = *potušit'* [*kostër*] 'extinguish [a campfire].' [4]

Now let us look at another triplet of interrelated LFs: **Real$_i$**, **Fact$_i$** and **Labreal$_{ij}$**. The LFs **Real$_i$**, **Fact$_i$** and **Labreal$_{ij}$** are analogous to the LFs **Oper$_i$**, **Func$_i$** and **Labor$_{ij}$**, respectively, in that they imply the same participants of the situation W_0; thus, syntactically, **Real$_i$** is parallel to **Oper$_i$**, **Fact$_i$** to **Func$_i$**, and **Labreal$_{ij}$** to **Labor$_{ij}$**, so that in the former the subscripts have exactly the same meaning as in the latter. Unlike the 'empty' LFs **Oper$_i$**, **Func$_i$** and **Labor$_{ij}$**, however, the functions which we are now concerned with correspond to a specific content – 'to fulfill a demand contained in the meaning of W_0.' Different meanings can imply different demands. For example, the 'fulfillment,' or 'realization,' of a hypothesis is its confirmation; therefore, **Real$_2$**(*gipoteza* 'hypothesis') = *podtverždat'* 'confirm' [*Fakty podtverždajut gipotezu* 'Facts confirm the hypothesis'], and **Fact$_2$**(*gipoteza*) = *sootvetstvovat'* 'be in accordance with' [*Gipoteza sootvetstvuet faktam* 'The hypothesis is in accordance with the facts']. The 'realization' of an artifact is its utilization according to its intended function; thus **Fact$_0$**(*nož* 'knife') = *rezat'* 'cut' [*Ètot nož režet xorošo* 'This knife cuts neatly']. Further examples:

Real$_1$(*obvinenie* 'accusation') = *dokazyvat'* [*obvinenie*] 'prove [an accusation]'; **Real$_1$**(*učebnoe zavedenie* 'educational institution') = *prepodavat'* [*v učebnom zavedenii*] 'teach [at an educational institution].'

Real$_2$(*obvinenie* 'accusation') = *soglašat'sja* [*s obvineniem*] 'agree [with an accusation]'; **Real$_2$**(*učebnoe zavedenie* 'educational institution') = *izučat'sja, prepodavat'sja* [*v učebnom zavedenii*] 'be studied, be taught [at an educational institution],' while **Real$_3$**(*učebnoe zavedenie* 'educational institution') = *učit'sja* [*v učebnom zavedenii*] 'study [at an educational institution]'; **Real$_2$**(*soblazn* 'temptation') = *poddavat'sja* [*soblaznu*] 'yield [to a temptation].'

Fact$_0$(*somnenie* 'doubt')=*podtverždat'sja* 'to be corroborated,' *opravdyvat'sja* 'to prove justified'; **Fact$_0$**(*nadežda* 'hope') = *sbyvat'sja* 'to come true'; it also applies to substantives **Fact$_0$** (*sudno*[1] 'ship') = *plyt'* 'sail.'

$\text{Fact}_1(o\check{c}ered'\,\text{'turn'}) = byt'\,[za\ kem\text{-}l.]$ 'be [someone's turn]' [*Očered' za vami* 'it's your turn']; $\text{Fact}_1(\grave{e}ksperiment\,\text{'experiment'}) = udavat'sja\ [komu\text{-}l.]$ 'work out [for someone].'

$\text{Fact}_2(sudno^1\ \text{'ship'}) = vezti,\ perevozit\ [gruzy,\ passa\check{z}irov]$ 'convey, transport [cargo, passengers]'; $\text{Fact}_2(sosud\ \text{'vessel'}\ [\text{container}]) = soder\check{z}at'\,[\check{c}to\text{-}l.]$ 'contain [something].'

$\text{Labreal}_{12}(viselica\ \text{'gallows'}) = vzdermut'\,[kogo\text{-}l.\ na\ viselicu]$ 'string up [someone on a gallows]'; $\text{Labreal}_{12}(obed\ \text{'dinner'}) = est'\,[\check{c}to\text{-}l.\ na\ obed]$ 'eat [something for dinner].'

The LFs **Real**, **Fact** and **Labreal** can be superscripted [with Roman numerals] for the degree of the 'realization,' or 'fulfillment': e.g., the superscript ^{I} can mean 'fulfillment at the psychological level,' with the superscript ^{II} meaning 'fulfillment at the physical level,' cf. $\text{Real}_2^{\text{I}}(prigla\check{s}enie$ 'invitation') $= prinimat'$ 'accept,' while $\text{Real}_2^{\text{II}}(prigla\check{s}enie) = sledovat'$ 'take up'; or Fact_1^{I} (*čuvstvo* 'emotion') $= govorit'$, *podskazyvat'* lit. 'tell,' while, on the other hand, $\text{Fact}_1^{\text{II}}(\check{c}uvstvo) = zastavljat'$ 'force.'

Manif – 'manifest itself in something,' 'become apparent': $\text{Manif}(vina$ 'guilt,' 'fault') $= obnaru\check{z}ivat'sja$ 'become apparent'; $\text{Manif}(udivlenie$ 'surprise') $= skvozit'$ 'show through'; $\text{Manif}(bezgramotnost'$ 'ignorance') $= projavljat'sja\ [v\ ego\ rabote]$ 'manifest itself [in his paper].'

Sympt – 'symptom,' i.e., a verb phrase denoting a bodily reaction that is the symptom of an emotional or physical state; **Sympt** is a two-argument lexical function [see Iordanskaja 1972]: $\text{Sympt}(udivlenie$ 'surprise,' *glaza* 'eyes') $= glaza\ na\ lob\ polezli$ 'his eyes started from his face'; $\text{Sympt}(udivlenie$ 'surprise,' *rot* 'mouth') $= razinut'\ rot$ 'open one's mouth wide'; $\text{Sympt}(strax$ 'fear,' *volosy* 'hair') $= volosy\ vstali\ dybom$ 'his hair stood on end.'

Prepar – 'prepare' 'get ready for use or normal functioning': $\text{Prepar}^{\text{I}}\text{-}\text{Fact}_0(revolver$ 'gun') $= zarja\check{z}at'$ 'load'; $\text{Prepar}^{\text{II}}\text{Fact}_0(revolver) = vzvodit'\ kurok$ 'cock.' Roman superscripts, in much the same manner as with **Real**, **Fact** and **Labreal**, express the degree of readiness. Compare also: $\text{Prepar}_1\text{Oper}_1(obed$ 'dinner') $= vyxodit'\ [k\ obedu]$ 'appear [for dinner]'; $\text{PreparOper}_2(obed$ 'dinner') $= podavat'\ [na\ obed]$ 'serve [something for dinner]'; $\text{PreparFunc}_1(obed) = podavat'\ [obed\ komu\text{-}l.]$ 'serve [somebody the dinner].'

Prox – 'be about to/on the verge of': $\text{ProxOper}_1(ot\check{c}ajanie$ 'despair') $= byt'\ na\ grani\ [ot\check{c}ajanija]$ 'be on the edge [of despair]'; $\text{ProxFunc}_0(groza$ 'thunderstorm') $= sobirat'sja$ 'brew.'

Degrad – 'degrade,' 'become worse or bad': $\text{Degrad}(moloko\ \text{'milk'}) = skisnut'$ 'go sour'; $\text{Degrad}(mjaso\ \text{'meat'}) = isportit'sja,\ protuxnut'$ 'go bad'; $\text{Degrad}(disciplina\ \text{'discipline'}) = ra\check{s}\check{s}atat'sja$ 'crumble.'

Son – 'to emit characteristic sounds': **Son**(*sobaka* 'dog') = *lajat'* 'bark'; **Son**(*banknoty* 'banknotes') = *xrustet'* 'rustle'; **Son**(*sneg* 'snow') = *skripet'* 'crunch'; **Son**(*vodopad* 'waterfall') = *šumet'*, *revet'* 'roar.'

Imper – conventional command [expressed in a manner other than the regular imperative form]: **Imper**(*streljat'* 'shoot') = *ogon'!* 'fire!'; **Imper**(*brat' oružie* 'seize arms') = *v ruž'ë!* 'pick up arms!'; **Imper**(*govorit' tixo* 'speak low') = *ts-s-s !* 'sh-h-h !'; **Imper**(*brat'* 'take') = *na[te]!* 'take it!'

Perf – 'perfective,' i.e., 'have the process carried through to its natural limit': **Perf**(*vstavat'* 'be standing up') = *vstat'* 'have stood up' or **Perf**(*rešat'* 'be solving [a problem]') = *rešit'* 'have solved it.'

Imperf – 'imperfective,' i.e., 'be carrying out the process': for example, **Imperf**(*vstat'*) = *vstavat'*, **Imperf**(*rešit'*) = *rešat'*.

Result – 'resultative,' i.e., 'the state of affairs that normally results from the completion of the process': **Result**(*pokupat'* 'buy') = *imet'* 'have'; **Result**(*ložit'sja* 'lie down') = *ležat'* 'be lying'; **Result**(*naučit'sja* 'have learnt') = *umet'* 'know,' 'have necessary skills.'

Along with the standard basic LFs listed above, two more types of LFs are extensively used in the ECD: **NON-STANDARD** and **COMPOUND** LFs.

A **NON-STANDARD** LF is a meaning which, while it can be idiomatically expressed with a certain word or words, has either a rather limited range of expressions, or a strongly limited combinability, or both. In other words, it is too specific, too particular to be granted the status of a standard LF. Non-standard LFs are written in plain, but standardized Russian, which is glossed in the same kind of English in this chapter. Some examples:

AREST 'arrest'
such that Y is confined
      to his home   : *domašnij* 'house [arrest]'

DOLG 'debt'
such that it is the result
of a loss at cards that was
not immediately paid   : *kartočnyj* 'card [debt],'
                               obsolete [*dolg*] *česti* '[debt] of honor'

UČIT'SJA 'study'
a short time and/or not
very intensively with the
purpose of knowing Y better   : //*podučit'sja*
                               'study a little bit more'

A **COMPOUND** LF is a combination of syntactically related basic LFs that has a single lexical expression covering the meaning of the combination as a whole. Compound LFs are written as strings of basic LFs, standard as well as non-standard ones. We have presented numerous examples of compound LFs above; here we give some more illustrations, with the key word printed in boldface:

AntiMagn:*židkie* **aplodissmenty** 'thin applause,' *slabye* **dovody** 'weak arguments,' *nizkaja* **temperatura** 'low temperature,' *neznačitel'nye* **poteri** 'negligible losses.'

AntiVer:*ložnyj* **styd** 'false shame,' *lživoe* **obeščanie** 'false promise,' *ošibočnoe* **predstavlenie** 'a wrong conception,' *bezosnovatel'nye* **opasenija** 'unfounded misgivings.'

IncepOper$_1$: *priobretat'* **populjarnost'** 'acquire popularity,' *vpadat' v* **otčajanie** 'sink into despair,' *vstavat' na* **put'** **predatel'stva** 'take the path of treason,' *perexodit' v* **pike** 'go into a dive [as of an aircraft].'

CausOper$_2$: *sdavat' v* **èkspluataciju** 'put into operation,' *vvergat' v* **rabstvo** 'force into slavery,' *stavit' pod* **kontrol'** 'put under the control of.'

AntiReal$_2$: *zavalit'* <*provalit'*> **èkzamen,** *provalit'sja na* **èkzamene** 'flunk an examination,' *otvergat'* **sovet** 'reject somebody's advice,' *otklonjat'* **xodatajstvo** 'turn down an application.'

The following four remarks bearing on all LFs are in order here:

(i) A LF may have a FUSED expression, i.e., a single lexical unit covering both the meaning of the function itself and that of its argument (= key word). The fusion is shown by the symbol //, separating all the fused values (on its right) from all the non-fused ones. For example:

Magn(*dožd'* 'rain') = *prolivnoj* 'heavy' // *liven'* 'shower' (i.e., *liven'* = *prolivnoj dožd'*);

Magn(*vkusno* 'delicious') = *očen'* 'very' // *pal'čiki obližeš'*, lit. 'You'll lick your fingers.' (*pal'čiki obližeš'* = *očen' vkusno* 'finger-lickin' good.')

(ii) Several LFs having the same key word but unrelated to each other syntactically may simultaneously be expressed by one lexical unit covering the meanings of all the LFs involved. This is what we call a CONFIGURATION of LFs, as opposed to compound LFs, in which all the constituent basic LFs are syntactically related. In a configuration of LFs, the '+' sign is used to separate the constituents. For example, when in the entry SUD'BA^1 'fate, destiny' we write:

Fact$_3^{II}$ + AntiBon$_2$: *presledovat'* 'persecute.' It means that fate adversely [= **AntiBon$_2$**] affects [= **Fact$_3^{II}$**] the person in question.

Two more examples:

A$_1$(*vosxiščenie* 'admiration') + Magn(*vosxiščenie*) = *preispolnennyj* [*vosxiščenija*] 'full [of admiration]';

Oper₁(*otčajanie* 'despair') +**Magn**(*otčajanie*) = *byt' vo vlasti* [*otčaja-nija*] 'be seized with [despair].'

(iii) Some LFs [most often, **Magn** or **Real** and its relatives **Fact** and **Labreal**] may be subscripted with a semantic component of the key word's definition [in square brackets] to indicate that the meaning of this LF interacts exactly with this component of the key word's meaning. Thus:

Labreal₁₂[*xranit′ keep*](*pamjat'* '[computer] memory') = *xranit'* [*v pamjati*] 'store [in memory]';

Labreal₁₂[*vydavat′ output*](*pamjat'*) = *izvlekat'* [*iz pamjati*] 'extract [from the memory]';

Magn[*terjat′ kontrol′ losecontrol*](*strax*[1] 'fear') = *paničeskij*, lit. 'causing panic';

AntiVer[*poražat′ hit*](*streljat'*[1] 'shoot') = *ploxo* 'badly,' *skverno* 'poorly';

AntiVer[*cel′ target*](*streljat'*[1]) = *v vozdux* 'into the air.'

(iv) Furthermore, some LFs may be superscripted with semantic labels, like 'usual,' 'loc[ation],' 'temp[oral],' 'quant[itative],' to make their meaning more precise:

Magn[temp](*opyt* 'experience') = *dlitel'nyj* 'long';

Magn[quant](*opyt* 'experience') = *bol'šoj* 'considerable.'

In concluding this survey of LFs we would like to emphasize the fact that they are used for two main purposes:

- for the description of idiomatic or restricted lexical co-occurrence relations,
- and for specifying some universal synonymic transformations of utterances at the deep-syntactic level.

It is clear, for example, that (9) holds in any language:

(9) $W_0 = $ **Oper₁** $\rightarrow$ **S₀** $[W_0] = $ **Oper₂** $\rightarrow$ **S₀**$[W_0] = $ **Func₁** $\rightarrow$ **S₀**$[W_0]$
$= $ **Func₂** $\rightarrow$ **S₀**$[W_0] = $ **Labor₁₂** $\rightarrow$ **S₀**$[W_0]$; and so on.

The transformations presented in (9) can be exemplified as follows:

(10) *vlijat'* '[to] influence' = *okazyvat'* [= **Oper₁**] *vlijanie* 'have influence'
$= $ *byt'* <*naxodit'sja*> [= **Oper₂**] *pod vlijaniem* 'be under someone's influence,' etc.

Compare (11):

(11) *Ivan durno vlijaet na Petra* 'Ivan adversely influences Peter' = *Ivan okazyvaet na Petra dumoe vlijanie* 'Ivan has an adverse influence on Peter' = *Pëtr naxoditsja pod dumym vlijaniem Ivana* 'Peter is under the adverse influence of Ivan.'

Rules of type (9) allow one to establish a **PARAPHRASING SYS-TEM** for synonymic transformations of sentences and/or discourses. Such a system can automatically produce for any given text a set of its synonymous or nearly-synonymous paraphrases. It can also automatically derive a canonical invariant for a set of synonymous texts. This indicates yet another promising direction for the practical use of the ECD, namely in the domain of automatic text processing. [For more details about paraphrasing systems using LFs as a tool see, e.g., Zholkovskij and Mel'chuk 1967, 1970, or Mel'čuk 1988c.]

By making extensive use of LFs, the ECD aims at presenting the restricted lexical co-occurrence of the entry lexeme and the set expressions involving it as fully and systematically as possible.[5]

8. *Examples.* The use of the entry lexeme and the corresponding LFs is exemplified by actual sentences.

9. *Encyclopedic information.* We admit encyclopedic information to the extent to which it is vital for the correct use of the entry lexeme. This information includes, among other things, an indication of the different species or different stages of the object or process denoted by W_0, the main types of behavior of this object or process, its co-species, etc.

10. *Idioms.* The last part of every dictionary entry contains a list of semantically unanalyzable idiomatic expressions in which the given entry lexeme appears. Our treatment of idioms coincides in general with the treatment of phraseology in ordinary monolingual dictionaries. However, the number of genuine idioms in the ECD turns out to be smaller than in traditional dictionaries because a significant amount of phraseology is covered by LFs, and the combination of a LF with its key word is not considered an idiom in the ECD.

Another important feature of the treatment of idioms in the ECD is the effort to classify them logically wherever possible. Such classification is achieved on the basis of connotations, as in the entry VETER 'wind,' for example, where the idioms are categorized according to the connotations of the entry lexeme, i.e., the semantic features 'quickness of movement,' 'changeability,' and 'lack of seriousness.'

Note that part 10 is used for cross reference only. In principle, the idioms are not provided with any information in this part since they are fully described in entries of their own.

Possible uses of the ECD

Here we limit ourselves to a brief characterization of three areas in which an ECD, that is a monolingual dictionary of any language designed along the same lines as the specific ECD we are discussing now, can find application.

(1) The ECD is likely to become a central component of automatic text synthesis and analysis systems because it presents all the essential information about the vocabulary of the language in question in an explicit and systematic way.

(2) The ECD, we hope, represents a contribution to language theory, at least in so far as it provides for the development and refinement of a semantic metalanguage, the systematic account of phraseology, and the development of a multifaceted approach to the word taken as the sum of all its semantic and syntactic characteristics.

(3) Various potential advantages are provided by the ECD in the area of language instruction (of both native and foreign tongues), as well as in any activity connected with the development of language skills. Textbooks, pedagogically-oriented dictionaries, reference works, etc. can be successfully developed along the format of the ECD.

It is obvious that a short introduction cannot clarify all difficulties and answer all questions. It is impossible to discuss here at length many of the technicalities of presentation, not to mention important theoretical matters which belong instead to general linguistics. Yet we hope this chapter will give the readers a foretaste of ECD lexicography and thus entice them into reading Mel'čuk and Zholkovsky 1984 and considering its entries. We feel confident that many fine points will become clear after repeated perusal.

For those who find it difficult to read Russian dictionary entries but would like to have a better understanding of what the Russian ECD is like, one of the very first entries of this dictionary – AGRESSIJA 'aggression' – is reproduced, in Latin transliteration and with complete English glosses, in the Appendix to this chapter. Let us also emphasize that now two volumes of a French ECD are available: [Mel'čuk et al. 1984 and 1988].

Notes

1. Since the notions of lexeme and vocable are crucial for the ECD, let us elaborate on them.

A **LEXEME** is an elementary lexical unit of the language, or one word taken in one well-defined sense with one set of syntactic, combinatorial and morphological properties. Each lexeme is described by one dictionary entry, and each dictionary entry describes one lexeme (or one idiom in a given sense; however, we will not consider idioms here).

Lexemes L_1 and L_2 are said *to be semantically linked in a direct way* if their signata share a non-trivial semantic component, which occupies (almost) the same position in the structure of the signata. Two lexemes connected by a sequence of direct semantic links are said *to be semantically linked* . Thus let L_1 = 'ABC,' L_2 = 'BDE,' L_3 = 'DFG,' and L_4 = 'GHK.' Lexemes L_1 and L_2 are semantically linked in a direct way, their signata sharing the component 'B,' as are L_2 and L_3 ['D'] and L_3 and L_4 ['G']; but L_1 and L_4 (or L_2 and L_4) are semantically linked even though they do not share any semantic components – since L_1 and L_4 are, respectively, the first and the last terms in a sequence of direct semantic links:

$$L_1 \longleftrightarrow L_2 \longleftrightarrow L_3 \longleftrightarrow L_4.$$

A **VOCABLE** (the term, coined after the Latin *vocabulum* 'word, term,' is borrowed from French) is the set of all lexemes such that:
  (i) all of them have an identical signans;
  (ii) any one of them is semantically linked to all the others.
Two lexemes that have different signantia belong to two different vocables. Two lexemes that have an identical signans but are not semantically linked also belong to two different (this time homonymous) vocables; such lexemes stand in the relation of homonymy. Two lexemes that belong to the same vocable stand in the relation of polysemy.
A lexeme of the ECD is roughly analogous to what is now known as a 'word sense,' and a vocable, to a 'full word,' i.e., to an entry in traditional dictionaries. In the ECD, a lexeme is an entry, and a vocable, a family of closely related entries. Examples:
LABOR I.1 'physical or mental efforts of a practical nature = work'; LABOR I.2 'a specific task = a piece of LABOR I.1'; LABOR I.3 'workers collectively = LABORING I.1 class'; and LABOR II 'the physical efforts of childbirth' are lexemes belonging to the same vocable LABOR.
TICK[1] 'a recurring sharp, clicking sound,' TICK[2] 'a blood-sucking insect,' and TICK[3] 'the cloth case of a mattress or pillow' are lexemes of three different vocables.

2. Instead of the more familiar direct, indirect and prepositional objects, we speak, when discussing surface-syntactic actants, of the 1st, 2nd, 3rd, ... complements. They are ranked according to the following three criteria:
  • morphological marking [the accusative precedes the genitive, the latter precedes the dative, etc.; all cases precede an infinitive, and the infinitive, a prepositional phrase];
  • omissibility [the less omissible a complement is, the lower its number];
  • word order [the nearer to the governor a complement must be in a neutral sequence, the lower its number].
For example, in *Ivan kolotil Petra* [ACC] *kulakami* [INSTR] *po spine*, lit. 'Ivan thrashed Peter with his fists on the back,' *Petra =* the 1st complement, *kulakami =* the 2nd complement, and *po spine =* the 3rd complement.

3. These verbs may be empty in the language, like OKAZAT' in Russian, which does not mean anything definite and cannot be translated in isolation; or else they are meaningful, their meaning being, however, included in that of their key word.

4. In instances where the first actant of a **Caus**, **Perm** or **Liqu** verb is also a participant of the situation W_0, the function symbol is subscripted with the number of this participant. Specifically, $\mathbf{Liqu_1Func_0}(W_0)$ indicates that the situation W_0 is liquidated by its own first participant (and not by someone not directly involved in the situation).

5. The only predecessors of the ECD in this domain are, to the best of our knowledge, the following:

Reum, A. 1953. *Petit dictionnaire du style à l'usage des Allemands.* Leipzig: VEB Bibliographisches Institut.

Reum, A. 1955. *A Dictionary of English Style.* Leverkusen: Gottschalksche Verlagsbuchhandlung.

Agricola, E. 1970. *Wörter und Wendungen. Wörterbuch zum deutschen Sprachgebrauch.* Leipzig: VEB Bibliographisches Institut.

Rodale, W. 1976. *The Word Finder.* Emmaus, PA: Rodale Books Inc.

Moliner, M. 1980. *Diccionario de uso del español.* Madrid: Gredos.

Katsumata, S. 1958. *Kenkyusha's New Dictionary of English Collocations.* Tokyo: Kenkyusha.

However, none of these dictionaries arranges the collocations and phrases it gives in semantically motivated patterns.

Other monolingual dictionaries which are close to the ECD in their treatment of definitions and cross-references to synonyms and antonyms, although not in their treatment of collocations, are:

Morris, W., ed. 1971. *The American Heritage Dictionary of the English Language.* New York: American Heritage Publ. Company and Houghton Mifflin Company, 1971.

Gove, P. B., ed. 1971. *Webster's Third New International Dictionary of the English Language.* Springfield, MA: G. & C. Merriam Company.

Robert, P. 1977. *Le Petit Robert. Dictionnaire alphabétique et analogique de la langue française.* Paris: Société du Nouveau Littré.

In this connection, we would also like to mention two more recently published dictionaries:

Apresjan, Ju. D., V. V. Botjakova et al. 1979. *Anglo-russkij sinonimičeskij slovar'* [English-Russian Synonym Dictionary]. Moscow: Russkij Jazyk. This dictionary follows, in an explicit form, some principles of the ECD (in definitions, presentation of combinability and co-occurrences, etc.).

Apresjan, Ju. D., and E. Páll. 1982. *Russkij glagol – vengerskij glagol. Upravlenie i sočetaemost'* [Russian Verb – Hungarian Verb. Government and Co-occurrence], vols. 1-2. Budapest: Tankönyvkiadó. This dictionary also has several features in common with the ECD.

Acknowledgments

We are indebted to a number of people who have commented on previous versions of this introduction. Our special gratitude goes to L. Elnitsky, B. and J. Grimes, R. Ilson, L. Iordanskaja, R. Kittredge, and J. Steele for their valuable remarks and suggestions.

Appendix – a dictionary entry from the ECD adapted for English readers

The entry given below is slightly abridged. All metalinguistic statements are in English; all Russian lexical material is glossed. This version has been prepared by L. Elnitsky and I. Mackenzie.

AGRESSIJA 'aggression'

AGRÉSSI|JA, *i*, pl undesirable, fem.

agressija X-a protiv Y-a 'aggression of X against Y' = protivorečaščee meždunarodnomu pravu vtorženie vojsk gosudarstva X na territoriju gosudarstva Y, javljajuščeesja načalom voennyx dejstvij meždu X-om i Y-om 'intrusion, in violation of international law, by the armed forces of a state X into the territory of another state Y, leading to hostilities between X and Y.'

Cf. BLOKADA 'blockade'; INFIL'TRACIJA 'infiltration'; ZAXVAT 'seizure'; OKKUPACIJA 'occupation'; ANNEKSIJA 'annexation.'

Government Pattern

I = X (aggressor)	II=Y (victim)
1. N_{gen} 'N's' 2. *so storony* N_{gen} 'by N' 3. A	1. *protiv* N_{gen} 'against N'

(1) M_2 = the second deep-syntactic actant denotes a state or the people of Y.

agressija (Kembrii) (protiv Muraka) '(Cambria's) aggression (against Muraq),' *agressija (so storony Kembrii) (protiv Muraka)* 'aggression (by Cambria) (against Muraq),' *kembrijskaja agressija (protiv Muraka <≅ protiv murakskogo naroda>)* 'Cambrian aggression (against Muraq <≅ against the Muraqi people>).'

Impossible: **agressija protiv murakskogo pravitel'stva* 'aggression against the Muraqi government' (1), but cf. *agressija kembrijskogo pravitel'stva protiv Muraka* 'agression by the Cambrian government against Muraq.'

Lexical Functions

$\mathrm{Syn}_{\supset}$	:	*napadenie* 'attack,' *vtorženie* 'invasion'
Anti	:	*nenapadenie* 'non-aggression'
A_0	:	*agressivnyj 1a* 'aggressive 1' [*plan* 'design' *politika* 'policy,' *vojna* 'war']
$S_{1\cap}$	:	*agressor 1,2* 'aggressor'
S_2	:	*ob'ekt* 'target' [$\sim i$]
$S_1\mathrm{Real}_2$ or S_{2C}	:	*žertva* 'victim' [$\sim i$] [the target of a successful act of aggression]
S_{res}	:	*posledstvija* 'consequences' [$\sim i$]
Sing	:	*akt* 'act'[$\sim i$], [*agressivnyj 1a* 'aggressive 1'] *akt* 'act'
Able_1	:	*agressivnyj 1b* 'aggressive 2'
$S_1\mathrm{Able}_1$	:	*sily* 'forces' [$\sim i$], [*agressivnye 1b* 'aggressive 2'] *sily* 'forces'
Qual_1	:	*voinstvennyj* 'bellicose,' *militaristskij* 'militaristic'
$\mathrm{Magn}_{[unlawful]}$	:	*nesprovocirovannaja* 'unprovoked'; *prjamaja* 'open,' *neprikrytaja* 'undisguised,' *otkrovennaja* 'naked'
$\mathrm{AntiBon} + \mathrm{Magn}_{[unlawful]}$	:	*prestupnaja* 'criminal'; *naglaja* 'flagrant'
$\mathrm{Magn}_{[hostilities]}$	:	*varvarskaja* 'barbarous,' *krovavaja* 'bloody'
Magn^{temp}	:	*prodolžitel'naja* 'prolonged,' *dlitel'naja* 'continuous'
$F_1 = \mathrm{IncepPredPlus}^{refl}_{[intrusion]}$	:	*usilivat'sja* 'increase'
S_0F_1	:	*usilenie* 'increase,' *èskalacija* 'escalation' [$\sim i$]
$\mathrm{IncepPredPlus}^{refl}_2$	:	*rasširjat'sja* 'expand'
$F_2 = \mathrm{Caus}_1\mathrm{PredPlus}^{refl}_2$	:	*rasširjat'* 'expand' [$\sim ju$]
S_0F_2	:	*rasširenie* 'expansion' [$\sim i$]

Adv_1	:	*v xode* 'in the course of'$[\sim i]$
$Oper_1$	:	*soveršat'* 'commit,' *osuščestvijat'* 'carry out' $[\sim ju]$
$IncepOper_1$	:	*načinat'* 'start,' *razvjazyvat'* 'embark on' $[\sim ju]$
$ContOper_1$	:	*prodolžat'* 'carry on'$[\sim ju]$
$FinOper_1$	:	*prekraščat'* 'cease' $[\sim ju]$
$CausOper_1$	:	*tolkat'* 'incite, push' $[N_{acc}$ *na* 'to' $\sim ju] // natravlivat'$ 'set' $[S_{acc}$ *na* 'against' $S_{acc} = Y]$
$Oper_2$	:	*podvergat'sja*, lit. 'undergo' $[\sim i]$
$Func_0$	:	*proisxodit'* 'take place, occur'
$F_3 = IncepFunc_0$	:	*načinat'sja* 'begin'
$S_{loc}(PredAble_1)F_3$	:	*očag* 'source' $[\sim i]$ [cf. *poroxovaja bočka* 'powder keg' in VOJNA 'war']
attempt to $CausFunc_0$	:	*provocirovat'* 'provoke'$[\sim ju]$
$PermFunc_0$	:	*popustitel'stvovat'* 'connive at,' *potvorstvovat'* 'abet' $[\sim i]$
$AntiPermFunc_0$	:	*sderživat'* 'contain,' *obuzdyvat'* 'curb' $[\sim ju]$
$LiquFunc_0$	:	*ostanavlivat'* 'stop,' *presekat'* 'stop short' $[\sim ju]$, *položit' konec* 'put an end to' $[\sim i]$, *pokončit'* 'end' $[s \sim ej]$
$Func_2$	:	*byt' napravlena* 'be directed' $[protiv$ 'against' $S_{gen}]$
$S_{res}Real_1$	:	*plody* 'rewards' $[\sim i]$
$AntiReal_2$	:	*otražat'* 'repel' $[\sim ju]$
$Prepar_1^I$	:	*vynašivat' plany* 'hatch plans' $[\sim i]$
$Prepar_1^{II}$	:	*gotovit'* 'prepare' $[\sim ju]$
A. committed by means of aircraft	:	*vozdušnaja* 'aerial'
a treaty to mutually renounce A.	:	$// pakt < dogovor > o$ *nenapadenii* 'non-aggression pact <treaty>'

Examples

Podobnye akcii pravjaščix krugov Danirei mogut liš' sprovocirovat' agres-
siju so storony Kembrii protiv Muraka $<\cong$ ... *tolknut' Kembriju na agres-*
siju protiv Muraka> 'Such action by the ruling circles of Danirea can only

provoke aggression on the part of Cambria against Muraq $<\cong$ ... push Cambria into aggression against Muraq>.' *S prixodom nacistov k vlasti v Evrope voznik opasnyj očag agressii* 'When the Nazis came to power, a dangerous source of aggression appeared in Europe.' *Pravitel'stvo Muraka vyrazilo ènergičnyj protest protiv oblëta sudov, obstrela pograničnyx punktov i drugix aktov agressii $<=$ agressivnyx aktov>*. 'The Muraqi government protested energetically against the overflight of its ships (by Cambrian aircraft), against attacks on its border posts, and against all other acts of aggression $<=$ aggressive acts>.'

References

Apresjan, Ju. 1974. *Leksičeskaja semantika: Sinonimičeskie sredstva.* Moscow: Nauka.

Apresjan, Ju. 1980. *Tipy informacii dija poverxnostno-semantičeskogo komponenta modeli "Smysl ⟺ Tekst."* Vienna: Wiener Slawistischer Almanach.

Apresjan, Ju., Mel'čuk, I., and Žolkovskij, A. 1973. Materials for an Explanatory Combinatory Dictionary of Modern Russian. In F. Kiefer, ed., *Trends in Soviet Linguistics.* Dordrecht: Reidel, 411-438.

Apresyan, Y., Mel'čuk, I., and Žolkovsky, A. 1970. Semantics and Lexicography: Towards a New Type of Unilingual Dictionary. In F. Kiefer, ed., *Studies in Syntax and Semantics.* Dordrecht: Reidel, 1-33.

Apresjan, Ju., Žolkovskij, A., and Mel'čuk, I. 1968. O sisteme semantičeskogo sinteza. III. Obrazcy slovarnyx statej. *Naučno-texničeskaja informacija, serija 2,* **11**, 8-21.

Iordanskaja, L. N. 1972. Leksikografičeskoe opisanie russkix vyraženij, oboznačajučšix fizičeskie simptomy čuvstv. *Mašinnyj perevod i prikladnaja lingvistika,* **16**, 3-30.

Iordanskaja, L. N. 1973. Tentative Lexicographic Definitions for a Group of Russian Words Denoting Emotions. In F. Kiefer, ed., *Trends in Soviet Linguistics.* Dordrecht: Reidel, 389-410.

Iordanskaja, L. N. 1979. The Semantics of Three Russian Verbs of Perception: VOSPRINIMAT' 'to perceive,' OŠČUŠČAT' 'to sense,' and ČUVSTVOVAT' 'to feel.' *Linguistics,* **17**, 825-842.

Iordanskaja, L. N., and Mel'čuk, I. 1984. Connotation en sémantique et lexicographie. In Mel'čuk et al. 1984, 33-40.

Mel'čuk, I. A. 1973. Towards a Linguistic 'Meaning ⟺ Text' Model. In *Trends in Soviet Linguistics.* Dordrecht: Reidel, 33-57.

Mel'čuk, I. A. 1974. Esquisse d'un modèle linguistique du type "Sens ⇔ Texte." *Problèmes actuels en psycholinguistique. Colloques intern. du CNRS*, **206**, 291-317.

Mel'čuk, I. A. 1978. A New Kind of Dictionary and its Role as a Core Component of Automatic Text Processing Systems. *T.A. Informations*, **2**, 3-8.

Mel'čuk, I. A. 1981. Meaning-Text Models: A Recent Trend in Soviet Linguistics. *Annual Review of Anthropology* **10**, 27-62.

Mel'čuk, I. A. 1982. Lexical Functions in Lexicographic Description. *Proceedings of the VIIIth Annual Meeting of the Berkeley Linguistic Society*. Berkeley, CA: UCB, 427-444.

Mel'čuk, I. A. 1988a. *Dependency Syntax: Theory and Practice*. Albany: State University of New York Press.

Mel'čuk, I. A. 1988b. Description sémantique des unités lexicales dans un dictionnaire explicatif et combinatoire: principes de base et critères heuristiques. In Mel'čuk et al. 1988.

Mel'čuk, I. A. 1988c. Paraphrase et lexique dans la théorie linguistique Sens-Texte. *Lexique*, **6**, 13-54.

Mel'čuk, I. A., Arbatchewsky-Jumarie, N., Elnitsky, L., Iordanskaja, L., and Lessard, A. 1984. *Dictionnaire explicatif et combinatoire du français contemporain. Recherches lexico-sémantiques. I*. Montreal: University of Montreal Press.

Mel'čuk, I. A., Arbatchewsky-Jumarie, N., Dagenais, L., Elnitsky, L., Iordanskaja, L., Lefebvre, M-N., and Mantha, S. 1988. *Dictionnaire explicatif et combinatoire du français contemporain. Recherches lexico-sémantiques. II*. Montreal: University of Montreal Press.

Mel'čuk, I. A., Iordanskaja, L. N., and Arbatchewsky-Jumarie, N. 1981. Un nouveau type de dictionnaire. *Cahiers de lexicologie*, **38**, 3-34.

Mel'čuk, I. A., Iordanskaja, L. N., Arbatchewsky-Jumarie, N., and Lessard, A. 1983. Trois principes de description sémantique d'une unité lexicale dans un dictionnaire explicatif et combinatoire. *Revue Canadienne de Linguistique*, **28**, 2, 105-121.

Mel'čuk, I. A. and Zholkovsky, A. K. 1984. *Explanatory Combinatorial Dictionary of Modern Russian. Semantico-Syntactic Studies of Russian Vocabulary*. Vienna: Wiener Slawistischer Almanach.

Mel'čuk, I. A. and Žolkovskij, A. K. 1970. Towards a Functioning Meaning-Text Model of Language. *Linguistics*, **57**, 10-47.

Zholkovskij, A. K. and I. A. Mel'chuk. 1970. Sur la synthèse sémantique. *T.A. Informations*, **2**.

Žholkovskii, A. K. and I. A. Mel'chuk. 1967. Semantic Synthesis. *Systems Theory Research - a translation of Problemy kibernetiki*, **19**, 179-243.

3
The dictionary and the
thesaurus can be combined *

Nicoletta Calzolari
Istituto di Linguistica Computazionale
Università di Pisa

Abstract

This paper discusses the design and implementation of a large lexical data-base that combines dictionary information with that typical of a thesaurus. It contains the syntactic information and the definitions from a traditional dictionary for more than one hundred thousand Italian words, as well as the synonyms, antonyms, hyponyms, and hyperonyms used to relate words in a thesaurus. In spite of its very large size the entire database is stored in such a way that it is always accessible interactively both to human questions and queries from computer programs.

Introduction

For several years our team at the University of Pisa has been working on the development of a large lexical database designed to be a repository of the entire vocabulary of Italian [Calzolari 1982, 1983a, 1983b; Calzolari

* This work was supported by the Istituto di Linguistica Computazionale del CNR, Pisa.

and Ceccotti 1981]. We have now collected approximately 106,000 lemmas or root forms, more than one million word forms, and approximately 186,000 definitions. The data and the database organization are described in Gruppo di Pisa 1979.

Now that we have captured syntactic information about our lexical entries, we have turned our attention toward the study of semantics. As we examined the definitions we discovered that they contain a great deal of implicit information about lexical and semantic relationships between words. The research described in this chapter focusses on the problem of making this implicit relational information entirely explicit. Using these relationships, words can be accessed not just alphabetically but from any point in the semantic field. Every word can be viewed as the center of its own lexical universe; we can trace out all its derivational morphology and all its semantic correlates. Our ultimate goal is to make our lexical database function both as a dictionary and a thesaurus [Michiels and Noel 1982, Calzolari 1984].

What advantages does a computerized lexical database give us that cannot be found in a printed dictionary? For the ordinary person who uses the computer only for word-processing, the potential benefit is relatively small – the convenience of having spelling correction and thesaurus lookup available immediately online [Fox et al. 1980]. For the scholar using an information retrieval system the benefits may be much larger – the addition of terms from the thesaurus to an otherwise unsuccessful query may improve recall significantly [Calzolari and Picchi 1984]. To the computational linguist a lexical database is an absolutely essential tool – this kind of information is precisely what is needed by natural language processing programs that try to understand and generate text [Smith and Maxwell 1977; Byrd 1983]. Until now most of this research has been purely experimental, dealing with toy systems; a large lexical database is a key element in moving from the experimental to the practical in machine translation, in question-answering, and in natural language front-ends [McNaught 1983; Kay 1983; Amsler 1984]. Recently the publishers of commercial dictionaries have begun to build lexical databases for themselves with the intent of using them as a source for a whole family of dictionaries [Hultin and Logan 1984; Brustkern and Hess 1983; Nagao et al. 1982]. Most important, from my point of view, is the resource that the lexical database provides to the linguist and the psychologist studying language. We are constantly learning more about language from our work with the database, deriving new information from the database itself to enrich it further.

The aim of this paper is to discuss the ways in which a lexical database can be structured and exploited in order to investigate the semantic structure of the lexicon, and to consider how database facilities can be used to capture eventual generalizations from already available dictionary data. This can be achieved with two apparently opposite strategies: either by explicitly displaying a number of lexical relations which in lexicographic definitions are only implicit, or by eliminating many redundancies and discrepancies (due to the use of natural language), i.e., by formulating rules to produce, implicitly, much of what is now explicitly repeated in identical or similar definitional patterns or terms. With this aim in mind, we can examine the possibility of modelling a new type of computerized dictionary able to overcome some of the drawbacks of traditional machine-readable dictionaries. The computational aids described make it possible to conceive a new model of a database dictionary including features of both the dictionary and the thesaurus, two different viewpoints on the lexicon which up until now have traditionally been considered as alternatives.

The Italian lexical database

The Italian Machine Dictionary is organized as a Database (DMI/DB) in separate archives. The main archives of the database are the Lemmas (approx. 106,000), the Word-Forms (more than one million), and the Definitions (approx. 186,000). The Definitions archive was the starting point for this research. Other archives (partly virtual archives) of Synonyms, Antonyms, Derivatives, Hyponyms and Hyperonyms, have been recently implemented and constitute a logical extension of the original database.

The entire database is recorded on Mass Storage devices; it is always on-line and is interactively accessible despite its very large size. The application of database methods and techniques for the organization of this dictionary makes it possible to extract completely different types of information (i.e., structured in several distinct ways and at various levels) from the same basic data. By using a large number of secondary or alternate indexes, or inversions, each record can be directly accessed by many different "search keys," i.e., the values of all the relevant attributes of an archive. For example, one can ask for all the entries beginning with a certain substring, and query all their definitions, or their synonyms, or hyponyms in the dictionary by an interactive information retrieval procedure. One can also select, for instance, all the lemmas ending in -TADE and, furthermore, one can ask whether they are graphical variants of other entries. In this way, it clearly appears on the screen that almost all these lemmas are archaic variants of lemmas ending in -TÀ (see Figure 1). The same query for lemmas ending in -TATE will result in an overlapping of many forms.

In a certain sense, the user can create his own "virtual database," tailored for his particular interests, using a simple query language. This query language, i.e., the logical access to the system, activates one or another of the many different paths connecting the entries. In fact, this capability of

Has Variants:

'gioco'	→	GIOCO	SM	→	GIUOCO	SM
					IOCO	SM 1
'io'	→	IO	PQ	→	EO	PQ 1
					ME	PQ
					MECO	PQ 3
					MEVE	PQ 1
					MI	PQ
					NOI	PQ

Is a Variant of:

'la'	→	LA	R	→	IL	R
		LA	PQ	→	ESSA	FS
		LA	SM		without pointer	
suff.'-tade'	→	ETADE	SF 1	→	ETÀ	SF
		CAPARBIETADE	SF 1	→	CAPARBIETÀ	SF
		SOCIETADE	SF 1	→	SOCIETÀ	SF
		PENTADE	SF		without pointer	
		EMPIETADE	SF 1	→	EMPIETÀ	SF
		. . .				
		. . .				
suff.'-tate'	→	ETATE	SF 1	→	ETÀ	SF
		SOCIETATE	SF 1	→	SOCIETÀ	SF
		PIETATE	SF 1	→	PIETÀ	SF
		EMPIETATE	SF 1	→	EMPIETÀ	SF
		ESTATE	SF		without pointer	
		. . .				
		. . .				

Figure 1. Example of interactive retrieval of variants
(SM = masculine noun, SF = feminine noun, PQ = relative pronoun,
R = determiner, 1 = archaic, 3 = rare)

a completely different access to the data, i.e., direct access to each entry and to each attribute, is of crucial, decisive importance in the design of a new computerized dictionary model, compared to the sequentially ordered machine-readable dictionaries. Easy extraction and distribution of information is achieved by the alphabetical ordering of entries in traditional dictionaries, or by the grouping of items according to concepts and topics in thesauruses. These two traditionally very distinct approaches to lexical data can be combined and merged into a single dictionary, if it is a database dictionary.

The dictionary as a means to investigate the structure of the lexicon

Let us examine how a database dictionary of this type can be exploited to analyze extensively the semantic content of the lexicon, and to encode in specified formats the results of this analysis. Within this framework, the dictionary is used to investigate aspects of the lexical system, as they have been traditionally coded by the lexicographer, more or less consciously, and often not explicitly or systematically. First of all, a database dictionary makes it possible to overcome the inadequacy of the simple alphabetical ordering of entries which, in a certain sense, obscures the rich potentiality of information contained in a standard dictionary. By using a database dictionary it is instead possible to obtain a number of different orderings, according to different kinds of logical arrangements within the lexicon.

This organization is based on relationships which are linguistically more relevant than the purely extrinsic alphabetical relation (which will obviously not be discarded, but will remain simply as one among the others). These other dispositions are in fact determined by the various logical, conceptual, semantic or lexical relations which are discovered and established between the entries, according to the various points of view from which each entry is considered. All these different ordering relations divide the lexicon into subsets, which intersect and overlap, forming an intricate network based on many distinct types of links or relations. Let us list some of the possible relations which can be detected in a database dictionary. Some of these can now be extracted automatically (or at least semi-automatically) from the Italian machine-dictionary definitions, and can thus be better analyzed in view of their successive formalization and implementation in the database dictionary. They are:

(a) hierarchical relations;
(b) synonymy relations;
(c) derivational relations;
(d) other taxonomies not organized on the IS-A relation;
(e) co-occurrence or collocational relations;
(f) terminological sublexicons;
(g) restriction or modification relations;
(h) case-type or argument relations;
(i) lexical fields.

Once these semantic relations have been included, the dictionary has also been given a thesaurus-type organization.

From lexical definitions to semantic links

One of the aims of this study is to examine the possibility of automatically obtaining information regarding semantic links and connections like those listed above from the definitions of a standard printed dictionary. My purpose is to evaluate to what extent the computational exploitation of natural language definitional sentences can help in discovering and implementing these types of links. At this point, I should like to make a few suggestions as to how it is actually possible to work on normal definitional data in order to establish and to generate a preliminary set of basic links, which must of course be extended.

The definitions, in fact, present many regularities in their lexical and/or syntactic patterns. The example in Figure 2 shows different generic terms (in italics) used to define words ending in -METRO, which are all related to the concept of "Instrument": why should INSTRUMENT not be automatically assigned to these terms as the main semantic marker? The same applies to the notion of "Measuring" which always links the generic and specific parts of these definitions, even if expressed in different ways (in inverted commas). These regular patterns should be exploited. As a matter of fact, natural language definitions, if appropriately ordered in logical subsets, convey information that can be used to attempt a normalization and then a formalization of the semantic content of a dictionary, i.e., to reduce definitions to standardized canonical forms. Some brief considerations of some of the relations listed above will appear below in the form of examples. These semantic links and relations are actually obtained or obtainable in the DMI/DB, while rearranging the definitional data into a thesaurus-like or conceptual organization.

Hierarchical relations

When querying our dictionary database, many virtual paths can be traced upwards and downwards between the entries, and this allows the interactive retrieval of hyponyms and superordinates up to n levels within the entire lexicon. A virtual network of IS-A links was thus constructed, by which it is possible to select coherent semantic subsets, e.g., all the names of tools, or machines, dogs, fish, etc. The semantic chains which produce these subsets must obviously be evaluated and controlled manually to verify their validity, and to examine the coherency and consistency of the definitions from which these chains originated. When we move upwards along these chains, we find that they are usually halted after 2, 3 or 4 steps in one of the two following ways:

a) a semantically almost empty word is reached (e.g., CHE (*what*), CHI (*who*)) which has no content definition, but only a functional definition;

b) a set of circular definitions is found, i.e., a loop is established through definitions (as happens for items defined as PARTE DI (*part of*), because PARTE references to PEZZO (*piece*) which references back to PARTE). In this case it is interesting to see how some of these loops actually function as primitive, undefinable concepts [see Calzolari 1977; Amsler 1980, p.92].

VOLTAMETRO	→	*strumento* "che misura" quantità di elettricità
MACHMETRO	→	*strumento* "indicatore" del numero di mach
ASSORBIMETRO	→	*apparecchio* "che misura" l'assorbimento di gas
CAPACIMETRO	→	*strumento* "per misurare" capacità elettriche
ALCALIMETRO	→	*apparecchio* "per determinare" l'alcalinità delle soluzioni
ESTENSIMETRO	→	*dispositivo* "per misurare" deformazione di corpi
DECOMPRESSIMETRO	→	*apparecchio* "per calcolare" dati di decompressione
GRAVIMETRO	→	*strumento* "per la misura" di variazioni di accelerazione
CURVIMETRO	→	*strumento* "atto a determinare" la lunghezza dell'arco di curva
SOLCOMETRO	→	*strumento* "che serve a misurare" la velocità di una nave
. . .		. . . . . .

Figure 2. Retrieval of words with identical endings
(271 lemmas ending in "-METRO")

It is now necessary to make these semantic IS-A links more flexible and compact. Up until now we have only been able to retrieve automatically, but separately, all the entries in whose definitions appears the word *strumento* (*instrument*), then those with *arnese* (*tool*), with *dispositivo* (*device*), and so on. These should not be kept as separate distinct subsets, instead all these related key-words (and consequently their connected subsets) should be grouped under an appropriate heading, which should be the most generic possible (in this case it could be STRUMENTO), considered this time not as a simple lexical item, but as a lexical item with the function of semantic marker. After this operation of unification of subsets, it would be more appropriate to speak of retrieval of entries associated to a semantic marker, or pertaining to an identical, more inclusive underlying concept.

Table 1 presents some quantitative data for the DMI definitions. The definitions have been divided according to the number of words for each definition. There is a total number of approximately 790,000 words, of which about 75,000 are coded as synonyms. For all these words (excluding one, two, and some three letter words) the semantic chains described above have been constructed automatically, and they can be traced in interactive mode to check their consistency.

Table 1. Some quantitative data for the DMI definitions
(The definitions contain approximately 790,000 words
with about 75,000 synonyms)

Number of Words per Definition	Number of Definitions
0	12,397
1	21,358
2	26,171
3	23,721
4	21,421
5	18,850
6	17,421
7	17,760
8	12,792
9	8,181
10	4,045
11	1,419
12	381
13	53
14	8
15	1
	185,979

Table 2 provides a frequency list of the most frequent words used in the defining vocabulary: we notice that DI (*of*) represents 6.27% of the word-forms (tokens), while the first half-full words are ATTO (*act*), EFFETTO (*effect*), PERSONA (*person*), PARTE (*part*), QUALITÀ (*quality*), NUOVO (*new*), MODO (*mode*), ESSERE (*being*), RELATIVO (*relative*). A comparison of these quantitative data with analogous data for dictionaries of other languages would be interesting.

Table 2. Frequency list of the most frequent words in definitions

RANK	FREQ.	TOTAL	WORD
1	49,513	49,513	di
2	20,635	70,148	che
3	11,329	81,477	del
4	11,059	92,536	a
5	10,907	103,443	o
6	10,786	114,229	in
7	9,760	123,989	e
8	8,683	132,672	per
9	7,905	140,577	un
10	7,124	147,701	chi
11	6,737	154,438	col
12	6,548	160,986	da
13	6,360	167,346	si
14	6,064	173,410	è
15	5,701	179,111	atto
16	5,195	184,306	una
17	5,093	189,399	della
18	5,079	194,478	la
19	5,004	199,482	il
20	4,949	204,431	l'
21	4,139	208,570	dell'
22	3,373	211,943	dei
23	3,191	215,134	detto
24	3,116	218,250	effetto
25	3,004	221,254	delle
26	2,997	224,251	come
27	2,822	227,073	ciò
28	2,705	229,778	non
29	2,647	232,425	al
30	2,443	234,868	d'

Table 2. Frequency list of the most frequent words
in definitions (continued)

RANK	FREQ.	TOTAL	WORD
31	2,397	237,265	alla
32	2,344	239,609	q.c.
33	2,265	241,874	cui
34	2,229	244,103	persona
35	2,167	246,270	verbo
36	2,135	248,405	aggettivo
37	2,134	250,539	considera
38	2,125	252,664	ha
39	2,117	254,781	participio
40	1,996	256,777	le
41	1,889	258,666	parte
42	1,864	260,530	più
43	1,860	262,390	qualità
44	1,850	264,240	i
45	1,786	266,026	nel
46	1,716	267,742	nuovo
47	1,675	269,417	c
48	1,647	271,064	modo
49	1,591	272,655	essere
50	1,535	274,190	relativo

Figure 3 shows a hierarchical tree (incomplete on the horizontal lines) which has been constructed following the definitional chains for Animals, a typical taxonomic field. At the lower levels, the ordinary taxonomic distinctions into families, classes and groups are quite well respected. At the higher levels, however, we do not have a tree, but loops, and more than one root [see Amsler 1980, 86 ff.]. Another hierarchy which has been extracted on the basis of the definitions refers to vehicles (see Figure 4). A loop is also found here at the very beginning. The empty arrows lead to vehicle subfields. The subfield of "vehicles" intersected by "drawn by horses" is represented in Figure 5. An initial loop between VETTURA (*vehicle*) and CARROZZA (*coach*) is seen here as well. We can also observe how, given the definitions of the root terms, and once the dependency links between the terms in the tree are established, it is possible to eliminate part of what is now explicit information for each entry, but which proves to be essentially redundant (such as "drawn by horses" for the entire set, and "public" for the subtree on the left), as this information could be implicitly inherited by the higher terms. A much more compact and efficient organization of lexical information could be achieved in this way.

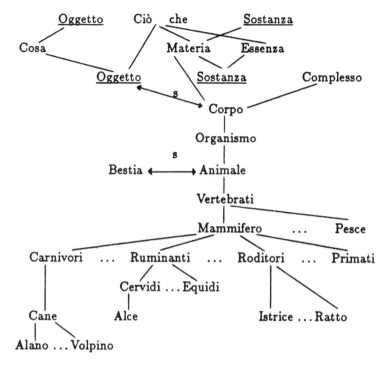

Figure 3. Part of the hierarchical tree for animals.

Synonymy relations

Synonyms can also be retrieved interactively in the database, using the database query language. Furthermore, a distinction can be made between the synonyms of a given word, and the other entries with which the given word is synonymous. For example CASA has the following synonyms: CASATO, STIRPE, DINASTIA, PATRIA, CONVENTO, MONASTERO, DITTA, AZIENDA, SOCIETÀ, but it is also found as a synonym of completely different words: ABITAZIONE, ALBERGO, DOMICILIO, DOMO, FOCOLARE, MAGIONE, PENATI, STABILE, TETTO. The same phenomenon is frequent for other words. Therefore, we find that under the label "Synonym," lexicographic definitions only give "quasi-synonyms," where the reverse relation is not really applied, i.e., synonymy in the dictionary is not used as a symmetrical relation, but as a relation with one preferential direction.

Figure 4. A hierarchy for vehicles

Derivational relations

A descriptive analysis of the phenomenon of suffixation has been made, and
so far a certain number of endings have been dealt with exhaustively [see
Calzolari 1983c, for more details]. In the associated definitions, we find
for each ending some recurrent patterns, or defining formulas, or recurrent generic terms ("genus" terms). These regular relationships between
meanings must be treated systematically throughout the lexicon. Table
3 schematically represents a hypothesis for a possible new organization of
derivatives in the database. The rules given are associated with the more
frequent patterns of change in meaning involved in suffixation. These rules

concern the meaning of derived words, by which we intend the modification effected by the suffix on the base. These rules connect bases and sets of observed derivatives, so that the meaning of the derivative becomes a function of the meaning of the base.

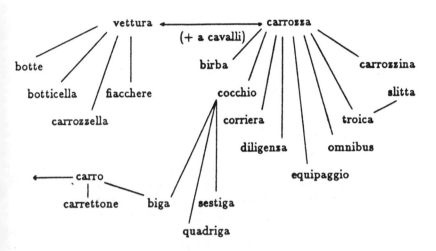

Figure 5. A subfield of vehicles

CARROZZA → vettura per persone a 4 ruote trainata da cavalli
    VETTURA → carrozza a cavalli per servizio pubblico
    Some information could be inherited, not repeated –
    in each entry "a cavalli," on some entries "pubblico."

Table 3. A new organization for derivatives in the dictionary

Keywords	Label of a Rule		Pointer to the Base	
legALITÀ	COND	No.L10 →		LEGALE
regALITÀ	COND	No.L20 →		REGALE
...	...		...	
...IERO	REL		...	
...	...		...	
...OSO	REL		...	
...OSO	FULL		...	
...OSO	AFF		...	
...	...		...	
...ICO	REL		...	

Rules for derivatives in Table 3

$$COND = \text{``condition of being''} + Adj. \; base$$

$$REL = \left\{ \begin{array}{c} \text{``relating to''} \\ \text{``proper of''} \\ \text{``concerning''} \\ \cdots \end{array} \right\} + Nom. \; base$$

$$FULL = \text{``full of''} + Nom. \; base$$

$$AFF = \text{``affected by''} + Nom. \; base$$

$$\cdots$$

In the record of each derivative there is a label which points to a rule, and a pointer to the base. Inversions on these fields will also provide the paths from each base to the set of its derivatives, and to other generalizations. As these rules express general lexical relations, they must be stored in the lexicon and should offer a higher level of abstraction. In this way, it will be possible to immediately retrieve, for example, all the terms denoting "action of" + Verbal base, i.e., all the deverbal nominalizations, which are treated by the same or by similar rules. Similarly, it will be possible to request interactively both the inflectional paradigm of lemmas (as can be done at present), and the derivational paradigm, with all the implications also from the syntactic point of view.

Other taxonomies

I refer here to taxonomies organized on relations other than the inclusion or IS-A relation, such as, for example, Part-Whole, Set-of, Process-of, Act-of, Effect-of, Cause-of, etc., which are certainly very important in structuring the lexicon. With regard to these taxonomies, little work has so far been done on our data, but some information can surely be automatically retrieved for the above relations, by exploiting the regular patterns used by lexicographers to indicate them in the definitions.

Terminological subsets

Using the existing codes for "Specialized Languages" (106 codes) the DMI/ DB can be queried for terminological subsystems. An example can be taken from the Legal Lexicon, which already contains 1078 coded terms. A test was carried out to see whether this first nucleus of terms could be extended by using some basic legal terms (such as *judge, law, legal*) as key-words in an interactive search for other semantically connected lemmas. As a matter of fact, using only 52 word-forms relative to 32 lemmas, the Legal Lexicon can be extended to cover some other 785 definitions of legal terms (see Figure 6). The exploitation of the semantic links processable within the lexicon proved to be useful in improving the terminological codings in the dictionary.

	TOTAL	WITH CODE	CODE TO BE INSERTED
DIRITTO	332	49	208
. . .			
GIUDICE	34	11	23
GIUDIZIALE	6	2	4
GIUDIZIARIO	64	20	43
GIURIDICO	148	51	96
GIURISDIZIONALE	25	14	11
GIURISDIZIONE	36		35
GIURISTA	8		8
. . .			
IMPUTATO	26	9	16
. . .			
PENALE	39	10	29
. . .			
REATO	66	30	36
. . .			
SENTENZA	36	8	19

**Figure 6. Quantitative results of an interactive search
of legal terms.** (We can add the code to 785 definitions
with the forms of only 32 keywords.)

Restriction or modification relations

By restriction or modification relations I intend those recurrent definitional patterns which are used to restrict the meaning of the "genus" term. These patterns should be examined exhaustively in order to obtain an idea of the most frequently used functions, and also of the different ways in which the same function can be expressed. In Figure 7 a number of different lexicalizations of the function SCOPO (*goal*) are listed. Not only the lexical but also the syntactic means of expression change. In a more formalized structure of definitional information, all these definitional patterns should obviously be subsumed under a single name or label of "functional link." In Figure 8 an example is shown of how some of these functions have a preferential combination with certain kinds of "genus" terms. This time, the "genus" terms are those which could be normalized and subsumed under the semantic marker STRUMENTO (*instrument*).

SCOPO (GOAL)

TENDENTE A	(tending to)
DIRETTO A	(directed to)
VOLTO A	(aimed at)
CON LO SCOPO DI	(with the purpose of)
A SCOPO DI	(for the purpose of)
CHE HA LO SCOPO DI	(which has the purpose of)
CHI MIRA A	(which aims at)
MIRANTE A	(aiming at)
RIVOLTO A	(turned to)
PER CONSEGUIMENTO DI	(for achieving)

Figure 7. Lexicalizations of the function SCOPO

ATTO A   (APT TO)
selects a particular marker:

ACCIARINO	=	Dispositivo atto a determinare l'accensione
ARCHIPENDOLO	=	Strumento atto a rendere orizzontale una retta
CARICATORE	=	Attrezzatura atta al carico e allo scarico di materiali
SPEZZATRICE	=	Macchina atta a tagliare la pasta in pezzi

Figure 8. A preferential combination of one function with one kind of "genus" term

Case-type relations

Let us now make a few brief observations as to how natural language definitions can be exploited to obtain information also concerning case-type or argument relations associated with typical actions. The first observation is in the form of an example taken from the Legal terminology sublanguage. It is interesting to notice how the terms selected by the key-word

CONTRATTO (*contract*), found in 125 definitions mostly of legal terms, are articulated around the concept of "Contract." It appears that in 64 definitions the word CONTRATTO is used as the "genus" term (formally determined by its being in the first position) and the defined words are particular "kinds-of" contract, while other less numerous but quite homogeneous groups of definitions can be retrieved denoting the objects, persons, actions, money, documents, which are apt to fill the typical or more important roles connected to the event implied by "Contract." We can thus very easily begin by implementing a hierarchical organization of underlying hyponymy relations. In a second stage, we can start to think about a model including more complex relations, so that this conceptual node "Contract" can be linked, through different paths, to some of the names of or "types-of" documents (linked by hyponymy relation to "Document"), and to some of the names for money, and to some of the many possible names denoting Persons in the dictionary database, etc. This is conceived as a model of an extended inter-connected conceptual network.

The way in which case relations can be evidenced by querying the database for connected terms can also be seen from the inflectional and derivational paradigm of the verb VENDERE (*to sell*). Table 4 shows the total number of definitions in which each given form (used in definitions) of this verb appears (first column), while the other columns evidence some of the cases or roles, associated with the case-frame of *sell*, which could be filled by the terms defined by these forms.

Table 4. How case relations can be displayed in the lexical database. Example root is **VEND-** *to sell.*

	Total Definitions	Agent	Action	Object	Locative
'ENDE	202	178		1	14
'ENDERE	33	5	22	1	
'ENDEVA	4	4			
'ENDEVANO	1				1
'ENDIBILE	1		1		
'ENDITA	64	2	11+(10)	4	19
'ENDITE	8	1	2		
'ENDITORE	130	123	(2)		
'ENDITORI	6				2
'ENDITRICE	4	4			
'ENDONO	33				33
'ENDUTA	3			1	
'ENDUTE	1		(1)		
'ENDUTO	8			4	

In particular the 3rd person sing. of the present tense, VENDE, appears in 202 definitions, and in 178 of them (i.e., the wide majority of cases) it serves to define a lexicalized name of Agent, going from the generic name *venditore (seller)* to the more specific names *fruttivendolo, giornalaio, lattaio,* etc.; obviously the key-form VENDITORE (*seller*) is typical for defining Agent names; while VENDONO (*they sell*) typically defines, quite unexpectedly, names of Places in which the action of selling is performed. In fact it is used in patterns such as "luogo, negozio, bottega, ecc. in cui si vendono" (*place, shop, etc., where ...are sold*) + the name of the thing sold. Some examples taken from these subsets of definitions are shown in Figure 9. This figure lists names of Agents (Figure 9a) – what is interesting is the recurrent connection with other types of actions such as FABBRICARE (*to make*), RIPARARE (*to repair*), etc., of Places (figure 9b), of Objects (Figure 9c); the underlined entries are the typical generic names for the main case arguments or roles.

ARGENTIERE	→	chi vende oggetti d'argento
ARMAIOLO	→	chi fabbrica vende ripara armi
BANCARELLISTA	→	chi vende oggetti su bancarelle
CARCIOFAIO	→	chi coltiva o vende carciofi
COCCIAIO	→	vasaio / chi fa o vende cocci
COCOMERAIO	→	chi vende coltiva cocomeri
. . .		
VASAIO	→	chi vende vasi di terracotta
<u>VENDITORE</u>	→	chi vende
. . .		
ABBACCHIARO	→	venditore di abbacchi
ARCHIBUGIERE	→	fabricante o venditore di armi
BORSETTAIO	→	fabbricante o venditore di borse
. . .		
VINAIO	→	venditore fornitore di vino
. . .		
CAMICIAIA	→	fabbricante o venditrice di camicie
. . .		
SIGARAIA	→	venditrice di sigari sigarette

Figure 9a. Definitions based on the agent case relation

BIRRERIA	→	locale pubblico dove si vende birra
CANTINA	→	osteria / bottega ove si vende il vino
. . .		
LATTERIA	→	negozio dove si vende e si consuma il latte
. . .		
PANIFICIO	→	negozio in cui si vende il pane
VENDITA	→	spaccio / negozio bottega dove si vende
. . .		
EDICOLA	→	chiosco adibito a vendita di giornali
LIQUORERIA	→	mescita e vendita di liquori
. . .		
BIGLIETTERIA	→	luogo in cui si vendono biglietti
CAMICERIA	→	negozio in cui si vendono camicie
. . .		
UTENSILERIA	→	bottega in cui si vendono utensili

Figure 9b. Definitions based on the locative case relation

MERCE	→	prodotto da vendere
ARTICOLO	→	oggetto capo di mercanzia posto in vendita
ASSORTIMENTO	→	disponibilità e varietà di merci in vendita
. . .		

Figure 9c. Definitions based on the object case relation

It should not be very difficult to utilize these systematic associations of "words used in definitions" and of "roles," for example, by labeling the definienda almost automatically with, e.g., a case-indicator. In this way it would be possible to query not only the words defined by VENDITORE, for example, but also all the lexicalized Agent-role fillers in the case-frame of VENDERE, or perhaps the name of the person who sells newspapers, or the name of the place where newspapers are sold, and so on. Obviously, it should be possible to reach this information starting both from *to sell*, and from *newspapers* and from this point moving towards the place where they are sold, or made, etc.

In particular, I am thinking of a model of a dictionary in which the user can enter where and how he wants, and at the level he prefers, and can move in different directions, guided by many types of relations, corresponding, at an external level, to internal links or physical pointers between entries.

Final observations

I should now like to stress the following general issues. A large quantity of information can be, and actually is, extracted from the definitions of a standard printed dictionary. These dictionary definitions, if appropriately exploited, lead us to primitive concepts (Semantic Markers) and to relations which do not greatly differ from those used, for example, in Artificial Intelligence systems, but which are empirically determined mostly by frequency and position in the definitions, and procedurally extracted by means of pattern-matching procedures. The logical schema designed and implemented for our database dictionary provides a basis for the identification of a large number of regularities and interrelationships, and this enables us to enter the structure – in particular the semantic structure – of the lexicon.

If it is viewed as a complex system of relationships and is rearranged accordingly, the dictionary can also become a thesaurus, thus overcoming what appeared as an insurmountable dichotomy simply by the use of computational tools. This can be achieved by using the quite different and various points of view or perspectives from which the same single entry can be considered. In this framework the dictionary can be eventually conceived more as a flexible and dynamic system for the representation of lexical data than as a static reference object, and the lexeme is seen more as a set of multi-level relationships than as an autonomous and self-contained unit.

References

Amsler, R. A. 1980. *The Structure of the Merriam-Webster Pocket Dictionary*, Ph.D. Thesis, Department of Computer Sciences, University of Texas, Austin.

Amsler, R. A. 1984. Machine-Readable Dictionaries, in *Annual Review of Information Science and Technology (ARIST)*, ed. by M.E Williams, ASIS, Knowledge Industry Publications, Vol. 19, 161 209.

Brustkern, J. and Hess, K. D. 1983. Machine Readable German Dictionaries – From a Comparative Study to an Integration, *Linguistica Computazionale, III, Supplement*, 77-93.

Byrd, R. J. 1983. Word Formation in Natural Language Processing Systems, *Proceedings of the 8th International Joint Conference on Artificial Intelligence*, Karlsruhe, 704-706.

Calzolari, N. 1977. An Empirical Approach to Circularity in Dictionary Definitions, *Cahiers de Lexicologie*, 31, 118-128.

Calzolari, N. 1982. Towards the Organization of Lexical Definitions on a Data Base Structure, *COLING82*, Prague: Charles University, 61-64.

Calzolari, N. 1983a. Semantic Links and the Dictionary, *Proceedings of the Sixth International Conference on Computers and the Humanities*, Raleigh, North Carolina, Computer Science Press, 47-50.

Calzolari, N. 1983b. Lexical Definitions in a Computerized Dictionary, *Computers and Artificial Intelligence*, **II**, 3, 225-233.

Calzolari, N. 1983c. On the Treatment of Derivatives in a Lexical Database, *Linguistica Computazionale*, **III**, Supplement, 103-113.

Calzolari, N. 1984. Detecting Patterns in a Lexical Data Base, *Coling84*, Stanford University, Association for Computational Linguistics, 170-173.

Calzolari, N. and Ceccotti, M. L. 1981. Organizing a Large Scale Lexical Database, *Actes du Congrès International Informatique et Sciences Humaines*, Liège, 18-21 November, 155-163.

Calzolari, N. and Picchi, E. 1984. The Machine Readable Dictionary as a Powerful Tool for Consulting Large Textual Archives, in L. Corti, ed., *Automatic Processing of Art History Data and Documents*, Pisa: Scuola Normale Superiore, 275-288.

Fox, M. S., Bebel, D. J., and Parker, A. C. 1980. The Automated Dictionary, *Computer*, July, 35-48.

Gruppo di Pisa. 1979. Il Dizionario di Macchina dell'Italiano, in Gambarara, D., Lo Piparo, F., Ruggiero, G., eds., *Linguaggi e Formalizzazioni*, Roma: Bulzoni, 683-707.

Hultin, N. C. and Logan, H. M. 1984. The New Oxford English Dictionary Project at Waterloo, *Dictionaries*, 6, 182-198.

Kay, M. 1983. The Dictionary of the Future and the Future of the Dictionary, *Linguistica Computazionale*, **III**, 161-174.

McNaught, J. 1983. The Generation of Term Definitions from an On-Line Terminology Thesaurus, *Proceedings of the First Conference of the European Chapter of the Association for Computational Linguistics*, Pisa, 90-95.

Michiels, A. and Noel, J. 1982. Approaches to Thesaurus Production, *COLING82*, Amsterdam: North-Holland, 227-232.

Nagao, M., Tsujii, J., Ueda, Y., and Takiyama, M. 1982. An Attempt to Computerize Dictionary Data Bases, in Goetschalckx and Rolling, eds., *Lexicography in the Electronic Age*, Amsterdam: North-Holland, 51-73.

Smith, R. N. and Maxwell, E. 1977. An English Dictionary for Computer-
    ized Syntactic and Semantic Processing, in Antonio Zampolli and
    Nicoletta Calzolari, eds., *Computational and Mathematical Lin-
    guistics*, Vol.I, Florence: Olschki, 303-322.

4

A lexicon for a medical expert system*

THOMAS AHLSWEDE AND MARTHA EVENS
COMPUTER SCIENCE DEPARTMENT
ILLINOIS INSTITUTE OF TECHNOLOGY
CHICAGO, IL 60616

Abstract

This paper describes the organization of the lexicon designed for the Michael Reese Hospital Stroke Consultant, a medical decision support system. The lexicon is structured as a semantic network using a number of lexical-semantic relations. It is intended to contain enough syntactic, semantic, and pragmatic information to support the automatic generation of case reports and also explanations for recommendations made by the Consultant.

Introduction

The Michael Reese Hospital Stroke Decision Support System is an expert system for stroke diagnosis being developed jointly by the Computer Science Department at Illinois Institute of Technology and the Department of Neurology at Michael Reese Hospital. One of its features is a text generation module which produces multiparagraph discharge summaries in a style similar to that used by doctors. We are also building a module that will generate explanations of recommendations made by the system in natural English.

---

* This research was supported by the National Science Foundation under grant IST 5-10069.

The relational lexicon – a definition

A fundamental requirement of any text generation system is a dictionary. Another requirement for any system capable of generating text beyond the "canned" level is a knowledge base. We intend to combine these functions in a single module: the relational lexicon.

The relational lexicon consists of a set of nodes, one for each entry in the vocabulary. (See below for a sample entry.) These nodes contain some definitional material specific to the word in question, but the essence of the relational lexicon is that the nodes are connected by labeled arcs denoting lexical-semantic relations. Our ideas about what information belongs in the lexicon have been much influenced by Igor Mel'čuk and his colleagues [Apresyan et al. 1970].

Some lexical-semantic relations are familiar, like synonymy. Some are less familiar but still very common: examples are taxonomy (the "is-a-kind-of" relation) and the part-whole relation. We can represent individual relational arcs as triples consisting of two words connected by a relation, thus:

artery	TAX	blood_vessel	(taxonomy)
cerebellum	PART	brain	(part-whole)

It is a matter of personal taste how far the lexicon should include regular derivations (e.g., *weakness* from *weak*), morphological forms (such as plurals), and other "computable" word forms as separate entries rather than leaving them to be computed. To the extent that we are trying to model human mental processes, we should probably lean toward storing these forms for lookup rather than computing them in cases where one approach is not overwhelmingly more reasonable than the other. This means that our list of relations will include things like:

reactions	PLURAL	reaction
weakness	STATE	weak

The lexicon also should not be limited to "words" in the narrow sense o items which contain no internal blanks. Following Becker [1975], we trea phrases as atomic lexical elements if they are stereotyped or difficult to analyze – or if they occur often enough that our intuition suggests they are not analyzed every time they appear.

An example of such a "lexical phrase" from the vocabulary of strok diagnosis is the expression *doll's head maneuver*, the name of a test in whicl the doctor turns the patient's head from side to side. (If the patient's eye do not move in response, this indicates a specific kind of brain damage. The phrase is metaphorical and any attempt to analyze it would lead u completely out of the realm of stroke diagnosis, so it clearly makes sense t treat it as if it were a single lexical item.

Automatic lexicon generation

Initially, we generated much of the lexicon "by hand" – identifying relational arcs by a careful study of some texts associated with the stroke decision support system. These were (1) a questionnaire used to enter stroke case histories into the database ("the questionnaire"); (2) a collection of definitions and explanations of stroke-related medical terms ("the stroke definitions"); and (3) a set of human-written reports summarizing stroke case histories ("the reports"). The reports also serve as the model for the reports that our text generation module is to produce (see Figure 1).

CLINICAL SUMMARY PATIENT NUMBER 6

This 78 yo woman was admitted on November 12, 1983 for evaluation of left hemiparesis.

She had no known prior neurological history including TIA or stroke and no previously detected hypertension or cardiac disease. One day before admission she abruptly became lightheaded while walking to the bathroom and collapsed to the floor with loss of consciousness of uncertain duration. On awakening she noted slurred speech and left sided weakness. She recalled no headache, nausea, or vomiting. She refused to come to the hospital until the following day when her friends brought her in. She had no worsening at home.

She consumes a moderate amount of alcohol, most recent drink two days before. No history of seizures or withdrawal.

On admission BP was 180/100. General medical exam was unremarkable. She was alert, aware of her deficit, and showed no neglect. She had a mild left hemiparesis and left hemisensory deficit. A CT scan showed a small hemorrhage in the putamen on the right. Routine labs were notable for mild renal insufficiency, no evidence of coagulopathy, and the EKG showed LV strain versus lateral ischemia. She was unchanged until the third hospital day when she spiked a temperature to 101 accompanied by lethargy and worsening of her left hemiparesis. No source of fever was determined and routine labs were unremarkable. The CT was unchanged. Decadron was begun. She improved to her baseline within 48 hours. She continued to improve over the next 3 weeks while undergoing evaluation for renal disease.

Figure 1. Sample stroke case report.

However, during the time we have worked on this project, we have developed techniques for automatic lexicon generation through the analysis of definitions from the machine-readable version of Webster's Seventh New Collegiate Dictionary (W7) prepared by John Olney [1968]. Hence the lexicon contains abundant information extracted automatically from W7 – especially taxonomy relations for nouns [Ahlswede et al. 1986]. Most of this information concerns the nontechnical part of the stroke vocabulary, but it also includes some medical terms which overlap with the general vocabulary (such as *cerebellum, paralysis,* etc.).

Strategy for building a lexicon

Tools

The first step toward creating the lexicon, and the first step in the text generation process overall, is to analyze the texts which are the basis of the system.

We already have ideas about how to build a lexicon [Evens and Smith 1978; Ahlswede 1985a, 1985b; Ahlswede and Evens 1988]. Furthermore, we would like to automate the process as much as possible even at the pilot stage, since even a relatively small lexicon such as this one is quite big; the three basic texts have a combined vocabulary of 1,979 lexical forms (counting abbreviations and morphological variants separately, but not including lexical phrases). This is already a big enough project to make a computer useful.

We arrived at the figure of 1,979 words with the help of one of the utility programs we have written for the early stages of analysis: a phrase counter. This program gives the number of occurrences of each phrase of some specified number of words ("word" here is used in the crude visual sense, as a character string separated by blanks or punctuation). Counting the phrases one word in length gives us the vocabulary, which can then be sorted alphabetically or by number of occurrences.

Another tool we are using in preliminary analysis is the KWIC (Key Word In Context) index. The KWIC index shows each occurrence of each word, preceded and followed by its context in the original text (see Figure 2). This tells us, for any word or phrase in the text, what other words and phrases co-occur with it. KWIC indices were valuable for finding relations in dictionary definitions [Ahlswede 1985a]; they have also been helpful in analyzing stroke texts.

On the day of	admission	her boyfriend called her about
On	admission	her examination was normal.
days following	admission	patient became quadriplegic.
On the day of	admission	Pt was found to be globally
Since	admission	she has made a very slow
At the time of	admission	she had BP 200/100, pulse 90.
the day following	admission	showed a modest non-ulcerative
Examination on	admission	showed a tendency to lean to
CT scan on	admission	was normal.
at the time of	admission	was unknown, but subsequently
local NJ hospital	admission,	where he was begun on Amicar,
recovery since	admission.	Some believe her to be able
This 47 YO BF was	admitted	25 August 1983 for right sided
He is a 56 YO WM	admitted	26 September 1983 for
When he was	admitted	he had a mild left sided

Figure 2. KWIC index of case reports.

A third and even more powerful tool of analysis which we have used is Naomi Sager's Linguistic String Parser (LSP) [Sager 1981]. The LSP has been useful not only in analyzing stroke reports but even more in generating them [Collier et al. to appear; Li et al. 1986].

An incidental advantage of using the LSP is that Sager and her coworkers have done extensive work in natural language processing, especially in medical applications. They have elaborated the concept of sublanguage [Sager 1986] – the language used in specialized applications such as stroke diagnosis, where the semantic universe is much smaller than that of the general language so that a great deal of semantic information can be determined by an apparently "syntactic" analysis. Even more importantly, they have developed the *information format* [Sager et al. 1987; Friedman et al. 1983; Friedman 1986] as a tool for extracting semantic information from medical texts. We have found that Friedman's information formats apply neatly to our stroke report texts, although we have had to expand them somewhat to handle some information that apparently did not appear in Friedman's texts.

Despite its power, the LSP is not a complete solution to the analysis of stroke texts. Its main drawback is that development of a reasonably complete grammar and vocabulary is very laborious. Our dictionary definition grammar [Ahlswede 1988; Ahlswede and Evens 1988] parses about two thirds of its input successfully, and has reached the stage where each additional rule change nets, on the average, about one new successful parse in the 8,000-definition development data sample.

Therefore we have supplemented the LSP with a semi-intelligent text processing strategy. Words in the text are tagged by part of speech (without trying to resolve ambiguous cases) and the tagged text is analyzed with one of several very simple heuristic grammars written in the Unix *awk* language. The *awk* grammar does not attempt to generate a full parse but only some specific item such as subject-verb-object sequences, heads of noun phrases, etc. This method has been very effective in identifying triples for various relations, especially noun taxonomy [Ahlswede and Evens 1988].

Finding relations

With the help of the word and phrase lists, KWIC indices, parse trees and *awk*ed sentences, we identify relations among the words and phrases in the text.

This is a time-consuming process, even after automation; the output of the parser or the *awk* grammar inevitably contains at least a few misidentifications (about 3 percent of noun taxonomies, for instance) and must be hand edited.

The first step is to determine what relations to include in our lexicon. Students of lexical-semantic relations differ wildly in the number of distinct relations they recognize, from Werner's three [Evens et al. 1980] up into the hundreds [e.g., Smith 1981]. Although we would like to avoid excessive splitting, we have found it simplest to recognize a fairly large number of relations, including some which could easily be analyzed as compound relations but which occur often enough in stroke texts to be treated as atomic.

An important part of any medical expert system is a knowledge of anatomy, which is largely a matter of spatial relationships:

temporal_lobe	ABOVE	third_nerve
frontal_lobe	BEFORE	parietal_lobe

A common relation in the stroke sublanguage is that between a bodily or mental function and the name of a pathology affecting that function:

aphasia	DYSFUNC	speech
dysphagia	DYSFUNC	swallowing

Our texts contain an interesting pair of relations, syntactic variations on taxonomy and part-whole. A condition such as aphasia can have many different forms, which may be identified in full, e.g., *Broca's aphasia, global aphasia*, etc., or referred to elliptically as *Broca's* or *global*. Taxonomy is combined here with a syntactic modification relation, and we find it convenient to treat the combination as a unit:

Broca's	PTAX	aphasia
global	PTAX	aphasia
global	PTAX	amnesia

as we do also with similar combination of modification and part-whole:

visual	PPART	cortex
motor	PPART	cortex

The result of this step of the work is a long list of word-relation-word triples, along with various syntactic and semantic information associated with each word.

Generating a relational network

The final step in the process is to convert the list of triples into an actual network in storage in the system. This network is the relational lexicon. Gannon [1981] and Ahlswede [1981] have written simple programs, in Lisp and Fortran respectively, to do this. The nodes of the networks generated by these programs are simply character strings representing the words in the lexicon; no information is associated with a node except relational arcs to other nodes. Also, neither program generates any relational arcs except those explicitly defined by triples in the input.

In fact, there is a great deal of information about most words which is most conveniently stored in some format other than that of the relational arc. For example, information about permissible categories of subject for a verb could be expressed in relational form by a mass of relational arcs pointing to all permissible subject nouns in the lexicon:

experience	$\overline{\text{PSUBJ}}$	patient
experience	$\overline{\text{PSUBJ}}$	he
experience	$\overline{\text{PSUBJ}}$	she

or as a single arc to a pseudo-lexical entry representing the attribute. The permissible nouns would be similarly linked to a corresponding attribute:

experience	$\overline{\text{ATTRIBUTE}}$	human_subject

(The bar over the relation name indicates an inverse relation – *human subject* is an attribute of *experience*, not the other way around.)

patient	$\overline{\text{ATTRIBUTE}}$	human
he	$\overline{\text{ATTRIBUTE}}$	human
she	$\overline{\text{ATTRIBUTE}}$	human

It probably makes more sense, however, to include this information as a "unary" attribute of the verb, to be compared with a similarly "unary" attribute of any nouns that might be proposed as a subject of the verb. This strategy would be similar to the last-described approach but without the ATTRIBUTE and $\overline{\text{ATTRIBUTE}}$ relations. Information to be stored in unary form would have to be entered in some form other than as triples.

Another important consideration is that relations imply other relations. Some, though not all, relations are reflexive: x SYN x but not x ANT x. Some are symmetric: x SYN y implies y SYN x. Some are transitive: x TAX y and y TAX z imply x TAX z. And some fit together in more complicated ways: x TAX z and x SYN y imply y TAX z. (That is, if a rabbit is "a kind of" mammal and a rabbit is "the same as" a bunny, then a bunny must be "a kind of" mammal.)

Most such properties of individual relations must be determined "by hand" but, once they are known, the relational arcs implied by these properties can and probably should be put into the network automatically. Also, every relation has an inverse relation (symmetric relations are their own inverses) which may be just as useful as the original relation. For instance, if TAX links an item to a category or family to which it belongs, the inverse relation $\overline{\text{TAX}}$ associates a category with a convenient list of all its members.

Sample lexical entries

The verb *admit* and its derivatives will be useful to illustrate the organization of the lexicon. Although the word *admit* appears only once in that form anywhere in our texts, *admission* appears 33 times, *admitted* (past participle) appears 12 times, and the abbreviation *adm.* (for *admitted*) appears once. Since the lexicon is to be used for text generation, we should also include entries for *admits* and *admitting*.

The entry consists of four components:

1. Attributes, with a value assigned to each attribute. The relevant attributes depend on the part of speech of the word.
2. A table of appropriate arguments (cases for verbs, appropriate noun classes for adjectives, prepositions for nouns, etc.).
3. A predicate calculus definition, if it is desirable to clarify the meaning of the word.
4. Relational arcs to other words in the lexicon. Comments are in [square brackets].

---

admitted

    [attributes]
      PART-OF-SPEECH   VEN [past participle – an LSP term]
                          TV   [tensed verb – an LSP term]
    [don't need predicate calculus definition –
    see *admit* for that]
      PAST   admit(1)
                           admit(2)
      PASTP   admit(1)
                           admit(2)

---

admission

[attributes]
    PART_OF_SPEECH   NOUN
    CATEGORIES   –CONCRETE
                         –ANIMATE
                         –HUMAN [or compute this from –ANIMATE]
                         –HUMAN_COLLECTIVE
                         –MALE
                         +COUNT
[no need for predicate calculus definition – admission is
TRESULT of admit]

[relations]
    TRESULT   admit(1)
                       admit(2)

---

admits

           [attributes]
             PART_OF_SPEECH   TV

           [relations]
             3SING   admit(1)
                            admit(2)

admitting

[attributes]
    PART_OF_SPEECH   VING   [verb + *ing* – LSP]
[relations]
                         PRESP   admit(1)
                                       admit(2)

---

admit(1)

[attributes]
    PART_OF_SPEECH   VERB
    PASSIVE   SINGLE   [direct object can be
                                          subject of passive]
    ACTION   YES   [can be used in the imperative]
    COMPLEMENTIZERS   none

    [case structure]
        [syntactic role]   [case]   [optionality]   [semantic categories]
    1. SUBJECT   AGENT OBLIGATORY +HUMAN (doctor)
        [in our texts the verb is always passive with no agent, so this
        case role is somewhat conjectural]
    2. DIR. OBJECT   OBJECTOBLIGATORY +HUMAN (patient)
    3. OBJ. OF PREP. PLACE ELLIPTICAL +CONCRETE

    [predicate calculus definition – very schematic here]
    (X admits Y to Z) = (X causes (Y becomes patient at Z))

                  [relations]
                    HOMONYM   admit(2)
                    SEMANTIC_FIELD patient_management
                    CAUSE   enter
                    ANT   reject
                    CONV   release

---

admit(2)

    [attributes]
        PART_OF_SPEECH   VERB
        PASSIVE   SINGLE
        ACTION   YES   [can be imperative]
        COMPLEMENTIZERS THATS, TOVO
                          [LSP terms: *that* +
                          sentence, *to* + verb + object]
        IMPLICATIVE   FACTIVE
    ["X admits Y" and "X does not admit Y"
      both imply that Y is true]
        PERFORMATIVE   EXPOSITIVE
    [to say "I admit X" is to admit X]

    [predicate calculus]
      (X admits Y) $\Rightarrow$ (Y is true) and (X says that Y is true)

        [relations]
            HOMONYM   admit(1)
            SEMANTIC_FIELD   communicate
            SYN   confess
            TAX   say
                          communicate
            ANT   deny

Problems

Up to now, almost all the work we have done with relations has been at the level of relating individual words to each other. Ahlswede [1985a] analyzed dictionary definitions in order to generate relational triples from them. This was possible because dictionaries represent relations by consistent use of specific phrases, the "defining formulas" [Smith 1981; Ahlswede 1985a].

The relational lexicon, by its very nature, works at the level of individual words. Much of the information in the knowledge base consists of propositions which can be expressed in the form of relational arcs, but only as arcs between complex phrases or even whole sentences.

Consider a sentence from the stroke definition corpus: "Failure of a pupil (of the eye) to react to light may reflect either an afferent or efferent defect." Here the verb phrase "may reflect" indicates a relation – at least a possible relation – between an event (the failure of a pupil to react to light) and a pathological condition (an afferent or efferent defect). The analysis (failure of a pupil to react to light) REFLECT (afferent or efferent defect)

is not the same as, say,

failure   REFLECT   defect

which, by itself, is so vague as to be useless. It is not at all clear at present
how this high-level relational arc can be expressed meaningfully as a set of
relational arcs between individual words or "lexical" phrases.

Another problem is that relations prove to be slippery when one attempts
to cover a large, varied sublanguage with them. This is connected to the
question of how many relations ought to be defined.

Some relations are fairly precise and consistent in their meaning: the
"child" relation, as in

lamb   CHILD   sheep

applies to several other pairs of words with exactly the same significance in
each case. Other relations, however, including such very important ones as
synonymy, are notoriously imprecise. Every pair of approximate synonyms
is linked by a unique relation – at least a unique variation on the general
notion of synonymy. Thus from a certain point of view, there are almost
as many different relations as there are pairs of words in the language.

An example of two almost but not quite identical relations from the
world of dictionary definitions is the difference between the adjective defining formula *having*, which describes an attributive relation, and the formula
exhibiting, which describes a more specific attributive relation. The definition

browed adj. having a brow or brows

would not be significantly changed in meaning if we substituted the formulas
possessing, marked by, or *characterized by*:

* browed adj. possessing a brow or brows
* browed adj. marked by a brow or brows
* browed adj. characterized by a brow or brows

but if we substitute

* browed adj. exhibiting a brow or brows

we are saying something we did not say in the previous definitions, where
the brow or brows are present but not necessarily "exhibited." In the adjective definition grammar [Ahlswede 1985a] we treated the formulas *having*,

possessing, marked by, and *characterized by* as denoting a single relation, while *exhibiting* denoted a similar but slightly different relation. Clearly there is a connection between the two relations: if *having* denotes attribution, then *exhibiting* denotes attribution plus something else. We still need to figure out how to represent that "something else."

Advantages of the relational lexicon as a knowledge base

We expect to be able to overcome the problems we have identified and hope that they will not be too difficult, since the relational lexicon has some admirable qualities fitting it for use as a knowledge base.

One is that it is conceptually simple. The lexicon consists basically of word nodes and labeled arcs connecting them. Some information is best stored as attributes attached to individual words, but how much information is to be stored this way and how much in relational form, is flexible.

It is also concise. Information need only be stored in one place; material associated with one word may be accessed by way of any related word. In principle it should be possible to reach any word through any other. In practice, the information most relevant to any particular word is associated either with that word or with words closely related to it, accessible through one or a very few arcs. The amount of information readily available through a particular word, even with this limitation, is a sizable fraction of the entire contents of the lexicon.

Plans for the future

We still have much work to do in identifying relational triples through parsing and text processing, and incorporating the triples into the lexicon. Furthermore, in the time we have been working on this project, we have acquired a large collection of source texts relating to stroke. Some of this text needs to be put on line, and all of it needs to be analyzed.

It is important to note that although our current application is medical, none of our techniques are limited to the medical domain. Some of the vocabulary is domain specific, as are some of the relations. We are still looking for a relational formalism that will allow us to express such relations as PTAX or DYSFUNC as compounds of more general relations in a computationally convenient way. Our goal is to create a large, general purpose lexicon, that could be used on its own or from which more specialized lexicons could be extracted.

We also envision the lexicon in many applications besides text generation. We have used the relational network component of the lexicon in an enhanced information retrieval system [Fox et al. 1988]. The possibility of using relations to make inferences may also be exploited in question answering systems or database interfaces.

References

Ahlswede, Thomas. 1981. Computer program to generate a relational network. Available from the authors.

Ahlswede, Thomas. 1985a. A Linguistic String Grammar of Adjective Definitions. In S. Williams, ed., *Humans and Machines: The Interface Through Language*. Norwood, NJ: Ablex, 101-127.

Ahlswede, Thomas. 1985b. A Tool Kit for Lexicon Building. *Proceedings of 23rd Annual ACL*, Chicago, 268-275.

Ahlswede, Thomas. 1988. *Syntactic and Semantic Analysis of Definitions in a Machine-Readable Dictionary*. Ph.D. thesis, Department of Computer Science, Illinois Institute of Technology.

Ahlswede, Thomas, Evens, Martha, Markowitz, Judith, and Rossi, Kay. 1986. Building a Lexical Database by Parsing Webster's Seventh Collegiate Dictionary, *Advances in Lexicology*. University of Waterloo: Centre for the New OED, 65-78.

Ahlswede, Thomas, and Evens, Martha. 1988. Generating a Relational Lexicon from a Machine-Readable Dictionary. *International Journal of Lexicography*, special issue edited by William Frawley and Raoul Smith.

Apresyan, Yuri, Mel'čuk, Igor, and Žolkovsky, Alexander. 1970. Semantics and Lexicography: Towards a New Type of Unilingual Dictionary. In Ferenc Kiefer, ed., *Studies in Syntax and Semantics*. Dordrecht, Holland: Reidel, 1-33.

Becker, Joseph. 1975. The Phrasal Lexicon. In Roger Schank and Bonnie Nash-Webber, eds., *Theoretical Issues in Natural Language Processing*, Association for Computational Linguistics, 38-41.

Collier, John, Evens, Martha, Hier, Daniel, and Li, Ping-Yang. To appear. Generating Case Reports for a Medical Expert System, *International Journal of Expert Systems*.

Evens, Martha, Litowitz, Bonnie, Markowitz, Judith, Smith, Raoul, and Werner, Oswald. 1980. *Lexical-Semantic Relations: A Comparative Survey*. Edmonton, Alberta: Linguistic Research, Inc.

Evens, Martha, and Smith, Raoul. 1978. A Lexicon for a Computer Question-Answering System. *American Journal of Computational Linguistics*, 4, 1-96.

Fox, Edward A., Nutter, J. Terry, Ahlswede, Thomas, Evens, Martha, and Markowitz, Judith, 1988. Building a Large Thesaurus for Information Retrieval. *Proceedings of the ACL Conference on Applied Natural Language Processing*, Austin, Texas, 101-108.

Friedman, Carol. 1986. Automatic Structuring of Sublanguage Information – Application to Medical Narratives. In Ralph Grishman and Richard Kittredge, eds., *Analyzing Language in Restricted Domains: Sublanguage Description and Processing*. Hillsdale, NJ: Erlbaum, 85-102.

Friedman, Carol, Sager, Naomi, Chi, Emile S., Marsh, Elaine, Christenson, Catherine, and Lyman, Margaret S., 1983. Computer Structuring of Free-Text Patient Data. *Proceedings of the 7th Annual Symposium on Computer Applications in Medical Care*. IEEE Computer Society, 688-691.

Gannon, Stephen. 1981. Computer program to generate a relational network. Available from the authors.

Li, Ping-Yang, Evens, Martha, and Hier, Daniel B. 1986. Generating Medical Case Reports with the Linguistic String Parser, *Proc. AAAI*, Philadelphia, August, 1069-1073.

Olney, John. 1968. To All Those Interested in the Merriam-Webster Transcripts and the Data Derived from Them. Santa Monica, CA: Systems Development Corporation L-13579.

Sager, Naomi. 1981. *Natural Language Information Processing*. Reading, Massachusetts: Addison-Wesley.

Sager, Naomi. 1986. Sublanguage: Linguistic Phenomenon and Computational Tool. In Ralph Grishman and Richard Kittredge, eds., *Analyzing Language in Restricted Domains: Sublanguage Description and Processing*. Hillsdale, NJ: Erlbaum, 1-18.

Sager, Naomi, Friedman, Carol, and Lyman, Margaret. 1987. *Medical Language Processing: Computer Management of Narrative Data*. Reading, MA: Addison-Wesley.

Smith, Raoul N. 1981. On Defining Adjectives, Part III. *Dictionaries: Journal of the Dictionary Society of North America*, 3, 28-38.

5
Using a lexicon of canonical graphs in a semantic interpreter

JOHN F. SOWA
IBM SYSTEMS RESEARCH
500 COLUMBUS AVENUE
THORNWOOD, NY 10594

Abstract

The parts of speech and word features in traditional dictionaries are adequate for a purely syntactic parser. But semantic analysis requires a more detailed representation of the patterns of relationships between concepts. This paper starts with examples that illustrate semantic patterns that must be represented in the lexicon. It then presents *canonical graphs* as purely declarative structures for representing those patterns. Canonical graphs are similar to the case frames of case grammar, but they are generalized to handle all parts of speech and a broader range of linguistic phenomena. An important aspect of the theory is a set of formal rules for manipulating the graphs. By applying the rules systematically, a semantic interpreter can use canonical graphs from the lexicon as building blocks for reconstructing the meaning of a sentence.

Semantic interpretation

The meaning of a sentence is derived from the meanings of its individual words together with its syntactic structure and surrounding context. The interactions of all those elements pose serious problems for any theory of understanding:

- *Multiple word senses.* Each word form may have several different parts of speech and many different meanings.

- *Syntactic ambiguity.* The grammar may permit more than one parsing with no clear guidelines for attaching modifiers and grouping words into phrases.

- *Implicit relationships.* The relation between a modifier and the word it modifies may not be specified by an explicit word, affix, or syntactic structure.

- *Long-range relationships.* Words in distant parts of a sentence or even in different sentences may have connections that are not signalled by the syntax.

Separately, these problems are unsolvable. But an integrated theory should determine how semantic patterns for each word interact with syntax and context. Several approaches to such an integration have been proposed:

- *Projection rules for combining markers.* Katz and Fodor [1963] proposed that the dictionary entry for a word contain a list of semantic markers, such as +CONCRETE or +ANIMATE. Projection rules associated with each grammar rule would enforce selectional constraints by checking the compatibility of possible conjunctions of markers.

- *Function application.* Montague [1974] introduced more complex rules based on functional forms. His semantic representation had more structure than Katz and Fodor's conjunctions of markers, but he did not address all the kinds of ambiguities.

- *Filling slots in templates.* Wilks' preference semantics [1975], McCord's slot grammars [1980], and frame-based systems such as Absity [Hirst 1987] use templates or frames with slots to be filled from words in the sentence. Such systems can handle ambiguities better than Katz and Fodor's projection rules, while supporting structures as rich as or richer than Montague's.

- *Building graph structures.* Schank and his students and colleagues [Schank and Riesbeck 1981] have used conceptual dependency graphs to represent arbitrarily complex relationships. Their approaches have a lot in common with template-filling methods, but their strong bias against syntax leads to procedural parsers that are difficult to maintain and extend.

This paper presents an approach based on conceptual graphs, which are generalizations of all of the above [Sowa 1984]. As a form of logic, the graphs are as powerful as Montague's intensional logic. As templates, they are generalizations of frames. And as a graph notation, they can represent Schank's graphs (as well as other kinds of graphs) directly. Unlike the Schankian procedural parsers, however, this paper presents a syntax-directed approach that combines the best features of a syntactic parser with a slot-filling style of interpretation. A semantic interpreter for this approach was implemented by Sowa and Way [1986]; variations on this approach were implemented by Fargues et al. [1986] and Velardi et al. [1988].

The semantic interpreter that comes closest to the approach described here is Hirst's Absity [1987]. Hirst also used a syntax-directed parser, but with frames as the semantic representation rather than graphs. Yet graphs have important advantages over frames:

- Frames can be combined into tree structures, but trees must be supplemented with *ad hoc* cross links to express all the relationships in graphs.

- Trees arbitrarily designate one element as the root or privileged node. Graphs allow the option of re-orienting the perspective with any node as the privileged one.

- In parsing, syntactic rules designate one node of each conceptual graph as the head. But the head is a temporary choice for a particular parsing. From the same graph, a different node might be chosen as head by a different rule.

- Maximal joins, which are a version of graph unification, are the operations that build the semantic interpretation. They are essentially graph-oriented operations that are difficult to express in a frame notation.

The limitations of frames caused problems for Absity. Conceptual graphs avoid those problems with their ease of changing perspective and their rules for maximal joins. The next section will present a number of problems that must be handled by any theory of semantics. Some parsing programs can handle them by *ad hoc* code for each special case. But conceptual graphs can handle them all with a principled, systematic mechanism.

Examples of semantic patterns

Associated with most words in the lexicon are complex patterns of relationships. As examples, consider Chomsky's old sentences [1965]:

> John is easy to please.
> John is eager to please.

Chomsky observed that *John* is the object of *please* in the first sentence, but the subject of *please* in the second. He did not, however, propose any mechanism that would enable a parser to determine the correct relationships in each instance. What determines those relationships is not a syntactic feature of the word forms, but a pattern associated with the underlying concepts: the concept EASY tends to link with the patients of verbs, and the concept EAGER links to agents. Those tendencies also appear with the adverbs *easily* and *eagerly*. The following two sentences have identical surface structures:

> John easily does the homework.
> John eagerly does the homework.

In some theories of syntax, these two sentences also have the same deep structures. But consider the following transformations:

> The homework is easy for John to do.
> John is eager to do the homework.

These sentences are not exactly synonymous with the originals because of differences in focus and emphasis. But the impossibility of the following transformations shows that EASY and EAGER have very different structural properties:

> * The homework is eager for John to do.
> * John is easy to do the homework.

The structural differences between EASY and EAGER appear in other syntactic patterns as well: one could say *John is an easy person to please*, but not *an eager person to please*.

When one noun modifies another, the relationships between them are not shown explicitly. Determining those relationships can be difficult. Consider the sentence:

Mary is Bob's philosophy teacher.

Interpreting the noun phrase, *Bob's philosophy teacher*, requires a case frame for *teach*:

- Bob is the recipient
- philosophy is the patient
- Mary is the agent

Apparently, complex noun phrases cannot be interpreted without something like the case frames commonly associated with verbs. How are those case frames represented in the lexicon? If nouns, verbs, and adjectives in the same sentence all have case frames, how could they combine or interact?

Prepositions cause problems because most of them do not specify a unique conceptual relation: *with* may represent accompaniment or instrument; *to* may represent destination or recipient; and *of* has so many meanings that it is almost meaningless. Consider the sentences:

The teacher with a beard is taller than the one with glasses.
The teacher of English is taller than the one of physics.
The chalice of gold is heavier than the one of silver.

The problems arise in the final noun phrases: *the one with glasses* sounds normal; *the one of physics* sounds odd or unnatural; and *the one of silver* sounds normal. Why? What information must the lexicon contain that would enable a parser to select the correct relationships for these three phrases? Is that information associated with the prepositions *with* and *of*, with case frames for the nouns, or with both?

Complex information may be stated in a single sentence or in multiple short sentences. Consider the next two examples:

The janitor opened the door with an old key.
The janitor opened the door. He used an old key.

A reader would normally assume that the old key is the instrument of *open* in both instances. In the first instance, it is the object of the preposition *with*. But in the second, it is the object of a separate verb *use*. By what rule can the patient of one verb be transferred to the instrument slot of another verb? What information in the lexicon would permit such a transfer or trigger some rule that does the transfer?

Other kinds of words also require information to be combined from separate sentences. Consider the following passage:

Today, I will give you a problem in long division.
The dividend is 12,593, and the divisor is 57.
Find the quotient and remainder.

The definite articles in *the dividend* and *the quotient* indicate references to something introduced earlier. Somehow, the word *division* carries with it a structure or pattern of relationships to an implicit dividend, divisor, quotient, and remainder. How is that structure represented in the lexicon, and how is it used by the language analyzer?

A complex verb may presuppose the existence of some associated action that may not be stated explicitly. To threaten, for example, is to communicate an intention to perform a second, presumably harmful act. Consider the next two sentences:

Tom threatened to beat Bill with a wet noodle.
Tom threatened Bill with a wet noodle.

In the first sentence, the wet noodle is the instrument and Bill is the object of *beat*. The means of communicating and the person who received the threat are not mentioned. (Tom may have mailed a threatening letter to Bill's mother.) In the second sentence, Bill is the recipient and the wet noodle is the instrument of the threat. (Tom may have waved it at him in a menacing fashion.) But by default, Bill is also the expected object and the wet noodle is the expected instrument of some unspecified act. How is that implicit act specified in the lexical entry for *threaten*?

Another pattern of relationships between actions is represented by verbs like *give* and *take* with nominalized actions as direct object; e.g., *give someone a kiss, bath, kick, slap* or *take a bath, walk, swim, pee*. The act occurring as patient of *give* is normally transitive, with the giver as agent and the recipient of *give* as the object of the act. The act occurring as patient of *take* is normally intransitive with the taker as agent. When *bath* is used after *give*, it is transitive; after *take*, it is reflexive with the same person as agent and patient. These are not frozen idioms, but productive paradigms that extend to other verbs, such as *want, need, get, receive,* and *have*. Such patterns must be represented in the lexical entries for those verbs.

These examples illustrate patterns that occur constantly in the normal use of language. They lie at the borderline between purely linguistic concerns and knowledge of the world. Yet they depend on shallow knowledge that one would expect to find in a dictionary rather than a detailed encyclopedia. The language analyzer must know, for example, that a quotient is the result of division, but it need not have an algorithm for computing a quotient. Such information must be represented in a systematic, principled way. And the representation must support the rules and mechanisms that analyze language and build a semantic interpretation.

Type hierarchy

A hierarchy of concept types is central to most knowledge representation systems. In the theory of conceptual graphs, the hierarchy is assumed to be a lattice with the universal or undefined type $\top$ at the top. To complete the lattice, the absurd type $\perp$ is assumed to be a subtype of all other types. All lattice operations (subtype F, maximal common subtype $\cap$, and minimal common supertype $\cup$) may be performed on types:

- PERSON < ANIMAL < ENTITY

- PET-CAT = CAT $\cap$ PET

- CARNIVORE = CAT $\cup$ DOG

Since the lattice of all sets of existing things is not isomorphic to the type lattice, the set versions of $\cap$ and $\cup$ do not produce equivalent results. For this example, the set of pet cats happens to be the intersection of the set of pets with the set of cats. But the set of carnivores is much bigger than the union of the sets of cats and dogs. For further discussion of this point, see Sowa [1983].

The lexicon maps word forms to syntactic categories and concept types. Since issues of morphology and syntax are comparatively well understood, this section will concentrate on the concept types and their relationship to semantic features. Following is a selection of words that might appear in the lexicon:

The word *hand* may be a noun with type HAND or a verb with type HAND-GIVE, a subtype of GIVE with instrument HAND. The word *ship* is either a noun or a verb; the type SHIPMENT will distinguish the act of shipping from the entity SHIP. The noun *shipment* may designate either the act of shipping (as in *The shipment took five days*) or the object that is shipped (as in *The shipment weighed 50 pounds*). In general, nominalized verbs may refer either to the process or action of the verb or to some entity in a case frame for the verb; e.g., *the process of generalization* vs. *a generalization, rapid growth* vs. *a growth on the brain*, or *a loud crack* vs.

Word Form	Syntactic Category	Concept Type
hand	count noun	HAND
	verb, ditransitive	HAND-GIVE
ship	count noun	SHIP
	verb, ditransitive	SHIPMENT
shipment	count noun	SHIPMENT
	count noun	SHIP-OBJ
jack	count noun	JACK
Jack	name	PERSON: Jack

a crack in the wall. In lower case, *jack* refers to an object of type JACK; in upper case, *Jack* refers to someone of type PERSON with a name Jack in the referent field of the concept.

The type hierarchy includes all concepts – actions and attributes as well as entities. The type GIVE, for example, has many subtypes besides HAND-GIVE:

- COMMUNICATE is giving where the patient is information;

- DONATE is giving for a worthy cause;

- SEND is giving across some distance;

- SHIPMENT is sending by means of a ship or other mode of transportation.

The type MOVE is a supertype of all kinds of motion: GO, for example, is a subtype of MOVE where the agent of GO is both the agent and patient of MOVE. The type ACT is still more general, having subtypes MOVE and GIVE as well as any other EVENT caused by an agent.

Natural types and role types

Subtypes of ENTITY are of two kinds: *natural types*, which have no required set of linguistic associations; and *role types*, which are subtypes of natural types in some particular pattern of relationships. PERSON, for example, is a natural type, and TEACHER is a subtype of PERSON in the role of teaching. Other examples of role types include

CHILD < PERSON

PET < ANIMAL

PEDESTRIAN < PERSON

QUOTIENT < NUMBER

FOOD < PHYSICAL-SUBSTANCE

Each of these role types has an implicit pattern of relationships that are always associated with it:

- A child is a role played by one person with respect to another person who plays the role of parent;

- A pet is an animal owned by some person and treated in a friendly manner, as opposed to livestock, which is typically raised for food;

- A pedestrian is a person walking on the street, as opposed to a hiker, who may be walking in the woods or mountains;

- A quotient is a number that is computed as the result of division.

- Food is a substance that is considered edible by some animal.

Note that a single entity may play many different roles: a person could be a child, parent, wife, friend, pedestrian, lawyer, employee, manager, gardener, and skier. A pea could be considered food, something to plant, or ammunition for a pea-shooter. The number 4 is the quotient of 20 divided by 5, the sum of 2 plus 2, and the difference of 13 and 9.

Bruin and Scha [1988] distinguish a class of relational nouns, such as *brother, commander, coauthor, speed, distance,* and *rating.* In their system, relational nouns are associated with explicit relations in a database or expert system. Every one of their relational nouns corresponds to a role type in conceptual graphs, but the role types are much broader since they include nouns like *pedestrian, thief,* and *food.* These nouns also have a pattern of relationships, but it is not possible to find the related items simply by searching a database. There is a test for distinguishing role types from natural types:

- τ is a natural type if something can be identified as type τ in isolation.

- τ is a role type if something can only be identified as type τ by considering some other entity, action, or state.

By this criterion, HOUSE and BUILDING are natural types, but HOME and DWELLING are role types. SENTENCE is also a natural type, but QUOTATION, ASSERTION, and BELIEF are role types.

A language might have a single word for some role types, or the role may be left implicit. In English, for example, the word *country* typically refers to a place, but *nation* refers to a society. A name like *America* might refer to either the country or the nation. A name like *Boston* might also refer either to the city as place or the city as society; but English has no word to distinguish the two. Therefore, a complete type lattice must be supplemented with type labels such as CITY-PLACE for CITY ∩ PLACE and CITY-SOCIETY for CITY ∩ SOCIETY. A parser must use selectional constraints to determine the correct role in a given sentence.

Natural types tend to form a strict tree, such as the biological classification tree. Role types, however, create tangles in the tree. When the role type PET is introduced, it induces a new subtype for every animal: PET-CAT, PET-SPIDER, PET-ELEPHANT, and even PET-PARAMECIUM. To save space and time in storing and searching the type hierarchy, it is possible to represent all the natural types directly, but show only the maximal common supertype for each role. For example, ANIMAL is the maximal common supertype of all pets; special cases like PET-ELEPHANT could be computed as needed. Metaphorical extensions like PET-ROCK can be computed by dynamically extending the type hierarchy, as Way [1987] has shown.

Canonical graphs

Canonical graphs are conceptual graphs that specify the patterns of relationships associated with a type. They show the selectional constraints expected for the types of concepts and relations they contain. The case frames of case grammar [Fillmore 1968] are examples of canonical graphs. Following is one of Fillmore's frames written in conceptual graph notation. (To save space, examples in this paper will use the linear notation for conceptual graphs rather than the box and circle notation.)

```
[OPEN]-
    (AGNT)→[ANIMATE]
    (PTNT)→[ENTITY]
    (INST)→[¬ ANIMATE].
```

This graph declares that OPEN takes an animate agent, any entity as its object, and an inanimate instrument. Adjectives also have canonical graphs, as in the following example for WARM, which was also adapted from Fillmore:

[WARM]–
    (EXPR)→[ANIMATE]
    (INST)→[PHYS-OBJECT].

This graph declares that an animate being must be the experiencer of warmth, and a physical object is the instrument of causing warmth. The set of all such graphs in the lexicon, called the *canonical basis* or *canon*, determines selectional constraints. By definition, all graphs in the canon are canonical. All other canonical graphs are derivable from the canon by four formation rules: copy, restrict, join, and simplify. Any graph derived by these rules will observe the constraints in the canon.

One of the ancestors of conceptual graph theory is Tesnière's dependency grammar [1959]. A related offshoot of Tesnière's work is valency theory [Allerton 1982], which counts the number of primary arguments of each verb:

- Intransitive verbs have valence 1: *cough, stumble, sleep.*

- Transitive verbs have valence 2: *eat, like, use.*

- Ditransitive verbs have valence 3: *give, tell, cost.*

Valency is a purely syntactic property. Canonical graphs add further information about the semantic roles that each argument plays. The verbs *eat, like,* and *use,* for example, have the same valence, but their subjects and objects play very different semantic roles:

[ANIMAL]←(AGNT)←[EAT]→ (PTNT)→[FOOD]

[ANIMATE]←(EXPR)←[LIKE]→ (PTNT)→[T]

[ANIMATE]←(AGNT)←[ACT]→ (INST)→[T]

The subject of *like* is not an agent, but an experiencer. The verb *use* does not have its own concept type; instead, it expresses the type ACT, but with its direct object in the role of instrument.

Adverbs derived from adjectives have the same canonical graphs. Following are the canonical graphs for the concepts EASY and EAGER, which are used for the adjectives *easy* and *eager* as well as the adverbs *easily* and *eagerly*:

```
[EASY]–
    (ATTR)←[ENTITY]←(PTNT)← [ACT: *x]
    (MANR)←[ACT: *x].
```

```
[EAGER]–
    (ATTR)←[ANIMATE]←(AGNT)← [ACT: *x]
    (MANR)←[ACT: *x].
```

The first graph says that EASY is an attribute of some ENTITY, and it is also the manner of some ACT. That ENTITY also happens to be the patient of the same ACT. The graph for EAGER has the same shape as the graph for EASY, but EAGER is an attribute of some ANIMATE being that is the agent of some ACT.

In the linear notation, the symbol *x is a variable indicating that the two occurrences of the concept [ACT] represent the same node. Converting from the box and circle notation to the linear notation causes cycles to be broken, and variables like *x are needed to show cross-references. The point at which the cycle is broken is purely arbitrary; the following graph is an equivalent representation of the canonical graph for EASY:

```
[ACT]–
    (MANR)→[EASY]←(ATTR)← [ENTITY: *x]
    (PTNT)→[ENTITY: *x].
```

In this graph, the variable *x shows that the two occurrences of [EN-TITY] represent the same node. Redrawing the graph with [ACT] at the top instead of [EASY] is an operation that frame systems do not support. Graphs make such a change of perspective simple and natural.

Role types always have canonical graphs that show the associated pattern of relationships. The canonical graph for PERSON is just the single concept [PERSON]. But the canonical graph for TEACHER includes the case frame for TEACH:

```
[TEACHER]←(AGNT)←[TEACH]–
              (RCPT)→[ANIMATE]
              (PTNT)→[SUBJECT-MATTER].
```

Nominalized verbs inherit the case frames of the verbs they were derived from. For the noun *maintenance,* the concept type is MAINTAIN, with the canonical graph

[MAINTAIN]–
   (AGNT)→[ANIMATE]
   (PTNT)→[T].

Not all role types are derived from verbs. The canonical graph for PRO-FESSOR would be similar to the graph for TEACHER, and the canonical graph for PEDESTRIAN would be:

[PEDESTRIAN]←(AGNT)←[WALK]→(LOC) →[STREET].

This graph happens to contain sufficient information to serve as a definition, but canonical graphs are usually not so detailed. They only represent the implicit pattern of relationships necessary for a semantically well-formed sentence. In general, a type definition is much more detailed than a canonical graph. In fact, as Wittgenstein [1953] pointed out, there are serious philosophical questions about whether adequate type definitions for most words are possible. That issue is discussed further in Sowa [1984].

Metaphors raise further questions about canonical graphs. In Goodman's terms [1968], a metaphor is a "calculated category mistake" – a systematic transfer of the patterns associated with one concept type to another concept type. Although metaphors violate the rules for combining canonical graphs, they do not refute the theory – they presuppose it. Way [1987] developed a technique for handling metaphors by dynamically extending the type hierarchy. For literal statements, the semantic interpreter uses a fixed hierarchy with associated canonical graphs. For metaphors, it first extends the hierarchy by introducing a new concept type; then it generalizes the canonical graphs for the old types. After the new type has been added to the hierarchy, the semantic interpreter can proceed to handle the metaphor by exactly the same mechanisms that it uses for literal statements.

Using canonical graphs in parsing

Conceptual graphs could be generated by a wide variety of parsers. In this section, a conventional phrase-structure grammar is assumed, but the parsing method could proceed in a top-down, bottom-up, or look-ahead fashion. Following are the essential ideas:

. The lexicon associates one or more canonical graphs with each word (or terminal symbol in the parse tree). For natural types, the graph may consist of a single concept. For verbs, adjectives, and role types, it may be a complex case frame.

2. Each canonical graph associated with a node in the parse tree has one concept designated as its *head*. The head concept is the starting point for joining that graph to graphs for other nodes.

3. Each phrase-structure rule is represented in an X-bar form,

$$X' \longrightarrow YXZ$$

where the category X' is a generalization of the category X with possible left and right adjuncts Y and Z. (The techniques in this paper are consistent with X-bar syntax [Jackendoff 1977], but they do not critically depend on its other assumptions. The reader may adapt the approach to other syntactic theories, as long as this feature is retained.)

4. To form the canonical graph for category X, the head concepts for categories Y and Z are joined either to the head for X or to some other concept in the graph for X. The head concept for X' is the same concept as the head for X.

5. When the head concept of one graph may be joined to any of several possibilities in another graph, the syntactic rule may specify a list of preferred relations connecting the two heads. The rule S → NP VP, for example, would specify preferences in Fillmore's order: AGNT, EXPR, INST, etc. The rule VP → V NP, however, would prefer PTNT to AGNT.

6. Syntactic ambiguities are resolved by constraints on joining conceptual graphs; if a join required by some syntactic rule is blocked, that rule is rejected, and some other parse must be found.

The conceptual graph for a sentence is determined by purely declarative grammar rules and canonical graphs. But the order in which the graphs are generated is determined by the parsing and interpretation procedures. In the conceptual graph generator CGEN [Sowa and Way 1986], the interpreter followed the above steps as closely as possible. It started with a parse tree from PEG [Jensen and Heidorn 1983] and generated the semantic interpretation from the bottom-up: it looked up each word in the lexicon to retrieve its canonical graph, and it joined the graphs in the order determined by the parse tree. If more than one interpretation was possible, it carried along a list of possibilities at each level; the ambiguities were resolved when joins were blocked by selectional constraints at higher levels in the tree. The theory, however, is consistent with many other strategies. For the DANTE text analysis system [Velardi et al. 1988], the canonical graphs were never represented explicitly in the lexicon. Instead, the equivalent information was distributed in separate Prolog rules for each conceptual relation. Instead of joining entire graphs in one step, DANTE joined one relation at a time to the new graph that was being created. If CGEN and DANTE started with the same grammar, lexicon, and canonical graphs, they would generate the same conceptual graphs for the same input sentences. But the order in which the graphs were generated would be very different. Other strategies would also be consistent with the theory. In a Schankian parser with expectation-based lookahead [Schank and Riesbeck 1981], a canonical graph could serve as a template for extracting concepts from a sentence and inserting them into the correct slots. The abstract theory determines the final result of semantic interpretation; the implementation determines how that result is computed.

The head concept of a graph determines its point of attachment to other graphs. Yet the choice of head is not an intrinsic property of a canonical graph; instead, it is determined by the syntactic category of the corresponding word or phrase. For nouns and verbs, the head concept of the graph is the one whose type label corresponds to the word itself: for *teacher*, the head concept is [TEACHER]; for *went*, the head concept is [GO]. For adjectives and adverbs, however, the head concept is the one associated with the noun or verb. Following is the canonical graph for the type EAGER, which may be expressed as the adjective *eager*, the adverb *eagerly*, or the noun *eagerness*:

$$[\text{EAGER}]-$$
$$(\text{ATTR}){\leftarrow}[\text{ANIMATE}]{\leftarrow}(\text{AGNT}){\leftarrow}[\text{ACT: }^*x]$$
$$(\text{MANR}){\leftarrow}[\text{ACT: }^*x].$$

For the adjective, the head concept is [ANIMATE], which corresponds to the noun that the adjective would modify. For the adverb, the head is [ACT]. For the noun, the head is [EAGER].

When prepositional phrases are used as adverbs, the head concept of the corresponding graph is the one associated with the verb. When used as adjectives, the head is the concept associated with the noun. Following are two canonical graphs for different senses of the preposition *with*:

$$[\text{ACT}]{\rightarrow}(\text{INST}){\rightarrow}[\neg \text{ ANIMATE}]$$

$$[\text{ENTITY}]{\rightarrow}(\text{ACCM}){\rightarrow}[\text{ENTITY}]$$

The first graph corresponds to an adverbial use for expressing an instrument, and the head is the concept [ACT]. The second graph corresponds to an adjectival use for expressing accompaniment. The head is the left occurrence of [ENTITY], the one accompanied by the other entity.

In English, the determiners *the* and *a* have many complex uses. In this article, only one use for each will be considered: the definite article *the* will have the canonical graph [T: #]; and the indefinite article *a* will have the canonical graph [T]. The universal type label T may be joined to any other type, and the symbol # in the referent field indicates a reference to be resolved by searching for something of a compatible type within the current context or some containing context. For the rule NP ⟶ Det N, the concept for the determiner is joined to the head concept for N. Following are the results of the joins for *the teacher* and *a teacher*:

[T: #] + [TEACHER] → [TEACHER: #].
[T] + [TEACHER] → [TEACHER].

In resolving anaphora, the system would start with [TEACHER: #] and search for another teacher that might be coreferent with it. But for the indefinite form [TEACHER], no searching is performed. For further discussion, see Sowa and Way 1986.

Parsing the examples

With the theory just presented, the series of examples at the beginning of this paper can be explained in a systematic way. For the sentence *John is easy to please*, assume that the grammar contains the following rules:

S → NP BE ADJP
ADJP → ADJ INF

The rule that combines an adjective ADJ with an infinitive INF joins the head of the INF graph (the verb concept) to some slot in the ADJ graph. This join is only possible for adjectives whose canonical graphs contain an appropriate slot. Assume the following canonical graph for PLEASE:

[PLEASE]–
    (AGNT)→[ANIMATE]
    (PTNT)→[ANIMATE].

The head of this graph is [PLEASE], which is joined to the concept [ACT] in the graph for EASY. Extending that join to a maximal join produces the following graph for the phrase *easy to please*:

[EASY]–
    (ATTR)←[ANIMATE]←(PTNT)←[PLEASE: *x]
    (MANR)←[PLEASE: *x]→(AGNT)→[ANIMATE].

Since this graph was constructed for an adjective phrase, its head is the concept linked by ATTR to [EASY]. Joining that head to the concept [PERSON:John] for the subject NP produces the graph

[EASY]–
    (ATTR)←[PERSON: John]←(PTNT)←[PLEASE: *x]
    (MANR)←[PLEASE: *x]→(AGNT)→[ANIMATE].

For the sentence *John is eager to please*, the same technique would produce the following graph:

[EAGER]–
    (ATTR)←[PERSON: John]←(AGNT)←[PLEASE: *x]
    (MANR)←[PLEASE: *x]→(PTNT)→[ANIMATE].

Canonical graphs determine the correct relationships without the need for traces in the parse tree. In fact, the graph derived as the semantic interpretation shows where the traces should go. These and other examples do not refute Chomsky's trace theory; they simply show that a parse tree festooned with traces is unnecessary as an intermediate stage in semantic interpretation.

The next example was the sentence, *John easily does the homework.* Assume that the underlying concept type for *do* is ACT, with the following canonical graph:

[ACT]–
    (AGNT)→[ANIMATE]
    (PTNT)→[ENTITY].

For the phrase *does the homework*, this graph must be joined to the graph for *the homework*, which has the single concept [HOMEWORK:#]. Since the rule VP ⟶ V NP prefers the PTNT relation to the AGNT relation, the result is

[ACT]–
    (AGNT)→[ANIMATE]
    (PTNT)→[HOMEWORK: #].

The next step is to apply the rule VP ⟶ Adv VP, and join the graph for EASY. Since *easily* is an adverb, the concept [ACT] is selected as the head in the canonical graph for EASY. After the initial join of [ACT] to [ACT], the extension to a maximal join forces [HOMEWORK:#] to merge with [ENTITY] to form the graph

[ACT]–
   (AGNT)→[ANIMATE]
   (PTNT)→[HOMEWORK: # *x]
   (MANR)→[EASY]←(ATTR)←[HOMEWORK: # *x].

As before, the variable *x indicates that the two occurrences of [HOME-
WORK:#] represent the same node. Finally, the highest-level rule, S $\longrightarrow$
NP VP, directs the join of [PERSON:John] to the agent [ANIMATE] to
form the final graph

[ACT]–
   (AGNT)→[PERSON: John]
   (PTNT)→[HOMEWORK: # *x]
   (MANR)→[EASY]←(ATTR)←[HOMEWORK: # *x].

For the sentence, *John eagerly does the homework*, the corresponding
steps generate the graph

[ACT]–
   (AGNT)→[PERSON: John]
   (PTNT)→[HOMEWORK: #]
   (MANR)→[EAGER]←(ATTR)←[Person: John].

The name *John* serves to show that the two occurrences of the concept
[PERSON: John] represent the same node. An additional variable is not
needed.

Generating language from a conceptual graph is based on a graph-scan-
ning algorithm described by Sowa [1983, 1984]. The scan begins at a conceptual relation chosen as the main link between the subject and the predicate. If the AGNT relation is chosen, the original sentences are produced:
John easily does the homework and *John eagerly does the homework*. If
the ATTR relation in each graph is chosen, the resulting sentences are *The
homework is easy for John to do* and *John is eager to do the homework*.
See the other references for details of this method.

When one noun modifies another, the last noun is the head. The head
concept of its graph becomes the head of the graph for the entire noun
phrase. To determine how the modifying noun is related to the head noun,
some canonical graph must be found for one noun or the other. There are
four possibilities:

1. The head noun: *philosophy teacher, jewelry thief, chicken coop.*

2. The modifying noun: *mother hen, pet cat, maintenance man, discussion topic.*

3. Both: *employee compensation, bus ticket, discussion leader.*

4. Neither: *gold bar, cat people.*

In the first case, the modifying noun must fit in some slot in the canonical graph for the head noun. For the sentence, *Mary is Bob's philosophy teacher*, type constraints in the canonical graph for TEACHER determine that Bob is the recipient, and philosophy is the subject matter. Finally, the subject graph [PERSON:Mary] is joined with the predicate NP graph to form

[TEACHER: Mary]←(AGNT)←[TEACH]–
    (RCPT)→[PERSON: Bob]
    (PTNT)→[PHILOSOPHY].

For the second possibility, when the modifying noun has the canonical graph, the modifier may specify the role, as in *mother hen* or *pet cat*. For these examples, the role concept is joined to the head of the modified concept, whose type label is restricted to the subtype MOTHER∩HEN or PET∩CAT. If the modifier is a nominalized verb, as in *maintenance man* or *discussion topic*, some concept in the verb's case frame is joined to the head concept: the man is the agent of MAINTAIN, and the topic is the patient of DISCUSS. For the third possibility, when both nouns have canonical graphs, either graph may determine the relation, although the graph for the head noun (the one modified) is preferred: employee compensation is compensation with recipient EMPLOYEE; a bus ticket admits a person to a bus; a discussion leader leads people in a discussion. The last possibility, when neither noun has a canonical graph, is the most ambiguous. One noun or the other must be restricted to some role type: for *gold bar*, either gold plays the role of material of which the bar is composed, or the bar plays the role of blocking the movement of gold; for *cat people*, either the cats play the role of the people's pets, or the people play the role of behaving or looking cat-like.

The phrases *one with glasses, one of physics*, and *one of silver* illustrate an important principle: the canonical graphs used to interpret each phrase are normally selected by words in that phrase; they are not carried anaphorically from some other word in the larger context. Both prepositions *with* and *of* have multiple senses with different canonical graphs for each sense.

For the phrase *one with glasses,* the instrument relation is not possible, and
the normal interpretation would be accompaniment. For the phrase *one of
silver,* the silver is the material of which the thing is composed. That relation is one of the normal senses of the preposition *of,* and silver satisfies
the selectional constraints; there is no need to consider any special relationships for CHALICE. But the phrase *one of physics* sounds odd because
no canonical graph for any word in that phrase can determine that physics
is the subject taught by the one. Determining that relationship requires a
separate step of transferring the canonical graph for TEACHER from the
earlier part of the sentence. Such a transfer is an exceptional step; an English speaker would normally repeat the word *teacher* as in the sentence,
The teacher of English is taller than the teacher of physics.

Resolving anaphoric references is a complex topic that will be saved for
another paper. But the combining rules for conceptual graphs help to re-
construct relationships once the referents have been determined. Consider
the sentence, *The janitor opened the door,* which has the following interpretation:

```
[OPEN]-
    (AGNT)→[JANITOR: #]
    (PTNT)→[DOOR: #]
    (PAST)
```

The symbol # marks definite references that must be resolved to some
occurrence of a janitor and a door in the current context. Following is the
graph for *He used an old key:*

```
[ACT]-
    (AGNT)→[MALE:#]
    (INST)→[KEY]→(ATTR)→[OLD]
    (PAST)
```

The concept [MALE:#] is the canonical graph for *he.* If the only suitable
referent is the janitor, that concept is joined to [JANITOR:#]. When the
join is extended to a maximal join, the result is:

```
[OPEN]-
    (AGNT)→[JANITOR: #]
    (INST)→[KEY]→(ATTR)→[OLD]
    (PTNT)→[DOOR: #]
    (PAST)
```

This is the same conceptual graph that would be obtained for the sentence, *The janitor opened the door with an old key*. Several aspects of conceptual graph theory facilitate this derivation: the type hierarchy, which specifies OPEN < ACT; the canonical graphs, which specify INST as the relation corresponding to the direct object of *use*; and the rules for maximal joins, which allow the graphs to be combined.

Anaphoric references are resolved to concepts that may be introduced into the context by several different means: by an explicit word or phrase; by their tacitly assumed presence in the current situation; or by their occurrence in the canonical graph of some word explicitly mentioned. For the noun *division*, the concept type is DIVIDE with the canonical graph:

```
[DIVIDE]–
    (PTNT)→[DIVIDEND]
    (INST)→[DIVISOR]
    (RSLT)→[QUOTIENT]
    (RSL2)→[REMAINDER].
```

When the word *division* occurs in a sentence, the entire pattern of relationships is potentially available. Subsequent references to *the quotient* may be resolved to the implicit slots in the canonical graph for DIVIDE. Note that the graph has two results, marked by the relations RSLT and RSL2. Since the syntactic patterns of English cannot express such a complex case frame, the semantic pattern is often expressed with two verb forms: *20 divided by 3 is 6 with 2 left over*; or *20 divided by 3 gives a quotient 6 and a remainder 2*.

Many verbs have complex complement structures, which must be expressed in their canonical graphs. The graph for THREAT includes a slot for an ACT that is being threatened:

```
[THREAT]–
    (AGNT)→[ANIMATE: *x]
    (RCPT)→[ANIMATE: *y]
    (PTNT)→[ACT]–
            (AGNT)→[ANIMATE: *x]
            (PTNT)→[ANIMATE: *y]
```

This graph declares that the agent *x of the threat is also the agent of the ACT that is the patient of the threat. The recipient *y of the threat is also the expected patient of the threatened act. For the sentence *Tom threatened Bill with a wet noodle*, one can assume that Tom would perform some unspecified act on Bill. Note that the canonical graph does not imply that the threatened act is harmful to Bill. It only states constraints on associated concepts; other implications would be determined by associated background knowledge in rules and definitions.

When the verb *give* has a patient of type ACT, its associated canonical graph has the same structure as the graph for THREAT:

```
[GIVE]–
    (AGNT)→[ANIMATE: *x]
    (RCPT)→[ANIMATE: *y]
    (PTNT)→[ACT]–
              (AGNT)→[ANIMATE: *x]
              (PTNT)→[ANIMATE: *y].
```

If Tom gave Bill a kick, Tom would be the agent of KICK and Bill would be the patient. When *take* has a patient of type ACT, the act is normally intransitive:

```
[TAKE]–
    (AGNT)→[ANIMATE: *x]
    (PTNT)→[ACT]–
              (AGNT)→[ANIMATE: *x].
```

If Bill takes a walk, he must be the agent of WALK.

Scope and limitations

Canonical graphs represent semantic patterns in a more general way than binary features or simple case frames. They are flexible enough to handle a wide range of linguistic phenomena:

1. Extended case frames for verbs that can include related verbs with complex interconnections;

2. Complex patterns of relationships for other parts of speech besides verbs;

3. Implicit relationships between words in the same sentence or different sentences;

4. Interactions between semantic patterns for different words.

What makes conceptual graphs especially powerful are the formal rules for combining and manipulating them. Frames can represent each pattern well enough, but none of the frame systems support combining operations as simple and powerful as maximal joins. Nor do frames allow a change of perspective as easily as graphs — note the canonical graph for EAGER, in which any of the three concepts could be taken as head, depending on the part of speech: adjective, adverb, or noun. Presumably, frames could be augmented with operators for maximal join and change of perspective. But if enough of these extensions and modifications were made, frames would just evolve into a notational variant of conceptual graphs.

Conceptual graphs handle many linguistic phenomena better than other theories, but they are not magic: they cannot solve problems that people fail to solve. For example, a broiler is a chicken that is cooked by broiling, and a steamer is a clam that is cooked by steaming. But the duck called a steamer is one that resembles a paddlewheel steamboat when it flaps its wings while swimming. Without prior knowledge, neither a person nor a computer could determine the meaning of that term.

In summary, canonical graphs are purely declarative patterns that can account for a wide range of linguistic phenomena. They support an elegant parsing technique and have important implications for the structure of a lexicon. But building a lexicon of canonical graphs involves many subtasks:

- Defining an ontology of concept types;

- Ordering the types in a lattice and adding all the implicit types that are required for the ∩ and ∪ operators (or providing a method for generating them as needed);

- Analyzing all of the variations of case grammar to develop a standard set of conceptual relations;

- Developing guidelines and tests (such as co-occurrence patterns) for identifying the relations associated with each concept type;

- Applying those guidelines to a large number of words in building up a lexicon.

Building such lexicons is a major effort. The CGEN interpreter demonstrated feasibility with a few dozen concept types, later extended to a few hundred. The DANTE system had much better coverage with about a thousand concept types. As an aid for constructing the DANTE lexicon, Magrini [1987] implemented a tool for generating entries automatically from a corpus of about 100,000 words of text. It started with a small, hand-coded dictionary to parse the text; then for each concept type, it determined what relational patterns actually occurred; it then generalized those patterns to form a hypothesis about the canonical graph for that type. It was only necessary for a linguist to check the entries and edit or correct them. With the original hand-coded entries, it took nearly a day to write the entry for each concept type; with Magrini's semi-automated tools [1987], the time to check and edit an entry was about half an hour.

References

Allerton, D. J. 1982. *Valency and the English Verb*, Academic Press, New York.

Bruin, Jose de, and Remko Scha. 1988. The interpretation of relational nouns, *Proceedings of the ACL*, Buffalo, NY.

Chomsky, Noam. 1965. *Aspects of the Theory of Syntax*, MIT Press, Cambridge, MA.

Fargues, Jean, Marie Claude Landau, Anne Dugourd, and Laurent Catach. 1986. Conceptual graphs for semantics and knowledge processing. *IBM J. of Research and Development* 30, 1, 70-79.

Fillmore, Charles J. 1968. The case for case. In E. Bach and R. T. Harms, eds., *Universals in Linguistic Theory*, Holt, Rinehart and Winston, New York, 1-88.

Goodman, Nelson. 1968. *Languages of Art*, Bobbs-Merrill, Indianapolis.

Hirst, Graeme. 1987. *Semantic Interpretation against Ambiguity*. Cambridge University Press, Cambridge.

Jackendoff, Ray. 1977. *X-bar Syntax: A Study of Phrase Structure*, MIT Press, Cambridge, MA.

Jensen, Karen, and George E. Heidorn. 1983. The fitted parse: 100% parsing capability in a syntactic parser of English. *Proceedings of the Conference on Applied Natural Language Processing*, Association for Computational Linguistics, Santa Monica, CA, 93-98.

Katz, Jerrold J., and Jerry A. Fodor. 1963. The structure of a semantic theory, *Language*, 39, 170-210.

Magrini, Stefano. 1987. *Realizzazione di un Sistema per la Definizione semi-automatica di un Dizionario semantico per l'Analisi del Linguaggio naturale*, Thesis, Università la Sapienza di Roma.

McCord, Michael C. 1980. Slot grammars, *American Journal of Computational Linguistics* 6, 1, 31-43.

Montague, Richard. 1974. *Formal Philosophy*, Yale University Press, New Haven.

Schank, Roger C., and Christopher K. Riesbeck, eds. 1981. *Inside Computer Understanding*. Lawrence Erlbaum Associates, Hillsdale, NJ

Sowa, John F. 1983. Generating language from conceptual graphs. *Computers and Mathematics with Applications* 9, 1, 29-43.

Sowa, John F. 1984. *Conceptual Structures: Information Processing in Mind and Machine*, Addison-Wesley, Reading, MA.

Sowa, John F., and Eileen C. Way. 1986. Implementing a semantic interpreter using conceptual graphs, *IBM J. of Research & Development*
30.

Tesnière, Lucien. 1959. *Eléments de Syntaxe Structurale*, 2nd edition,
Librairie C. Klincksieck, Paris, 1965.

Velardi, Paola, Maria Teresa Pazienza, and Mario De' Giovanetti. 1988.
Conceptual graphs for the analysis and generation of sentences,
IBM J. of Research & Development, **32**, 2, 251-267.

Way, Eileen C. 1987. *Dynamic Type Hierarchies: An Approach to Knowledge Representation through Metaphor*. PhD dissertation, Systems
Science Department, SUNY at Binghamton.

Wilks, Yorick. 1975. An intelligent analyzer and understander of English,
Comm. ACM, **18**, 5, 264-274.

Wittgenstein, Ludwig. 1953. *Philosophical Investigations*, Basil Blackwell,
Oxford.

Part II:
Representing lexical knowledge

6
How to teach a network: minimal design features for a cultural knowledge acquisition device or C-KAD

OSWALD WERNER
DEPARTMENT OF ANTHROPOLOGY
NORTHWESTERN UNIVERSITY

Abstract

My goal is to establish a minimal set of features for a cultural knowledge acquisition device (C-KAD). Two important "values" of the device are a "thirst for knowledge" and a relentless "need to inform." Another non-trivial aspect of C-KAD is its inability to "forget" who said what – expert systems must not be allowed to forget their sources. This makes them very different from humans. I start describing the learning device by setting up all possible interrogatives, giving each a "home" taxonomy. These rudimentary taxonomies become the point of departure for the acquisition of the device's knowledge without much additional apparatus. The fixed overhead of features needed for C-KAD to perform appropriately is still considerable. My hunch is that future experience will *expand* rather than reduce this list. This chapter is intended to represent a beginning in the investigation of minimum requirements for an effective Cultural Knowledge Acquisition and Information Dispensing Device (C-KAIDD).

Introduction

You may wonder why an anthropologist would be interested in semantic networks, in teaching semantic networks to acquire information automatically, and in the resulting expert systems. Let me explain.

Ethnographies as expert systems

Cultural anthropologists do many different things. One of these is to write ethnographies – "qualitative descriptions" of social systems, based on extended fieldwork during which we "gather the data" on which our ethnographies are based. Ideally, an ethnography is an expert system. A user could utilize it by asking questions about a given social system and its distinct culture and receiving reasonable answers. In other words, I see an ethnography as a queriable expert system about the cultural knowledge of a social group. This is why I see the task of the ethnographer and the task of the "knowledge engineer" to be convergent, or possibly even identical. The difference is perhaps that a knowledge engineer and his expert system may be more restricted to a subset of all cultural knowledge, while the ethnographer tries to be more global (or exhaustive).

In practice the difference may be minimal. An ethnographer can rarely (if ever) explore literally "everything." He or she too must restrict the task to limited cultural domains. Nevertheless, what I am describing has been called the "encyclopedic" approach to ethnography.

Similarities

Let me list the similarities (identities) between the two fields:
(1) Expert systems and ethnographies are both encyclopedic.
(2) Both deal with large systems of knowledge.
(3) For both the acquisition of expert knowledge is a serious problem.
(4) For both automation of the acquisition of expert knowledge is imperative.
(5) For both the fixed "overhead" needed for getting the acquisition' process under way should be minimal.

Therefore, the task I have set for myself is to present some thoughts concerning this minimal fixed "machinery" that is requisite for an efficient, automatic acquisition of expert knowledge by an appropriate computer program.

Semantic networks

I have been involved in the design of semantic networks for some time – some readers may have heard of my so-called MTQ schema through Evens et al. [1980]. More recently, the main features of the model have been described in Werner and Schoepfle [1987].

In this model, which I also call SIM (Synthetic Informant Model – a theory – to be distinguished from SID, a Synthetic Informant Device – a computer program based on SIM [Werner 1978]), I took aspects of the relevant anthropological and related literature from allied fields and reduced the proposed semantic relations to a minimal inventory. I have called this model the MTQ schema. For those who are interested in problems of knowledge representation I will summarize the MTQ schema here very briefly. Others should skip to the next section.

The organization of an entire language system in the MTQ Schema can be imagined from the illustration in Figure 1 [adapted from Werner and Schoepfle 1987].

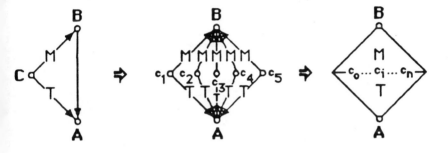

Figure 1. Aristotelian definition to lexical/semantic field

Based on Aristotelian definitions of the form "**A** is a **B** which **C**" this formula can be represented as in Figure 1. If **C**, most usually a paragraph, is complex it can be broken down into simple sentence. The "smooth" **M** and **T** triangle (far right in Figure 1) symbolizes the fact that most definitional paragraphs (differentiae) are open, i.e., there is no longest encyclopaedic definition. The graph in Figure 2 illustrates what an extended lexical/semantic field might look like.

What does C-KAD need to learn?

In the following pages I speculate on the minimal features of a cultural knowledge acquisition device (C-KAD). But first I describe some prerequisites for a C-KAD and explain some of its general features.

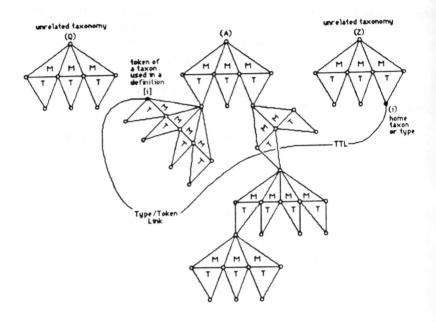

Figure 2. View of an extended lexical/semantic network

Expert systems and children

Culture is sometimes defined as learned cultural knowledge. Language is learned knowledge (disregarding for the moment the apparently genetic human predisposition for learning a language). Following this definition language is "in" culture. Thus human children learn their culture and their language at the same time at least initially. At around age five the child's syntactic patterns become fixed. A gradual shift occurs in which hereafter most of the cultural knowledge is acquired *through* language. Not surprisingly, in many cultures the onset of formal education begins at this age.

C-KAD, the automated acquirer of cultural knowledge, cannot take the time we grant human children to acquire their language and their culture. While many of us find it amusing, interesting, or even insightful to watch our children learn their language and culture, I doubt that machines imitating children will ever be very amusing. In the case of ethnographies and expert systems we want the learning process to take place as fast as possible and to be as automatic as possible. We need to utilize these devices for practical ends, not watch their learning processes.

C-KAD must therefore spring into life "fully" formed, like Athene out of Zeus' head. The key question is, of course, what "fully" means in this context. More precisely, the problem before us is how minimal can we make C-KAD and still consider its capacity to learn some area of general expert knowledge as "full."

Meta-meta...- grammars

At this stage of our discussion we may want to consider Chomsky's postulate: the construction of a meta-grammar (or perhaps several levels of meta-meta...-grammars) that underlie all human languages. The meta-meta...-grammar could be part of the fixed overhead features of C-KAD. Given English sentences, C-KAD could eventually acquire English and whatever information was contained in the set of English sentences to which it was exposed. Given Native American, for example, Navajo sentences, it would do the same with Navajo, and so on.

Unfortunately, I see little progress toward a Chomskian meta-meta... -grammar, at least in the sense that if C-KAD is given this meta-meta ...-grammar and a large set of sentences of language X, then a language specific grammar would emerge that C-KAD could then further utilize.

Conceptual universals

The problem of conceptual universals seems infinitely more difficult when compared to the surface forms of individual languages, yet most of the effort in semantic networks has concentrated on universal lexical/semantic relations and fields [e.g., Cohen and Feigenbaum 1982; Werner and Schoepfle 1987]. We all seem to think – perhaps mistakenly – that a C-KAD processing concepts in relative independence from specific natural languages, could be constructed more easily than a universal meta-meta...-grammar.

My MTQ schema works (more or less informally) in Navajo, Rapa Nui (Easter Island) and, of course, English and Hungarian. Some of my students found these relations without difficulty in African languages (e.g., Gourma [Swanson 1976]). Other ethnographers have found them just about anywhere they have looked among the languages/cultures of the world. Work by Hamill [1978], Hutchins [1980], and others is accumulating evidence that human logic is the same wherever we go. All this seems to give credence to the idea that the conceptual level is more fundamental, more similar from language to language (or culture to culture) and perhaps therefore also simpler. If we accept my assertion that all lexical/semantic relations proposed thus far are translatable unambiguously into the MTQ schema (plus symbolic logic), then we do have a meta-conceptual schema that fulfills the requirements for a minimal C-KAD.

Nature of expert knowledge

Most expert systems seem to assume, at least implicitly, that expert knowledge is homogeneous, or that experts in a field always agree among themselves about what constitutes appropriate knowledge and what constitutes proper action based on a body of knowledge. If that were truly the case, then there would be no point in having conferences, meetings, symposia, or discussions in general. Controversies could not exist.

Even if C-KAD does not deal with controversies directly, an expert system ought to remember who gave it which piece of information. Ideally C-KAD needs to mark every piece of information and remember its source. It should also create a profile on each information giver. For example, C-KAD should know that Joseph Weizenbaum is a computer scientist and Roy D'Andrade an anthropologist. Therefore, C-KAD must know that on anthropological matters D'Andrade's knowledge should be more highly valued than Weizenbaum's. In matters concerning computers the reverse should hold true. Unfortunately, that is too simple-minded: both Weizenbaum and D'Andrade are very smart people, so occasionally Weizenbaum may have anthropological insights superior to D'Andrade's and D'Andrade may see things in computer science that Weizenbaum may have missed.

Epistemological windows. There is a way out of this dilemma. Based on many sources in psychology, sociology, philosophy and related fields [e.g., Kuhn 1962], Alan Manning and I [1979] concluded that a culture is better known if we know the issues that people disagree about. The same applies to expert systems. In a recent book [Werner and Schoepfle 1987] and an article [Ward and Werner 1984] we demonstrate that any discrepancy in an ethnographic (or any other) data base is a potential source of new insights. We call these opportunities for learning "epistemological windows."

Expert systems need to be able to deal with controversy. By this I do not mean taking sides – that is the easy way out and ultimately resolves nothing. My concern is with tracking down the sources of controversy, whenever possible.

Let me illustrate this point with a well-known anthropological example. In a classic article Edward Sapir [1938] describes a case of ethnographic controversy noted and resolved by George Dorsey, a 19th century American ethnographer. Dorsey's curiosity was aroused when all his Omaha Indian consultants claimed the existence of eight clans, while a knowledgeable Chief called Two Crows said there were only seven. Who was right? Should the ethnographer's expert system side with the majority, or with an expert witness?

In this case, as I suspect in most, the resolution of the controversy leads to a deeper understanding of Omaha cultural knowledge: both information

givers were correct. Upon further inquiry Dorsey discovered that traditionally the Omaha did indeed have eight clans; that is, the majority of Omaha
Indians were correct. However, there were no surviving members of the
eighth clan. They had all died out. Therefore Two Crows was also correct.
The story has a punch line – an even deeper insight into Omaha social
dynamics: Two Crows had no use for any of the members of the eighth
clan and he was glad to be rid of them. On a still deeper level it would be
interesting to know why he disliked them so much. Sapir does not tell.

I cannot guarantee that all controversies between experts can be resolved
this easily. However, the lesson is clear: we know more about the Omaha
Indians because of Dorsey's persistence in querying, and because of his
reluctance to take sides.

In other words, an expert system must recognize controversy and resolve
it. The situation is relatively simple if consultant A claims that q is true and
consultant B that not-q is true. Perhaps anything that A said that B did
not, and any statements of A's that raise doubts about B's statements (and
vice versa), should also be treated as "controversy" in need of resolution.
In some cases the simplest resolution may be an appeal to one human
consultant's forgetfulness. In others a "real" controversy may reveal the
dynamics of a knowledge system. As we know from the literature [e.g.,
Kuhn 1962] anomaly – or controversies – are the germs of change.

Thirst for knowledge – need to inform. That brings up another related
issue. C-KAD must have a built-in "value": a "Thirst for Knowledge,"
including a need for resolving (understanding) controversies.

I envision this "Thirst for Knowledge" as a persistent need to expand its
knowledge base, fill apparent gaps and find out why two consultants failed
to mention the same information or why they are claiming the truth of
contrary propositions.

This "Thirst for Knowledge" must be accompanied by an equally intense
'Need to Inform." Given half a chance, the machine must provide all
information that a human user requests. At the same time, the user must
be alerted by the expert system to other kinds of information pertaining to
the topic of inquiry that it may also possess.

The main problem I foresee is that a machine with an insatiable "thirst for
knowledge" and an equally insatiable "need to inform" is a conversational
'crashing bore" who will not let go – the proverbial dog with a bone.

Metaphors. That brings up the ability of the C-KAD to understand metaphors. Perhaps the easiest way to deal with this problem is to introduce
metaphoric thinking into the logical apparatus of the expert system. In

Werner et al. [1975] we did just that. We noted that postulating a "syllogism of metaphor" (one of the invalid Aristotelian syllogisms) can account for many (perhaps all?) metaphors. This syllogism follows:

If A has a set of attributes q
and
if B has a set of attributes q

then A is B

The example is from our article on schizophrenic speech (Werner et al. 1975):

If socks smell, ...
and
if men smell, ...

then men are socks

Admittedly this is a bizarre metaphor, but our expert system should be able to "understand" it, that is, resolve (if necessary by further questions) why anyone would want to assert it. Less bizarre metaphors may be more transparent (e.g., the heart is a pump). Obviously C-KAD needs to work backward from "Men are socks" to an understanding why anyone would want to utter such a sentence presumably because of the possible shared attributes of "men" and "socks."

Minimum capabilities of C-KAD

The fixed features of a Cultural Knowledge Acquisition Device (C-KAD) leading to a cultural knowledge expert system must contain at least the following capabilities:
(1) A built-in "value," "Thirst for Knowledge" and an equally persistent "Need to Inform."
(2) The ability to recognize and resolve controversies. C-KAD should be able do this, in part, by remembering who said what and by asking further questions if two statements are contradictory, or two texts match imperfectly ("Why does A know more about topic X than B?").
(3) The ability to recognize and resolve metaphors. C-KAD can do this in part by constructing the syllogism of metaphor and comparing attribute fields (most simply lists of attributes).
These general capabilities must be met before we can construct any part of a teachable lexical/semantic network.

Specific features of C-KAD

The specific features of C-KAD address the question about which minimal part of the network should be constructed initially, literally, to get the system off the ground.

Getting started

Following the MTQ Schema, C-KAD interprets every declarative sentence taxonomically. It assumes that the focal subject of a sentence represents a known superordinate taxon which the predicate modifies and thus in effect creates a new taxon: the sentence. Figure 3 illustrates this idea.

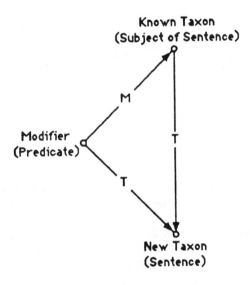

Figure 3. The taxonomic interpretation of a declarative sentence

This arrangement will work properly with declarative sentences. C-KAD, upon receiving a new declarative sentence, identifies the subject, determines if the subject has a known superordinate taxon, and places the subject into

that taxonomy. If it finds no superordinate taxon, it sets up a new taxonomy with the subject of the sentence as its root node (unique beginner). A
note is made (below I symbolize it by (?)) to query when given a chance,
the taxonomic status of the new subject. The predicate (new information)
meanwhile is set up as a modifier (attribute) of the subject and the sentence
represents the new taxon that was thus created.

To the question "Who are you?", for example, my response would be "I
am Ossy," a declarative sentence that is interpreted as shown in Figure 4.

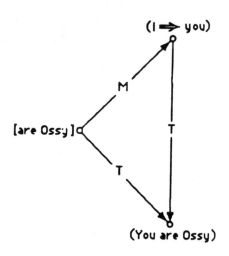

Figure 4. The establishment of a taxonomy of others (yous)
(Note that C-KAD automatically transforms my "I" into its "you")

C-KAD thus establishes a taxonomy of all people who come in contact
with it. Later, through additional inquiry the "yous" can be linked to a
taxonomy of people in general. Each "you," of course, receives, as time goes
on and contact and knowledge of the "yous" increases, additional modifiers
– a deeper knowledge of C-KAD's consultants. If I answer C-KAD's query
with "My name is Ossy," the internal response is similar (as you can see in
Figure 5).

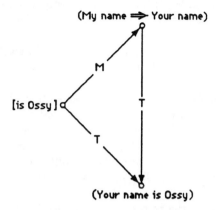

Figure 5. The establishment of a "name" taxonomy

In this case C-KAD establishes a "name" taxonomy. Furthermore, it must have the capability of recognizing "your name" as composite and parse it as "name" modified by "your" and set up the taxonomy in Figure 6.

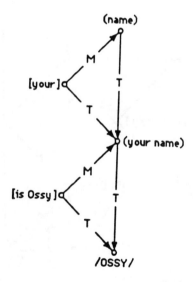

Figure 6. The beginning of a classification of names
(Note that the full text of the final node is abbreviated.)

Several things are notable about this taxonomy. This classification of names is ultimately (on the bottom level) a classification of phoneme or letter sequences (symbolized by placing capital letters between slashes). However, the classification of Figures 4 and 5 is a classification of concepts – symbolized by round parentheses. Modifiers placed in square brackets are always tokens of concepts. The two are linked by type-token links (TTL), following Quillian [1968].

Any classification of names must refer to a classification of concepts (and vice versa). This follows Chomsky's [1965] notion that every lexical entry consists of an ordered pair (C,P) where C is the conceptual/semantic part and P is the phonological/orthographic part of an entry. Strictly speaking in the MTQ Schema there are no lexical entries, but every pronounceable concept must have a link to a classification of names, that is, ultimately to phonetic matrices or letters.

It can be easily seen that the responses "I am Ossy" and "My name is Ossy" create the same linked structure, one from the conceptual side, the other from the name or phonological/letter side. The resulting structure appears in Figure 7.

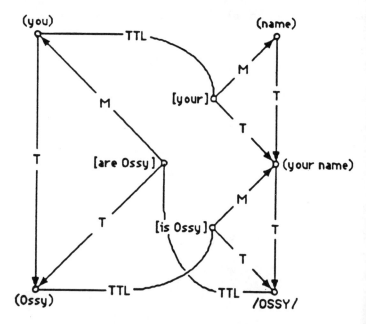

Figure 7. The type-token linkage
of concept and name taxonomies

The situation becomes more complex if I respond to the computer's "Who are you?" with "I am called Ossy."

First, before proceeding with the analysis, this response has uncovered another general principle: How far do we go in allowing paraphrases? The answer is simple. Since we are dealing with the design of software that imitates human intelligence, a device that does not possess human-like flexibility from the outset remains unacceptable. This simple answer unfortunately requires complex solutions.

The first taxonomic interpretation of "I am called Ossy" is straightforward, as shown in Figure 8.

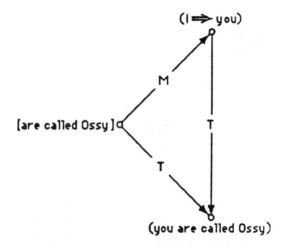

Figure 8. Taxonomic representation of "You are called Ossy"

For the second time we have to call upon the parsing capabilities of C-KAD and a slightly different representation of verbs. The device recognizes 'are called" as a passive construction with the verb "to call" and its complement "Ossy." It is clear from the context that "you" is the object of he verb with an indefinite agentive phrase. This leads to the structure in Figure 9.

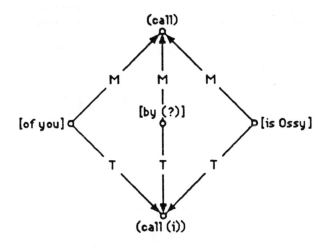

Figure 9. The MT representation of "call"
(Note the possible reading of the structure as
"The calling of you by (?) is Ossy.")

The (?) in the above figure could be called *a place holder for ignorance.*
The "thirst for knowledge" of C-KAD requires that, given a chance, it tries
to eliminate all question marks. Thus we can now represent Figure 9 in
abbreviated form as in Figure 10.

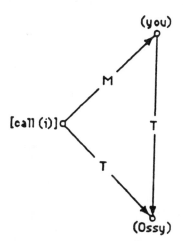

Figure 10. Simplified taxonomic representation of
"You are called Ossy"
(Here [call (i)] and (call (i)) are linked through a type-token
link (TTL) between Figures 9 and 10 – not shown.)

nterrogatives. A general principle that also emerges out of specific design features of C-KAD is its response to ambiguity/uncertainty/controversy. Whenever in doubt, the device must ask clarifying questions. The "thirst or knowledge" (or the elimination of (?)'s) is part of this capability. Thus if C-KAD finds in its data base (?)'s, ambiguities, uncertainties, and controversies (different information from different expert consultants is included n the latter), then it *must ask more questions.*

There are question words in all languages of the world that elicit a response to all types of needs for information. The following examples are suggestive rather than definitive or exhaustive.

(1) (?) = what: e.g., "What calls you Ossy?" Obviously, the next example (2) sounds better, but at this stage C-KAD does not know yet that generally only people call me (or any human being) "Ossy."

(2) (?) = who: e.g., "Who calls you Ossy?"

his interrogative explains the mysterious (*ex nihilo*) appearance of C-AD's first question "Who are you?" at the beginning of the session.

Part of this must apparently be pre-programmed. The goal is to keep all pre-programmed questions or other 'canned' programming to the barest minimum.

I assumed in the section called "Getting Started" that C-KAD already "knew" that only people (in the vast majority of cases) have names. In addition, until we are able to hook up two (or more) machines all of C-KAD's tutors will be human. But for C-KAD to fully appreciate this, the rudimentary taxonomy shown in Figure 11 must be set up ("canned") in advance.

Figure 11. The "what" and "who" taxonomies.

The origin of "Who are you?" is now clear. First, it is part of C-KAD's "thirst for knowledge" to ask questions whenever a (?) appears in its internal structure. Turning on the computer presents the first such opportunity. Second, Figure 4 is not an independent taxonomy. Considering the right side of Figure 3, it was already part of the "people" taxonomy.

In analogous fashion C-KAD must have taxonomies pre-programmed for places and for times.

(3) (?) = where: Introduces a taxonomy of places.

(4) (?) = when: Introduces a classification of times.

(5) (?) = how: Introduces manner adverbials, all kinds of formal and informal measurements, e.g., how big, large, small, little, long (length or duration), short (length or duration), tall (vertical length), wide (at right angles to length), narrow, etc. Possibly all adjectives and adverbs can be queried in this manner.

Questions about how to do something introduce plans and scripts – and information relevant to procedures. (The representation of plans involve the Queuing relation Q. This is elaborated further in the section on the verbs *Teach* and *Learn*.)

(6) (?) = why: Usually this interrogative requests information about motivation of an actor or actors. It is also the major interrogative for resolving incomplete or controversial information. For example, "If person A says q, and if person B says not-q, then [tell me] why?"

These are the basic interrogatives. There are others that must be part of C-KAD's repertory as well. For example,

(7) (?) = whom: This is the proper query if the direct object of a verb (sentence) is human but unknown to C-KAD.

(8) Who did it? ((?) = subject)

(9) What did she do? ((?) = verb)

There is a need for asking about quantities and numbers. This set of questions needs to query the entire domain of quantification – from universal to existential quantification and everything in between.

(10) How much? ((?) = price, quantity)

(11) How many? ((?) = number)

Earlier I set up two classifications: the domain of concepts and the domain of names. The first creates the need for C-KAD to ask for folk definitions, rather than merely a list of individual attributes. As a result, attributes can be simple (mono-morphemic) or complex. The second is the source of C-KAD's need to ask for the names of things.

(12) What is (?)? and in a more complex manner "What does (?) mean?" where taxonomically the meaning of (?) is its folk definition. Note that these kinds of folk definitions are open, that is, tend to be encyclopaedic. The "openness" implies that there is no longest encyclopaedic folk definition. There is always more left to be said.

(13) What is (?) called? (or better "What is the name of (?))"

It may be interesting to speculate that the installation of this baker's dozen of interrogatives (and probably additional ones) lays the foundations for *all knowledge structures*. This base, combined with C-KAD's "thirst for knowledge," represents perhaps its single most important feature.

Equivalence rules. Though various levels of politeness could be built into C-KAD, it is preferable if the device acquires and internalizes these (integrates them into its lexical/semantic networks) in the course of its "duties." To manage identical (or very similar) requests for information on different levels of politeness, C-KAD needs equivalence rules. These establish the equivalence between, for example,

(1) (Who are you?) $\cong$ (Who am I talking to?) $\cong$ (Who do I have the pleasure of talking to?) $\cong$ ...
(I use $\cong$ for the equivalence relation)

The level of politeness in (1) is increasing from left to right. However, equivalence rules are not restricted to phrases conveying different levels of politeness. The following examples illustrate such extensions.

(2) (Person A is male person B's father) $\cong$ (Person B is male person A's son)

(3) (Person A buys C from person B for D $) $\cong$ (Person B sells C for D $ to person A)

The equivalence relation can also be used for referential identity:

(4) (hognose snake) $\cong$ (heterodon)

These equivalence rules are closely related to the deductive capabilities of C-KAD because they can be represented as double implications.

Variations of "OK". The major exception of the avoidance of fixed messages within C-KAD may be certain formulas of politeness which at first need not be broken down into constituent parts but can be utilized whole. Another exception may be various levels of "OK" and its paraphrases of increasing politeness. I will present example variants of "OK" through sample conversations.

1. Ossy: [Turns on computer]

2. C-KAD: Who are you? (on the basis of a (?) in the person and "you" taxonomy)

3. Ossy: I am Ossy.

4.1 C-KAD: "OK" (paraphrase: "I have created you in my data base,") or

"Nice to meet you," or if consultant was encountered previously,

"Good to talk to you again."

Another alternative is

4.2 C-KAD: "OK?" (paraphrase: "At your service, what do you want to do?")

or, all of the above (4.1) and

"At your service."

In polite conversation combinations of all of these are conceivable: the response by C-KAD of "OK, OK?" seems a bit aggressive but not out of line with C-KAD's general "thirst" for information.

The following example is based on the rudimentary knowledge available so far to C-KAD:

1. Ossy: "Who am I?"

2. C-KAD: "You are a people."

"OK?" (paraphrase: "Am I correct?")

3. Ossy: "Yes, but 'human being' is better."
(The quotes represent orthographic convention.)

4. C-KAD: "OK" (paraphrase: "I accept")

"You are a human being. This is better."

"And also you are a people."

"OK?" (paraphrase: "Am I doing all right?")

5. Ossy: "OK" (paraphrase: "You are doing fine.")

The list of OK's in the preceding examples is not exhaustive. I present below a tentative summary in tabular form.

OK(1):   "I have integrated your statement with my data base. I accept."

OK(2):   "Nice to meet you."

OK(3):   "Good to talk to you again" (perhaps two versions, one at the beginning of a conversation and one at the end of a conversation with C-KAD).

OK(4):   "Am I doing all right?"

OK(5):   "You are doing fine."

Verbs: teach and learn

In the section on **Interrogatives** I found it necessary to set up rudimentary start up taxonomies for "people," "things," "places" and "times," etc. This provided the appropriate interrogatives with taxonomic "homes" on which to build the knowledge base of C-KAD. A similar rudimentary taxonomy of verbs is also needed to allow C-KAD to expand its repertory of verbs.

In addition the device can ask questions to fill in further detail. There are two types of questions that must be answered. First, C-KAD asks for folk definitions. These are much harder to formulate for verbs even for experienced human tutors. Nevertheless, it is a first step toward understanding verbs.

Second, C-KAD asks about prepositions, a much more difficult question procedure. In the MTQ schema every verb has a set of appropriate prepositions (see Figure 9). Some of these are always shown explicitly in declarative sentences. These present no problem if the device has at its disposal a list of all possible prepositions. Prepositions in texts can then be identified by looking them up.

A small set of prepositions may or may not appear in declarative active sentences, for example "to" in indirect object constructions and "with" in instrumentals.

Two prepositions, "of" for the direct object with transitive verbs and for the subject with intransitive verbs, and "by" for the agent with transitive verbs, never appear in (English) active declarative sentences. In the case of these two sets of preposition C-KAD must make a guess and submit its guess to the tutor, but only at the time of the first occurrence of the verb or in cases where a verb exhibits more than one prepositional pattern.

In English a test for prepositions is relatively easy. In other languages it may be more difficult.

Upon receiving a sentence with an unknown verb, C-KAD transforms it into a noun phrase with the verb as its head. The following example illustrates this procedure:

   1. Ossy: "I teach you about plants"
                  (I am purposely avoiding complex tenses.)

   2. C-KAD: "OK" (performs I → you
                  and you →I transformation first).
                  "Teaching of me by you about plants?"

   3. Ossy: "Yes" (or OK).

Another, more complex example:

   1. Ossy: "Let me learn algebra from you."

   2. C-KAD: "OK" (performs I→you,
                  you→I transformation).
                  "Letting of you by me learning of algebra
                  by you from me?"

   3. Ossy: "Yes" (OK)

The internal representation of the structures in Figure 12 and 13 follows the conventions of diagramming verbs (sentences) in the MTQ schema, as introduced in Figure 9. Figure 12 represents the algebra sentence. Figure 13 shows a taxonomic representation of the same sentence. All sentences have taxonomic representations of this type.

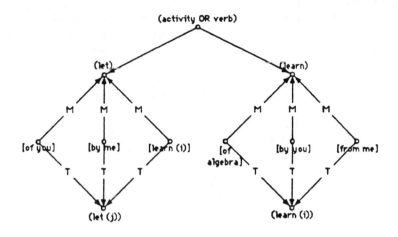

Figure 12. The representation of the sentence
"Let me (you) learn algebra from you (me)."

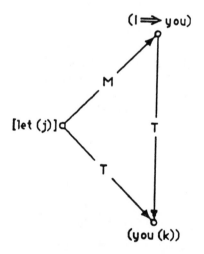

Figure 13. The sentence of Figure 12 as modifier of "you"
(Note that (let (j)) and [let (j)] and (learn(i)) and [learn(i)]
are connected by Type-Token links)

The sentence "Let me (you) learn algebra from you (me)" is in the "you" taxonomy, where "you" is the known subject of the sentence and the predicate is the modifier creating a new "you" (you(k)), that is, one who wants to learn algebra from C-KAD.

Notice that any folk-definition of the verbs "to teach" or "to let" would appear on the upper level of Figure 12. The form of such definitions is in canonical form or can always be transformed into the form:

A is a B, which C

where A is the taxon to be defined, B its superordinate taxon, and C usually a paragraph (or more) of attributes both complex and simple. This canonical form is, of course, the form of definition first proposed by Aristotle: A is the *definiendum*, B is the *genus*, and C the *differentiae*.

Other verbs may follow "teach" and "learn" and are added to the data base as conversations (teaching sessions) are conducted with C-KAD. No doubt C-KAD will be starting with no verbs and no nouns, so the beginning will be very tedious, but after C-KAD achieves a certain level of basic knowledge the going should be considerably easier and quicker. This basic knowledge system may then be cloned to form the starting point of differentiated partial knowledge bases.

I am well aware that I have glossed over some fairly complex detail. However, in principle, there seems to be good reason for utilizing the MTQ schema for a Cultural Knowledge Acquisition Device that starts with a minimal structure and a minimal fixed, built-in basic knowledge from which it constructs complex expert systems.

Summary and conclusions

Let me summarize first the general requirements for C-KAD and then some of its specific features.

General requirements

Most important among these is the device's "thirst for knowledge." Given his "thirst" and its interrogative capability, it can resolve controversies in the knowledge base because every incomplete set or contradictory set of propositions from different consultants of the device demands a "why" question. When this question is answered, the resulting resolution or understanding of the controversy allows C-KAD deeper insight into the knowledge system.

Metaphors are resolved by a built-in syllogism of metaphor and, if necessary, by follow-up questions to determine the common attribute spaces of a term and its metaphoric explanation. This syllogism of metaphor is invalid in the Aristotelian system, but must be added to the logical capabilities of C-KAD.

Finally, the paraphrase capabilities of C-KAD must be as flexible as possible – approaching human skills in this area. The reason is simple: a device simulating human intelligence must come as close to human performance levels as possible. This ability to paraphrase intelligently may be the most difficult part in the design of an expert system.

Specific capabilities

Chief among these specific capabilities is the MTQ Schema. Unfortunately, I was able to sketch only its most salient features.

The second most important feature, building upon the MTQ System, is to start with all possible interrogatives, giving each a "home" taxonomy. Once this is accomplished, these rudimentary taxonomies become the point of departure for the expansion of the device's knowledge without much additional apparatus.

I also postulate a "home" taxonomy for verbs. However, here it becomes necessary to provide C-KAD with an exhaustive list of prepositions. This becomes necessary because there seems to exist no easy way to elicit a taxonomic (or some other) classification of prepositions.

There is a need for two systems of classification – all of sociolinguistics is based on this. One for conceptual content and a different one for phonological variants ("names") used in different contexts (e.g., a colloquial versus a scientific context). That is, C-KAD has a taxonomic/modification structure for concepts and another parallel one for names of things.

Occasionally, I made reference to parsing and synthesizing capabilities of C-KAD. However, the requirements of this skill seem to be relatively simple. Furthermore, any new hypothesis about the assignment of the set of usually implicit prepositions in active declarative sentences is checked by C-KAD's "need" to request the human consultant's approval. C-KAD does this every time a new verb form appears in the conversation with the consultant. The same applies to, for example, passive constructions.

In order to resolve data sets from different consultants that do not match (different levels of detail), or that contradict each other, C-KAD keeps track of who said what. It does this by creating a taxonomy of consultants ("yous") just as it interprets almost everything else taxonomically. Part of the attribute space of each consultant is his or her specific knowledge on a variety of subjects.

A non-trivial aspect of the planning of C-KAD is its inability to "forget" who said what as the device fills its memory. It is conceivable that expert systems must not be allowed to forget their sources. This incapability to forget would make them very different from human beings. That is a C-KAD is not only a "crashing bore" (informing when it knows and relentlessly questioning when it doesn't). It has no opinions of its own and manifests therefore a poorly developed ego, attributing all that it knows to someone else.

Since C-KAD can make mistakes, consultant responses of "no," or "not OK" must be added to its fixed repertory of several variants of "OK's."

The equivalence relation ≅ is needed but can be viewed as the logical double implication. It is thus part of C-KAD's logical capability.

The fixed overhead of features needed for C-KAD to perform appropriately is still considerable. I have discussed some of these. My hunch is that future experience will expand rather than reduce this list. However, I hope this chapter represents a starting point, for further investigations of minimum requirements for an effective Cultural Knowledge Acquisition and Information Dispensing Device (C-KAIDD).

Acknowledgements

A preliminary version of this chapter was presented at the *Workshop on Relational Models* organized by Martha Evens at Stanford University in conjunction with COLING84. The comments of the participants in this symposium helped to shape this paper. A thorough critique of every detail of this paper by my friend and former student Richard Sun, MD, has further improved it and brought it to its present form.

References

Chomsky, N. 1965. *Aspects of a Theory of Syntax*. MIT Press, Cambridge, MA.

Cohen, P. R., and E. A. Feigenbaum, eds. 1982. *The Handboook of Artificial Intelligence*, Volume 3. William Kaufmann, Inc., Los Altos, CA.

Evens, M., B. Litowitz, J. Markowitz, R. N. Smith, and O. Werner. 1980. *Lexical-Semantic Relations: A Comparative Survey*. Linguistic Research, Edmonton, Alberta.

Grindall, B. T., and D. M. Warren, eds. 1979. *Essays in Humanistic Anthropology: A Festschrift in Honor of David Bidney*. University Press of America, Washington, D.C.

Hamill, J. F. 1978. Transcultural Logic: Testing Hypotheses in Three Languages. In Loflin and Silverberg 1978, 19-43.

Hutchins, E. 1980. *Culture and Inference: A Trobriand Case Study*. Harvard University Press, Cambridge, MA.

Kuhn, T. S. 1962. *The Structure of Scientific Revolutions*. University of Chicago Press, Chicago, IL.

Loflin, M. D., and J. Silverberg, eds. 1978. *Discourse and Inference in Cognitive Anthropology: An Approach to Psychic Unity and Enculturation.* Mouton Publishers, the Hague.

Quillian, M. R. 1968. The Teachable Language Comprehender: Simulation Program and Theory of Language. *Communications of the ACM* **12**, 8, 459-476.

Sanches, M. and B. Blount, eds. 1975. *Sociocultural Dimensions of Language Use.* Academic Press, New York.

Sapir, E. 1938. Why Cultural Anthropology Needs the Psychiatrist. *Psychiatry*, **1**, 7-12.

Swanson, R. 1976. *Gourma Ethnoanatomy: A Theory of Human Being.* Ph.D. Dissertation, Department of Anthropology, Northwestern University, Evanston, IL.

Ward, J. and O. Werner. 1984. Difference and Dissonance in Ethnographic Data. *Communication and Cognition* **17**, 219-243.

Werner, O. 1978. The Synthetic Informant Model: On the Simulation of Large Lexical/Semantic Fields. In Loflin and Silverberg 1978, 45-82.

Werner, O., G. Levis-Matichek, with M. W. Evens and B. E. Litowitz. 1975. An Ethnoscience View of Schizophrenic Speech. In Sanches and Blount 1975, 349-380.

Werner, O., and A. Manning. 1979. Tough Luck Ethnography versus God's Truth Ethnography in Ethnoscience: Some Thoughts on the Nature of Culture. In Grindall and Warren 1979, 327-374.

Werner, O., and G. M. Schoepfle. 1987. *Systematic Fieldwork*, Volume 1. *Foundations of Ethnography and Interviewing.* Volume 2. *Ethnographic Analysis and Data Management.* Sage Publications, Newbury Park, CA.

7

Information dependencies in lexical subentries*

Joseph E. Grimes
Department of Modern Languages and Linguistics
Cornell University, Ithaca, New York 14853 and
Summer Institute of Linguistics

Abstract

Lexical information required by linguistic theory can be put into relational normal form by allowing certain types of information to appear in distinct contexts. The normalization yields twelve clusters of information fields: (1) language and name-form, (2) homograph and sense, (3) phonology and etymology, (4) syntax and morphology, (5) definition and field of reference, (6) lexical relations, (7) examples, (8) linkage to grammar, (9) encyclopedic information, (10) housekeeping details, (11) cross references to other subentries, and (12) an index of lexical relations.

Introduction

The attempt to understand the nature of the **lexicon**, an object defined by linguistic theory, is sometimes obscured by commercial limitations placed on the publication of **dictionaries**, which present certain information drawn from the lexicon in a stylized way. Now that information storage techniques

*Part of the work on which this chapter is based was supported by a grant from the National Science Foundation.

allow us access to gigabytes, we are free to visualize just what information needs to be in the lexicon. The lexicon itself is simply the totality of all the information there is about words and word-like objects in a natural language; it registers items and their properties in contrast to the **grammar**, which registers combinations of items and their properties.

This paper is part of the design specification for a multilingual lexical data base, intended as a tool to be used in the field investigation of living languages, or in the organization of information gleaned from texts in extinct languages.

The information structure of entries in such a lexical data base is defined in terms of single-valued and multivalued information dependencies. These are part of the theory of relational data bases [Codd 1970; Date 1981; Ullman 1980; Smith 1985]. One kind of information is said to **depend** on another kind if at any point in time a fact of the independent kind determines one or more facts about the dependent kind.

A lexical data base is composed of **records**. Each record corresponds to one sense or subentry of a word, as is explained more fully later. A record contains several different kinds of information, each considered a different **attribute**, which are kept together by the data base management system. Each attribute is associated with a **field** designator that identifies the kind of information it is expected to contain.

One or more fields of a record are designated as its **key** fields. Together they identify that record uniquely. Smith [1985] gives a simple set of criteria for organizing a data base into a number of relations, each with its own key and nonkey fields, based on the information dependencies that are inherent in the subject matter.

Until Smith's paper appeared, I regarded it as impractical to put lexical information into strict data base normal form. Multivalued dependencies such as lexical relations, and multiple grammatical manifestations of semantic actants, both seemed to me to require a denormalized treatment; furthermore, the fact that one example may be pertinent for several subentries, and one subentry may have several examples, each of which may be part of a whole set of cross reference notes, argued against normalization [J. Grimes 1984]. Smith's use of separate contexts for the same information, and of surrogate fields, here treated as pointers, made it practical once again to think of full normalization.

The term **word** is used throughout these specifications in a sense peculiar to lexicography. Usually it refers to an ordinary orthographic word such as is customarily written between spaces. Sometimes, however, it means more than a word: a cluster of words that has a sense of its own that is not just the resultant of the senses of its components: "teddy bear," for example, is a culturally distinct object that has the form, but not the biology, of bears, and neither the form nor the biology of people nicknamed "Teddy"; so it has to be treated as a separate lexical item. Sometimes *word* covers only part of an actual word: an affix like the plural *-s* or part of a compound like the *green* in *greenhouse*. In short, *word* is used for any lexical item, whether that item is represented by an orthographic word, a string of orthographic words, or a fragment of an orthographic word.

At the same time, the true focus of lexicography is not the word itself, even taken broadly as just described, but each individual sense of a word. The unit of information having to do with one sense of a word is technically called a **lexeme**, but that can also be referred to as a *sense* or *subentry*.

Information clusters

The different divisions of a subentry yield twelve clusters of information fields. Following Smith [1985], these clusters express an organization of the fields in a subentry that facilitates their storage and access while eliminating anomalies that could otherwise occur in updating, an organization that at the same time matches the thought processes of the lexicographer.

One basis for clustering is the minimization of the number of fields in a key. If subentries in the lexicon were stored as simple records, their keys would be five fields long; but by partitioning using surrogate key pointers the keys can be reduced to series three fields long, which is more manageable in some data base systems. In addition, one simple record would have many fields; another kind of surrogate concept here called an **organizing** relation allows the fields to be grouped in a way that is meaningful to the lexicographer. A description of each information cluster follows.

Languages and their entries

The main division of this kind of lexical data base is between information about the language under investigation, known as *Language 1*, and parallel information on other languages, known as *Language 2, 3, 4 . . .*, that are used for communicating information about Language 1. A monolingual dictionary has only Language 1. In the mini-dictionary I compiled as background to research on the properties of the lexicon [J. Grimes et al. 1981], Language 1 is Huichol, a Uto-Aztecan language spoken by about 12,000 people in the mountains of west central Mexico. It has a unique three-letter identifying code [HCH] taken from the worldwide list published in the *Ethnologue* [B. Grimes 1984]. Language 2 is Spanish [SPN], the language used with greater or lesser proficiency by those Huichol speakers who are to some degree bilingual. It is the language of the national school system. Language 3, not included in the published monograph, is English [ENG], the language most widely used for scientific communication about linguistics in general.

Each of the languages has a language name and a three-letter code taken from the *Ethnologue*. It also has a set of table pointers specific to that language: one to a table that tells how forms in that language are alphabetized, another to a table that tells how the name-forms under which words are catalogued are derived from the technically complete transcription given as a specification for the pronunciation. Others point to tables that define the script in which that language is written on the computer screen and on the printer.

For English all these tables are empty, since the computer was designed for English. Spanish needs a sorting table to put **ch, ll, ñ**, and **rr** after **c, l, n**, and **r** respectively. It needs screen and printer tables for its accented letters, special punctuation marks, and n̈. Huichol has its own sorting table and name-form table, the latter because its writing system collapses distinctions of rhythm, length, and tone that are part of the full scale account of pronunciation. It also has its own screen and printer tables to take care of **ü**, ', and accents.

The published form of a dictionary consists of **entries** that are multiply dependent on the language; that is, each language has more than one entry (a lot of them, in fact) attached to it. Entries are distinguished in the first instance by their sort key, which is an arbitrary string of letters produced from the sorting table that gets them into the right sequence so that they can be looked up. They are distinguished more precisely by their name-form, since it is possible for two or more entries to have the same sort key.

To summarize the dependencies in the information, the following representations use the symbol ">" for single-valued dependencies and ">>" for multivalued dependencies. Names to the right identify information categories that depend on information categories to the left. When several categories all depend on the same higher category they are put one under the other, as in an outline.

Pointers to other clusters of information dependencies are tagged with an asterisk, as in **entry***. Names of dependency clusters that are introduced for clarity rather than because the information structure itself requires them are tagged with an exclamation point, as in **grammar!**. They are always single-valued dependents of a pointer.

Categories of information that are included for cross reference between clusters begin with a semantically relevant label followed by "/" and the actual category designation. **Type/example*** is an ordinary **example*** pointer being used to identify the particular example chosen to display the meaning and use of a sense most typically. **Trace/note*** appears in many places; it points to a cross reference note that has been made for the field it is attached to, and provides a path by which the editor can make changes to the cross references when he or she changes a subentry.

language-number [1, 2, ...] >   language-name
                            >   *Ethnologue*-code [**AAA** ...**ZZZ**]
                            >   sort-table*
                            >   name-form-table*
                            >   screen-table*
                            >   printer-table*
                          >>   sort-key >> name-form >
                                entry*

Subentries

Each entry consists of one or more **subentries**. Each subentry gives one **sense** of a word.

Entries divide into subentries at two levels. The first is a split into **homographs**, words that are spelled alike whether they are pronounced alike or not, yet whose meanings have nothing in particular to do with each other. (Strictly speaking, different words that are spelled alike because they are pronounced the same are also **homophones**, but as far as information processing is concerned they are one kind of homograph.) In English, for example, *lead* as a metal and *lead* as a verb for going ahead of someone are spelled alike but are not pronounced alike and are not related in meaning. In an English dictionary we need a homograph tag for each: *lead A* for the noun, say, and *lead B* for the verb. Capital letters are used throughout the dictionary to distinguish homographs. [1]

Subentries that are written the same because they are senses of a single word and share part of their meaning are not homographs. They are properly considered subentries. They may be numbered in a way that shows which subentries are closer in meaning and which are farther away, though distance is hard to calibrate in meaning.

In many dictionaries physically based meanings are given lower numbers: *lead B 1*, for example, might denote the situation where one person goes

---

[1] In system development, if there is only one form, it is automatically tagged as homograph "A" to keep the information structure intact, but that "A" should never be seen by the linguist unless there is also a homograph "B." The same is true of the subentry numbers in the next paragraphs: if there is only one subentry, it is automatically tagged as "1" to keep the information structure intact, but a "1" not followed by another subentry number should never be seen.

ahead of another along a path. It would be numbered lower than a social
meaning *lead B 2* in which someone motivates someone else to act even
if neither of them actually moves. This area of meaning might split into
lead B 2.1 having to do with general leadership and *lead B 2.2* having
to do with the highly patterned activity of leading a symphony orchestra.
Lead B 3 could be logical or abstract as in "this leads us to conclude...."
Higher numbers are usually assigned to more abstract, more specialized,
and metaphorical senses.

entry* >> homograph-letter >> subentry-number > sense*

Lexemes

The sense or subentry or lexeme is the core information management unit of
all lexicography. Different senses of the same word often differ slightly but
significantly in the social usage of their pronunciation variants, their grammatical properties, their meaning, their linkage to grammar, their neighborhood of lexically related words, and their encyclopedic properties. The
information structure for each sense of a word, therefore, is divided for
clarity into these headings, each of which is further elaborated. There is
also a group of housekeeping fields used by the person who compiles the
dictionary.

The information structure has to have room for all possible differences
between senses. When different senses have properties in common, either
those properties are not mentioned in any but the first sense for which
they hold true, or there is a statement that says they are the same as the
corresponding properties of some other sense.

sense*   >   sound!
         >   grammar!
         >   meaning!
         >   linkage!
         >   neighborhood!
         >   encyclopedia!
         >   housekeeping!

Sound

Information about the **sound** of a word includes a phonological or phonetic specification of its ordinary pronunciation and the pronunciation of
each of its variants that cannot be predicted by a simple, overall rule. (Standard German has an overall pronunciation rule for words whose spelling

ends in the voiced stops *b*, *d*, or *g*: if the word has no endings that begin with voiced sounds, or no following compound members that begin with voiced sounds, pronounce *b d g* as if they were their voiceless counterparts *p t k*. If there is a rule like this, the variant forms that result do not need to be in the dictionary.)

If there are variant pronunciations, the regional or social contexts where they are most likely may be able to be specified along with them.

The **etymology** or history of a word, attested or reconstructed, is at least partly connected with its contemporary phonological form; therefore what information is available about it can be included here. Separating etymology from information about meaning is also appropriate in that it creates less of a risk that someone will confuse the history of a word with its contemporary meaning and use – the fallacious but widespread idea that if we only knew what a word meant at some earlier stage in its history, we would understand more precisely what it means now. (The reason earlier meanings are unreliable as guides to contemporary ones is that meanings change with time just as forms do; but they change along more dimensions, and in less predictable ways.)

> sound! > pronunciation >> variant >> social-context
>> trace/note*
> etymology

Grammar

Part of the **grammar** of a word is put on record by identifying its major part of speech classification (N noun, V verb, A adjective for those languages that have them, P preposition or postposition, and Adv adverb). Another part involves the pattern or patterns by which the word is inflected if it is inflected. Function words like question words, conjunctions, articles, auxiliaries, and quantifiers need to be specified more exactly, since they do not fall into large general categories.

Information about inflection and other matters of word structure may be covered best by identifying the paradigm type or types to which the word belongs as a way of defining the general pattern of inflection. There may, however, be irregularities when the inflection of the word being considered is compared with that of others of the same paradigm type. There may also be gaps in the inflection, forms that simply aren't there when we would expect them. And there may be additional forms in the paradigm: English, for example, has both *burned* and *burnt* as past participles of *burn* in spite of the fact that most verbs (like *turn*) have only one past participle.

```
grammar!  >   part-of-speech
          >>  paradigm-type  >>  irregularity >>
                                    trace/note*
                             >>  gap
                             >>  additional-form >>
                                    trace-note*
```

Meaning

Information about the **meaning** of a subentry centers on its **definition**. The definition is in prose, but it is built around a **framework**; that is, a systematic representation of those aspect-related elements of meaning that define the thematic role set of the word. In addition to the semantic information in the framework, the definition contains information that distinguishes the word from others with the same framework. This additional information may be in the form of manner conditions, or (following Jackendoff) of **conditions** that are typically true or that are at least true of central, obvious cases of the word.

The framework elements determine the valence of the word for purposes of linkage with grammatical patterns. They are defined within the limits of a semantic theory, for which the most satisfactory seems to be along the lines proposed by Ray Jackendoff [1983], with heavy input from David Dowty [1979] and Roger Schank [1977].

Along with each definition there should be one **type example**, chosen to typify the sense and display the full actant structure.

Since definition frameworks may be common to a whole set of words – for example, verbs of motion or verbs of carrying or names of snakes – it is useful to know what other words have **conformable** definitions; that is, definitions with shared frameworks. This is achieved by identifying each entry in the set of conformable definitions by its name form, if necessary adding its homophone letter and subentry number.

There may also be one or more comments on the **usage** of the sense with examples, and remarks on **connotations** with examples.

For general positioning of a word relative to other words in semantic space a **field of reference** indicator gives an overall grouping. I am using an adaptation of a set proposed by Mantaro J. Hashimoto for Newari [1977]; Brent Berlin and Terrance Kaufmann have worked out another. Carl Darling Buck's [1949] work on Indo-European synonyms gives a broad basis for this kind of thinking.

Various kinds of **lexical relations** define clusters of words in a lexical neighborhood [Mel'čuk and Zholkovsky 1984]. These relations fall into several groups. Mel'čuk originally grouped them according to whether they were related paradigmatically to their head word by substituting for it syntactically, or syntagmatically by accompanying it syntactically. Another potentially useful breakdown is the one I suggest here, which views lexical relations in terms of the role they play in inferencing and similar manipulations for the purpose of arriving at likely deductions. This approach has the potential of bringing together lexicography as an expression of linguistic theory and the information needed for expert systems in artificial intelligence.

Mutual relations apply to the word as a whole, and include words that are the same in meaning but are in different grammatical categories (like "accompany" and one sense of "with"), symmetries like synonyms, antonyms, and conversives (like "buy" and "sell"), words in inverse relation to each other (like "strep throat" and "fever," antecedent and consequent) and words higher or lower in one of several hierarchies (like "junk food" and "potato chips" in an inclusion hierarchy, "opera" and "overture" in a part-whole hierarchy, "sergeant" and "platoon" in an organizational hierarchy). For synonyms it helps to attach synonym discriminating information to all the synonyms listed under the entry for one member of each set of synonyms. [2]

The **augmenting** relations bring another actant into a situation; they include causatives and a couple of others.

Detail relations pick out one part of a situation and name it: one of the actants (like "game" in relation to one sense of "play"), a peripheral element (like "quiver" as the place where "arrow" is typically found), an aspect of the temporal progress of things (like "resound" and "die away," said of sounds), measures and degrees of activity (like "worsen") and factives that indicate progress in some process (like "adopt" in relation to "program").

Most users of a dictionary of a language not their own want a simple translation equivalent or *gloss* in another language. The gloss is not a definition; in fact, it has no place at all in semantic theory. But people have expected glosses since before the Rosetta Stone was carved. In the absence

---

[2] Treating generic-specific and whole-part relations as lexical relations, and thereby making the relation mechanism a part of the inferencing system, was first suggested by Martha Evens. Her 1978 article with Raoul Smith gave the arguments for recognizing inverse and symmetric relations. Later development of the idea is summarized in Evens, Vandendorpe, and Wang 1985. I see the possibility of refinements of their scheme that go back to the Mel'čuk group's insight that lexical relations, except for the ones that act specifically on syntactic category membership, tend to ignore major category lines.

of any explicit theory of what is involved in the translation process, we do the best we can, realizing how infrequently a gloss provides an accurate characterization of what a word means.

Idioms that make use of the head word are simply listed as separate senses, rather than being included under some less specialized sense.

```
meaning!  >    definition   >    framework
                            >>   conditions
                            >>   trace/note*
          >    type/example*
          >>   conformable/full-lemma
                    [=name-form (homophone-letter)
                                    (subentry-number)]
          >>   usage >> example*
          >>   connotation >> example*
          >    field-of-reference
          >>   mutual/relation* >> synonym-discriminator
          >>   augmenting/relation*
          >>   detail/relation*
          >>   gloss/language-number >> gloss
```

Lexical relations

Since **lexical relations** come up here, the information they represent is given here before proceeding with the other parts of the sense description of a word. There is a pointer to the relation, which has a **relation-ordinal** to get multiple relationships into a canonical order. Relations can be simple or composite, and so the relation ordinal corresponds to the last relation in a **symbol-string**, which represents one or more relation symbols concatenated without space, each beginning with a capital letter. (If the relation is idiosyncratic, an arbitrary number greater than 500 is given it as relation ordinal.) The symbol string leads to a pointer to a **value**.

The value in turn has one or more **value-strings** dependent upon it. Value-strings may have the number of one or more of the other languages, each followed by one or more **glosses**; they don't for a monolingual dictionary, and they do for a bilingual or multilingual one. In addition each value-string may have one or more pointers to examples attached to it.

```
relation*   >    relation-ordinal > symbol-string > value*
                 [the ordinal goes with the last symbol in the
                 string; > 500 for individual relations]
```

value* >> value-string >> other/language-number >> gloss
                      >> example*
                      >> trace/note*

Examples

Each example pointer identifies one example expression in a particular language. It may also identify a citation of the source of the example. For a bilingual or multilingual dictionary it has one or more numbers to identify other languages, each with one or more translations of the example expression into that language.

example* > language-number > expression
         > citation
         >> other/language-number >> translation
         >> trace/note*

Linkage

The **linkage** information about a word includes a description of each of its actants and the grammatical manifestations possible for each. This includes restrictions on meaning or grammar in linkage. There are a group of detail lexical relations that go with various actants and that could be incorporated here; but my present strategy is to keep all the lexical relations together.

linkage! >> actant-rank > meaning-role
                        >> restriction >> trace/note*
                        >> grammar-number > mapping*
         >> syntactic-compatibility
         >> semantic-compatibility

The details of how each actant of a word maps to its possible grammatical manifestations follows Mel'čuk's work on diathesis closely, though it does not use his tabular format as in the 1984 work on Russian.

mapping* > grammar-role [grammatical relation]
         > grammar-form
         >> example*
         >> restriction >> negative/example*
         >> word-feature

Encyclopedic information

Encyclopedic information covers what a user of the language needs to know about a word that is not directly connected with either defining it or giving its grammatical and phonological properties. **Inclusion** information has been treated as encyclopedic, at least in the sense that it is essential for drawing inferences in which the word plays a part; but here it has been treated as the Generic and Specific lexical relations instead. **Part** or **phase** information – the former for things that maintain their shape, the latter for things that happen – gets into spatial and temporal constituency and is the basis for scripts and for some aspects of frame-based logic. Mel'čuk and his group originally treated it as encyclopedic, but to present it in a form more accessible to inference tracing it is now included as the Whole and Part lexical relations. The **situations** in which the word normally plays a part can be enumerated or characterized. Objects needed to **exploit** what the word refers to, associated with it functionally, belong here (like "ski poles" and "bindings" along with "skis"). **Activities** that are carried out in connection with instances of what the word refers to, and **typical names** given to people connected with it, complete the encyclopedic picture.

encyclopedia! >>   situation >> trace/note*
            >>   needed-for-exploitation >> trace/note*
            >>   activity >> trace/note*
            >>   typical-name >> trace/note*
            >>   [type, handled as Generic-Specific
                   relations]
            >>   [phase, handled as Whole-Part relations]

Housekeeping

Housekeeping information helps the dictionary compiler keep track of his or her work. Dates when an entry is begun, last modified, and written off as complete can be entered, as well as an indication of the quality of the entry. If a picture is associated with it, the size of the area to be left blank for it goes here.

Sources of the information in the entry, whether informants, consultants, other dictionaries, or citations in the literature, can be added. Cross reference notes have pointers here.

```
housekeeping!  >    begun
               >    last-modified
               >    written-off
               >    quality
               >    picture-size
               >>   source
               >>   note*
```

Cross reference

Notes for cross reference are produced by the system in order to open
slots for subentries that should eventually be written. They tell what real
entry they came from, what field in that entry, and they point back to the
contents of the field. The dictionary editor thus has enough information
to begin work on the subentry they represent, realizing that the dictionary
has to account for at least the use given in the note, and probably for a lot
more as well.

```
note*  >   label [symbol-string or other field-name]
       >   context
       >   full-lemma
               [=name-form (homophone-letter)
               (subentry-number)]
       >   example*
```

Relation index

An index to the lexical relations helps the linguist keep track of some of the
information. This index also keeps track of inverse relations, important for
information processing that makes use of lexical information.

```
relation-ordinal  >    relation-symbol
                  >    relation-name
                  >    relation-sketch
                  >    relation-definition
                  >    inverse/relation-ordinal
                  >>   similar/relation-ordinal
                                    >    relation-discrimination
                  >>   probe-question
```

A set of computer programs for an unnormalized version of substantially the same information was written in 1979 using merges to tapes; tape cartridges at that time were the only physically reliable medium available that could be taken into the field for lexicographic research. Now that portable random access media are available, and we understand the nature of the lexicon a little better than we did at that time, a major redesign is in order. The first versions were written in PTP (Programmable Text Processor, [Simons 1984]). The new design is being implemented in Prolog.

References

Buck, Carl Darling. 1949. *A Dictionary of Selected Synonyms in the Principal Indo-European Languages.* Chicago: University of Chicago Press.

Codd, E. F. 1970. A relational model of data for large shared data banks. *Communications of the ACM,* **13**, 6, 377-387.

Date, C. J. 1981. *An Introduction to Database Systems,* 3rd edition. Reading MA: Addison-Wesley.

Dowty, David R. 1979. *Word Meaning and Montague Grammar: The Semantics of Verbs and Times in Generative Semantics and in Montague's PTQ.* Dordrecht: D. Reidel Publishing Company.

Evens, Martha W. and Raoul N. Smith. 1978. A lexicon for a computer question-answering system. *American Journal of Computational Linguistics,* microfiche 83.1-98, Appendix in *The Finite String,* AJCL microfiche 81.16-24.

Evens, Martha, James Vandendorpe, and Yih-Chen Wang. 1985. Lexical-semantic relations in information retrieval. In S. Williams, ed., *Humans and Machines.* Norwood NJ: Ablex, 73-100.

Grimes, Barbara F., ed. 1984. *Ethnologue: Languages of the World,* 10th edition. Dallas TX: Wycliffe Bible Translators.

Grimes, José E. et al. 1981. El huichol: apuntes sobre el léxico. Technical report no. 5. ERIC document ED 210 901, microfiche.

Grimes, Joseph E. 1984. Denormalization and cross referencing in theoretical lexicography. *COLING 84.* Stanford CA: Association for Computational Linguistics, 38-41.

Hashimoto, Mantaro J. 1977. *The Newari Language: A Classified Lexicon of its Bhadgaon Dialect.* Tokyo: Institute for the Study of Languages and Cultures of Asia and Africa.

Jackendoff, Ray. 1983. *Semantics and Cognition.* Cambridge MA: The MIT Press.

Mel'čuk, Igor A. and Alexander K. Zholkovsky. 1984. *Explanatory Combinatorial Dictionary of Modern Russian.* Vienna: Wiener Slawisticher Almanach.

Schank, Roger C. and Robert P. Abelson. 1977. *Scripts, Plans, Goals and Understanding: An Inquiry into Human Knowledge Structures.* Hillsdale NJ: Lawrence Erlbaum Associates.

Simons, Gary F. 1984. *Powerful Ideas for Text Processing.* Dallas: Summer Institute of Linguistics.

Smith, Henry C. 1985. Database design: composing fully normalized tables from a rigorous dependency diagram. *Communications of the ACM* **28**, 8, 826-838.

Ullman, Jeffrey D. 1980. *Principles of Database Systems.* Rockville MD: Computer Science Press.

8
Determination of lexical-semantic relations for multi-lingual terminology structures

JOHN S. WHITE
MARTIN MARIETTA DATA SYSTEMS
ENGLEWOOD, COLORADO 80112

Abstract

This paper describes a methodology for generating multilingual taxonomic hierarchies for specific and general terminological systems, using the lexical relations derivable from machine-readable dictionaries. Taxonomic structures can be optimized to provide data for a knowledge base facilitating the automatic disambiguation of text in one language into lexical senses of terms in the same or another language. Such a capability, in turn, contributes a multi-directional translation dimension to automatic paraphrase and content analysis. As part of a full natural language processing machine translation system, the knowledge added by the structures derived from a machine-readable dictionary can assist in sense selection, grammar rule-base composition, and generation. The methodology for the development of these structures is described here, consisting of a manual pre-disambiguation task, and computational creation of parallel taxonomic structures in each language. The rationale behind deriving lexical semantic structures in this way is discussed.

Introduction

An emerging line of research and development in recent years has centered around the manipulation of machine-readable dictionaries (MRD's) to extract various sorts of representations of lexical relations, and to create data structures of use in natural language processing (NLP). At the same time, there persists a concern about whether such activities constitute a legitimately scientific, computational linguistics study. This is a fruitful question, serving as it does to challenge those interested in MRD's to show what it is about dictionaries, and their manipulation, that furthers the aims of computational linguistics. Simply stated, a dictionary is, while a description of an aspect of some language, at the same time a linguistic phenomenon of that language. For this reason the relations which can be elicited from the dictionary, if this elicitation is performed with a consistent, well-motivated methodology, are at once descriptions and evidentiary data. The structures revealed in elicitation undertakings say something about the language at the same time as serving as tools in natural language processing.

This paper describes a methodology for using the principles of internally valid relations to create a multi-lingual hierarchical structure. Such a structure could form a component of a translation-paraphrase routine, via automatic disambiguation by taxonomic, collocational, and translation links among entry words. The methodology for the development of these structures is described here, consisting of a manual pre-disambiguation task, and computational creation of parallel taxonomic structures and collocational associations in each language.

The task described here draws from progress in two areas, namely that of online translation glossaries, and of automatic structure generation from machine-readable dictionaries. The first area has arisen primarily from the need to support machine-aided translation environments. The second has emerged as a means of studying the organization of concepts in human language as revealed in the semantic structure of its dictionaries. Translation dictionaries link together terms which are translations of each other, under specified conditions. The recent dictionary hierarchy models link terms with the semantically superordinate terms in their definitions, under specified constraints, from a monolingual terminology set. The method described here combines the translation linking of the one with the semantic linking of the other.

Derivation of semantic relations

The original formulation of computational principles for deriving structured semantic information from a dictionary comes from the work of Amsler

[Amsler and White 1979, Amsler 1980]. In Amsler's approach, syntactic criteria are used to build taxonomic links, called "ISA" links by Norman and Rumelhart [1975], between a dictionary entry and the grammatical head of its definition text. The constraint that semantic links are bound to syntactic criteria guarantees that no inconsistencies in semantic relations may be imposed externally, as can be the case in a purely intuitive semantic linking exercise. In an internally complete dictionary, i.e., one like the Merriam-Webster Modern Pocket Dictionary in which every word in a definition is also an entry in the dictionary, a taxonomic structure can be grown recursively via ISA links from an entry to its definition head, which is linked to its own definition head, and so on until a few words are defined in terms of each other.

The Amsler project was undertaken in two phases, which parallel the methodological description of the multilingual task below. First, because of homography (separate entries with the same spelling) and polysemy (multiple sense-definitions of an entry), designations of sense had to be assigned to the syntactic heads of definition texts. This allowed the taxonomic link to obtain between particular senses of words, rather than among orthographic strings. This task was performed manually, by looking up a definition head word in the same dictionary and determining the sense of its use in that definition text.

The second phase of the Amsler project was the creation of the taxonomic structure itself, which is a tangled hierarchy of ISA links among senses of entries and senses of definition heads. The following is an example of a subset of the Modern Pocket Dictionary tree, showing the ISA links from an entry term to a term or terms in the text, and showing the taxonomic level of those links [excerpted from Amsler 1980].

01	MEAL-1.2A	= AN ACT-1.1B OR THE TIME-1.3A OF EATING A MEAL
02	BREAKFAST-.0A	= THE FIRST MEAL-1.2A OF THE DAY
03	BRUNCH-.0A	= A LATE BREAKFAST-.0A, AN EARLY LUNCH-1.1A,OR A COMBINATION-.2A OF THE TWO
02	BUFFET-3.2B	= A MEAL-1.2A AT WHICH PEOPLE SERVE THEMSELVES...
03	SMORGASBORD-.0A	= A LUNCHEON OR SUPPER BUFFET-3.2B CONSISTING OF MANY FOODS...
02	DINNER-.0A	= THE MAIN MEAL-1.2A OF THE DAY

This automatically generated structure shows MEAL (sense 1.2A) at the top level (01) to have three hyponyms (at level 02), BREAKFAST-.0A, BUFFET-3.2B, and DINNER-.0A. BUFFET-3.2B itself has a hyponym SMORGASBORD-.0A (at level 03). BREAKFAST has a hyponym, also, BRUNCH-.0A (at level 03).

Note that the text of a definition is potentially available at its associated node in the structure; that is, a mechanism can be implemented which relates a term to the words with which it co-occurs in a definition text as well as to its superordinates ("hyperonyms") and hyponyms. A structure with both taxonomic and and collocational dimensions [see Sinclair 1966 for a valuable discussion of Firthian collocation theory] has a potential application as a knowledge base possessing a sense-specification capability to enable both automatic disambiguation of text, and paraphrase through generalization via ISA links.

Internally derived relations

The significant awakening of interest in manipulating MRD's in recent years has been motivated in different ways, though most often by a desire to create large NLP lexicons quickly. In the course of these studies, much discussion has centered around the methods by which relations in the dictionaries are to be discovered and exploited. The practice of simply asserting these relations has well-known consequences of duplication, inconsistency, overlap of categories, etc. So the methodological issue of rigor in the assertion of relations has been complicated by such problems as requirements for useful analysis and description.

The method for relational validity pursued by Amsler was based on an information elicitation technique analogous to that of the anthropological discipline of ethnosemantics. In the theory underlying this discipline, the criteria for the determination of lexical relational primitives must be derived from organizing principles internal to the data itself. These principles must be discovered along with the organization which these principles impose upon cognitive concepts.

Thus, if an ethnosemantic analysis of, say, musical instruments used some feature "+/- reed," there must be evidence in a native speaker's use of the language that such a feature is actually one of the ones ordinarily used by the speaker to make segregations within the domain of musical instruments. The domain of musical instruments must also be provable as a concept inherent in a native speaker's cognition, i.e., it must be a way that he/she actually thinks about things like musical instruments.

The ultimate value of the ethnosemantic requirement for "psychological validity" [Burling 1964] has proven to be a re-emphasis of the need for explicit evaluation matrices, and an assertion that the best configuration of relations is discoverable from within the corpus of observed phenomena itself.

The project described in this paper is aimed at an application, and thus does not have to pose the questions of those observing a dynamic interplay of language and social interaction. But there is a point at which the perspectives are similar. The task here is to determine which and how many relations are necessary to accomplish automatic lexical structure generation, and we make this determination based upon what the corpus of phenomena itself reveals.

This was the philosophy underlying the method employed in Amsler's original studies. In this work Amsler sought to avoid any imposition of structure a priori; rather, the methodology was to use, to the greatest extent possible, consistent, verifiable criteria for postulating the presence of lexical semantic relations in the corpus. This approach was intended to avoid the consequences of the imposition of categories or relationships which would tend to obscure, rather than elucidate, the relations expressed in the dictionary itself. Thus the basis for the determination of the existence of a semantic relation (the sense of a word used in the definition of another word) was syntactic. The judgment depended entirely on the syntactic head of the defining text.

The dictionary as a linguistic artifact

The notion that elicitation, rather than imposition, of relational expressions in dictionaries is desirable or possible relates to the anthropological orientation alluded to above. Specifically, a dictionary is a naturally occurring linguistic artifact, created by human native speakers with the intention, at least, of carrying out a consistent plan of organization, which possesses in addition to that attempted organization a definite embodiment of the lexicographers' intuitive grasp of the lexical semantics of the language. Thus the organizing principles in the dictionary, i.e., the lexical-semantic relations explicitly or implicitly present among the entries and definitions, are either exactly indicative of ordinary natural language organizing principles, or somewhat inexact in random ways. This is also the most that can be said for an externally imposed system of lexical-semantic relations, one in which semantic primitives are postulated to describe natural language derived by observation. This is the most common type, of course, employed in every NLP system that has semantics, and, indeed, in any pedagogical language text.

The conclusion to be drawn is that the imposition of a system of lexical-semantic relations upon a corpus which is created for the purpose of expressing lexical-semantic relations (i.e., the dictionary itself) is likely both to compound the possible errors in the organization, and also to obscure consistent, well-formed relations.

To pursue the issue a step further, it is clear that there are obvious relationships, such as the ISA relation, which are overtly expressed in the layout of the dictionary entry itself, i.e., between the entry term and the definition text of each of its senses (specifically between the defining term and the syntactic head). There are many other relations expressed, of course, but the idea of elicitation of the inherent properties expressed in the dictionary itself can be taken to a heuristically beneficial extreme. The first cut is into two relations: the ISA relation between the entry term and the sense-definition head, and the simple collocational relation between the defining head and the other words in the definition. Obviously there is more expressed in the definition text than just these two relations. But the extraction of these two relations provides us with much useful information without imposing relations that are not actually in the dictionary.

Suppose now that an effort is made to refine the collocational axis to elicit other lexical relations. This can be done by attempting to identify textual patterns ("one of," "any of a class of," "used for," "used as," etc.), as described in other recent dictionary work [Evens and Smith 1983, Chodorow et al. 1985, Markowitz et al. 1986, Slator and Wilks 1987]. Evidently, these patterns express a relation between the entry word and the syntactic complement of these phrases. Further, these patterns can be combined into heuristic relational classes (e.g., the phrase "any of a class of X" and "any X" can be taken as expressing the same relation). There is no particular problem with naming that relation, say "member," except that we may freeze these heuristic combinations into imposed structures that may not actually be present in the data. It is easier from a bookkeeping point of view, and is at the same time more consistent with the philosophy by which the ISA axis is built, to give the relation expressed by a particular text pattern a name that includes the pattern itself. This method assures that patterns mistakenly combined into a class of relational expressions can immediately be separated again.

So, heuristically, the value of manipulating the dictionary comes from the ability to hypothesize or to posit relations as atomically as needed, while being assured that no new, unmotivated relations are being imposed.

Application of relational structures

The elaboration of elicited relations into a structure, even a two-dimensional structure using explicit ISA and collocational associations, can in theory be employed to disambiguate free text, and then to extract relationships from that text with minimal processing effort. The MRD-derived lexical network can be used to look at free text and find a collocational fit between a datum point in the text and the other words around it, or the hyperonyms of the other words around it, or the collocations of the hyperonyms of the other words around it, or the collocation of the hyperonyms of the datum point.

Each lateral step (hyperonym of collocate or collocate of hyperonym) of course imposes a distance weight that can be used in judging the felicity of a hypothetical relationship.

If there is no fit, or if the fit that is achieved is intolerably weighted, this strategy is repeated for a different sense of the datum point word. This ability to access taxonomic trees, collocates of tree members, and tree associates of collocates, with no particular processing effort, should theoretically allow the disambiguation of a significant number, perhaps a majority, of the words in free text. From there, the words that have not been disambiguated can be included in the pile of known (though not sense-disambiguated) collocates. It is convenient to think of this side effect as an automatic learning capability, since these collocational misfits can be employed as (cautiously weighted) collocates for disambiguating the next text.

The net power of just an MRD-derived model, particularly one with somewhat refined relational dimensions, should be sufficient to disambiguate text to the point that the relations can be extracted by automatic abstraction and paraphrase routines. With just a two-dimensional structure (i.e., with the ISA hierarchy in place and an undifferentiated collocational relation) determination of the topic of the text should be possible.

It is from this methodological tradition that the development of multilingual semantic structure is undertaken, employing machine readable general dictionaries and a specialized terminology database which contains both translations and definitions.

The TEAM terminology database

The Siemens AG TEAM terminological database is a terminology bank for use by translators working for Siemens Language Services. There are over two million entries in 760 subject fields. Each entry contains the entry term, the document source, a definition, and translation information in nine languages. Not every entry contains definitional or synonymy information for every transfer. The following are typical entries:

10:Dekontaminationsfaktor
11:m.
14:...Das Verhältnis der Aktivitätskonzentrationen oder der Aktivitätsflächendichten einer kontaminierenden radioaktiven Substanz vor und nach der Dekontamination.

20:...decontamination factor
24:...The ratio of activity concentrations or activity surface
densities of a contaminated radioactive substance before or after
decontamination.

10:Verhältnis
11:n.
20:ratio
21:n.

10:Geiger-Müller-Zähler
16:Geiger-Müller-Zählrohr
20:Geiger-Müller counter
24:A gas-filled counter operated under such conditions that the
magnitude of each pulse is independent of the energy of ions
initiating it.
26:Geiger-Müller tube; Geiger counter

The above examples are of: a) an entry with a link from the German entry
term (Dekontaminationsfaktor) to a head term in its definition (Verhältnis),
and a link from the English term (decontamination factor) to a term in
its definition (ratio); b) the entry record for the previous defining head
(Verhältnis; note that this one has no definition in either language, and
is indeed a redundant entry, since definitions exist for both in the previous entry); and c) an entry which has no German definition, but does
have a definition for the English entry term, and synonym terms for both
languages.

These examples show bilingual German-English records which can be
accessed through either the German or English entry term. Two facts
should be noted here. First, while the entry record is capable of containing
a definition in every language, it often contains a definition for only one.
Secondly, the definition head for an entry term tends to have a rather
general reference (e.g., "counter" in the example above), of a sort which
would not be likely to appear in a specialized glossary. This fact has the
consequence of producing very shallow hierarchies if we attempt to build
structures from within the glossary alone.

For both these reasons, a manual coding phase of the multilingual semantic network project must include an analysis of the lexemic status of phrases
containing the defining head word, and a means of manual disambiguation
of sense into general on-line dictionaries in English and German.

Coding phase

The procedure for the manual coding phase is as follows, using nouns as an example:

> **A.** For each language in an entry record, the head noun phrase of its definition is queried as an entry term in the database, using these patterns:
>
> > 1. Noun
> > 2. Adjective*-(Prepphrase-Participle)-Noun
> > 3. (Adjective*)-Noun-PrepPhrase
>
> The synonym is used if there is no definition given for the term.
>
> **B.** If an entry term is found from a query of one of the above patterns, the successful pattern is marked as the "defining head" of the original entry term, and the procedure in A is repeated. In this way, ISA links are derived from entry-term plus defining head pairs, for each language in the record.
>
> **C.** If an entry term does not have a definition, the head noun of the entry term is looked up in a general, online dictionary and assigned a sense value. If the entry term does have a definition but the patterned query failed to find an entry term that corresponds to its defining head, the head noun of the definition (or synonym) text is looked up in the general dictionary and assigned a sense value. In either case, the results of the lookup in the general dictionary are themselves looked up in the same dictionary, using the Amsler criteria, until the tree-tops of the general dictionary are reached.

At this point, each language has specific, usually multi-word terms which may be in ISA relations with other such terms, all ultimately linked to senses of entries in general terminology dictionaries. Thus the lowest nodes in the taxonomic structures will tend to be multi-word and not sense-disambiguated (subject-field specificity is presumed adequate at the lowest level). The higher nodes will be generally single-word and disambiguated according to the dictates of the dictionary.

Tree generation

The procedure consists of linking marked defining head strings with their defining heads, carrying along the sense designation where present. Each defining string (a sense-designated word, or a marked defining head) is indexed to all the definition texts in which it occurred. Every TEAM entry term is linked to the translation entry term in its same entry record.

Every term, then, may be seen as the intersection of values in three di mensions: the hierarchical (represented by its ISA link to its immediate superordinate), the collocational (the list of words with which it occurred in definition texts), and the transfer (the corresponding entry term in the target language, itself an intersection of three dimensions). Using this struc ture, a collocation set can associate a term in a free text with a sense based upon collocational matchings in the text. An ISA path may then be exploited to conceptually generalize a term matching a lower node, be translated into the target language anywhere along that path, and proceed upward in generality in the target language.

There are two reasons for maintaining such a fundamental separation between the technical-set terms and the general-set terms, that is, for no including a general multilingual dictionary in the structure. First, the na ture of the task presumes disambiguation of texts in a specific field. (The automatic prediction of field based on scanning passes is seen as an ex ternal process.) Second, a general translation dictionary usually provide multiple senses, and there is no automatic way at such a link to know the ascendancy on the target side. In order to identify an ascendancy path in such a corpus, an additional manual disambiguation task would have to be undertaken. Consequently, an entry term from a general dictionary has direct hierarchical/collocative provenience, and inherits a translation lin from its hyponym path.

The following small subset of the networks is formed by following all the possible upward ISA paths for the translation pair "ratio" and "Verhältnis.

Verhältnis .1a   Messbare oder vergleichbare Beziehung; Proportion

Beziehung .4a   Etwas mit ihm oder damit zu tun haben

Proportion .0b   Verhältnisgleichung

Wahrig's monolingual *Deutsches Wörterbuch* [1967], has ISA links from *Verhältnis* to both *Beziehung* and *Proportion*. The sense of *Beziehung* that is being used in the *Vehältnis* definition is, in turn, ISA linked to the (se mantically vacuous) *etwas*, and *Proportion* to *Verhältnisgleichung*. From these associations among syntactic heads and defining words, the dictio nary elicits both the ISA links from a sense of *Verhältnis*, to *Proportio* o *Verhältnisgleichung,* and a set of collocational links among, for example, *Beziehung, messbar,* and *vergleichbar.*

atio .1b	The relationship in quantity, amount, or size between two or more things
elationship .1a	The state or character of being related or interrelated
tate 1.1a	Mode or condition of being
haracter 1.2a	One of the attributes or features that make up and distinguish the individual

On the English side of the translation link established by the *ratio –* *Verhältnis* pairing in the technical translation dictionary, the trees elicited om *Webster's Seventh Collegiate Dictionary* [1967] provide some rather eep paths, of which only a small sample is given here. A sense of *ratio* is nked to *relationship,* as the head of its definition text. The sense of *relationship* used in the *ratio* definition is in turn ISA-linked to senses of both tate and *character.* Thus, collocational sets are also established among e members of the definition texts, such as that among the (now known) nses of *state* and *character,* and *related* and *interrelated.*

Using this structure, a collocation set can associate a term in a free text ith a sense based upon text collocational matchings. An ISA path may en be exploited to conceptually generalize a term matching a lower node, translated into the target language along that path up to the most neral ISA link in the TEAM portion, and proceed upward in generality the target language. A general term in free text may use collocation nks to direct a downward ISA path, translate along the path from the ost general TEAM entry downward, and have available the ISA tree for neralization in the other language.

It is interesting to note a similarity between this structure and the digraph rategy employed by Litkowski [1978] in a lexical decomposition task. His ees are built on the relation $R(x,y)$ such that x is used to define y. In rms of our present structure, the relation expressed describes x as either the set of collocates of y, or as the superordinate of y. While Litkowski's sk was different, the conclusions he has drawn should be of considerable edictive value for our model, since R can be derived algorithmically from e taxonomy/collocation/translation structure.

Beyond disambiguation

As we have described the system so far, there are only three of what ma
be called lexical-semantic relations being exploited, each of which has a
indicator external to semantics. The ISA relation is signalled by the dicti
nary format by which an entry term is defined by a phrase with a syntact
head. The translation relation is the explicit listing of one word as th
transfer equivalent of another word. The range of the collocation relatic
is the list of words with which a word (which is elsewhere given as an entr
term) co-occurs in a definition text. The fact that the motivation for thes
relations is derived from attributes inherent in the dictionary text, rath
than imposed from without, provides a strong claim for the intrinsic vali
ity of any structure which derives from them. Structures distilled by th
strategy exploit the relations inherent in the corpus itself. We are, hov
ever, trying to build an application, and so the ultimate measure is wheth
these three relations can in fact serve to disambiguate free text in certa
technical fields, and to what extent (if any), and by what criteria, the li
of relations should be extended to accommodate the needs of a functic
such as translation paraphrase.

It is believed that the three relations form a sufficient grid for the pu
pose of disambiguating text of a known specialized field, with little or
grammatical parsing. A paraphrase, for example, into a summary-ty
template, would have to be able to manipulate generality and report sen
ing information, but also would have to instantiate formulaic slots referrir
to, e.g., temporal, spatial, and use relations with respect to the object
discourse. The instantiations must be discoverable from the disambiguat
text, and so must be added to the set of relations that can be determin
for words in the definition corpora. We find ourselves, from a slightly d
ferent perspective, in accord with Werner's position [this volume], name
that the basic relations are few and that more relations are added for a
plication tasks. The present approach makes no claim, of course, about t
dynamics of the lexicon of native speakers, and does not necessarily ne
to distinguish lexical from semantic relations [see Evens and Smith 1978 f
a discussion of such distinctions].

There are as many ways to add relations to the lexical-semantic netwc
as there are relational (or componential) schemes, of course, but there a
also means of maintaining the metric of validity. These consist of tact
for extracting relations via consistent, syntactic or formulaic patterns, ju
as we did for the three relations now employed, from what we now cc
sider the collocational axis. The collocational relation simply represe
the co-occurrence of a word with other words, regardless of the seman
relationships expressed among the referents of those words.

A growing body of work in machine-readable dictionaries has demonstrated that refinement from within the collocational corpus is not only possible in internally consistent ways, but is actually necessary for the purpose of capturing truer hierarchical links. Research in the area of semantic networks and dictionaries has demonstrated the need for optimization of the automatically generated trees. Beyond the question of the internal consistency of general dictionaries discussed earlier, false paths can be generated by the tree-growing procedure, as when upward OR-links degrade the transitivity of ISA relations. These problems are compounded with those associated with the maintenance of collocational links. It is presently believed that the collocational dimension may well suffice to disambiguate text in concert with the taxonomic dimension; yet there is certainly reason to speculate on the value (both to accuracy and to combinatory parsimony) of distilling subsidiary relations (e.g., "use," "part," "sequence") out of the collocation dimension if syntactic criteria (i.e., phrasal patterns in the definitions) reveal their presence. Much promising work has been performed recently with respect to the problems of extracting relations from textual patterns. Evens and Smith [1983] and Michiels and Noel [1982, 1983] have demonstrated the feasibility of deriving semantic relations in an internally consistent manner from syntactic cues in definition text, in a way ultimately compatible with the present approach. The fairly exhaustive set of "lexical functions" of Apresyan et al. [1970] is useful as well, even though the means by which the consistency of extraction of relations from syntactic patterns, and the completeness of the description itself, are not directly verifiable. The fact that their evaluation metric (three criteria by which an association among words may be identified as an axiomatic lexical function) is explicit makes their model of 46 functions a useful standard against which to make predictions about the possibility of extractable relations inherent in the definition texts. ISA links can in fact appear in definition texts in ways other than the standard pattern used for them; White [1983] demonstrates at least one grammatical pattern ("related to") which seems to signal covert ISA links in monolingual dictionaries.

Discovering the distribution of relation-revealing patterns such as these is facilitated by growing the tree ISA/collocational so as to structure the terminology set along the principal semantic relation (ISA). The semantic relations discovered by consistency of patterns arrayed on this structure can be included in the overall semantic structure via an augmentation procedure, or by re-growing the trees with the marked text patterns indicating newly separate semantic dimensions. The task of optimizing the multilingual terminological structure proceeds in precisely the same way as has been shown valuable for the monolingual structure. Semantic relations which reveal themselves from consistent syntactic patternings arrayed along the

ISA hierarchical structure are distilled from the collocation set, both for ir creased precision in disambiguation, and for a more streamlined taxonomi dimension.

Use of MRD-driven disambiguation in full NLP

The target of the previous discussion has been the application of MRL driven structures to tasks which strive to minimize parsing effort to th point where they are not natural language processing tasks. There a applications, however, to full NLP systems, especially ones concerned wit both interpretation and generation, as well as machine translation.

In a transfer-type machine translation system, lexicons are maintaine separately for each language, maximizing transportability to other langua pairs. The entries in the two lexicons are related via the transfer lexico which however typically suffers in one-to-many transfer situations. Di ambiguated text helps here to specifically resolve these transfer problem Less obvious, but perhaps more important, is the capability to exploit i ferences about the topic in order to improve grammar rule application an generation.

Texts about different topics, particularly technical texts which have pr scribed stylistic conventions, will differ not only in their collocational di tribution, but also in their syntactic patterns. These differences sugge ad-hoc handling in practical applications, except that this violates genera ity of handling and can interfere with parsing in cases where these syntact patterns do not occur. Knowing what the text is about can allow the sy tem to load ad-hoc rules in as needed. This would seem not to be su a problem for a whole text (the user can set a topic flag at runtime), b the disambiguation power enables much more, namely the ability to r compute topic on a paragraph-by-paragraph basis, adjusting the rule ba accordingly. This same capability can enhance the discriminatory ability generation, so as to adjust the output stylistics to accommodate detecte internal, local changes in topic. In machine translation, these changes ca be made to correspond with stylistic expectations in the source languag

Conclusion

The project design described here employs recent work in elicitation machine-readable dictionary structures to perform multi-lingual processin The lexical-semantic structures, when optimized, form a base in which ea term has a value in at least three dimensions. A matching term in a te then, can be disambiguated by matching collocations, can be generaliz by following its taxonomic pathways, and can be manipulated in either these ways in any of the languages for which it has a transfer dictiona equivalent.

References

Amsler, R. A. 1980. *The Structure of the Merriam-Webster Pocket Dictionary.* PhD Thesis, Austin: University of Texas.

Amsler, R. A., and J. S. White. 1979. *Development of a Computational Methodology for Deriving Natural Language Semantic Structures via Analysis of Machine-Readable Dictionaries.* NSF Technical Report MCS77-01315.

Apresyan, Y. D., I. A. Mel'čuk, and A. D. Žolkovsky. 1970. Semantics and Lexicography: Toward a New Type of Monolingual Dictionary. In F.Kiefer, ed., *Studies in Syntax and Semantics.* Dordrecht, Holland: Reidel, 1-33.

Burling, R. 1964. Cognition and Componential Analysis: God's Truth or Hocus-Pocus? *American Anthropologist*, 66, 1, 20-28.

Chodorow, M. S., R. J. Byrd, and G. E. Heidorn. 1985. Extracting Semantic Hierarchies from a Large On-Line Dictionary. *Proceedings of the 23rd Annual Meeting of the Association for Computational Linguistics*, Chicago, June, 299-304.

Evens, M. and R. N. Smith. 1978. A Lexicon for a Computer Question-Answering System. *American Journal of Computational Linguistics*, Microfiche 81, 1-99.

Evens, M. and R. N. Smith. 1983. Determination of Adverbial Senses from Webster 7th Collegiate Definitions. Paper presented at the 1983 Workshop on Machine Readable Dictionaries, SRI International, April, 1983.

Litkowski, K. 1978. Models of the Semantic Structure of Dictionaries. *American Journal of Computational Linguistics*, Microfiche 81, 24-74.

Markowitz, J., T. Ahlswede, and M. Evens, 1986. "Semantically Significant Patterns in Dictionary Definitions," *Proc. 24th Annual Meeting of the ACL*, New York City, June, 112-119.

Michiels, A. and J. Noel. 1982. Approaches to Thesaurus Production. *COLING 82*, 227-232.

Michiels, A. and J. Noel. 1983. Automatic Analysis of Texts. Paper presented at the 1983 Workshop on Machine Readable Dictionaries, SRI International, April,1983.

Norman, D. A., and D. E. Rumelhart. 1975. *Explorations in Cognition.* San Francisco: W.H.Freeman.

Sinclair, J. McH. 1966. Beginning the Study of Lexis. In C. E. Bazell, J. C. Catford, M. A. K. Halliday, and R. H. Robins, eds., *In Memory of J.R. Firth*. London: Longmans, 410-430.

Slator, B. M. and Y. Wilks. 1987. Towards Semantic Structures from Dictionary Entries. *Proceedings of the 1987 Rocky Mountain Conference on Artificial Intelligence*, June, Boulder, CO, 85-98.

Wahrig, G. 1967. *Deutsches Wörterbuch*. Bertelsmann Lexikon-Verlag.

Webster's Seventh New Collegiate Dictionary. 1967. G&C Merriam Company, Springfield, MA.

Werner, O. 1988. How to Teach a Network: Minimal Design Features for a Cultural Knowledge Acquisition Device or C-KAD. This volume.

White, J. S. 1983. An Ethnosemantic Approach to a Dictionary Taxonomy. Paper presented at the 1983 Workshop on Machine Readable Dictionaries, SRI International, April, 1983.

9

Improved retrieval using a relational thesaurus for automatic expansion of extended Boolean logic queries

Edward A. Fox
Department of Computer Science
Virginia Polytechnic Institute and State University
Blacksburg VA 24061

Abstract

The aim of an information retrieval system is to aid users in locating items of interest from large collections of messages, bibliographic citations, or other types of documents. Since searchers' queries often do not employ precisely the same terminology as the stored full text, it is desirable to identify words which are closely related to those in the original query and which occur in relevant documents. A lexical-relational thesaurus, containing entries of the type suggested by Apresyan et al. [1970] and by Evens and Smith [1978], should be of value in this regard. Earlier experimentation by this author and by Wang et al. [1985] made it clear that further study would be of value to determine the most effective way to incorporate lexically related terms in queries. A collection of 1460 highly cited documents in information science and a set of thirty-five natural language questions were selected to evaluate experimentally the applicability of a relational thesaurus for improving the effectiveness of information retrieval methods. Three searchers formulated Boolean logic versions of each query which were then interpreted as "p-norm" expressions and which yielded higher precision and recall than standard vector techniques. Adding in entries that would be present in a relational thesaurus to the extended Boolean logic (i.c., p-norm) queries led to even further gains in retrieval effectiveness. Further study by this author on the possibility of automatic construction of a relational thesaurus and on determination of the optimal method for using related words to improve queries is underway.

Introduction

To function effectively in today's information society it is extremely important for individuals to be able to locate specific entries out of the vast collections of data now in existence. Consequently, database management systems have been developed which store and retrieve groups of values from pre-structured repositories. Question answering systems typically obtain specific facts in response to a natural language query. *Information retrieval* systems, on the other hand, usually locate messages, bibliographic records, or text-based items which for convenience will all be referred to herewith as *documents.*

While considerable attention has been given to improving the efficiency of database management systems or the comprehensiveness of question answering systems, much of the research in the area of information retrieval has focussed on devising more *effective* methods to retrieve exactly those entries which the end-user desires. It is important to find as many as possible of the items a user deems relevant to a query, thus giving high *recall*, while at the same time keeping *precision* high by not retrieving non-relevant documents. Unhappily, one usually finds that if one aims for high recall then precision declines, and that one often must expect no more than 50% precision when 50% recall is achieved [Salton and McGill 1983].

It is natural for information scientists to turn to the field of computational linguistics to try to improve upon this situation [Sparck Jones and Kay 1973]. While it would be most useful for computers to record the deep semantic structure of millions of documents and to locate relevant items quickly in response to a natural language statement of a user's interest, this is currently not feasible. What should soon be practical, however, is to utilize more effectively the information available in machine readable dictionaries and other reference works which could lead to a comprehensive computerized lexicon. This paper describes one methodology for improving the effectiveness of an information retrieval system through the use of lexical relations, and gives experimental evidence of the viability of that approach.

Relational thesaurus

Information retrieval systems have typically employed some type of thesaurus so that the terminology of an author or indexer can be reconciled with that of a user or searcher. Frequently a committee is charged with devising a specialized controlled vocabulary, or constructing a hierarchical classification so that similar, broader, or narrower terms can be readily identified. Years of tedious work are often needed since groups of people with differing ideas must agree on semantic interpretations in spite of ongoing fluctuations in usage and frequency of terms. For maximum effectiveness certain rules must be obeyed: term classes should be composed of entries which have roughly the same occurrence frequency in the collection; all allowed terms should have some relevance to the subject matter; and use of correct word senses should be enforced [Salton and McGill 1983].

A number of studies have considered the problem of automatic thesaurus construction. Terms occurring in documents were grouped together if their occurrence characteristics in those documents were similar and if certain other requirements were met; slight improvements in retrieval resulted when such classes were used as the basis for query-document matching operations [Sparck Jones 1971]. Early methods of clustering to identify classes were not very efficient and did not allow overlap between classes. Later experiments focussed on reducing the computational complexity and expense, and on increasing the likelihood of associations being semantically meaningful [Yu and Raghavan 1977]. Finding classes for low frequency terms (which should be in classes, since each one occurs in only a small number of documents) is difficult since the co-occurrence data is scanty. For this and other reasons, a priori automatic construction of a thesaurus based on term-term co-occurrence for a given collection has not become a practical reality.

What should be generally feasible and useful is the enhancement of queries by addition of suitable terms, rather than the construction of term classes in advance. One method, a form of feedback, is to supplement queries by terms found in relevant documents located by a prior search. Selecting "searchonyms," which occur near query words in the original sentences of some relevant documents, and whose presence can be considered equivalent to the presence of query terms for the purpose of searching, should be particularly valuable [Attar and Fraenkel 1977]. Another method is to construct a maximum spanning tree which inter-relates all collection terms based on co-occurrence behavior and then to select entries that are adjacent in that tree to query terms [Van Rijsbergen 1979].

Of particular interest, however, would be to employ term relationships applicable to a number of diverse document collections. The development of an *Explanatory Combinatorial Dictionary* by a group of Soviet linguists seemed particularly promising [Apresyan et al. 1970]. Supplementing the morphological and syntactic details in their comprehensive lexicon, they sought to spell out for each entry all other words with important lexical or semantic relationships. It seemed reasonable to consider using such relationships for information retrieval as well as for other purposes like translation or language learning [Leed and Nakhimovsky 1979]. An important consideration is the availability of such lexicons for languages besides Russian.

Several Western efforts were closely allied. The study of semantic relations was carried forward by Casagrande and Hale [1967]. Evens and Smith [1978] sought to adapt and reorganize earlier notions into a suitable form for a lexicon that would be applicable to question answering systems. More recently, attention has turned to the automatic construction of a relational thesaurus through appropriate analysis of machine readable dictionaries [Ahlswede and Evens 1988].

Given such a thesaurus, it was necessary to devise techniques to improve queries by adding in appropriate information. One study by this author, using a small test collection and very simple methods, showed the approach resulted in noticeable improvement [Fox 1980]. A more thorough study by Wang et al. [1985] confirmed the earlier tests. However, both of these investigations employed so-called vector queries, and since extended Boolean queries seem to be more effective in most cases [Salton et al. 1983], it was decided that a further study should be undertaken using such query forms.

Vector queries

The vector space model of information retrieval can be easily understood if one pictures any given document as a point in a vector space whose dimensions are the concepts (e.g., terms) in a document collection. The vector space is constructed by an automatic indexing process where stop words are removed and remaining terms are stemmed and counted. Retrieval then requires indexing of the query to locate it in the same space, and selecting documents which are suitably "close" to the query's location [Salton et al. 1975]. Formally, let

$$
\begin{aligned}
N &= \text{number of documents in the collection} \\
T &= \text{number of terms in the collection dictionary} \\
t_j &= j\text{-th term in the dictionary} \\
D_i &= i\text{-th document} \\
C &= \text{collection of documents} \\
&= (\, D_1,\ D_2,\ \ldots,\ D_N \,)
\end{aligned}
$$

Each document and query vector is obtained from the original natural language text by the automatic indexing procedure. One key benefit of such processing is that through the use of statistics, the weight or importance of a term in a query or document can be measured as a real value instead of just having a 0 or 1 (i.e., using binary weights). Both the frequency of occurrence in a document and the number of documents containing the term can be used to determine a suitable weight. Then

$$
\begin{aligned}
d_{ij} &= \text{weight of } j\text{-th term in } D_i \\
D_i &= i\text{-th document} \\
&= (\ d_{i1},\ d_{i2},\ \ldots,\ d_{iT}\ ) \\
q_j &= \text{weight of } j\text{-th term in query } Q \\
Q &= \text{query} \\
&= (\ q_1,\ q_2,\ \ldots,\ q_T\ )
\end{aligned}
$$

$SIM_{COS}(Q, D_i)$ measures the vector similarity between the query, Q, and the i-th document, D_i, by determining the cosine of the angle between the two vectors. Similarity is inversely related to the distance in the vector space, and measures the correlation between query and document. Documents are presented to a user in decreasing order of

$$
SIM_{COS}(Q, D_i) \quad = \quad \frac{\sum_{j=1}^{T} q_j d_{ij}}{\sqrt{\sum_{j=1}^{T} q_j^2 \ \sum_{j=1}^{T} d_{ij}^2}}
$$

Extended Boolean queries

While the vector space model leads to effective retrieval results, especially when vectors are not overly short, it has seldom been used outside of laboratory systems. Rather, the Boolean model is typically adopted in commercially available retrieval services. No automatic indexing of natural language queries takes place then. A search intermediary transforms a user's original interest statement, such as "understanding communication," into a roughly equivalent Boolean expression, i.e.,

understanding AND communication,

so that a system can quickly retrieve only those documents which contain both terms. More complex Boolean queries can be devised to specify desired documents more accurately. Thus, if the above query did not retrieve enough documents (i.e., had low recall), an experienced searcher might extend the query by adding a related word to get

understanding AND (communication OR speech)

Boolean systems are widely used since they are easy to implement on computers and since librarians and other information specialists have been trained to serve as intermediaries following a long tradition of intellectual indexing and searching. Though intermediaries are not available to aid novice searchers in all applications (e.g., searching one's archive of personal electronic mail messages), millions of documents in a wide variety of retrieval systems are accessible today using Boolean logic. Consequently it would be particularly valuable if Boolean queries could be somehow extended to include several of the insights of the vector space model, yielding a new, more effective scheme. The "p-norm" or extended Boolean model was originally developed by Wu and was thoroughly tested by this author [Fox 1983a]. The five points given below explain in part how the p-norm model generalizes and improves upon both the vector and Boolean models [Salton et al. 1983].

First, consider the relative importance of terms, as in a given document. Whereas vector methods measure this with a real-valued weight, thereby capturing important statistical information, Boolean schemes only consider whether or not a document is indexed by a term. In the p-norm model, a real value similar to the term weights of the vector model is used, namely:

d_{ij} = fuzzy set membership function value indicating the degree to which the i-th document should be indexed by the j-th term.

Real valued query weights can also be associated with query terms or clauses based on, for example, user perception of the relative importance of each disjunct and conjunct.

Second, consider the real meaning of the OR and AND operators. From a linguistic perspective, one would use OR to link together alternatives which have similar meaning, and use AND to combine concepts that should appear together, as in a phrase. When one links many concepts in this fashion, the usual Boolean operators seem overly restrictive. Thus,

$$x_1 \ AND \ x_2 \ AND \ x_3 \ AND \ x_4$$

will not retrieve a document containing three of the four specified terms. Similarly,

$$x_1 \ OR \ x_2 \ OR \ x_3 \ OR \ x_4$$

will not present to the user documents containing all four terms as being better than documents having only one of them. The p-norm scheme solves these problems by suitably defining the OR and AND operators, so that a ranked list of matches is obtained. When a query is to express the disjunction of the k and m-th terms, the similarity between the i-th document and that query is defined as the normalized distance between the origin and the projection of D_i onto the k-m plane. The origin represents the least desirable case of indexing, since then

$$d_{ik} = d_{im} = 0.$$

Substituting in a suitable metric, namely the L_p-norm, as the distance function, leads to the following "p-norm" definition of the OR connective:

$$SIM\big((t_k \; OR^p \; t_m), \; D_i \big) = \left(\frac{\big(t_k d_{ik}\big)^p + \big(t_m d_{im}\big)^p}{t_k^p + t_m^p} \right)^{1/p}$$

When a query specifies the conjunction of terms, it is sensible to measure similarity between query and documents so as to favor those documents which are closest to being indexed fully by all terms. Good documents are those with smallest distance from the point

$$d_{ik} = d_{im} = 1$$

The corresponding definition of similarity is then given by:

$$SIM\big((t_k \; AND^p \; t_m), \; D_i \big) = 1 - \left(\frac{\big(t_k(1 - d_{ik})\big)^p + \big(t_m(1 - d_{im})\big)^p}{t_k^p + t_m^p} \right)^{1/p}$$

Other definitions have been made by Wu to handle the complete range of forms that can occur in arbitrarily complex Boolean expressions [Salton et al. 1983].

Third, note that since the similarity of a p-norm query can be computed using real values, then a ranked set of documents can be presented to the user. The user can simply view whatever number are desired, with the initial ones more likely to be relevant, rather than being faced with a retrieval set of arbitrary size.

Fourth, note that the "p-value" in previous formulas serves as a parameter which enables one to model either the vector or the Boolean schemes. When $p = 1$ one has behavior similar to the vector model, while when $p = \infty$ one has essentially the Boolean case. In between p-values are also allowed and reflect variations in the degree of "ANDness" or "ORness" that is desired. Usually low p-values on the order of 1 to 3 should be selected.

Finally, experimental tests with five collections have shown that the p-norm scheme outperforms both the Boolean and vector methods, when precision at various recall levels is measured. Even further improvements are possible through p-norm feedback techniques [Fox 1983a]. Consequently, it seems appropriate to explore the extension of p-norm queries with entries from a relational thesaurus.

Experimental study

To compare the effectiveness of information retrieval methods, one needs a collection of documents, a set of queries, and indications regarding the relevance of each of the documents to each query. In the initial retrieval test of lexical relations, done in 1980 by this author, 82 documents in information science were used along with 35 queries. Matching of query and document vectors was based upon the SIM_{COS} measure explained above [Fox 1980]. Wang's recent study employed 222 papers in computer science, 29 queries, and vector processing, but only had binary weights in the document vectors [Wang et al. 1985]. For this current study, 1460 articles in the field of information science were employed along with 35 p-norm queries [Fox 1983b].

Table 1. Collections

Study	Subject	Docs	Queries	Query Form
Fox 80	Inf. science	82	35	vector
Wang 85	Comp. science	222	29	vector
current	Inf. science	1,460	35	p-norm

The method used to extend queries so as to incorporate lexically related terms is an important distinction between these three studies. The initial study by this author simply added in terms to the original query vector. The weights of added terms were multiplied by a constant (e.g., 0.25) so as not to swamp the effects of the original query terms. The study of Wang et al. [1985] used binary weights so that document and query terms had a weight of 1, which is unfortunate since having good real valued weights in document vectors often leads to important performance improvements. However, Wang et al. [1985] devised a very clever scheme of weighting for added terms, leading to values in the interval between 0 and 1. The weights were inversely proportional to the number of related terms for the original query word – a more flexible scheme than the above mentioned fractional constant weighting technique.

When using extended Boolean queries, however, it was possible to arrange the method of adding terms more carefully. Specifically, the following procedure was adopted:

1. Each of the 35 natural language queries was given to 3 searchers, namely this author and two librarians. Each searcher constructed a Boolean query based upon the natural language statement.

2. All unique terms in those queries were identified and a list made up of those which appeared in at least one document but which did not appear in a large percentage of the documents. Thus, high frequency terms which are often inappropriate for thesaurus classes were omitted.

3. Each term in the resulting list was considered appropriate to look up in a relational thesaurus. Since such a thesaurus was not available, this author generated a table of related words. An example is shown in Table 2 below. Only related terms that appear somewhere in the dictionary of terms for the collection were recorded.

Table 2. Words lexically related to *communicate*

Word	Relationship	Explanation
speech	Cont	Continue (predicate)
speaker	Tsource	Source (case)
word	Tinst	Instrument (case)
phoneme	Part	Has part (part whole)

4. For each term, a new replacement Boolean expression was devised. Its form was the disjunction of the original term with a clause containing all related terms. It should be noted that due to the normalization process for p-norm queries, the original query term will automatically count as much toward overall similarity as does the entire clause of related entries. Thus the p-norm query form automatically adjusts for the effect of adding any number of related terms to a query by localizing the effects of addition. Furthermore, a relative weight (e.g., 0.5) can be applied to the newly added clause, to reduce its effect significantly in comparison to the original query term. For example, the clause which would replace *communication* in a query would be based on the corresponding verb form and hence employ the related words shown in Table 2:

$$communicate \; OR^p$$
$$<(\; speech \; OR^p \; speaker \; OR^p \; word \; OR^p \; phoneme \;),0.5>$$

5. In each query, every occurrence of one of the above mentioned terms was replaced by the corresponding Boolean expression. For example, the query shown earlier in this paper about "understanding communication" would become

$$understanding \; AND^p$$
$$(\; communicate \; OR^p$$
$$<(\; speech \; OR^p \; speaker \; OR^p \; word \; OR^p \; phoneme \;),0.5> \;)$$

Given the above query collection, it was then possible to compare the effects of using lexically related terms. For brevity, the experimental results will be greatly condensed in the following discussion. Instead of showing a complete table of precision values for recall levels 0.0, 0.1, ..., 0.9, 1.0, only a single average precision value is given for each retrieval test run. Furthermore, only the most important combinations of weighting method and "p-value" are shown.

Table 3. Average-precision results

Searcher Used	Strict Boolean	Cos Vector	P-Norm Original	P-Norm W. Lexrel	Lexrel vs. Orig. P-Norm
Author	.1118	.1569	.1835	.1869	+1.9%
Librarian 1	.0549	.1569	.1604	.1694	+5.6%
Librarian 2	.0653	.1569	.1802	.1949	+8.2%

From Table 3 it can be readily seen that for all three searchers the vector and p-norm schemes were clearly superior to the Boolean case. In addition, the p-norm scheme is superior to the vector method. Finally, the use of lexically related terms caused the p-norm scheme to give even better retrieval.

To gauge the degree of improvement of the p-norm scheme with related terms versus the p-norm case before expansion, percentage improvements are shown in the last column of Table 3. While these figures are not definitive statistics, they do suggest that 2-8% improvement might result using rather simple techniques. Reasonable benefit from expansion seems likely, especially since the case with lowest improvement is rather atypical – it was for queries devised by this author, where considerable pains were taken to include synonyms and other related words in the original forms.

Conclusions and future plans

Two studies by this author and one by Wang have all demonstrated the value of expanding queries through the use of lexically related terms. Since the p-norm or extended Boolean notation outperforms other query methods, and since lexically related terms are readily added to queries through the use of p-norm expressions, it seems particularly appropriate to consider using such a scheme in connection with a relational thesaurus.

Further investigation by this author is planned so as to lead to a better understanding of the relationship between p-norm queries and lexically related words. While $p = 1$ was used in the p-norm runs mentioned above, other settings should be considered inside the clauses of lexically related terms. These tests should lead to a better understanding of the OR^p operator as well.

Another planned study is to compare the effects of how lexically related terms are obtained. In all previous studies, terms that were lexically related were first identified manually and then used. An alternative scheme would be to use any word that appears in the appropriate entry of a machine readable dictionary or thesaurus. If such an approach gives reasonable results, the above mentioned p-norm query expansion scheme could be applied to retrieval systems even before a complete relational thesaurus becomes available. In any case, it seems worthwhile for efforts to proceed on devising an

English relational thesaurus, and to utilize that to enhance the effectiveness of information retrieval systems.

References

Ahlswede, Thomas and Martha Evens. 1988. Generating a Relational Lexicon from a Machine-Readable Dictionary. *International Journal of Lexicography*, Fall.

Apresyan, Yuri, Igor Mel'čuk and Alexander Žolkovsky. 1970. Semantics and Lexicography: Towards a New Type of Unilingual Dictionary. In F. Kiefer, ed., *Studies in Syntax and Semantics*, D. Reidel, Dordrecht, Holland, 1-33.

Attar, Rony and Aviezri S. Fraenkel. 1977. Local Feedback in Full-Text Retrieval Systems. *JACM*, **24**, 3, 397-417, July 1977.

Casagrande, Joseph and Kenneth Hale. 1967. Semantic Relations in Papago Folk Definitions. In Dell Hymes and W. E. Bittle, *Studies in Southwestern Ethnolinguistics*, Mouton, The Hague, 165-196.

Evens, Martha and Raoul N. Smith. 1978. A Lexicon for a Computer Question-Answering System. *Amer. J. Comp. Ling.*, Microfiches 81:16-24 and 83:1-98, 1978.

Fox, Edward A. 1980. Lexical Relations: Enhancing Effectiveness of Information Retrieval Systems. *ACM SIGIR Forum*, **15**, 3, 5-36, Winter 1980.

Fox, Edward A. 1983a. *Extending the Boolean and Vector Space Models of Information Retrieval with P-Norm Queries and Multiple Concept Types*. Dissertation, Cornell Univ., Ithaca, NY.

Fox, Edward A. 1983b. Characterization of Two New Experimental Collections in Computer and Information Science Containing Textual and Bibliographic Concepts. Tech. Report 83-561, Cornell Univ., Dept. of Comp. Sci., Ithaca, NY.

Leed, Richard L. and Alexander D. Nakhimovsky. 1979. Lexical Functions and Language Learning. *Slavic and East European Journal*, **23**, 1, 104-113.

Salton, Gerard, A. Wong and C. S. Yang. 1975. A Vector Space Model for Automatic Indexing. *CACM*, **18**, 11, 613-620, Nov. 1975.

Salton, Gerard and Michael J. McGill. 1983. *Introduction to Modern Information Retrieval*. McGraw-Hill, New York.

Salton, Gerard, Edward A. Fox and Harry Wu. 1983. Extended Boolean Information Retrieval. *CACM*, **26**, 12, 1022-1036, Nov. 1983.

Sparck Jones, Karen. 1971. *Automatic Keyword Classifications*. Butterworths, London.

Sparck Jones, Karen and Martin Kay. 1973. *Linguistics and Information Science*. Academic Press, New York.

Van Rijsbergen, C. J. 1979. *Information Retrieval*: Second Edition. Butterworths, London.

Wang, Yih-Chen, James Vandendorpe, and Martha Evens. 1985. Relational Thesauri in Information Retrieval. *JASIS*, 36, 1, 15-27, Jan. 1985.

Yu, Clement and Vijay V. Raghavan. 1977. Single-Pass Method of Determining the Semantic Relationships between Terms. *JASIS*, 28, 5 (Nov), 345-354.

10

A lexical, syntactic, and semantic framework for TELI: a user customized natural language processor

BRUCE W. BALLARD
AT&T BELL LABORATORIES
MURRAY HILL, NJ 07974

Abstract

In constructing a domain-independent English-language question answering system, we have developed several formalisms for characterizing the various types of lexical, syntactic, and semantic information employed by the system. In this paper, we discuss these formalisms in detail, along with some alternatives and unresolved problems, with remarks on their possible use for languages other than English. The primary topics addressed involve parts of speech; lexical features, such as case, gender, and number; inflections; synonyms; hyphenations; idioms; selectional restrictions, including case frames for verb and other phrase types; and semantics for word and phrase modifiers. In addition to its obvious relation to interfaces between humans and machines, this work relates indirectly to the scientific study of language in its desire to identify a minimal amount of information that can support broad and robust language coverage.

Introduction

For the past several years, we have been developing a natural language processor that can be easily and reliably adapted to a large variety of database query applications. The system is called the *Transportable English Language Interface* (TELI), and is based on previous work with the LDC project [Ballard 1982, 1984, 1986]. Some of TELI's more distinctive goals are (a) to allow for customizations by the *users* of the system, as opposed to the system designers; (b) to provide *on-line* facilities to examine and update any domain-specific information being used by the system; and (c) to support *complex semantics*, where meanings of the English words and phrases to be processed may relate in complex ways to the information immediately available from the physical data files supplied to the system. An example from a sample session with TELI appears as Figure 1.

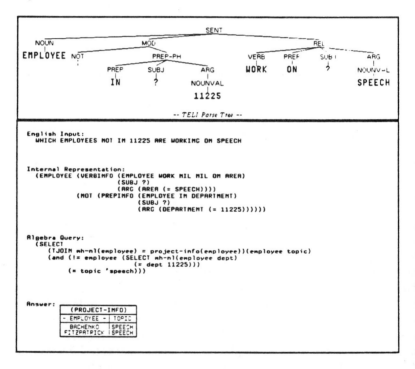

Figure 1. A sample TELI display screen.

Our selection of database query as an application area for TELI was initially based on (1) the thought of drawing from, as well as being able to compare our work against, a large amount of previous work in applied natural language processing, and (2) the belief that solutions to many of the referential issues arising in the domain of database query will apply to problems that arise in less well defined areas, such as expert systems. In addition to these motivations, we have recently come to believe that (3) developing a high-quality, domain-independent interface for database query represents an interesting, important, and elusive problem in its own right, and (4) our system can provide a reliable framework in which to conduct experimental work in higher-level aspects of computational linguistics (for example, pronouns, quantifier scope, or discourse).

In the remainder of the paper, we present an overview of the representational issues involved in the design of TELI, with comments on why various decisions were made, what some alternatives were, and some of the lingering problems.

Overview of TELI

The design of the TELI system began in the fall of 1984 as an extension of the Layered Domain Class (LDC) system. LDC was developed at Duke University from 1981 through 1984 by the author and two graduate students, John Lusth and Nancy Tinkham [Ballard et al. 1984]. The principal extensions provided by TELI over LDC are (1) a much broader grammar; (2) provision for an arbitrary number of database relations, rather than just one; (3) capabilities for more complex semantic definitions; and (4) an elaborate run-time customization module. As indicated in Figure 2, TELI comprises three top-level components, namely (1) a domain-independent natural language processor (NLP), (2) a Lisp-based database management system (DBMS), and (3) a collection of customization modules. To date, TELI has been customized by its designers for just over a dozen real and hypothetical databases, with applications involving AI research at Bell Labs, New Hampshire hiking trails, San Francisco restaurants, automated VLSI chip design, and several others.

As indicated by the ellipses in Figure 2, both the natural language and customization portions of TELI are parameterized to operate in a variety of settings: the NLP can adapt to various database applications, while the customization module can adapt to various NLP's. The current NLP processes its inputs in the context of five files, whose organization is defined for the customization modules by the file labelled "pre-defined specification of the NLP." This makes it possible to augment or refine the individual modules of the NLP without losing or having to resupply customization abilities. Three of these five files contain domain-specific information, which is acquired from the user by a collection of customization modules.

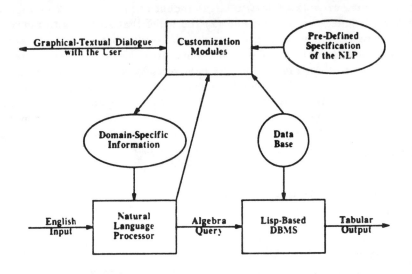

Figure 2. The top-level organization of TELI.

Since this paper will concern the capabilities of the natural language processor (NLP) and the customization module, with emphasis on the operation of the NLP, Figure 3 gives a more detailed view of the organization of the NLP. As indicated, English inputs pass through four successive refinements, with the final result being a relational algebra query, which is produced from an intermediate relational calculus query not shown in the figure.

When TELI begins its customization for a new application, it inquires about each column of each table of the database, as described in Ballard and Stumberger 1986. Thereafter, customization modules may be invoked either by the user or, when missing information is required, by the system itself. This allows users to type a question containing words or concepts not yet known to the system; the system responds by asking for the exact information it needs to process the input, saving its newly acquired information for use in subsequent interactions. Thus, each of the three domain-specific files is dynamic and grows as information about the application is supplied by users.

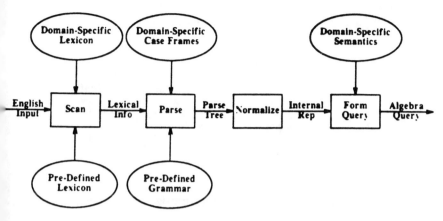

Figure 3. Organization of the NLP.

As the reader may infer from the remainder of the paper, TELI revolves around a simple but powerful model of its potential application areas. Specifically, the person customizing TELI for a new database is asked to specify a collection of *entities*, or object types, which are expected to collectively exhaust the objects in the database (for historical reasons, the term "nountype" will also be used to refer to entities). Then, each *single-word* modifier (e.g., adjective) applies to one of these entities, while each *phrasal* modifier (e.g., prepositional phrase) applies to an ordered set (not necessarily unique) of one, two or three entities (as indicated later, each word or phrase may have several definitions). Examples of single-word and phrasal modifiers are given in Figures 4a and 4b, where we assume a database consisting of the three entities: campsite, mountain, and trail. As indicated in Figure 4a, "tall" may exist as an adjective modifier of mountains, and "family" could be a noun used to modify campsites. As indicated in Figure 4b, the preposition "on" might relate campsites to trails, in that order, and "bubble" could exist as an intransitive verb having mountains as its subject (dashes and unattached circles denote unfilled optional slots, as discussed in the section on case frame specification).

In the remainder of the paper, we consider the structure and function of each type of representation associated with the lexical, syntactic, and semantic processing of TELI.

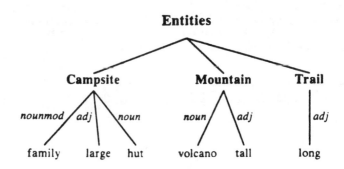

Figure 4a. Treatment of single-word modifiers.

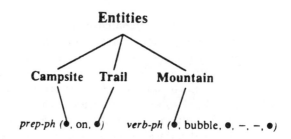

Figure 4b. Treatment of phrasal modifiers.

Primary lexical data structures

Lexical information resides in (1) the *lexicon*, which includes both pre-defined and domain-dependent terminology, and (2) a number of *auxiliary structures*, which contain information related to inflections, hyphenations and simple idioms, and patterns that specify the character-by-character morphology of any object types whose names can be captured in this manner (e.g., social security numbers comprise nine digits with hyphens appearing at specific places). Before TELI has been given any domain-specific information, its lexicon contains about 150 pre-defined items, including

five *imperative verbs*, such as "show;"
sixteen *verb forms* associated with
    the infinitives "be," "have," and "do;"
a handful of the *most frequently occurring vocabulary*
    items, including a dozen or so adjectives,
    some nouns, and all common prepositions;
the *cardinals* "one" through "ten;"
the *ordinals* "first" through "tenth," and "last;"
six *quantifiers*, such as "all" and "any;" and
five *relative pronouns*, including
    the adverbial relatives "when" and "where."

About twenty-five other items appear, many of which act as grammatical formatives (e.g., "than").

In addition to its pre-defined lexical items, TELI is initially supplied with (a) a short list of the most common *irregular inflections*, and (b) a *reserve list* of some of the most frequent adjectives and prepositions that are expected to arise. The reason for having this list, rather than placing the items it contains directly in the lexicon, is to prevent words that are irrelevant for a particular application from cluttering the various menus generated by the system. The structure for hyphenations and idioms is initially null, as is the highly domain-specific structure giving morphological patterns.

Following a customization, TELI's data structures will contain the information mentioned above, as well as information on domain-specific vocabulary, selectional restrictions for various phrase types, and so forth, as discussed below.

The lexicon

The lexicon is made up of a collection of *lexical entries*, each of which associates one or more *lexical definitions* with a given *word*. Each lexical definition consists of (a) the *word* being defined; (b) a unique *part of speech* for the word; (c) the *root form* of the word, which is often simply the word itself; and (d) zero or more *feature-value specifications*, each of which comprises (i) a *feature* name and (ii) zero or more *values*. For example, the lexical definition

    (directories noun directory (sp plural) (nt file))

says that the word "directories" is a plural (sp) form of the noun "directory" and refers to domain objects (nt) that are files. An example of a complete lexical entry is the following, which specifies "file" as either a singular noun, a verb infinitive, or a plural present-tense verb form.

```
(file
    (file noun file (sp sing) (nt file))
    (file verb file)
    (file vpres file (sp plural)))
```

Since verb collocations may involve more than one object type (e.g., they may have both subject and object), the "nt" information pertaining to them is stored not in the lexicon itself but rather as case frame information, as described below.

The responsibility of specifying the appropriate feature agreements that must obtain across phrases is assigned to the system grammar. For example, number agreement must occur between the italicized pair in each of the following phrases.

"the employees that *Ballard works* with"
"the *employees* that *work* with Ballard"

In addition to number agreement, TELI's selectional restrictions based on object type ("nt") must occur between similarly labelled items of the following.

"How many new(1) departments(1) are large(1)?"
"Which employees(1a) work(1b) for(1c) the newest(2a)
        manager(1d)(2b)?"

where 1a-1d denote case-frame agreement and 2a-2b indicate compatibility between "new" and "manager." The need to pass multiple agreement information into and out of phrases, as shown here in the case of "manager," derives from our desire to construct only semantically acceptable parses. As described in Ballard and Tinkham 1984, this causes some interesting complexities in the grammar and in the grammar interpreter.

Since the number of values associated with each feature is arbitrary, situations may arise in which, say, both salaries and offices could be large, as indicated by

```
(large adj large (nt office salary))
```

In terms of parser efficiency, this single lexical entry is preferable to a pair of definitions for "large," one related to office and the other to salary, since this avoids the need for backtracking at this point. In the event that a given definition contains a plurality designation for either singular or plural, the "sp" feature may be omitted entirely. For user-defined vocabulary, however, there is no guarantee that the customization module will produce such "optimized" definitions.

Although TELI presently employs only plurality ("sp") and object type ("nt") features, its formalism for lexical definitions allows for other features that would arise in a more general interface and also for some feature types that occur in languages other than English. Some examples of further use of features for English include *person* and *case*, for example,

> (me pron I (person 1) (case obj) (sp sing))
> (goes vpres go (person 3) (sp sing))

As a more elaborate example, French adjectives have both gender and number, and the plural feminine form of the adjective "joli" ("pretty") would be represented as

> (jolies adj joli (sp plural) (gender fem) ...)

Corresponding to the German word "sie," which means either "she" or "they," and can occur in either nominative or accusative case, would be the following lexical entry, where "*" appears as a place holder in the root position of a pronoun.

> (sie
>   (sie pron * (gender fem) (sp sing) (person 3)
>   (case nom acc))
>   (sie pron * (sp plural) (person 3) (case nom acc)))

In dealing with a morphologically rich language, one would be tempted to avoid storing inflected forms in the lexicon, at least for open categories. Instead, one could generate this information by simply storing the fact that, say, "jolies" is the feminine plural of "joli," after enabling the lexical processor to make appropriate modifications to the entry for "joli." To accomplish this, it would be sufficient to maintain a data structure with entries such as

> (jolies joli fem-plur-adj)

f morphemic modifications were to occur separately, to suggest an agglu- inating as opposed to inflecting tendency, entries of the form

(jolies joli adj fem plur)

would be appropriate. However, the process of suffix stripping can be a tricky business, especially if one wants to guard against spurious readings (e.g., "bes" is not a present tense third person singular form of "be" in standard English). Alternately, one could perform morphological analysis upon demand to discover that "jolies" consists of the known adjective "joli" followed by "es," which would then signal the same modification of the entry for "joli" ("e" denoting feminine and "s" denoting plural). In any of these situations, however, the sample scanner outputs shown above still indicate the format of the output produced by the scanner for use in parsing, regardless of how it is arrived at. A discussion of a scheme developed for German morphemic analysis, which is similar to the one just described, but which involves an even finer granularity, is given in Gehrke and Block 1986.

Inflections

When scanning an input during English-language processing, and at each of several points during customization, it is necessary for TELI to know the inflections of root words that admit morphological variants. For this reason, we have supplied the system with a simple set of heuristics (or "rules") that predict noun plurals, past tense verb forms, and so forth. In some cases, the prediction is for no variant (for example, the comparative of a lengthy adjective not ending in "y"). Since these heuristics are incomplete, the system maintains a list of exceptions to override the prediction by giving a different form, extra forms, or no form at all.

Initially, before TELI begins learning about a specific application, it will have been given the irregular forms of two adjectives (namely, "good" and "bad"), a handful of nouns, and about forty verbs. Incidentally, we consider it problematic to decide where the "rules" should leave off and the "exceptions" begin, and we have therefore adopted a pragmatically tenable solution.

The inflection list is indexed jointly by word and part of speech. Associated with each index is a list of lists whose first member is the name of a part of speech and whose tail indicates the allowable forms. For example, the entry associated with the verb "think" will be

((think . verb) (vpast thought) (ven thought))

Although the verb "think" has several other variants, only its simple past and past participle forms are irregular, so they are all that is stored. As a second example, if the user wishes to allow either "volcanos" or "volcanoes" as acceptable plural forms for "volcano," the associated entry on the inflection list would be

((volcano . noun) (noun-pl volcanos volcanoes))

As a third example, if the user wishes to allow "simpler" and "simplest," and the rules for comparatives and superlatives indicate that "simple" is paraphrastic (i.e., requires "more" and "most"), the following would arise as a variant list entry.

((simple . adj) (compar simpler))

An explicit specification of the superlative form is omitted because the *-est* form algorithm bases its predictions on the *-er* form. Conversely, to assure that no inflected form is accepted for some variant part of speech, a null list can occur. Thus, the entry

((president . noun) (noun-pl))

cancels "presidents" as the predicted plural of "president." This might be desirable for a company having only its own unique president in its database.

Each root form associated with a part of speech that may have inflections is placed on the inflection list, even if the inflectional heuristics correctly predict its variants. This is the system's way of noting that its predictions have been verified. Thus, assuming that the inflectional heuristics correctly predict the plural of "phone," we would have the entry

((phone . noun))

In some cases, our heuristics derive one inflected form from another, rather than from the root form itself. Specifically, superlatives are derived from comparatives, if possible (by replacing terminal "er" with "est") and participle forms are derived from past tense (past participle being identical, present participle by replacing terminal "ed" with "ing"). In this way, matters such as unexpected consonant doubling are resolved once rather than two or three times. For this reason, the entry for the verb "catch" is actually

((catch . verb) (vpast caught))

which correctly leads to a past participle of "caught" and a present participle of "catching." In the latter case, since the indicated past tense form cannot have a terminal "ed" removed from it, the present participle is derived from the root in the normal manner.

Supplementary lexical data structures

We now discuss the several auxiliary lexical data structures maintained by TELI.

Synonyms

The third component of a lexical definition, corresponding to the "root" word, permits both synonyms and inflected forms to be stored in the lexicon. Some example synonyms are

> (VP noun vice-president (sp sing) (nt employee))
> (dolphin noun porpoise (sp sing) (nt animal))

while an example inflection ("directories") was shown earlier. As seen here, abbreviations ("VP") may occur as one type of synonym.

Although the present scheme of maintaining synonyms and inflected forms in the lexicon has proven quite satisfactory, we consider it aesthetically unpleasing. More importantly, it causes unpleasant complexities for the customization modules, and leads to occasional lexical vestiges. For example, if we have inadvertently allowed "volcanos" as a plural and wish to replace it with "volcanoes," the latter term will be added without the removal of the previous one. For these and other minor reasons, we expect to restructure the scanner so that (a) a separate list is maintained for synonyms, and (b) the data structure just described for inflections is used by the scanner as well as the customization module.

Hyphenations and simple idioms

Although the TELI grammar has no direct provision for idioms, its scanner allows hyphenated words to occur separately, and this can be used for an interesting side effect: if an idiom is made to appear to the lexicon as a hyphenated word, then, since the scanner allows the components of hyphenated word to appear as separate words, without hyphens, an English sentence can contain the idiom in its usual form, and it will be recognized by the system. In these situations, one could speak of the idiom as being "parsed" (trivially) by the scanner, rather than the parser. Thus, if the terms that form the idiom are themselves meaningful to the system, an ambiguity may arise between the idiomatic and literal readings. Obviously, only very simple idioms whose components are contiguous can be captured in this way, and providing for more general idioms such as "give . . . a break" is a prime candidate for extension to TELI over the coming months.

In order to be able to determine quickly whether a given token begins a hyphenated form, and to support simple idioms, the scanner maintains a list associating with the first word in a hyphenation both the full hyphenated form and the list of remaining words. For example, the presence in the lexicon of entries for the singular and plural forms of "vice-president" would result in the following hyphenation list entries.

> (vice vice-president president)
> (vice vice-presidents presidents)

As a second example, the grammar's inability to handle two-word prepositions, such as "up with" in the context of "put up with," can be circumvented by including "up-with" in the lexicon, which would entail the system's putting

> (up up-with with)

onto its hyphenation list. Some alternatives would be to define either "put-up" followed by "with" or "put-up-with" as transitive; however, these would require a proliferation of hyphenations for "puts-up," "putting-up," and so forth. As a third example, a characteristic use of the hyphenation scheme is indicated by

> (above above-treeline treeline)

As a final example, one useful type of hyphenation involves compound proper names. For example, in a database containing a restaurant named "The Meeting Place," we would have the following entry.

> (the the-meeting-place meeting place)

For each token encountered by the scanner, any hyphenation list entries that it indexes (i.e., that it is the first member of) are used to construct auxiliary definitions for the token. In the event that such a token is not meaningful by itself, as perhaps is the case for "vice" in "vice president," these may in fact be the only definitions. As an example of the result of such derived meanings, suppose that the entry shown earlier for "up with" were present, and suppose further that "Up-and-Over" has been given as a nickname for Alaska. Then the scanner output for the word "up" would be as follows.

```
(up
   (up prep up)
   (up prep up-with (nextword with))
   (up nounval Alaska (nt state) (nextword and over)))
```

The "nextword" feature tells the parser that, if it is able to find the indicated list of tokens immediately following the position of the token being processed in parsing the current sentence, it may treat the entire list of tokens as though it were a single token with the lexical definition supplied, minus the "nextword" feature. This scheme enables us to account for a large variety of what some systems have resorted to a "chart" to accomplish, yet is simpler to create and probably simpler to interpret during parsing than these more sophisticated methods. A complementary use of the "nextword" feature accounts for contractions. For example, the lexical entry for "don't" could be

```
(don't verb do (nextword + not) (vpres plur))
```

Pattern-type morphology

We wish to allow TELI to recognize the occurrence of a database value in an input being processed without cluttering the lexicon any more than is necessary. To accomplish this, the customizer is asked, for each object type of the application at hand, which of three types of lexical treatment to apply to it. First, the values may be ignored; this is appropriate when all or most of them are not expected to appear in English inputs. Naturally, the tabular outputs produced by TELI can still contain arbitrary database values. Second, the system can be asked to construct one or more patterns that define the morphological structure of the values. This is appropriate for object types whose values exhibit a high degree of regularity, and is probably not appropriate for data values consisting entirely of letters. Examples appear below. Finally, the system can be instructed to enter each value into the lexicon, marked as a noun value (proper noun) and having the appropriate "nt" feature to specify its object type.

At present, our pattern generation algorithm considers letters, digits, and special characters such as hyphen or period. As a simple example, the morphological composition of zip codes, which consist of a sequence of 5 digits, is indicated by the pattern

```
((digit 5))
```

while the names of offices at the author's institution entail the two patterns

> ((digit 1) (letter 1) (hyphen 1) (digit 3))
> ((digit 1) (letter 1) (hyphen 1) (digit 3) (letter 1))

which respectively cover values such as "3C-235" and "3C-440A."

Having constructed one or more patterns for each of the object types whose values admit such treatment, TELI combines these patterns into a pattern file, whose entries consist of an object type followed by one or more patterns that describe it. For example,

> (office
> ((digit 1) (letter 1) (hyphen 1) (digit 3))
> ((digit 1) (letter 1) (hyphen 1) (digit 3) (letter 1)))

Patterns which are identical except for the number of adjacent occurrences of one or more types of characters are merged using "*" in the position of the count. For example, the course names "CS221" and "BIO14" would lead to the pattern

> ((letter *) (digit *))

Our use of patterns is similar to the methods described by Damerau [1985]; it differs in that we have chosen to conflate patterns that differ only in the number of times some symbol repeats.

Syntax-related data structures

As indicated in Figure 3, the data structures involved in parsing are (1) a domain-independent *grammar* and (2) a domain-specific collection of *case frames*. To improve the run-time efficiency of the top-down parser, auxiliary information, created automatically from the grammar when TELI is compiled, tells what surface words, parts of speech, and root words can begin each grammar routine.

The phrase-structure grammar

As described in Ballard and Tinkham [1984], TELI operates on an augmented phrase-structure grammar of our design. Two of the most important design considerations in developing this grammatical formalism, and its associated parser, are (1) allowing arbitrary "feature" information to be passed into and out of the nodes of the parse tree being constructed, and (2) determining the "deep case structure" of each input during parsing, so that the resulting parse structure will be immediately interpretable by the semantics module. For example, the parser will label the agent of a passive verb phrase as its (deep) subject.

The grammatical formalism developed for TELI is based on seven "command" types: three are associated with words and phrases (*Quote* for grammatical formatives, *Get* for parts of speech, and *Call* for grammatical categories) and four relate to interactions among words and phrases (*Seq* for sequence, *Alt* for alternation or choice, * for arbitrary repetition, and *Opt* for optionality.) Since complete information on this formalism, and comments on an early version of our parser, are available in the paper cited above, the remainder of this section is restricted to (1) a summary of the current grammatical coverage of TELI, and (2) a description of the current repertoire of selectional restrictions employed by the system.

The current TELI grammar, which includes about 85 grammatical categories ranging in specificity from *sentence* to *relative adjective phrase minus argument* (e.g., "that John is taller than"), is specified in about 18 pages of Lisp-like text. This grammar accounts for both (1) the English questions to be answered and (2) statements that supply the meaning of a new word or phrase in terms of language already known to the system.

The present top-level structures of the English inputs supported by TELI can be grouped into about eight categories (e.g., imperative, yes-no question, etc.), most of which can be further refined (e.g., yes-no questions may be either active or passive, may involve either a linking verb or a user-defined verb, and so forth). Within sentences, noun phrases may contain determiners, titles such as "Dr," possessive proper nouns (e.g., "Ballard's"), ordinals, adjectives, common or proper nouns occurring as prenominal modifiers, superlative forms of adjectives, and a host of relative clause forms including comparative and verb phrases. Certain linguistically sophisticated forms involving subtle features (e.g., mood and complex tenses) are also provided by the grammar but ignored during semantic interpretation. For example, the phrase

"the manager that has been being reported to by Smith"

is treated identically to "the manager that Smith reports to." Similarly, logical and some complex numerical quantifiers are supported by the grammar but are not currently being translated into database queries.

Case frame specifications

The case frames provided to TELI enable the parser to ensure that the parse structures being built satisfy whatever domain-specific selectional restrictions on phrases have been specified by the user. To achieve this, the customization module maintains, and the parser consults, a list of *ordered tuples* for each phrase, where each tuple is composed of words and object types of the domain at hand. The present repertoire of case frame types is as follows. Tokens that begin with a capital letter denote entities; the remaining tokens denote words; and parentheses denote optionality.

Adjective Phrase
Subject adjective preposition Argument

Noun-Modifier Phrase
Noun-Modifier Subject

Prepositional Phrase
Subject preposition Argument

Verb Phrase
Subject verb (Object) (particle) (preposition Argument)

Functional Noun Phrase
Subject noun Argument

During parsing, agreement is assured by constructing, for each phrase of the input, a similar list of tuples whose *word* slots are filled by the appropriate words of the input being processed and whose *object type* slots are filled by the object type ("nt") of the noun phrases being built. For example, from the input

"What trails on the Twinway lead to a volcano?"

the parser would construct the compatibility vector

prep-ph: (trail on mountain)

where *trail* and *mountain* give the object types of the common and proper nouns "trails" and "Twinway," respectively, and

verb-ph: (trail lead nil nil to mountain)

where *trail* and *mountain* are the object types of the common nouns "trails" and "volcano" and the *nil*'s correspond to missing optional slots for direct objects and prepositions used as particles.

Since TELI allows a given word to refer to an arbitrary number of object types, situations somewhat more complex than those just described can arise. For example, in one of our test databases, "Liberty Spring" is both a trail and a campsite, but the context of its occurrence is generally sufficient to enable the parser to decide which sense is being used. For example, if

trails can be on mountains but not on other trails, then a unique interpretation of the phrase "trails on Liberty Spring" would result from the
confluence of case frame specifications.

Semantic definitions

As described in Ballard and Stumberger [1986], TELI provides elaborate
run-time facilities for the user to define, examine, and update the definitions
of any domain-specific words or phrases known to the system. In our computational setting, each user-defined semantic definition may be regarded
as a *modifier* which is *predicative* in that it is used to form a *subset* of the set
of objects referred to by whatever it modifies. Thus, "tall mountains" will
be a subset of the set of mountains and, since nouns also act as modifiers,
"huts" would yield some subset of the set of all campsites. Since semantic interpretation in TELI is almost entirely compositional, "tall volcanic
mountains" would yield the set of mountains that are both tall and volcanic, as would "volcanic mountains that are tall" and other similar forms,
including "tall volcanoes" if the noun "volcano" has been given a definition
equivalent to that of the adjective "volcanic."

In associating predicative semantics with user-defined vocabulary, modifiers are treated as *N-place predicates*; specifically, each *word* meaning is a
1-place predicate, while each *phrase* meaning is a one, two or three place
predicate, depending on the number of entity slots its case frame contains.
Thus, as indicated in the list of case frame structures given above, adjective
phrases and prepositional phrases will act as 2-place predicates, intransitive
verbs without complements will act as 1-place predicates, and so forth.

For the reasons stated in Ballard and Stumberger [1986], we have found
it useful to distinguish between the *internal type* of a definition being used
by the system and the *modalities* with which this definition is made. Thus,
definition types comprise the algebraic, database, and indirect formats
discussed below, while modalities of specification involve mouse-sensitive
menus, type-in windows, and so forth. The remainder of this section is
concerned with the internal representations of semantic definitions, referring the reader to the paper cited above for a discussion of how semantics
are actually supplied by the user.

Semantic definitions in TELI are based upon three types of *primitive*
definitions. At present, each modifier is defined by a list of zero or more
primitive definitions, where the associated meanings are presumed to be
conjoined. Through the use of "not," and the provision for indirect definitions, *arbitrary Boolean combinations* may be formed. To prevent an
infinite loop from arising during production of a relational algebra query,
circular definitions are detected by the system. In addition to being able to

"point" from one meaning to another, as described below, users are enabled to *borrow*, or copy, an existing definition, thus enabling it to be modified without altering the original meaning.

Data structure semantics

The simplest type of primitive semantic definition involves a reference to the actual *data structures* which define the domain at hand. In our current context, this amounts specifically to a *database* reference, as indicated by

$$
\begin{array}{lll}
<\text{Spec}> & ::= & \text{in} <\text{rel}> <\text{Triples}> \\
<\text{Triples}> & ::= & <\text{Triple}> \mid <\text{Triple}> <\text{Triples}> \\
<\text{Triple}> & ::= & (\ <\text{field}> <\text{Relop}> <\text{Ref}>\ ) \\
<\text{Ref}> & ::= & <\text{param}> \mid <\text{constant}> \\
<\text{Relop}> & ::= & =\ \mid\ <\ \mid\ >\ \mid\ <=\ \mid\ >=\ \mid\ \sim=
\end{array}
$$

In this specification, *rel* is the name of a database relation; *field* is any field name of the specified database relation; *param* is a reference to one of the parameters of the N-place predicate being defined; *function* refers to one of an extensible list of 1-operand user-defined functions; and *constant* may be a number, a symbol, or a list. Some examples follow.

Modifier	Database Definition
(func-ph (size size department))	in dhead (dept=p-arg) (siz=p-subj)
(adj small department)	in dhead (dept=p-arg) (siz < 10)
(adj volcanic mountain)	in mnts (mountain=p-noun)(vol=y)
(noun volcano mountain)	in mnts (mountain=p-noun)(vol=y)

The definition shown here for "size of department" provides the information about physical data storage needed to make sense out of the algebraic definition of a "large department" to be given in the following section. An alternate method of defining an adjective modifier of department, somewhat simpler but with less generality and, we believe, less elegance, is shown above for "small department." Our preference is to separate conceptual properties, e.g., having a size less than 10, from specific data structure references. In this way, we expect both algebraic definitions and indirect definitions to transfer with minimal effort to applications areas less conventional than that of database query. For example, in an expert system, several rules may be involved in finding the size of a department, but the definition of a "small department" as one having a size less than 10 can occur just as in the database world.

Algebraic semantics

The second type of primitive semantic definition, which we shall refer to as *algebraic* semantics, involves a triple comprising (a) a referential left-hand side, (b) an equality or inequality symbol, and (c) a referential right-hand side. Algebraic triples have the top-level structure indicated by

$$
\begin{array}{lll}
<\text{Spec}> & ::= & <\text{Term}> <\text{Relop}> <\text{Term}> \\
<\text{Term}> & ::= & <\text{Ref}> \mid (<\text{function}> <\text{Term}>) \\
<\text{Ref}> & ::= & <\text{param}> \mid <\text{constant}>
\end{array}
$$

where *relop* is as indicated earlier. Some examples follow, where *p-adj* refers to the formal parameter of an adjective modifier and *p-subj*, *p-obj*, and *p-arg* refer to formal parameters of phrasal modifiers (the Subject, Object, and Argument positions named above).

Modifier	Algebraic Definition
(adj large department)	(size p-adj) > 20
(adj asian country)	(continent p-adj) = Asia
(adj oriental restaurant)	(cuisine p-adj) = '(chinese japanese)
(verb-ph (employee work nil nil for manager))	(manager p-subj) = p-arg
(func-ph (employee associate employee))	(manager p-subj) = (manager p-arg)
(prep-ph (house in state))	(state (county p-subj)) = p-arg

Note that, as indicated, our use of inequalities is *overloaded* in that we require them to act on lists as well as scalars. This may arise either explicitly, due to the presence of a list of values, such as that shown in the definition of "Oriental restaurant," or implicitly, whenever one of the "functions" being referred to is multiple-valued. In these situations, we define operators other than "~=" to yield true in precisely those cases where at least one of the values on its left stands in the indicated relation to at least one of the values on its right and, for "~=," we require that *none* of the values on its left equals a value on its right. In most of the sample databases we have worked with, only "=" requires a non-scalar interpretation.

Although algebraic definitions exhibit the flavor of the computational setting in which TELI operates, they contain no specific references to the location(s) where functional values can be found, or how they are to be computed. One of several planned extensions to the scheme shown above is to introduce functions of more than one argument. This would allow, for example, a definition of the adjective phrase "close to," or the prepositional phrase "near," in terms of a 2-place *distance* function. We are also considering ways of providing for *arithmetic* operations, to allow for expressions like

$$(\text{length p-subj}) > (*\ 2\ (\text{width p-obj}))$$

Indirect semantics

The third and final type of primitive definition involves making an *indirect* reference to a word or phrase already known to the system. Indirect definitions may be specified as follows.

```
<Spec> ::=  ( <Mod> <Params> ) |  ( not <Spec> )
<Mod>  ::=  ( <W-type> <word> <entity> ) |
            ( <Ph-type> ( <Tups> ) )
<Tups> ::=  <Tup>  |  <Tup> <Tups>
<Tup>  ::=  <word>  |  <entity>
```

where *W-type* refers to types of word modifiers (currently adjective, noun, and noun modifier), *Ph-type* refers to phrasal modifier types (verb phrases, prepositional phrases, and so forth), *word* and *entity* refer respectively to user-defined words and entities of the domain at hand, and *params* indicates a binding to a parameter of the existing word or phrase in terms of which a definition is being made (i.e., the definition associated with <Mod>). Some examples of indirect definitions follow.

Modifier	Definition
(adj silent mountain)	(not ((noun volcano mountain) p-adj))
(func-info (department abode employee))	((prep-ph (employee in department)) p-arg p-subj)
(adj lucky employee)	((prep-ph (employee in department)) p-adj 11384)

These examples illustrate (1) defining an adjective ("silent") as the negation of an existing noun ("volcano"), (2) defining a functional noun ("abode of ...") in terms of an existing prepositional relationship ("employee in department"), and (3) defining one item ("lucky") in terms of another item ("employee in department") having more operands, here involving the somewhat fanciful notion that employees are lucky precisely when they work in department 11384.

Discussion

This concluding section will address one general question and several more specific questions that elaborate on material presented earlier.

Why, whence, and whither TELI

In designing TELI, we have sought to develop an architecture that minimizes the *interactions* among the components responsible for syntax, semantics, and so forth. In addition to its importance for practical system design, this is important to basic research in natural language processing since an evaluation of methods for dealing with one type of problem sensibly includes asking how smoothly the associated module operates in the context of the remaining modules. For example, we have sought to provide for complex grammatical coverage that can be represented by parse structures that permit nearly compositional interpretation.

Despite the intermittent database flavor of our discussions, we have frequently avoided temptations to introduce features specifically targeted for database applications. At the same time, we provide a variety of linguistically attractive facilities, including passives and various forms of fronting, many of which are largely superfluous in the pragmatically based realm of database query. Thus, TELI can easily handle such deeply nested prolixities as "how many employees are in the departments that the employees not in the department Ballard is in are in?," but, until very recently, it failed to provide for some very simple inputs such as "give the manager and salary of Smith." Although the latter example contains an isolated and predictable type of conjunction that could be easily accounted for (e.g., an imperative verb may be followed by a list of attribute names), we hesitate to incorporate a feature (here, conjunction) until we are able to allow it to distribute freely throughout the grammar.

At the time of this writing (fall, 1986) we are engaged in (a) extending the already quite elaborate semantic definition facilities described above, (b) providing for complex numerical quantificational abilities in the grammar, and (c) adapting TELI to construct queries for multiple "back end" retrieval modules, including the initial database systems discussed in this paper and also more AI-based systems.

Elaborations on previous remarks

We stated above that our semantic definitions, by virtue of allowing free use of conjunction and negation, are able to provide for "arbitrary Boolean combinations" of primitive definitions. Thus, if $a(x)$ represents a one place predicate to be associated with (say) an adjective, and we want

$$a(x) => b(x) \text{ or } c(x)$$

we could make use of DeMorgan's rules and the fact that not(not(p)) is equivalent to p to rewrite the above as

b(x) or c(x) => not (not b(x) and not c(x))

which would lead us to the following definitions.

a(x) => not d(x)

d(x) => e(x) and f(x)

e(x) => not b(x)

f(x) => not c(x)

where d(x), e(x), and (fx) are the definitions of new and quite possibly otherwise useless modifiers. This points out the fact that our statement concerning the ability to define arbitrary Boolean combinations is mainly a formal statement, not one relating to the habitability of the interface. We make this point at length to suggest to the reader that any "formal" claims concerning TELI or any other system be carefully scrutinized before one forms any impression of their practical import.

We gave the case structure of the "functional noun phrase" as

Subject noun Argument

where Subject and Argument constitute entity slots and "noun" denotes a functional noun. During the past year, our treatment of this type of phrase has had anywhere from two to four components, nor are we now completely satisfied with the current scheme. At present, functional noun phrases arise either by the use of "of" in the places where a preposition would otherwise occur (and perhaps more, e.g., "that John is the father of" as well that "that is the father of Bill") or as a possessive ("Mary's ... salary" is treated as though it were "the ... salary of Mary," where "..." are optional adjectives or other pre-nominal, post-determiner items). The motivation for a fourth slot is to allow words other than "of," most often "to." The motivation for removing the noun position is the typical redundancy of having it be equal to the subject entity. However, the distinction does allow for words like "friend," "enemy," "colleague" and so forth which (unlike words like "employee" and "manager") cannot meaningfully be considered entity names.

Another frequent redundancy involves words appearing in one of the phrasal case frame slots, which the existing grammar asks for by both naming the part of speech to be allowed and specifying the case slot the word must fill. Since only prepositions occur in (say) the particle slot of verb phrase, or the preposition slot of a prepositional phrase, the grammar could just as well ask for any word at all that fills the required slot. In fact, isn't a word of a certain type precisely because it can occur in the positions where words of that type are expected?

Finally, we wish to point out the freedom allowed by the "Pre-Defined Specification of the NLP" file shown in Figure 2. As an example, we shall consider the part of speech called "title," which we introduced into TELI when we wanted to allow words like "mount" and "mt" to precede a proper name, as in "mt bond," where "bond" is the actual database entry for a mountain. Titles are defined in this file by the one-line entry

(title title (* title * nt))

and by an appearance in a list of open parts of speech (i.e., categories extensible by the user). On the other hand, they are not included in the list of user-definable parts of speech, so there is no real semantics associated with them. For this reason, the grammar indicates to the parser that, when a title is seen, it is not to be included in the tree under construction. However, as indicated by the entry above, titles can play an informative or a disambiguational role by their having an "nt" feature. Of course, in many envisionable situations, one would indeed want to associate meanings with titles. For example, in referring to "university instructors" "dr" could mean "has a PhD," so that "Dr Smith" could be an unambiguous reference whereas "Smith" could be ambiguous. At present, TELI does not ask specifically for plural titles, but the user could of course specify "mts," "drs," and so forth. To allow for plural titles would involve adding exactly one line and one symbol to the appropriate pre-defined file. Thus, the preceding example has shown that the repertoire of parts of speech is quite flexible, and that the properties of each part of speech (e.g., whether plural or other inflections may arise or whether semantics are to be associated with words in the class) can be specified easily and independently of one another.

Recent developments

Recently, TELI has been extended in a number of ways and tested in several new applications. It has been applied to the problem of retrieval from systems that are not databases, including the Kandor knowledge-representation system [Patel-Schneider 1984]. We have used TELI to populate the knowledge base of Kandor, and to *define concepts* for it. A sophisticated *logical form* language, which is an extension of first-order logic, has been devised and implemented, as described in [Ballard and Stumberger 1987]. The scheme for lexical storage has been simplified, so that features are attached to morphological variants (e.g., plural nouns and comparative adjectives) by the scanner, rather than by the customization module as was done in the earlier versions of the system.

Many redundancies of our grammar have been eliminated through provisions for *meta rules*, which create the grammar for relative clauses, yes-no questions, and a host of other categories (many of which are so-called "slash" categories) from a base grammar for declaratives. The facility we described for "indirect semantics" has been supplanted by a provision for definitions to be given using any English that the system can process (e.g., "large company" might be defined as a company "that makes more than 8 types of cars"). User-defined semantics may now be directly given as any Boolean combination of primitive definitions. Finally, additional grammatical and semantic coverage has been provided, including a wide variety of comparatives, quantifiers, and combinations of these, such as, "What foreign companies make at least 3 more than twice as many large cars as Buick?"

Acknowledgments

Doug Stumberger was entirely responsible for generating relational database queries, including the splicing of the definitions of English words and phrases. He also helped design and did the initial implementation of the domain-independent query generator alluded to in the last section. Doug Foxvog provided the facility for making definitions in terms of arbitrary Boolean complexity. Finally, I wish to thank Paul Martin for sending me a Lisp encoding of the world mountains database that appeared in Grosz et al. 1987, which furnished some of the examples in this paper.

References

Ballard, B. 1982. A "Domain Class" Approach tc Transportable Natural Language Processing. *Cognition and Brain Theory* **5**, 3, 269-287.

Ballard, B. 1984. The Syntax and Semantics of User-Defined Modifiers in a Transportable Natural Language Processor. *COLING84*, Stanford University, July, 52-56.

Ballard, B. 1986. User Specification of Syntactic Case Frames in TELI, A Transportable, User-Customized Natural Language Processor. *COLING86*, University of Bonn, August, 454-460.

Ballard, B., Lusth, J., and Tinkham, N. 1984. LDC-1: A Transportable Natural Language Processor for Office Environments. *ACM Transactions on Office Information Systems*, **2**, 1, 1-23.

Ballard, B. and Stumberger, D. 1986. Semantic Acquisition in TELI: A Transportable, User-Customized Natural Language Processor. *24th Annual Meeting of the Association for Computational Linguistics*, Columbia University, June, 20-29.

Ballard, B. and Stumberger, D. 1987. The Design and Use of a Logic-Based Internal Representation Language for Backend-Independent Natural Language Processing. AT&T Bell Laboratories Technical Memorandum, Department 11254, October 1987.

Ballard, B. and Tinkham, N. 1984. A Phrase-Structured Grammatical Framework for Transportable Natural Language Processing. *Computational Linguistics*, **10**, 2, 81-96.

Damerau, F. 1985. Problems and Some Solutions in Customization of Natural Language Database Front Ends. *ACM Transactions on Office Information Systems*, **3**, 2, 165-184.

Gehrke, M. and Block, H. 1986. Morpheme-Based Lexical Analysis. *Advances in Lexicology: Second Annual Conference of the UW Centre for the New Oxford English Dictionary*, Waterloo, November, 1-15.

Grosz, B., Appelt, D., Martin, P., and Pereira, F. 1987. TEAM: An Experiment in the Design of Transportable Natural-Language Interfaces. *Artificial Intelligence*, **32**, 2: 173-243.

Patel-Schneider, P. 1984. Small Can Be Beautiful in Knowledge Representation. *Proceedings of the IEEE Workshop on Principles of Knowledge-Based Systems*, Denver, Colorado, December.

Part III:
The nature of lexical relations

11
An exploration into graded set membership

Judith Markowitz
Navistar International Transportation Corp.
Oak Brook Terrace, Illinois 60521

Abstract

Seventy-six mature adults were interviewed about prototypicality and membership gradation for twenty-one categories of objects. These categories included a wide range of object types. Subjects' responses were analyzed using lexical-semantic relations, such as FUNCTION, PART-WHOLE, and AGENT. The results demonstrate that specific relations or factors are significant for entire classes of categories. The relative importance of specific lexical-semantic relations within and across categories also provides important insights into why certain category members are better exemplars, and what types of knowledge are used to characterize typicality.

Introduction

Fuzzy-set theory came into being as a formal discipline when Lotfi Zadeh [1965] noted that categories like *animal*, which were believed to have rigid membership criteria, have a "continuum of grades of membership." Zadeh's observations transformed the analysis of simple member/non-member judgments into the modeling of judgments about degree of membership.

While Zadeh and his colleagues were elaborating the theory of fuzzy sets [Zadeh 1971, 1976; Zadeh, Fu, Tanaka, and Shimura 1975; and Zadeh and

Lee 1969] other researchers were constructing empirical studies designed to identify and analyze the cognitive processes underlying membership gradation. This research has shown that the role of frequency of occurrence is minimal, but that word association or "category dominance" is related to judgments of membership typicality [Howell 1973; Malt and Smith 1982; McCloskey 1980; Mervis, Catlin, and Rosch 1976; and Rosch, Simpson, and Miller 1976].

Wittgenstein's [1953] concept of "family resemblance" was applied to membership gradation to account for the observation that highly typical category members tend to share the same general set of attributes [Rosch 1973; Rosch and Mervis 1975; Rosch, Mervis, Gray, Johnson, and Boyes-Braem 1976; and Tversky 1977]. *Birds*, for example, all share wings and feathers, but there are other attributes, like talons, which are strongly characteristic of the category yet are not possessed by all typical category members. Some researchers have also suggested that family resemblance attributes do not simply co-occur; they interact to increase typicality [Malt and Smith 1984; and Rosch, Mervis, Gray, Johnson, and Boyes-Braem 1976]. The family resemblance approach has also been used to develop and support the prototype theory [Rosch 1975, 1978; Rosch, Mervis, Gray, Johnson, and Boyes-Braem 1976; and Tversky 1977] which holds that membership gradation results from comparison of category members with a single category prototype. This theory has been very useful too, but recent research has shown that it may be simplistic [Malt and Smith 1984; Oden 1977; and Osherson and Smith 1981].

Three levels of categories were identified by Rosch, Mervis, Gray, Johnson, and Boyes-Braem [1976]: **Superordinate**, like *tree* and *furniture*, which are very heterogeneous and whose members share few attributes; **Basic**, like *oak* and *chair*, whose members share a "significant number of attributes," have "motor programs which are similar to one another," have similar shapes, and "can be identified from average shapes of members of the class"; and **Sub-Basic** like *white oak* and *kitchen chair*, whose members share many attributes with related categories. This classification has formed the basis for subsequent research. However, the greatest focus has been on the Basic Level categories.

The goal of this study is to expand the understanding of graded set membership through specific changes in methodology and analysis. One major change is the introduction of qualitative data. Most studies of graded set membership have relied primarily on quantitative techniques, such as response time, and have generally ignored the in-depth, qualitative data commonly used in the development of artificial intelligence expert systems. If the aim of research on membership gradation is to understand human cognition, qualitative data must be included. This is particularly true for models which use semantic relations because such models should represent the relations which are used in typicality decisions as well as those which are understood when presented to subjects in a study.

Another change is the population from which the study sample was taken. Most studies of membership gradation have been done on college sophomores. This is a highly homogeneous population. Such limited sampling not only restricts the generalizability of the research findings, it artificially enhances intersubject agreement. This study uses a more diverse sample of adults.

Finally, this study is primarily concerned with Superordinate Level categories, including highly non-visual categories, part-whole categories, and activity categories. Such diversity of category types provides some checks and balances on the application of the findings, particularly those regarding the importance and function of specific semantic relations. These checks are important because it is possible that one kind of relation may be important for typicality only in certain types of categories.

Methodology

All 76 subjects participating in this study were native speakers of American English. Their education ranged from two years of high school to eight years of college, and their ages ranged from 50 to 69. There were 40 women and 36 men and all were caucasian (see Table 1). These age and education ranges were selected to increase the likelihood of individual differences based on life-experience and expertise [Fillmore, Kempler and Wang 1978; Markowitz and Moses 1981; Rosch 1977; and Rosch, Mervis, Gray, Johnson, and Boyes-Braem 1976].

Table 1. Grouping of subjects by sex, age, and education

Education	Sex and Age			
	Men (50–59)	Women (50–59)	Men (60–69)	Women (60–69)
High school	6	6	4	9
1 to 3 years of college	6	6	5	5
4 or more years of college	6	8	9	6
Total	18	20	18	20

Twenty-one test categories, each with five or six members, were selected from Battig and Montague's [1969] list of category response norms. Table 2 shows that these categories include naturally-occurring objects (seven categories), manufactured objects (nine categories), highly non-visual categories (three categories), one part-whole category, and one activity category. One well-documented Basic Level category, *bird*, has also been included to serve as a bridge between the findings of this study and those of other studies.

Table 2. Categories used in the study

I.Naturally Occurring	II.Manufactured	III.Highly Non-Visual
Animal	Clothing	Drink
Bird (Basic Level)	Footwear	Fuel
Flower	Furniture	Seasoning
Fruit	Kitchen Utensil	
Insect	Musical Instrument	IV.Part-Whole
Tree	Tool	Body Part
Vegetable	Toy	
	Vehicle	V.Activity
	Weapon	Sport

Category members were selected from the Battig and Montague lists at the following frequency levels:

1. The item most frequently listed first;
2. Any items listed between 100 and 200 times;
3. Any item listed between 30 and 75 times; and
4. Any item listed fewer than 10 times.

An attempt was made to reduce the lack-of-familiarity factor [McCloskey 1980; and Malt and Smith 1982] but this was not always possible, especially at the lower frequency levels. At least one additional category member was selected at one of the frequency levels which was judged to be physically very different from the other member selected in that range.

The name of each category was printed on a 3 x 5 card. Member cards had the member name printed on one side and a picture of the member on the other. This was done to reduce the effects of picture vs. word presentation for picturable categories.

Each subject was interviewed individually by the experimenter. Subjects were told that they were to judge the goodness-of-fit of certain objects in several categories, and were assured that no special knowledge was needed. Each interview began with a folk definition [Spradley 1979; and Werner,

Schoepfle, Iris, and Bouck 1976]. Subjects were asked to explain the category as if they were talking to a child or to someone from another planet. The interviewer probed aspects of the folk definition and proposed category members. If, for example, the subject stated that *furniture* sits on the floor the interviewer asked about *built-in-tables*.

The category cards were then displayed and the subject was asked to rank them on the basis of typicality. The member rated most typical was assigned the rank of 1. Ties were permitted and were later examined to see if they were assigned to physically dissimilar objects. This phenomenon was described by Malt and Smith [1984] as an argument against single category prototypes. The subject was encouraged to verbalize while ranking.

After the ranking was completed the subject was asked which, if any, of the items were not members or were questionable members of the category. Finally, the subject was asked to name the most prototypical category member they could imagine. The order of presentation of categories was random, and half of the picturable categories were displayed using pictures and half with printed words.

A content analysis was done of the interviews to identify the semantic relations which played the greatest role in typicality and restriction of category membership. Table 3 lists and defines the relations used in the analysis. They are taken from Evens, Litowitz, Markowitz, Smith, and Werner [1980].

Overall intersubject agreement was assessed by t-test and Chi-square measures with significance set at the ninety-ninth percentile.

Results and discussion

Intersubject agreement

The overall levels of intersubject agreement on ranking were significant for all 21 categories. This substantiates the claim that ranking was not done at random. The 136 reports of questionable membership along with the 78 "I don't know if X is a member" responses also support Zadeh's [1965] observation that category boundaries are fuzzy.

As predicted, intersubject agreement was much lower than in studies using college sophomores. It ranged from 11 percent to 86 percent. Table 4 shows that the greatest agreement generally occurred on the best and poorest category exemplars; a result which agrees with the findings of McCloskey and Glucksberg [1978].

The Chi-square revealed no significant differences between groups of subjects except between the subjects who viewed pictures vs. words for the category *tree*. The difference between women and men for the category *kitchen utensil* also approached significance. These findings indicate that most of the lower intersubject agreement found in this study was not due to age, sex, education, or picture vs. word stimuli.

Table 3. Lexical-semantic relations used in the content analysis

Relation	Description	Examples
AGENT	A lexical relation which signals the instigator of an action.	Birds fly. People drive vehicles.
ANTONYMY	A relation which expresses oppositeness or complementarity. It often sets two or more attributes against each other.	Feathered vs. furry vs. scaly. Big vs. small.
FUNCTION	A relation expressing goal, use, or purpose. In English it is sometimes represented by "for."	Clothing is for warmth.
INSTRUMENT	A lexical relation showing an inanimate object which is involved in an action. In English it is often expressed by "with" or the verb "to use."	You use fuel to heat your house. You eat with a kitchen utensil.
LOCATIVE	A relation which signals place or position. In English it is frequently signaled by prepositions.	Animals walk on land. Body parts are inside the body.
MODIFICATION	A general attributive relation expressing such things as color, size, texture, evaluative judgment, source, and material. In English it typically, but not universally, appears as an adjective.	Birds are small. Furniture is made of wood.
OBJECT	A lexical relation which identifies something as the recipient of an action.	You eat chicken. People drive vehicles.

Table 3. **Lexical semantic relations (continued)**

Relation	Description	Examples
PART-WHOLE	A relation which identifies something as being a segment or a portion of something else. In English it is often expressed by "part of," the verb "to have," and the possessive.	A vehicle has a motor. A petal is part of a flower.
SYNONYMY	A relation which signals equivalence between words or verbal expressions. In English it often appears as the verb "to be."	A bug is an insect (meaning the word "bug" is just another word for "insect").
TAXONOMY	A relation showing the membership of an individual in a set or of a group of individuals in a larger group. In English it is often expressed by the verb "to be" or "is a kind of." Care must be taken to distinguish it from synonymy.	Ants and fleas are kinds of insects. A bug is an insect (meaning a bug is a kind of insect).

Some of the qualitative data supporting the high agreement items shown on Table 4 shed light on category dominance. *Rose*, for example, was not only the item with the greatest category association for *flower* in Battig and Montague [1969] and the one with the highest typicality ratings in this study, it was also the one which subjects reported "personified *flower*." *Rose, robin, oak, apple, piano,* and *eagle* are part of our cultural folklore. They tended to evoke stronger affect from subjects than other members of their categories and were often described as "more beautiful" or "enjoyable" as well. The *eagle* was described by some subjects as "American" which, for a few subjects, was sufficient to rank it the most birdlike of the candidate-members. Its cultural significance may also have been the reason other subjects ranked it below *robin* and just above *wren*, despite *wren*'s greater physical similarity to the highly typical *robin*.

In some instances ranking preferences were clearly tied to the life experiences, expertise, or interests of individual subjects. One subject, a furniture dealer, assigned *birch* a low rank for the category *tree* because it "has poor quality wood." Most subjects gave *birch* a much higher rank. Three other subjects who are good cooks assigned the highest *kitchen utensil* rating

Table 4. Members showing greatest inter-subject agreement
(using responses from 76 subjects)

Category	Member	Rank	Number of Subjects Giving Rank
Sport	fencing	4	67
	chess	5	71
Vehicle	ski	5	74
Musical Instrument	piano	1	67
Seasoning	nuts	5	73
Fruit	apple	1	68
	cherry	2	68
Clothing	necklace	6	75
Tool	hammer	1	67
Flower	rose	1	72
Footwear	shoe	1	73
	ice skate	4	66
	flipper	5	66
Tree	oak	1	67
Bird	robin	1	66

to *stove* whereas most subjects ranked it low in typicality. Knowledge of scientific definitions, particularly biological taxonomies, also affected rank assignments. Familiarity with such information varied from subject to subject, but generally appeared to represent a higher authority for the subjects. During the ranking task some subjects remarked that, contrary to common knowledge, a *tomato* is not a *vegetable* and a *bat* is not a *bird*. Subjects who were unaware of the biological classifications of these things tended to rank them higher in category typicality than subjects who knew their classifications. More extensive knowledge of, or expertise in, biological classification tended to produce tied ranks. One subject, for example, tended to separate the items into members and non-members on the basis of biological taxonomy. When he was asked to re-rank categories as other people might rank them he produced rankings which were very similar to those of other subjects. This indicated that, as with the subjects who only knew that *bats* are not *birds*, he elected to use the more highly-valued, scientific system, but that system was superimposed on the informal, fuzzy membership system he shared with other subjects.

Despite the lower intersubject agreement levels found in this study as compared with those of other studies, the mean ranks for members in ten categories generally agree with Rosch's [1975] "exemplariness ranks" (see Tables 5 and 6). However, five of these categories and 13 of the total 21 categories have members whose mean ranks are not significantly different from each other. Examination of these category members reveals that they are at the mid-level of typicality where the poorest intersubject agreement occurred. Some of these category members, such as *socks* and *pajamas* in the category *clothing* and *ostrich* and *chicken* in the category *bird*, were, in fact, often seen as occupying similar typicality levels. Subjects simply disagreed about which was slightly more typical than the other. Other examples, like *fly* and *ant* in *insect*, are a statistical by-product of disagreement about the relative typicality of entire subclasses of a category. This will be discussed further below.

Table 5. Comparison of ranking results obtained in this study with those of Rosch [1975] (– indicates disagreement, * agreement)

Category	Item	Exemplariness Rank Rosch [1975]	Mean Rank This Study
Bird	robin	1.02	1.132
	wren	1.64	2.276
	eagle	1.75	2.789
	chicken	4.02	*4.592
	ostrich	4.12	*4.605
	bat	6.15	5.500
Clothing	shirt	1.14	-1.750
	jacket	1.68	-1.487
	socks	2.13	*3.684
	pajamas	2.25	*3.803
	hat	4.20	4.250
	necklace	6.21	5.987
Fruit	apple	1.08	1.080
	cherry	1.86	2.013
	prune	3.30	3.093
	tomato	5.58	3.800

Table 5. Comparison of ranking results (continued)
(− indicates disagreement, * agreement)

Category	Item	Exemplariness Rank Rosch [1975]	Mean Rank This Study
Furniture	chair	1.04	1.382
	dresser	1.33	1.750
	lamp	2.94	-3.816
	stool	3.13	-3.092
	picture	5.75	4.868
Sport	baseball	1.05	1.227
	basketball	1.12	2.173
	tennis	1.15	2.613
	fencing	2.13	3.947
	chess	5.07	4.947
Tool	hammer	1.34	1.158
	screwdriver	1.56	*2.158
	tape measure	1.69	-4.342
	pliers	2.50	*2.434
	bolts	3.63	4.592
Toy	doll	1.41	1.667
	soldier	1.61	-2.837
	block	1.63	-2.187
	balloon	3.07	4.027
	swing	3.35	5.240
Vegetable	carrot	1.15	1.635
	spinach	1.22	2.108
	squash	1.83	*3.338
	onion	2.52	*3.486
	parsley	3.32	4.365
Vehicle	car	1.24	1.200
	bus	1.27	1.813
	motorcycle	1.65	3.053
	boat	2.75	3.893
	ski	5.40	4.960
Weapon	gun	1.03	1.263
	bomb	1.61	-2.882
	bow and arrow	1.98	-2.237
	stick	4.04	*3.776
	rock	4.18	*3.829

Table 6. Additional category members whose
ranks were not significantly different

Category	Members	Means
Animal	cow	2.200
	deer	2.347
Body Part	skin	3.865
	veins	4.000
Drink	milk	2.111
	coffee	2.306
	fruit juice	2.097
Fuel	oil	1.743
	coal	1.811
	paper	4.243
	steam	4.014
Insect	fly	1.947
	ant	1.920
	grasshopper	3.733
	flea	3.427
	grasshopper	3.733
	centipede	3.933
Kitchen Utensil	knife	1.947
	pan	1.671
	stove	4.079
	dish	3.658
	stove	4.079
	potholder	4.316
Toy	swing	5.240
	paint set	4.893
Tree (Test A:	pine	2.972
word stimuli)	birch	2.806
	weeping willow	3.111

Tied ranks

Thirty-four of the 76 subjects assigned tied ranks to at least two members of a single category. These subjects produced a total of 102 instances of tied rankings, including 69 two-member ties, 15 three-member ties, 14 four-member ties, three five-member ties, and 11 failures to rank any member. All categories except *weapon* had ties assigned to members by at least one subject. Table 7 shows the category members which were assigned tied ranks by four or more subjects. Many involve members which are physically dissimilar, which supports Malt and Smith [1984].

Table 7. Categories and members with four or more tied-rank assignments

Category Name	Category Type	Number of Tied Ranks	Members Assigned Tied Ranks
Footwear	Manufactured	8	flipper, ice skate
Toy	Manufactured	7	doll, toy soldier
Tool	Manufactured	6	hammer, pliers, screwdriver
Animal	Naturally Occurring	5	dog, cow
Flower	Naturally Occurring	5	tulip, poppy
Sport	Activity	5	baseball, basketball
Body Part	Part-whole	4	skin, veins
Drink	Non-visual	4	milk, coffee, juice, cider
Fuel	Non-visual	4	coal, oil
Kitchen Utensil	Manufactured	4	broom, stove
Kitchen Utensil	Manufactured	4	broom, dish
Tree	Naturally Occurring	4	oak, pine, birch, willow

The subjects accounting for three or more of the tied-rank assignments (15 subjects) tended to be younger (51-59 years), well-educated, and male. As mentioned earlier there is also evidence that adherence to non-fuzzy classification systems, such as biological taxonomy, contributed to the tied-rank assignments of some subjects.

Content analysis

The semantic relations which played the most important role in the ranking and restriction of membership were MODIFICATION, PART-WHOLE, FUNCTION, AGENT, and OBJECT. The other relations were also present in the data, but were rarely used to rank or to limit membership. INSTRUMENT, for example, was used to define categories of inanimate objects.

but the "effectiveness scale" for FUNCTION was more important in ranking and restricting membership in those categories. Each of the five major relations will be discussed separately.

MODIFICATION is an extremely important relation which was used in the definitions of all categories. It was a major factor in ranking and restricting membership for 17 of the 21 categories studied.

The most widely used type of MODIFICATION relation was the size scale. Many categories had a specific range of acceptable sizes which were sometimes expressed numerically (e.g., *tree*: "between 10 and 60 feet in height"; *insect*: "from hard-to-see to two inches"); sometimes with reference to specific category members (e.g., *tool*: "from jeweler's tools to machines"; *bird*: "hummingbird to ostrich size"); and at times using the human body as a guide (*tool*: "hand to machine size"). Beyond these ranges the categories blend into neighboring sets. *Kitchen utensils* which become too large become *appliances*, *tool* blends into *machine* with increased size, *bird* fades into *insect* making *hummingbird* a suspiciously small *bird* for some subjects, and *trees* that are too small are suspected of being *bushes*.

The typical size of category members was also expressed numerically (e.g., *bird*: "three or four inches long"), with reference to highly typical category members (e.g., *kitchen utensil*: "the size of a three-to-four-quart pot"), or compared with the human body (e.g., *vehicle*: "large enough to get into"; *kitchen utensil*, *bird*, and *tool*: "hand-size"). When subjects used a category member to specify typical size they frequently identified the same member as the best exemplar of the category later in the interview. Another important feature of typical size is that it was not necessarily midway between the largest and smallest acceptable size as can be seen in the examples given above for *bird* and *tool*.

Size was frequently used to eliminate members from categories of creatures, like *bird* and *insect*, and from categories of manufactured objects. Elimination of category members depended upon the size range a subject was willing to allow for a category.

Another frequently used MODIFICATION relation was the beauty/ugliness scale. It is an affective scale based on the perceived beauty/ugliness of both a category and category member which was generally applied to categories of animate objects. Ugly *insects* were judged more insectlike than beautiful *insects*, whereas beautiful *flowers* and *birds* were seen as more representative of their categories than plain category members. *Robin*, which was named the best *bird* exemplar by 66 subjects, was also frequently described as "beautiful" as was *rose* for *flower* and *oak* for *tree*. This scale could also be applied to entire subsets of categories. Cultivated *flowers*, for example, were more flowerlike for some subjects because they are "larger and more beautiful" than wild *flowers*.

Other MODIFICATION relations played important roles in specific categories. Material and form strongly influenced both the ranking and elimination of members in certain categories of manufactured objects: *clothing* must be made of fabric; *kitchen utensils* must have a rigid structure and are more typical if they are metal; and *furniture* which has a rigid structure is more furniture-like. For two of the three highly non-visual categories, form was also important. Granular *seasonings* are the most typical while thickness, especially when coupled with "nourishing," tended to shift members out of *drink* and into *food*. Raw *fruit* was more typical than cooked *fruit*, but this dichotomy did not appear to affect *vegetables* for most subjects. In the activity category, *sport*, "physicalness" was an extremely important criterion for membership as was "being organized or professional" and being "competitive." The team or individual nature of a *sport* varied in importance but was used in ranking. Some subjects used animacy to eliminate objects like *horse* from *vehicle* while other subjects simply rated animate *vehicles* less typical of the category. For the category *weapon* "accessible" was a ranking criterion as was "modern."

MODIFICATION relations operated jointly with other types of relations to rank and/or eliminate member-candidates from target categories. Some of these will be presented in the discussions of other relations.

The PART-WHOLE relation was important in all categories of naturally-occurring objects except the food-forms *fruit* and *vegetable*, the part-whole category (*body part*), two of the three highly non-visual categories (*drink* and *seasoning*), and one of the nine categories of manufactured objects (*vehicle*). It was used primarily to eliminate member-candidates from categories, but it was also employed in ranking. The unimportance of PART-WHOLE for ranking and limiting membership of categories of manufactured objects is partly explained by the greater importance of other relations. However, another factor is the physical variability which characterizes those categories as compared with categories of animate objects. It is possible that this marked asymmetry in the role of PART-WHOLE based on category type is an indication that Superordinate Level manufactured-object categories are farther from the Basic Level than other types of Superordinate categories.

When the PART-WHOLE relation was used to eliminate member-candidates from target categories it was generally attributed to lack of possession of important parts. *Turtles* and *snakes*, for example, were rejected from *animal* because they lack fur or "four legs." Less often rejected members were credited with having parts that are not acceptable in the category. *Turtles* were also rejected as *animals* because they "have a shell" and *soup* was eliminated from *drink* because it "has solids in it." In some cases the PART-WHOLE relation helped identify neighboring or contrast sets. *Flower* was distinguished from *plant* by some subjects because *flowers* "have blossoms" and *plants* do not; *insects* were separated from *bugs* based on the number of legs possessed; *animals* were different from *reptiles* because only *animals* have a combination of four legs and fur; and *birds* were distinct from other creatures because they have both wings and feathers, although for some subjects having feathers was simply a criterion for ranking in this category which allowed *bat* to remain in the category.

The highly non-visual categories and the part-whole category were distinguished from neighboring categories by virtue of being parts themselves. One way in which *seasoning*, for example, differs from *condiment* is that *condiments* were described as having *seasonings* in them; and not only should true *body parts* not contain well-defined sub-parts (as does the *face*), some subjects felt that they should also not be part of many other parts (like *skin* and *veins*). *Soup* was shifted in the direction of *food* rather than *drink* for a similar reason. Not only do *soups* tend to "have solids" in them, but *soup* can be "part of a meal" and *drinks* cannot.

Some PART-WHOLE relations were seen to operate in conjunction with other relations to rank and/or eliminate category members. In this discussion not only the instances of PART-WHOLE and MODIFICATION will be shown, but also the ways in which PART-WHOLE interacted with LOCATIVE, AGENT, and OBJECT.

Sometimes the relations were treated as if they simply joined forces. *Soup*, which was rated very undrink-like because of being "thick" and "nourishing" (MODIFICATION), was even less acceptable when it also "had solids" in it; *vehicles* were seen as being more typical when they had motors and wheels, especially when they were also large enough to "get into."

In other cases one of the relations took precedence. While size is important for the category *tree* it is less critical than "having bark and leaves" which allowed some subjects to accept *bonsai* as an atypical *tree*; having granular structure had a greater impact on acceptability as a *seasoning* than whether or not something contained other *seasonings*; both size and having feathers were important to the category *bird*, but subjects disagreed about which was more critical thus accounting for some of the variation on the relative rankings of *bat* and *chicken*.

FUNCTION proved to be an extremely important criterion for both ranking and restricting membership in all categories except the activity category and categories of naturally-occurring objects. Most of the categories affected by FUNCTION were described as having well-defined functions against which candidate-members were judged. Some of the rejected members were seen as having the wrong primary function for the target category. *Bulletproof vests*, for example, failed as *clothing* because they "protect peo-

ple from other people" rather than "from the environment"; *flipper* and
ice skate are not "for walking" so they were judged to be, at best, borderline *footwear* whereas *socks* were questionable because they act to "protect
the feet from *footwear*"; *milk* "nourishes" rather than "quenches thirst" as
drinks should do; the *tomato* is "used like a *vegetable*" and as a result is
unfruit-like; and a *paint set* is "educational" and "creative" while *toys* are
only supposed to "entertain" and "amuse."

Ranking using FUNCTION was done based on a scale which measures
the effectiveness or necessity of the candidate-member with regard to the
primary function of the target category. Members which were seen to perform the primary function well were described as "versatile," "necessary,"
and "effective" while members which were judged unable to meet the category function satisfactorily were labeled "limited," "unnecessary," or "non-
functional" and assigned borderline or non-member status. Among those
items suffering this fate were *hat* and *pajamas* for *clothing*, *nuts* for *seasoning*, *bolts* for *tool*, and *ski* for *vehicle*. Only for the category *weapon* was
an object denied membership because it met the function too well. Ten
subjects rejected *bomb* as a *weapon* because it could not only kill, it could
be used for "mass destruction."

The pre-eminence of FUNCTION in many categories not only supports
the use of semantic relations as a tool of analysis, it calls into question
the prototype theory as it is currently formulated. This theory constructs
prototypes based largely on physical attributes. However, for the Superordinate Level categories strongly influenced by FUNCTION, typicality has
little to do with physical appearance.

When FUNCTION relations were combined with other relations the
FUNCTION relation was often given more weight. In *furniture*, for example, lack of a rigid structure (MODIFICATION) caused *beanbag chair*
to be judged atypical for the category, but having the right FUNCTION
kept it from being eliminated from the category; atypical *necklaces* may be
made of fabric (MODIFICATION) but they still do not achieve membership in *clothing* because their FUNCTION is to adorn rather than cover
and protect; and a *machine* may have a motor and wheels, but if it was not
designed to carry people or objects it is not a *vehicle*. Counter-examples
include *stove*, which is used for cooking (FUNCTION) but, because of size
(MODIFICATION), stoves were often judged to be borderline members or
non-members of *kitchen utensil*; and *swing* which was seen as too large
(MODIFICATION) to be acceptable as a *toy* even though it is designed
to entertain children. These examples illustrate the importance of the size
scale of MODIFICATION.

The LOCATIVE relations were used to both rank and restrict membership for all types of categories except the activity category. This may be a

artifact of the particular activity category used in this study, however. One important way in which LOCATIVE relations contributed to ranking was in the identification of the typical context of a category. Subjects reported, for example, that "land" *animals*, "outdoor, land" *footwear*, "indoor" *furniture*, and "indoor" *toys* were the most typical subsets of their categories. Some subjects even restricted category membership to these groups. For other categories, subjects disagreed with each other about the typical context. Some stated that internal *body parts* are more body-partlike while others ranked external *body parts* higher in typicality; according to some subjects *insects* found outdoors are more typical, but other subjects felt that indoor *insects* are more *insect*-like; and to some subjects *weapons* that are used "in the street" are more typical while other subjects felt this was true of *weapons* used on a battlefield.

As with other relations already discussed LOCATIVE relations combined with other types of relations to change typicality and membership. Granular (MODIFICATION) *seasonings* which are effective in changing the taste of food (FUNCTION) and which are used in main courses (LOCATIVE) were identified as more typical than *seasonings* which are used in or on desserts; for some subjects parts (PART-WHOLE) of the *face* (LOCATIVE) are not *body parts*; *galoshes* fail as *footwear* because they protect *footwear* instead of protecting the foot (FUNCTION) and they are worn "on top of *footwear*" (LOCATIVE); and *drapes* do not satisfy the FUNCTION of *furniture*, they do not have a rigid structure (MODIFICATION), and they do not "sit on the floor" (LOCATIVE).

Subjects generally restricted the AGENT relation to the three categories of animate beings (*animal, bird,* and *insect*) where it was used to indicate typical behavior, especially modes of locomotion. In a few instances, such as "*seasonings* change the taste of food," subjects blurred the line between AGENT and INSTRUMENT. Unfortunately, it was not possible to explore such statements given the data volume and the goals of this study.

When the AGENT relation was used for the three animate-being categories it was important in both ranking and restriction of membership. *Birds* that fly were judged more *bird*like than those which do not, accounting for the lack of significant difference between the statistical means of *chicken* and *ostrich*; and *animals* that "walk on four legs" were considered to be more typical than *animals* which use other forms of locomotion. Subjects disagreed about whether crawling *insects* or flying *insects* are more *insect*like. Some subjects also used locomotion to distinguish *insects* from *bugs*, but there was disagreement about which fly and which crawl. Marked disagreements of this type sometimes surfaced as lack of statistical difference between the means of category members like *ant* and *fly* in *insect*.

As with other relations, AGENT relations were used as scales. The AGENT scale for *bird* was based on flying ability. Not only were flying *birds* as a group judged more *bird*like than non-flying *birds*, they were ranked on their flying ability. This explains, in part, the most common ranking for that category: *robin, eagle, wren* because many subjects reacted to the flying ability of the *eagle* (another factor is the previously mentioned cultural significance of *robin* and *eagle* as opposed to *wren*). This ranking was used by subjects who viewed pictured stimuli as well as those who saw printed words, and supports the work of researchers cited earlier who question the single category prototype as an adequate explanation for graded membership.

The strongly affective AGENT "pestiness" scale was important for *insect*. Some subjects revealed the significance of this scale from their very first response to the category name, which often was "Insects! I hate them!" One subject predicated so much typicality on this scale that the most insectlike *insect* he could think of was a *snake*. A few subjects applied a similar scale to *animal*. Some subjects rated "friendly" *animals*, like *dogs*, more typical than "vicious" ones while other subjects evaluated typicality the opposite way.

The AGENT relation interacted with other relations to affect typicality and membership. Subjects who highly valued good flying ability tended to rank *bat* above *chicken* in *bird*ness, but the lack of feathers (PART-WHOLE) and the *bat's* ugliness (MODIFICATION) kept it from being a typical *bird*. Similarly, walking (AGENT) combined with having four legs and fur (PART-WHOLE) and staying on land (LOCATIVE) made the subset *land mammal* the most typical members of *animal*.

Although the OBJECT relation was used for all types of categories, it was not as widely used as the other relations which have been discussed. It was most frequently used to eliminate members from categories. *Chickens* were rejected by several subjects as *birds* because "we eat them"; *soup* was not acceptable as a *drink* for the same reason; *swing* was shifted from *toy* to *playground equipment* by several subjects because "you can't pick it up"; and *bolts* were removed from the *tool* category because "you use *tools* on *bolts*." *Bolts* also "remain in the product" which is another way of indicating that they behave like OBJECTS rather than like INSTRUMENTS as *tools* should.

The OBJECT relation sometimes signaled typical agents or agents which were unacceptable for the target category. The typical agents of *weapon*, for example, which were identified by the OBJECT relation were "criminals," "police," "soldiers," and "hunters"; for *toy* it was "children"; for *tool* they were "carpenters," "janitors," and "mechanics." When a member-candidate had an atypical agent it was often rejected from the target category. *Wind chimes* were not acceptable as a *musical instrument* because they are not played by "people"; *broom* was rejected as a *kitchen utensil* by one subject because "janitors use them"; another subject eliminated *tape measure* from *tool* because "women use them" indicating that women were not seen as being carpenters, janitors, or mechanics; and one subject also rejected *chess* as a *sport* because "an older person plays it."

In two instances the OBJECT relation was used to rank within a category. *Stick* was judged by one subject to be a borderline *weapon* because it is used by "other cultures"; and subjects disagreed about whether *toys* used specifically by one sex are more or less *toy*like.

OBJECT relations also combined with other relations to eliminate member-candidates from target categories. Generally, however, OBJECT had less influence on decisions about membership than the other relations. *Sticks*, for example, were judged to be poor *weapons* more because they are not effective (FUNCTION) and because they have other primary uses (FUNCTION) than because other cultures use them (OBJECT); *brooms* failed as *kitchen utensils* primarily because they are not used to cook (FUNCTION) and as a result of their use in more places than the kitchen (LOCATIVE), but having an atypical agent added to their unacceptability; *chickens* were seen as bad examples of *bird* principally because they are big (MODIFICATION) and they are not thought to fly (AGENT), but the fact that we eat them (OBJECT) makes them even less *bird*like; and *soup*'s membership in *drink* was questioned on the basis of its thickness (MODIFICATION) and because it can have solids in it (PART-WHOLE) both of which make it more likely that we will eat rather than drink it (OBJECT).

Conclusions and recommendations

This study has shown that research on populations other than college sophomores is of value to the field of membership gradation. On the one hand, the role of expertise and of varying levels of knowledge of scientific classification systems in reducing intersubject agreement levels indicates that these factors are more widespread, complex, and influential than previously thought. On the other hand, agreement between the rankings done here and those done by college sophomores suggests that category typicality is a cultural phenomenon.

The use of semantic relations to analyze qualitative data provided clear support for the hypothesis that distinct category types exist and that they differ with regard to the characteristics which contribute to typicality. The analysis also showed that physical attributes, which have been pre-eminent in prior research, play a minor role in determining typicality for specific

Superordinate Level categories and category types, and that such things as function, location, and affect may be central to typicality. This helps account for Malt and Smith's [1984] observation that physically dissimilar objects may be assigned equivalent membership grades; but more importantly, it demonstrates that in order to understand membership gradation fully the research in this field must use powerful, highly-organized analytic tools, like semantic relations. The fact that semantic relations can also be used to construct complex models of concept structure is an added benefit.

Several areas of future research are suggested by the results of this study. Continued investigation using diverse populations would shed light on the extent to which typicality patterns are culturally shared. Such research could also clarify the roles of specialized knowledge and expertise in membership gradation patterns as well as the degree to which individual differences attenuate culturally shared information. Another benefit that could be derived from research on diverse populations is greater insight into the nature of category dominance. The findings of this study suggest that dominance and typicality are, in part, manifestations of cultural significance. To substantiate this, of course, would require continued use of qualitative, as well as quantitative data.

More research needs to be done on different category types and levels. This study found that Superordinate Level manufactured object categories, for example, are structured very differently from categories of naturally-occurring objects. By using semantic relations as an analytic tool it would be possible to explore non-physical as well as physical characteristics in a systematic fashion, the relative importance and roles of different types of information which may be used in decisions about typicality, and the interaction which exists among varying types of information.

Further research on tied ranks would also shed light on the relative importance of different types of information for membership gradation. If, for example, two category members differ in typical agent as well as specific MODIFICATION and PART-WHOLE relations, but are seen to have the same FUNCTION with equivalent effectiveness, will they be assigned similar membership grades?

Further exploration into fuzzy boundaries would contribute to the understanding of the kinds of information that most affect acceptability in a category as well as lending support to knowledge gathered in other types of studies regarding the interaction of semantic relations. At the same time it would offer valuable insights into how a larger taxonomy of categories might be structured.

References

Battig, W., and W. Montague. 1969. Category Norms for Verbal Items in 56 Categories: A Replication and Extension of the Connecticut Category Norms. *Journal of Experimental Psychology Monograph*, **80**, part 2.

Evens, M., B. Litowitz, J. Markowitz, R. Smith, and O. Werner. 1980. *Lexical-Semantic Relations: A Comparative Study*. Edmonton, Alberta, Canada: Linguistic Research, Inc.

Fillmore, C., D. Kempler, and W. Wang, Eds. 1978. *Individual Differences in Language Ability and Language Behavior*. New York: Academic Press.

Howell, W. 1973. Effects of Organization on Discrimination of Word-Frequency Within and Between Categories. *Journal of Experimental Psychology*, **99**, 255-260.

Malt, B., and E. Smith. 1982. The Role of Familiarity in Determining Typicality. *Memory and Cognition*, **10**, 69-75.

Malt, B., and E. Smith. 1984. Correlated Properties in Natural Categories. *Journal of Verbal Learning and Verbal Behavior*, **23**, 250-269.

Markowitz, J., and R. Moses. 1981. What is Rugtime? Linguistic Variation among First Graders. In C. S. Masek, R. A. Hendrick, and M. F. Miller, Eds., *Papers from the Parasession on Language and Behavior of the Chicago Linguistics Society*. Chicago: Chicago Linguistic Society, 156-164.

McCloskey, M. 1980. The Stimulus Familiarity Problem in Semantic Memory Research. *Journal of Verbal Learning and Verbal Behavior*, **19**, 485-502.

McCloskey, M., and S. Glucksberg. 1978. Natural Categories: Well-Defined or Fuzzy Sets? *Memory and Cognition*, **6**, 462-472.

Mervis, C., J. Catlin, and E. Rosch. 1976. Relationships among Goodness-of-Example, Category Norms, and Word-Frequency. *Bulletin of the Psychonomic Society*, **7**, 283-284.

Mervis, C., and E. Rosch. 1981. Categorization of Natural Objects. *Annual Review of Psychology*, **32**, 89-115.

Oden, G. 1977. Fuzziness in Semantic Memory: Choosing Exemplars of Subjective Categories. *Memory and Cognition*, **5**, 198-204.

Osherson, E., and E. Smith. 1981. On the Adequacy of Prototype Theory as a Theory of Concepts. *Cognition*, **9**, 35-58.

Rosch, E. 1973. On the Internal Structure of Perceptual and Semantic Categories. In T. Moore, Ed., *Cognitive Development and the Acquisition of Language*. New York: Academic Press.

Rosch, E. 1975. Cognitive Representation of Semantic Categories. *Journal of Experimental Psychology*, **104**, 192-233.

Rosch, E. 1977. Human Categorization. In N. Warren, Ed., *Advances in Cross-Cultural Psychology* (Volume 1). London: Academic Press.

Rosch, E. 1978. Principles of Categorization. In E. Rosch and B. Lloyd, Eds., *Cognition and Categorization*. Hillsdale, New Jersey: Lawrence Erlbaum Associates, Inc., 111-144.

Rosch, E., and C. Mervis. 1975. Family Rescmblances: Studies in the Internal Structure of Categories. *Cognitive Psychology*, 7, 573-605.

Rosch, E., C. Mervis, W. Gray, W. Johnson, and P. Boyes-Braem. 1976. Basic Objects in Natural Categories. *Cognitive Psychology*, 8, 382-439.

Rosch, E., E. Simpson, and S. Miller. 1976. Structural Bases of Typicality Effects. *Journal of Experimental Psychology: Human Perception and Performance*, 2, 491-502.

Spradley, J. 1979. *The Ethnographic Interview*. New York: Holt, Rinehart and Winston.

Tversky, A. 1977. Features of Similarity. *Psychological Review*, 84, 327-352.

Werner, O., G. Schoepfle, M. Iris, and D. Bouck. 1976. *Handbook of Ethnoscience*. Evanston, Illinois: Department of Anthropology, Northwestern University.

Wittgenstein, L. 1953. *Philosophical Investigations*. New York: MacMillan.

Zadeh, L. 1965. Fuzzy Sets. *Information and Control*, 8, 338-353.

Zadeh, L. 1971. Fuzzy Languages and Their Relation to Human and Machine Intelligence. Memorandum No. ERL-M302. Berkeley, California: University of California Electronics Research Laboratory.

Zadeh, L. 1976. A Fuzzy-Algorithmic Approach to the Definition of Complex or Imprecise Concepts. *International Journal of Man-Machine Studies*, 8, 249-291.

Zadeh, L., K-S. Fu, K. Tanaka, and M. Shimura, Eds. 1975. *Fuzzy Sets and Their Applications to Cognitive and Decision Processes*. New York: Academic Press.

Zadeh, L., and T. Lee. 1969. Note on Fuzzy Languages. *Information Sciences*, 1, 421-434.

12
Problems of the part-whole relation*

MADELYN ANNE IRIS
DEPARTMENT OF ANTHROPOLOGY
NORTHWESTERN UNIVERSITY
EVANSTON, ILLINOIS 60208

BONNIE E. LITOWITZ
DEPARTMENT OF LINGUISTICS
NORTHWESTERN UNIVERSITY
EVANSTON, ILLINOIS 60208

MARTHA EVENS
COMPUTER SCIENCE DEPARTMENT
ILLINOIS INSTITUTE OF TECHNOLOGY
CHICAGO, ILLINOIS 60616

Abstract

The nature of the part-whole relation has been particularly mysterious and controversial. Argument has centered around two basic issues: is this relation transitive? and should it be treated as a semantic primitive? On the basis of our analysis of dictionary data from *Webster's Seventh Collegiate Dictionary* (hereafter W7), we find the part-whole relation to have

* This research was supported by the National Science Foundation under grant IST 85-10069.

four different senses: the relation of the functional component to its whole,
the relation of the segment to the segmented whole, the membership relation, and the set-inclusion relation. These four senses generate four distinct
models of the part-whole relation. These four models explain some well-
known contradictions. First, some senses of part-whole are transitive while
others are not. Second, some authors claim part-whole is a logical primitive
while others view it as derived from more primitive components. Although
the part-whole relation is of prime importance in human cognitive processing, some senses of the relation seem to appear earlier than others; that
is, some are more primitive developmentally than others. In this paper
we argue that the part-whole relation should be treated as a collection of
relations, not as a single relation.

The problems

The part-whole relation has long been a source of confusion and controversy. Even within the same discipline scholars argue about whether it is
transitive or not. There are disagreements as well about whether it should
be treated as a semantic primitive. Lyons [1977] introduces the problem
of the transitivity of the part-whole relation with several illustrations that
have become notorious. He first gives an example in which transitivity
holds: "The sleeve has a cuff; the coat has a sleeve; the coat has a cuff."
Then he gives one where it fails: "The door has a handle; the house has
a door; the house has a handle." [Vol.I: p. 313]. He suggests a possible
solution to this problem:

> The fact that different authors disagree about this point is
> perhaps an indication that there are various kinds of part-
> whole relations in language .... [Vol.I: p. 312]

We have followed Lyons' suggestion of looking at different kinds of part-
whole, as have Winston, Chaffin, and Herrmann [1987], while others [Cruse
1979] have turned to contextual constraints for explanations.

There is an equally profound dispute about the primitiveness of the part-
whole relation. *Primitive* can have several meanings. [See Carey 1982 for
a discussion of this question.] First, primitive is related to *prime*, that is,
fundamental to the ways in which humans organize knowledge. In a second
sense, *primitive* is seen as initial or original in order of development. A
third sense of *primitive* is used in logic: we can ask whether the part-whole
relation is a logical primitive, whether it is an atomic concept or one with
meaning derived from others. It has been found that children do not often
use the term *part* in their definitions [Litowitz and Novy 1984], yet *part*
is the second most common noun appearing in definitions of other nouns

in W7 [Smith 1985]. We found that an examination of the ways in which different speakers express the part-whole relation could tell us more about the primitive nature of this relation.

The relational model of lexical/semantic knowledge

The theoretical context of this study of the part-whole relation is the relational model of human semantic memory. There are currently several major models of semantic organization, including field models, componential or feature models, and relational models. This paper is rooted in the relational approach, which focuses on semantic domains and accepts the supposition that there are common properties that bind the items in a semantic domain together, as well as properties that differentiate items from each other. However, the significant question in a relational model is how all the items are related. A relational model represents human semantic memory as a network in which each node is a concept and concepts are linked together by a variety of semantic and lexical relations.

Much of the major research in lexical-semantic relations has been reviewed in Evens et al. [1980] which includes a comparison of various relational models of semantic organization in anthropology, computer science, linguistics, and psychology. [See also Chaffin and Herrmann this volume; Cruse 1986.] Taxonomy, modification, synonymy, antonymy, and grading appear in some form in almost all relational models. In contrast, the part-whole relation is sometimes treated as fundamental, sometimes treated as a complex relation derived from other relations, and sometimes ignored altogether.

The part-whole relation seems to play a rather ambiguous role in anthropology. In their pioneering work in lexical-semantic relations Casagrande and Hale [1967] categorize the relations in 800 folk definitions in Papago. They did not find the part-whole relation in their sample. They classify as *spatial* the definition: "*tongue*: ... which stands in our mouth," and they use the name *exemplification* for the relation that appears in "*wing*: ... any kind of bird has wings." In the discussion section of their paper, however, on the basis of their experience as speakers of English, they posit a constituent relation, which applies when "X is defined as being a constituent or part of Y." The example they give is "a cheek is part of a face."

In the late 1960's Werner started the research on Navajo medical terms that led to the *Anatomical Atlas of the Navajo* [Werner et al. 1969/1981]. At that point he treated the part-whole relation, like the taxonomy relation, as a logical primitive. In later work, however, he concludes that the part-whole relation is a "complex" rather than an "atomic" relation. He now analyzes "a thumb is part of the hand" as "a thumb is a kind of hand-part" [Werner and Topper 1976], and derives the part-whole relation from taxonomy.

In one of the earliest psychological studies using the relational model, Collins and Quillian [1972] actually name this relation *Part* (giving *nose-face* as an example) and distinguish it carefully from the relation they call *Location*. Riegel [1970] separates *Part* and *Whole* into two distinct relations, labelling them both as infra-logical relations, i.e., relations based on the denoted objects, events, or qualities ...a product of abstracting physical features from items, as in "*zebra-stripes,*" or "*table-leg.*" Hermann, Chaffin, and Winston [1986] find that subjects analyze examples of parts and wholes into several different categories. Their experiment is discussed in some detail below, and their results compared with our findings.

The part-whole relation does not appear by name in the relational model of the Soviet linguists Apresyan, Mel'čuk, and Žolkovsky [1970]. Instead, they posit several more specific relations, such as the relation Cap as in Cap(*tribe*) = *chief*. The Centr relation expresses the relation between a concept and its central point or peak as in Centr(*life*) = *prime*. Sing designates the name for a countable chunk carved out of a mass, as in Sing(*news*) = *item*. When queried recently as to why the part-whole relation *per se* does not appear in their long list of lexical functions, Mel'čuk (personal communication) replied that he felt it was far too general to be useful. The implication of his statement is that the part-whole relation is too all-inclusive to serve as the basis for precise reasoning. Wierzbicka, on the other hand, treats part (with particular emphasis on body parts) as one of the thirteen semantic primes on which her whole semantic system is based in *Lingua Mentalis* [1980]. Cruse [1979] views part-whole as a unitary relation but attempts to untangle the transitivity issue by considering the physical context of specific parts and wholes. We will return to Cruse's position below in our discussion of transitivity.

Several computer scientists have used the part-whole relation in natural language processing systems. One of the first question-answering systems, Raphael's [1968] SIR system, uses a relation called Have-As-Parts. This relation holds between *people* and *hands* and also between *hands* and *fingers*. Raphael makes clear his conviction that this relation is transitive. In fact, he uses this transitivity to conclude that people have fingers as parts. In Simmons' [1973] question answering system this relation is called "HASPART." Simmons and Amsler [1975] apply the part-whole relation to verbs as well as to nouns; *to talk* is part of *to arbitrate*. The part-whole relation plays a very important role in Fahlman's [1979] computer model of semantic memory. He treats this relation, which he calls "PART-OF," as transitive and uses the same algorithms to exploit the transitivity of the PART-OF relation and the IS-A (taxonomy) relation.

While people in other disciplines seem uncertain about the primitive nature of this relation, major figures in modern philosophy unequivocally treat part-whole as a primitive term. In the 1920's the Polish philosopher Lesnièwski published a series of papers formulating the theory of this concept, which he termed Merology (the Greek word for part is *Meros*). This is just one component of a theory known in this country as the calculus of individuals [Rescher 1975]. In the the late 1930's the philosopher-biologist J.H. Woodger [1937] developed an axiomatic system to express the fundamental concepts of biology. This system is based on ten undefined terms, one of which is Part. His use of the relation is very general, including both spatial and temporal parts. The logician Tarski, who had studied in Warsaw under Lesnièwski and Lukasiewicz, developed a formal theory of *Part* and *Time*, which is an advance on both Woodger's and Lesnièwski's work and which appears as an appendix to Woodger's book. Both Woodger and Tarski treat the relation as transitive. More recently the American philosopher Richard Martin [1971] has reformulated the theory of the part-whole relation as part of his calculus of events, which gives an elegant basis for reasoning about both space and time. Martin treats the transitivity of the part relation as axiomatic.

The methodology

In this paper we examine the various ways in which English speakers express this relation. We ask if this variety reflects differences in both underlying knowledge and in labelling practices for parts and wholes. We are led to ask these questions for several reasons:

1. English has a wealth of terms, many of which are specifically collocational, for expressing the part-whole relations (in contrast to category membership, which is almost always expressed either by "is a" or "is a kind of").

2. Among all these terms, however, the word *part* is privileged; it gives its name to the relation and it also appears as the second most frequent noun (after *act*) in noun definitions in W7 [Smith 1981].

3. In spite of this frequency at the culturally consensual level, studies indicate that young children's use of *part* is rare and inconsistent [Litowitz and Novy 1984]. This early labelling practice seems to reflect what theorists claim is a preclass or precategorial cognitive structure based on physical not on logico-mathematical knowledge [Inhelder and Piaget 1964; Riegel 1970].

4. Among theorists who have examined it, the part-whole relation has been viewed as derived from taxonomy [Werner
and Topper 1976], made up of smaller semantic features
[Chaffin and Herrmann 1986, this volume], pervasive [Mel'-
čuk personal communication], and ambiguously related to
taxonomy [Winston et al. 1987].

If the conceptual underpinnings of partness remain tied to the highly
variable physical world, and if the ways that partness is appropriately labelled also change, then variability among theorists may mean that they
are looking at different aspects of these phenomena and looking at them in
different ways.

There have been three approaches to investigations of semantic relations.
The first is model-building, where theorists seek to create a system of relations that will account for a given body of conceptual, semantic or lexical
knowledge by means of an exhaustive number of specific relations or a par-
simonious few, more general ones. [See Werner this volume.]

A second approach focuses on testing the psychological reality of relations in general or of particular relations. Such studies employ measures
traditional in the psychological literature such as multidimensional scal-
ing of similarity judgments and elapsed response time analyses. A basic
assumption of this approach is that knowledge can be assessed on the basis of differential behavioral reponses to a problem-solving task which has
been constructed according to the underlying theoretical assumptions of
the experimenters; for example, longer response time on tasks of category
membership indicates a greater distance between the member and the center of the category; or stimulus items that vary along a particular dimension
will evoke responses that validate the reality of that dimension. [See Clark
and Clark 1977, for example.]

A third approach is to use naturally occurring language rather than behavioral responses to language stimuli as evidence. A basic assumption of
this approach is that differences in language performance constitute and
reflect underlying differences in knowledge. In this paper we use this third
approach to investigate the relations between parts and wholes, since we believe the more traditional approaches offered by psychology are inappropriate in this ill-defined situation. We are urged on by our diverse experience
with the use of the part-whole relation in natural language, in dictionaries,
and in computer question-answering systems. The approach used reflects
our multi-disciplinary biases; in particular, our concern with examining the
way lexical-semantic relations are used in various natural language contexts. Our tendency is to be more "ethnographic" and exploratory and less
concerned with hypothesis testing within pre-determined boundaries.

The data set

In our investigation of the problems of the part-whole relation, an English language dictionary was used as a source of information on the part-whole relation. A dictionary was chosen as a data source for several reasons. It is perceived to represent an ideal speaker with perfect control of the vocabularies of diverse subcultures. Entries in the dictionary we used, *Webster's Seventh Collegiate Dictionary* (W7), are based on a large collection of citations which is constantly augmented from a wide selection of American writers [Olney 1968]. Thus, this dictionary represents not only an ideal speaker but a consensual one as well. Furthermore, W7 represents a "literate" speaker, in which the Aristotelian model of the ideal definitional form is fully incorporated in the act of definition-making.

In previous writings [see Iris et al. forthcoming], we have discussed the developmental aspects of the part-whole relation and the way in which definition-making develops from a situationally-oriented to an Aristotelian form. As part of this initial inquiry into the nature of the part-whole relation, descriptions of parts were gathered from both children and university students. Data collection techniques included collecting verbal descriptions of parts and wholes from children [as described in Litowitz and Novy 1984] and written definitions of body parts and synonyms of *part* from university students. These activities produced a data set that exhibits numerous features associated with natural language, such as idiosyncratic usage and non-repetitiveness. Our findings were used to answer questions regarding the developmental aspects of the part-whole relation [described in Iris et al. forthcoming] as well as to generate initial versions of the various models of the part-whole relation described below. In our discussion here, however, we focus attention on the findings from the dictionary data alone, in order to refine the four models and address the questions of transitivity and primitiveness.

The analysis of the dictionary data was a multi-stage process. With kind permission of the G & C Merriam Company, we obtained a copy of the machine-readable version of W7 from Raoul Smith of Northeastern University. From these tapes we selected the definitions of those nouns that occurred more than eight times in Kučera and Francis' [1964] million words of running English text. Next, using a KWIC (Keyword in Context) index we examined all occurrences of *part* in these definitions. These were separated into two types: (1) Examples of the taxonomy of *part* itself, as in "edge...the narrow, adjacent part," "fat...the best or richest part"; and (2) Examples of the part-whole relation, as in "leaf ...part of a book" or "floor ... part of a room." The examples given here are all from W7.

Analysis of the dictionary data

By far the most common type of part used in noun definitions is the functional part. For example:

> *Drum* is a part of a *machine*
> *Horn* is a part of an *animal*
> *Disk* is a part of a *plow*
> *Finger* is a part of a *glove*
> *Knee* is a part of a *leg*

While most functional parts are discrete, named entities, some are continuous and are, therefore, really pieces that are not readily detachable. For example:

> *Flame* is a part of *fire*
> *Flesh* is a part of *fruit*
> *Green* is a part of the *spectrum*

In some cases, specific portions or segments of the whole are identified as a significant part. For example:

> *Gulf* is part of the *ocean* or *sea*
> *Knee* is a part of a *garment*
> *Ford* and *Harbor* are parts of a *body of water*
> *Echo* is part of a *wave*
> *Light* is part of a *range*

When the whole is a temporal or spatial sequence, parts become measured (or measurable) segments. For example:

> *Instance* is part of a *process* or *series*
> *Episode* is part of a *series*
> *Hour* is part of a *day*
> *Evening* is a part of a *day*
> *Half* is part of a *thing*

In fact, any entity can be segmented in this way to yield first or front parts; for example, the tip of a horn is the topmost part of a part of an animal. To express this fact, the dictionary lists many terms taxonomically related to *part*. For example:

> *Front* is the forward part or surface
> *Edge* is the narrow adjacent part

       Interior is the inland part
       Height is the highest part

Besides such locative distinctions, the dictionary definitely distinguishes evaluative and functional parts:

       Fat is the best or richest part
       Elite is the choicest part, esp. a socially superior group
       Grip is the part by which something is grasped
       Extension is the part constituting an addition

Such terms are generalizable distinctions of *part* as such and should be separated from specific instances of part-whole relationships that exist between specific parts and specific wholes. Of these latter, as we have seen, the functional and piece or segment relationships appear most frequently in the dictionary definitions of nouns containing the word *part*.

There are other terms, however, besides *part*, that are used in noun definitions. W7 distinguishes the synonyms of *part* as follows:

> PART is a general term interchangeable with any of the others; PORTION implies an assigned or allotted part; PIECE applies to a separated or detached part of a whole; MEMBER suggests one of the functional parts composing a body; DIVISION and SECTION imply a part made by cutting, ...; SEGMENT applies to a part separated or marked out by natural lines of cleavage; FRAGMENT applies to a part produced accidentally as by breaking off or shattering

We have examined definitions that used these synonyms of *part*, in addition to those using *part* itself. The general distinction between the use of *piece* and *segment* corresponds to the difference presented earlier between discrete entities which compose a whole and continuous wholes which are segmented. So, for example, *king* is a chesspiece and *kiss* is a piece of candy; whereas *lap* is a segment of a journey and *arc* is a segment of a circle. *Piece* can, in addition, be used for a discrete unit, as *item* of news or *job* of work. In these instances, *piece* becomes a unitizing noun [Jespersen 1933]. Occasionally, *piece* is used to indicate substance or provenience: *flag* is a piece of fabric; *fur* is a piece of pelt; *furniture* is a piece of wood. In these cases, a phrase – "is made from" – seems to have been elided. This use of *piece* seems to misdirect our attention from part to substance. Such usage may be the source of the "stuff" relations described by Chaffin and his colleagues [this volume].

Division is a general synonym for *segment* (*era* is a division of geological time; *field* is a division of activity). *Division* is also used as a synonym for functional part (*head* is a division of a body) and piece (*lesson* is a division of a *course*). *Portion* also identifies a part or piece segmented from the whole: *leg* is a portion of a trip (but *lap* is a segment of a journey); *heading* is a portion of a mast; *helping* is a portion of food. Portion may also be used as a synonym of part, in general. For example: *land* is a portion of the earth's surface; *gum* is a portion of the jaw.

Thus far, we have not discussed two other kinds of part-whole relationships, collection-member and set-subset. The dictionary indicates these relationships in noun definitions by *member, including, comprising,* and *containing. Element* is defined both as a constituent part and as a member of a set or class. There is a wide range of examples involving *member*:

> *Fellow* is a member of a *group* or *college*
> *Engineer* is a member of a *military group*
> *Duke* is a member of a *peerage*
> *Guerrilla* is a member of a *unit*

Occasionally, *member* also identifies functional parts instead of elements of sets (*fingers* are members of the hand) and subsets (*divisions* are members of a parliamentary body).

The partitive gerunds *including, comprising,* and *containing,* indicate many different part-whole relations. *Including* seems to be used very generally to indicate every kind of part-whole relation, such as,

> functional parts:
> *Eye* – including *eyelids, eyelashes, eyebrows*
> *Face* – including the *chin, mouth, nose, cheeks, eyes*
> *Life* – including *metabolism, growth, reproduction*

> segmented wholes:
> *Spike* is an ear including *seeds* and ...

> collection-member:
> *Light* is radiation including *infrared, visible, ultraviolet*

> set-subset:
> *House* is a family including *ancestors, descendants,* and *kindred*
> *Grain* ... including *cereal grasses*

Comprising seems to be almost as general though our examples do not include functional parts.

> segmented whole:
> *Foot* is a unit comprising twelve *inches*

> collection-member:
> *Labor* is a group comprising those who do manual labor
> *Heart* is a suit comprising *cards*

> set-subset:
> *Family* ...comprising *genera*

Containing and *contains* seem to be the most general of all – implying not just part-whole but substance; *consisting of* seems to imply substance primarily. For example:

> *Head* ...contains the *brain*
> *Ice* is a dessert containing *fruit juice*
> *Fountain* is a reservoir containing *liquid*
> *Food* is material containing or consisting of *carbohydrates*

Partitive gerunds focus on the whole and provide a means of listing parts relevant to that whole. The form of such definitions is Aristotelian with the partitive differentiae introduced by the partitive gerunds. In contrast, *part, piece, segment, portion*, and *division* focus on the part and mark its relation to the whole by a genitive phrase ("of –"). The need to shift foci between parts and wholes is related to the variety of expressions available for part-whole relations and has been noted elsewhere [e.g., Litowitz and Novy 1984]. For example, often children who use the word *part* explicitly when focus is on the part (*teeth* are part of the *mouth*) shift focus to the whole with *have* (the *mouth* has *teeth*).

In summary, two major types of part-whole relation appear very directly in the dictionary definitions of nouns: functional part and segmented whole. These relationships are directly labeled as *part* or by some variant of *part* specified as a synonym in the dictionary definition of *part*, such as *piece, segment, division*, or *portion*. Two additional types of part-whole relationships appear in the definitions: collection-element and set-subset. These tend to be expressed by some other term such as *member*, or, when the focus is on the whole, by *including, comprising*, or *containing*. We now turn to a more detailed discussion of these four types of part-whole relations, and to their implications for the problems identified earlier: transitivity and primitiveness.

Four models of the part-whole relation

Our analysis of the W7 data confirmed the conviction developed during our experiments with human informants [Iris et al. forthcoming] that the part-whole relation is best understood as a family of relations rather than as one single relation. We gradually developed four models or schemata of this family, expressing the functional component, the segmented whole, the collection-member, and the set-subset aspects of part-whole.

The functional component

The first schema views the part as a functioning unit in a whole, such as an organ of the body or an engine in a car. The part, in this sense, contributes to the whole, not just as a structural unit but as essential to the purposeful activity of the whole. Figure 1 illustrates this sense.

Figure 1. Functional component of a whole

In Figure 1 the parts may exist prior to their inclusion in the whole, as in the parts of a bicycle. In fact, the whole is built up out of the logical and systematic assemblage of its parts. However, this is not true in all instances, since the organs of the body, though they may exist outside of the body itself (due to the miracles of modern medicine), derive their meaning from their inclusion in the whole and function solely with reference to it.

The relation between an event and its features or a plan and its component activities also seems to partake in some abstract way of the notion of functional part, but these concepts also involve the notion of queuing or sequencing. Certainly setting the oven temperature and putting the mixture in the pan are both parts of the script for baking a cake, but it is important to perform these steps in the right time sequence or the cake will fall flat.

The segmented whole

This schema emphasizes the whole which is divided into pieces like a pie, as shown in Figure 2. This conception of the part-whole relation implies the removability of the part or the divisibility of the whole. Some sense of entatitivity is attributed to the part, even though it may be removed from its whole. In some cases the part has a predetermined size and shape. For example, we find naturally occurring segments, as in a grapefruit or layers of mica schist. A slice of bread, though not naturally occurring, also connotes a particular shape, size, and thickness. A piece of pie generally implies a consistent shape and maximum size (that is, less than a quarter of the whole). In contrast, other part-denoting words such as fragment or scrap carry with them the implication of entatitivity but no particular shape or size.

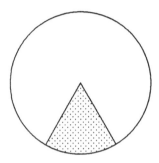

Figure 2. The segmented whole

In all these instances one senses that the whole must precede the part. One cannot have a piece of pie before the pie exists, nor does a section of fruit exist without reference to the whole fruit. This seems to be true even for those parts without a given size or shape; a handful of sand cannot exist without the sandpile.

The count/mass distinction reflects in language the difference between the discrete and the continuous whole. Count nouns label elements that the language considers distinguishable and discrete. Sometimes this distinction seems more conventional than actual: *bean* is a count noun, *rice* a mass noun. Count and mass nouns take different quantifiers: *many/few beans* vs. *much/little rice*. We also find a number of specialized terms for parts of mass nouns that do not necessarily apply to count nouns. Jespersen [1933] comments on the plethora of individuation terms in English, which give us names for countable chunks of masses. Some individuation nouns are highly specific, e.g., a *grain* of rice, a *lump* of sugar, while others are more generic, e.g., a *piece* of cake, a *slice* of pie. Jespersen notes the extension of these more generic terms to abstract, immaterial mass-words: a *bit* of information, a *piece* of folly, news, or advice. Masses tend to form amorphous wholes which can be given boundaries by general collective nouns, e.g., a *pile* of sand, a *bunch* of pebbles, or by measurement nouns, a *pail* of sand, a *cup* of rice. *Inch, foot,* and *yard,* like *cup, pint, quart,* and *gallon,* all give us names for segments of wholes. [See Sowa 1984.]

We also have a set of measurement nouns for time and names for time divisions, but these are, in an important sense, more complex and more abstract than the notion of the physical, spatial segmented whole. It might be argued that inches and feet are abstractions imposed upon the world by man, just like seconds, minutes, and hours, but we can see and feel inches and feet in a concrete and physical way not possible with time divisions.

Should named times like *Valentine's Day* be considered as parts? We could say that Valentine's Day is a part of the month of February and thus answer this question in the affirmative, but it is clear that the queuing or sequencing relation is at least as important as the part-whole relation here. We think of Valentine's Day as February 14, as coming after Lincoln's Birthday and before Washington's Birthday, not primarily as a part of February, although it is located in that month.

When the whole is not specified or discretely bounded, parts may be viewed as a collection, e.g., a collection of grains of rice, or of beans.

Collections and members

In this sense the relationship of part to whole is the relationship of member to collection or element to set. In its simplest form this schema denotes a physical collection or aggregate of objects that are spatially close together, but have no particular structural organization, as shown in Figure 3.

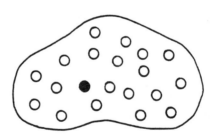

Figure 3. Member of a collection

English has a number of special words for collections, such as *gaggle* of geese or *pride* of lions or *flock* of sheep. The collection may well be transitory in time. The members of the flock may stray. The gaggle exists only as a more or less temporary unit which may vary in size, shape, membership, etc., from one time or instance to another. Sometimes there are names for special members of the collection. The boatswain has a special function among the hands that make up the crew.

This simple and concrete notion becomes abstract as we consider logical collections instead of physical collections. We can define a set or collection in terms of the properties of its members, e.g., the set of mammals can be defined as vertebrates with hair.

Sets and subsets

This model of part-whole is based on the more primitive one of member and collection. The set A is a subset of the set B if and only if every member of A is also a member of B. Figure 4A gives a simple illustration of a subset of a set. This notion of set is basic to the abstractions of modern mathematics.

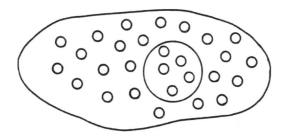

Figure 4A. A subset of a set

Often subsets within a set that have a special meaning acquire labels of their own. For example, within the collection of objects in the world which we, as native speakers of English and as members of the American culture, label food, there are subsets labeled meat and fruit.

Whenever we have sets and subsets we have a potential hierarchy. The subset of fruit can be broken down into smaller subsets containing apples, pears, and pineapples, among others. Hierarchies are often represented by tree diagrams, to make them easier to visualize. Figure 4B shows a partial tree of the domain of food.

As members of the western culture we are educated to think and particularly to make definitions in terms of hierarchies of sets and subsets. The "ideal" (Aristotelian) definition begins by specifying the "genus," the term in the hierarchy that comes next as we go up the tree. Thus, we learn to define *apple* as a kind of fruit.

The traditional notion that categorization and classification tasks are actually performed by reference to mental versions of these hierarchies in which lower members share properties which include them in the higher class and are differentiated from other members of that class by other, unshared properties has been called into question. Rosch's work [1978], based on Zadeh's [1965] notion of fuzzy sets, recasts Figure 4A as Figure 3 with some added internal structure. In this view members are related to the class of which they are a part by family resemblance; the most prototypic member is central, and less typical members are peripheral. So the internal structure of categories is portrayed not as an inclusive and contrastive hierarchy, but as a whole with spatially displayed parts. Markman et al. [1980] have emphasized the differences between collections and classes in such natural language pairs as *child-family* and *tulip-flower*.

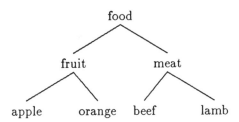

Figure 4B. Partial tree of the domain of food

Among all our models only that shown in Figures 4A and 4B, the setsubset model, carries the notion of class-inclusion and hierarchy. The other three share the notion of contrastive organization within a bounded whole, but not the multi-level hierarchic organization.

Discussion of the models

These various senses of part-whole lead us to examine variations in the naming or citing of parts and wholes themselves. For example, elements, as shown in Figure 3, tend to have labels, even though we do not necessarily distinguish them from each other (e.g., cells are parts of the body). Subsets, as shown in Figures 4A and 4B, and functional components, as shown in Figure 1, usually have individual labels. Segments (Figure 2) may have special labels or may be named by generic terms like *piece*. The wholes in Figures 1 and 2 are likely to have names, as do the top and bottom nodes in the hierarchy. Labels for intermediate nodes in hierarchies may be hard to elicit or only known by experts [Werner and Topper 1976].

In addition, changes in focus, context, or condition may make one part-whole relation merge into another. For example, if the bicycle is disassembled and its functional parts are laid out in a circle on the ground, they can be viewed as a collection of objects while their function is relatively obscure. This observation has led some authors to assume that relations are really complex sets of features rather than entities in themselves [e.g., Chaffin and Herrmann this volume]. We believe, rather, that a speaker chooses a particular model of the part-whole relation that best matches the physical attributes of the objects that he wishes to emphasize or, alternatively, best fits the abstract concepts he is trying to convey. One's language provides specific resources for meeting the needs of speakers along various axes from space to time or from physical to logical.

Among the linguistic resources available to English speakers are a large array of individuation or measurement nouns that can create discrete parts out of such continuous wholes as time, space, or matter. Thus, out of continuous experience language creates entities such as *hours* and *yards*, as well as *activities* and *events*. Masses can be made countable as in *cupfuls* and *pints*. Discrete wholes can also be created through language for ad hoc collections and aggregates as in *piles* and *bunches*. Therefore, speakers have at their disposal not only specific labels for parts and wholes but also other linguistic resources for labeling parts and wholes created as needed. The four conceptual models of part-whole relationships proposed here are designed to differentiate the existing labels and also to explain how speakers can generate new part-whole distinctions.

One important confirmation of the validity of these models is that they explain some of the contradictory assertions about the transitivity of the part-whole relation that appear in the literature.

The problem of transitivity

Our fourfold model of the part-whole relation has notable explanatory significance in understanding the controversy over the transitivity of the part-whole relation. The problem here is: supposing that we know that A is a part of B and B is a part of C, can we always be sure that A is a part of C? In more formal terms, does A *part* B and B *part* C always imply A *part* C?

The logicians answer with a resounding yes. Lesnièwski listed the transitivity of the part-whole relation as a fundamental axiom of merology [Rescher 1975]. Both Woodger and Tarski include transitivity in their axiom systems as well, and they specify explicitly that it applies to both spatial and temporal parts.

Computer scientists seem to be equally convinced that the part-whole relation is transitive. Raphael [1968] explicitly uses the transitivity of "Have-As-Parts" in making inferences. Simmons and Amsler [1975] develop a part-whole hierarchy for verbs based on transitivity. Fahlman [1979] lists transitivity as an axiom of his PART-OF relation and uses transitivity extensively in reasoning.

Linguists, on the other hand, have expressed serious doubts. Cruse [1979] tries to resolve the problems noted by Lyons in the excerpt quoted earlier by characterizing contexts where transitivity holds or does not hold. The context that he labels the "functional domain" corresponds fairly closely to our "functional aspect," as illustrated in Figure 1. The problem occurs because when we say that X is a (functional) part of Y, we usually mean that X is a major component of Y. Thus, it is appropriate to say that the house has a door and that the door has a handle, but not that the house has a handle. Cruse's analysis is perfectly correct. Transitivity does not hold in general for functional parts.

Nor does transitivity hold for the collection-element model of the part-whole relation shown in Figure 3. For example, each of the authors can be described as part of a pair. If we make a list of these pairs we get:

$$PLIST = \{\{Madelyn, \ Mark\}, \{Bonnie, \ Norman\}, \{Martha, \ Len\}\}$$

Bonnie is an element of the set *{Bonnie, Norman}*. The pair *{Bonnie, Norman}* is an element of *PLIST*, but *Bonnie* is not an element of *PLIST*; the elements of *PLIST* are pairs.

To consider another example where transitivity does not hold: each of the authors can be described as part of a university. (From our professorial point of view, the university is the faculty.)

$$Northwestern \ University = \{Madelyn \ Iris, Bonnie \ Litowitz, ...\}$$

$$Illinois \ Institute \ of \ Technology = \{Martha \ Evens, ...\}$$

We can also consider the set of universities in the Chicago area.

$$CU = \{Northwestern, Illinois \ Institute \ of \ Technology, ...\}$$

Bonnie is a part of *Northwestern University* and *Northwestern University* is a member of the set *CU* of universities in the Chicago area, but *Bonnie* is not a member of the set *CU*. The set *CU* consists of universities

Yet transitivity does hold for the subset model of the part-whole relation (Figure 4), sometimes called the set-inclusion relation. A set X is said to be a subset of a set Y if and only if every element of X is also an element of Y. Suppose we have three sets A, B, and C, and we know that A is a subset of B and B is a subset of C. The fact that A is a subset of B implies that every element of A is an element of B. But every element of B is an element of C, since B is a subset of C. So every element of A is also an element of C. That is, A is a subset of C. For example, let A represent the set of lions, B the cat family or Felidae, and C the set of all mammals. A is a subset of B; B is a subset of C; A is also a subset of C. All lions belong to the cat family; all members of the cat family are mammals; all lions are mammals.

When we view a part as a piece of segmented whole (as depicted in Figure 2), transitivity will still hold. If we cut a piece of pie into pieces, each new piece is still a piece of the original pie. If we dig a spadeful of clay out of an ant's nest and then in turn take a trowelful out of the spadeful, we still have a piece of the ant's nest.

In his computer model of semantic memory Fahlman [1979] is clearly thinking of part-whole in these terms. Fahlman treats his PART-OF relation as transitive, and the algorithms that exploit the transitivity of the taxonomy relation are used for the PART-OF relation as well. In addition, PART role-nodes are marked to key special routines to find all parts of a given whole and all wholes to which a given part contributes.

Fahlman uses these part-whole algorithms in making two important kinds of deductions. The first involves arguments about existence. If an object is said to exist in an area then it must exist within larger areas of which that area is a part but not necessarily in any one subarea. The example that he gives is: If coyotes exist within NEVADA, then they also exist in larger areas of which NEVADA is a part, WESTERN-USA, for example, but they do not necessarily exist within every part of NEVADA, particularly not in DOWNTOWN-LAS-VEGAS.

Arguments about the validity of statements make use of the part-whole hierarchy in a different way. The statement "gambling is legal" is valid for all parts of NEVADA, such as DOWNTOWN-LAS-VEGAS, but it need not be valid throughout WESTERN-USA. In general, if a statement is valid for a given area it must be valid in every subarea, but not necessarily in larger areas. Fahlman is clearly thinking of geographical parts in terms of the segmented whole, "piece of pie" aspect of the part-whole relation. In Fahlman's Nevada, transitivity holds without question. Parts of parts of Nevada are parts of Nevada as well.

Our analysis leads us to conclude that the validity of the transitive property depends on the particular model of part under discussion. Transitivity holds for the subset model (the set-inclusion relation) and for the segmented wholes. It is not valid for functional parts or for the collection-element model.

The primitive nature of the part-whole relation

Another controversy centers on the primitive nature of the part-whole relation. As we have seen, the question of primitiveness can be interpreted in three different ways:

1. Is the part-whole relation prime or first in order of importance?
2. Does it appear in the primitive, early stages of cognitive development?
3. Is the part-whole relation a logical primitive from which other relations can be derived?

In an attempt to answer these questions we have examined data from dictionary definitions and discovered that the part-whole relation may appear in many forms. Sometimes the word *part* appears itself; at other times a synonym such as *section, portion*, or *segment* appears instead. In addition, the part concept is often expressed using partitive gerunds, such as *including, comprising*, or *containing*.

To the first question we can answer an unqualified yes. The part-whole relation is of prime importance. This relation has played a central role in psychological studies and computer models of human memory. Linguists and anthropologists have discussed it at length and it plays a fundamental role in the calculus of individuals in modern philosophy. Smith [1985] has found the word *part* to be the second most frequent noun appearing in W7 definitions of other nouns. In the definitions that we studied, functional parts and segmented wholes seem to be most common among those that actually use the word *part*. Other kinds of part relations appear frequently but these more often use the word *member* or a partitive gerund to express the particular relationship. The part-whole relation clearly plays an important role in adult cognitive processes.

When it comes to the second sense of primitiveness, the developmental one, our answer must be qualified. Some aspects of the part-whole relation are formulated relatively early; for example, spatial expressions [see Litowitz and Novy 1984]. The collection-element and segmented whole aspects of the relation also appear fairly early. Definitions which invoke class inclusion and taxonomic concepts appear later. This question is discussed much more fully in our paper on children's definitions [Iris et al. forthcoming].

The third question – is the part-whole relation a logical primitive or not – is much more controversial. The answer depends on one's theoretical or formal perspective. Modern logicians, following Lesnièwski, take part-whole as a formal prime and derive other relations from it. Wierzbicka may have been influenced by Lesnièwski in her choice of the part-whole relation as one of the thirteen fundamental semantic primitives in her *Lingua Mentalis* [1980]. Fahlman, like Simmons and Raphael, treats part-whole as a primitive concept. Both the logicians and the computer scientists seem to be dealing with the segmented-whole relation. Transitivity holds for this model and thus they can safely use this property in making inferences.

Amsler [1980, 1981] also argues for the primitive nature of this relation. He has discovered that the part-whole relation appears at the top of a large "tangled hierarchy," in his study of definitions in the *Merriam-Webster Pocket Dictionary*. Tangled hierarchies occur when a group of terms can only be defined in terms of each other. Amsler makes a convincing argument that these tangled hierarchies point to semantic primitives.

On the other side of this question, there are important scholars who treat part-whole as a derived relation, not as a logical primitive. Werner derives the part-whole relation from taxonomy and modification. Mel'čuk sees part-whole as too vague and general to be a valid lexical function; rather, he sees it as a name for a group of lexical functions.

Our analysis of the fourfold nature of the part-whole relation could be used to support both sides of this argument. On one side, part-whole as a separate relation disappears, replaced by spatial, functional, and taxonomic relations; the part-whole relation is derivable from these relations. On the other side, however, the relationships of parts to wholes can be seen as fundamental and the variety of models we propose can be viewed as imply the derived manifestations which express this general and important underlying semantic relationship.

Discussion

Winston, Chaffin, and Herrmann [1987] also propose a multi-relational solution to problems of the part-whole relation. Arguing from a psychological perspective and using experimental data, they compile an ad hoc taxonomy of six types of part-whole relations. In addition to a collection of stuff relations, their taxonomy lists:

1. integral object – component
2. collection – member
3. mass – portion
4. activity – phase
5. event – feature
6. area – place

The first three share an affinity because they can be expressed by a possessive form (*has a*) as well as by the true partitive (*is a part of*). Mass-portion
can also be expressed by quantification (*is some of*). Stuff relations differ
from the other six in that they are expressed by *is partly* or *is made of.*

Five examples of each of these six types of part-whole plus the stuff
relations were given to subjects who were instructed to put similar relations (not concepts) together and also to provide a label for relations (with
the assumption that relations judged as similar would bear similar labels).
Analysis by a hierarchical clustering procedure confirmed the ad hoc list
and indicated to the experimenters multiple, specific relationships. Stuff
relations were separated from part-whole relations and the part-whole relations were themselves subdivided so that activity-phase was separated from
the other kinds of part-whole and homogeneous mass-portion from the heterogeneous examples. In addition, area-place, event-feature, time-occasion,
and measure-unit were distinguished from the other part-whole relations.
As a result, the authors suggest that merological relations consist of eight
semantic domains, cross-classified by three major "fundamental relations":
parts, stuff, and relational parts.

They also claim that merological relations are transitive so long as one
remains within a particular part-whole relation throughout the argument.
In the section on transitivity above, we show that transitivity does not hold
for the collection-member relation. Our argument that it does not hold for
functional parts either is essentially similar to one given by Lyons [1977]
and is not original with us.

In regard to primitiveness, Chaffin and Herrmann [this volume] hypothesize that it is the properties of the relations that are primitive, not the
relations themselves and that subjects decompose merological relations into
"simpler properties" to decide which type of part-whole relation applies in a
specific example. Properties include class-inclusion, spatial inclusion, possession, attachment, homogeneous vs. heterogeneous parts, constrained vs.
unconstrained location of parts. In addition, they say, word-pairs may represent more than one part-whole relation depending upon focus (i.e., upon
pragmatic considerations).

Decomposition of relations into properties raises the same difficulty encountered in earlier featural or componential semantic models: what is the
ontological status of a property? What is the relationship between properties and the relations that they define? It was precisely these issues that
gave rise to the relational theory of semantics, in which relations must be
made explicit and all terms must be elicitable in natural language from
native speakers [Evens et al. 1980].

In another paper, Chaffin and Herrmann conclude "that people can make graded similarity judgments about the similarity of semantic relations *and* that this ability is based on a comparison of the elements of which relations are composed" [1987, p. 30, italics ours]. These elements which the authors generate from the similarity judgment results are viewed as the "new primitive terms." Relations, then, are not viewed as unitary but as composed of various combinations of relational elements, some of which are more defining or typical for a specific relation than others (e.g., class inclusion for taxonomy).

That subjects can make similarity judgments about relations as well as about the concepts they link does not necessarily lead to these authors' causal conclusions, indicated by *and* in the passage quoted above. While prototypicality may be useful in identifying new instances of non-classic categories [Osheron and Smith 1981; Sowa 1984, pp. 16-17], it has not been established that semantic relations are categories of this kind.

Furthermore, it is not true that a unitary relational perspective fails to provide a basis for judging relationships among relations [Chaffin and Herrmann 1986, p. 6]. In Evens et al. [1980], we have discussed such relationships explicitly; for example, the interdependencies of taxonomy and modification; synonymy as a limiting case of taxonomy; the possibility of viewing antonymy as a kind of grading. In earlier papers one of us has discussed the connections between part/whole and spatial and possessive relations [Litowitz and Novy 1984]. In this paper we focus on part/whole as a set of relations, one of which touches on taxonomy, and we suggest that part/whole can shed light on the difference between sets/collections and classes/types.

Two further problems may be noted. Chaffin and Herrmann [1986] strongly insist on the mutual exclusion of part-whole relations and taxonomic relations. Taxonomic relations are, of course, hierarchic and transitive (i.e., they represent class-inclusion). Yet Winston, Chaffin, and Herrmann [1987] claim that class-inclusion is the one uniform property of all merological relations. A second difficulty arises from the ad hoc nature of the original list of examples that they used with their subjects, and their original classification of these items. For example, they classify refrigerator-kitchen as a functional part, not as a locative relationship. This seems to dunk the transitivity test that they themselves propose, i.e., that transitivity holds if one stays within a single family of part-whole relations. For example, in the functional part family, vegetable-bin FP refrigerator, and refrigerator FP kitchen should imply vegetable-bin FP kitchen, which seems somewhat problematic to us.

By the authors' own admission, many examples are ambiguously related. Subjects may vary in their interpretations of examples (and therefore sorting of word-pairs) for pragmatic reasons. Questionable examples in the ad hoc taxonomy and pragmatic shifts in task interpretation will skew the clustering solution, which in turn was used to create the fundamental relations. In other words, the results obtained by Chaffin and his coworkers indicate how their particular subjects performed on a set of words proposed by the experimenters; it is not clear how this performance relates to native speakers' abilities to identify and label parts and wholes. Nor is it necessary to suppose that in natural situations speakers use Chaffin's "decompositional strategy" in their decisions.

As an alternative hypothesis, we suggest that speakers use two sources of information to identify merological relations. The first is conceptual: subjects have models or schemata of at least four kinds of part-whole relationships. These differ in terms of discreteness and formedness (entatitivity) of whole and part, and in which came first, part or whole. The second is linguistic: subjects have labels for some parts but not their wholes (or vice versa) and a specific language determines which aspects of the models or schemata are eligible for more productive labeling. English, for example, provides many terms for collection (*pile, bunch, pride, brace*) and for unit/measure (*inch, foot, yard, cubit, rood, ...*) and individuation/ segmentation (*item, lump, loaf, ...*).

Our first three schemata are similar to Chaffin's integral object, collection-member, and mass-portion relations, respectively; these relations can be expressed by possession. The stuff relations can be better handled by non-merological relations such as composition (made-of) and provenience (comes-from) relations as described in Evens et al. [1980]. Events, named times, and time measures seem better handled by a sequencing or grading relation. Activity-phase seems to describe an aspect of scripts. Perhaps these can be handled by some combination of functional part and sequencing.

Conclusion

Working with dictionary data we have developed four models or schemata of the part-whole relation to support our belief that part-whole is really a family of four relations. These models have notable explanatory power when it comes to examining contradictory evidence about the transitivity of this relation. These models help to explain some of the questions about the primitive nature of the part-whole relation as well, but clearly the developmental history of merological relations is very complex.

All part-whole schemata are derived originally from physical knowledge of the world [Riegel 1970]. For this reason, discreteness, formedness, attachment, spatial inclusion, and questions of alienable vs. inalienable possession are all implicated. From the child's early experiences and the label learned for them, part-whole relations are extended to non-physical examples. In making decisions about parts and wholes, however, one returns to the prototypes that have resulted from one's early experiences. With maturity, as part of the process of becoming a literate member of a western culture, we develop a bias toward taxonomy [Iris et al. forthcoming] and part-whole relations are not immune to that structural pressure. As a result, our fourth schema, the set-subset model, develops [Markman et al. 1980]. In defining tasks the higher taxon *part* and collocationally specific superordinate parts (*limb, extension*) are increasingly used by adult English speakers. The fourth schema is a class-inclusion schema, while the other three are spatially bounded, and therefore inclusive in a locative sense.

Paraphrases can also capture the differences between part-whole relations where the whole precedes the part. For example, a face contains eyes, nose, and mouth, but we do not say that a bicycle contains a wheel, or a wheel contains a spoke. In contrast, a bicycle consists of wheels, pedals, etc. Conceptually, then, there seem to be two kinds of boundaries: one that preexists or predates its parts; another that can be drawn around existing parts. The latter corresponds to our segmented whole; the former to collections. Obviously very basic topological issues are implicated [Inhelder and Piaget 1964]; some objects are perceived as cavitied (closed, potential containers, e.g., the body contains the heart) while others are perceived as biplanar or open (e.g., arms have hands). With intellectual growth children overlay their earliest topological conception of space with a projective and then a Euclidean geometric conception. They learn that bikes have fronts, forests have edges, etc. [cf. the relational parts of Winston et al. 1987].

Developmental studies suggest that part-whole relations emerge out of spatial knowledge [Markman and Seibert 1976; Markman et al. 1980; Litowitz and Novy 1984] and become increasingly expanded but not necessarily replaced by class, superordinate, and taxonomic structures [Iris et al. forthcoming]. However, our earlier relations are retained, to be used when needed. These facts have led to several different kinds of investigations of parts and wholes. This is not surprising given the nature of the phenomena under study and the multiplicity of backgrounds of the investigators. Part-whole is, then, not one relation, or even two, but a whole family of relations. Our conception of this family is one of four overlapping related schemata.

References

Amsler, Robert. 1980. *The Structure of the Merriam-Webster Pocket Dictionary.* Ph.D. Dissertation, Computer Science Department, University of Texas at Austin, Austin, Texas.

Amsler, Robert. 1981. A Taxonomy for English Nouns and Verbs. *Proceedings of the 19th Annual Meeting of the Association for Computational Linguistics*, Stanford, California, June 29-July 1, 133-138.

Apresyan, Yuri, Mel'čuk, Igor, and Žolkovsky, Alexander. 1970. Semantics and Lexicography: Towards a New Type of Unilingual Dictionary. In F. Kiefer, ed., *Studies in Syntax and Semantics*. Reidel, Dordrecht-Holland, 1-33.

Carey, Susan. 1982. Semantic Development: the State of the Art. In E. Wanner and L.R. Gleitman, eds., *Language Acquisition: the State of the Art*. Cambridge University Press, Cambridge, 347-389.

Casagrande, Joseph, and Hale, Kenneth. 1967. Semantic Relations in Papago Folk Definitions. In D. Hymes and W.E. Bittle, eds., *Studies in Southwestern Ethnolinguistics*. Mouton, the Hague, 165-196.

Chaffin, Roger, and Herrmann, Douglas. 1986. Relation Element Theory: A New Account of the Representation and Processing of Semantic Relations. In D. Gorfein and R. Hoffmann, eds., *Learning and Memory: The Ebbinghaus Centennial Conference*. Erlbaum, Hillsdale, NJ.

Chaffin, Roger, and Herrmann, Douglas. This volume. The Nature of Semantic Relations: A Comparison of Two Approaches.

Clark, Herbert, and Clark, Eve. 1977. *Psychology and Language*. Harcourt Brace Jovanovich, New York.

Collins, Alan, and Quillian, M. Ross. 1972. How to Make a Language User In E. Tulving and W. Donaldson, eds., *Organization of Memory* Academic Press, New York, 310-354.

Cruse, D.A. 1979. On the Transitivity of the Part-Whole Relation. *Journal of Linguistics*, 15, 29-38.

Cruse, D.A. 1986. *Lexical Semantics*. Cambridge University Press, Cambridge.

Evens, Martha, Litowitz, Bonnie, Markowitz, Judith, Smith, Raoul, and Werner, Oswald. 1980. *Lexical-Semantic Relations: A Comparative Survey*. Linguistics Research, Edmonton, Alberta.

Fahlman, Scott. 1979. *NETL: A System for Representing and Using Real World Knowledge*. MIT Press, Cambridge, Massachusetts.

Herrmann, Douglas, Chaffin, Roger, and Winston, Morton. 1986. *Bulletin of the Psychonomic Society*, 24, 6, 413-415.

Inhelder, Barbel, and Piaget, Jean. 1964. *The Early Growth of Logic in the Child: Classification and Seriation*. Routledge and Kegan Paul, London.

Iris, Madelyn, Litowitz, Bonnie, and Evens, Martha. 1988. Moving toward Literacy by Making Definitions. In W. Frawley and R. Smith, eds. special issue of *International Journal of Lexicography*.

Jespersen, Otto. 1933. *Essentials of English Grammar.* Allen and Unwin, London.

Kucera, Henry, and Francis, W.N. 1964. *A Standard Corpus of Present-day Edited American English for Use with Digital Computers.* Brown University Press, Providence, Rhode Island.

Litowitz, Bonnie, and Novy, Forrest. 1984. Expression of the Part-Whole Semantic Relation by 3 to 12 Year Old Children. *Journal of Child Language,* **11**, 159-178.

Lyons, John. 1977. *Semantics.* Cambridge University Press. Cambridge.

Markman, E. M., Horton, M. S., and McLanahan, A. G. 1980. Classes and Collections: Principles of Organization in the Learning of Hierarchical Relations. *Cognition,* **8**, 227-241.

Markman, E. M., and Seibert, J. 1976. Classes and Collections: Internal Organization and Resulting Holistic Properties. *Cognitive Psychology,* **8**, 561-577.

Martin, Richard. 1971. *Logic, Language, and Metaphysics.* New York University Press, New York.

Olney, John. 1968. To All Interested in the Merriam-Webster Transcripts and Data Derived from Them. Systems Development Corporation, Santa Monica, CA, Document L-13579.

Osheron, Daniel, and Smith, Edward. 1981. On the Adequacy of Prototype Theory and a Theory of Concepts. *Cognition,* **9**, 35-58.

Raphael, Bertram. 1968. SIR, a Computer Program for Semantic Information Retrieval. In M. Minsky, ed., *Semantic Information Processing,* MIT Press, Cambridge, Massachusetts, 33-145.

Rescher, Nicholas. 1975. Applied Logic. In *Encyclopedia Britannica,* 15th ed., Macropedia, **11**, 28-38.

Riegel, Klaus. 1970. The Language Acquisition Process: a Reinterpretation of Related Research Findings. In L.R. Goulet and P.B. Baltes, eds., *Theory and Research in Life-Span Developmental Psychology,* Academic Press, New York, 357-399.

Rosch, Eleanor. 1978. Principles of Categorization. In Eleanor Rosch and B.B. Lloyd, eds., *Cognition and Categorization,* Erlbaum, Hillsdale, NJ, 27-48.

Simmons, Robert F. 1973. Semantic Networks: Their Computation and Use for Understanding English Semantics. In Roger Schank and Kenneth Colby, eds., *Computer Models of Thought and Language,* W.H. Freeman and Company, San Francisco, 1-113.

Simmons, Robert F., and Amsler, Robert A. 1975. Modeling Dictionary Data. In Ralph Grishman, ed., *Directions in Artificial Intelligence, Natural Language Processing,* Courant Institute Report #7, New York University, 1-26.

Smith, Raoul. 1981. On Defining Adjectives, Part III. *Dictionaries: Journal of the Dictionary Society of North America*, **3**, 28-38.

Smith, Raoul. 1985. Conceptual Primitives in the English Lexicon. *Papers in Linguistics*, **18**, 99-137.

Sowa, John F. 1984. *Conceptual Structures: Information Processing in Mind and Machine*. Addison-Wesley, Reading, MA.

Tarski, Alfred. 1937. An Alternative System for P and T. Appendix E in Woodger, 1937.

Webster's Seventh New Collegiate Dictionary. 1963. G & C Merriam Company, Springfield, Massachusetts.

Werner, Oswald, Austin, Martha, and Begishe, Kenneth Y. 1969/1981. *Anatomical Atlas of Navajo*. Handbook of North American Indians. Department of Anthropology, Northwestern University; U.S. Dept. of Public Health.

Werner, Oswald, and Topper, Martin. 1976. On the Theoretical Unity of Ethnoscience Lexicography and Ethnoscience Ethnographics. In Clea Rameh, ed., *Semantics, Theory and Applications, Proceedings of the Georgetown Round Table on Language and Linguistics*, 111-143.

Wierzbicka, Anna. 1980. *Lingua Mentalis: The Semantics of Natural Language*. Academic Press, New York.

Winston, Morton, Chaffin, Roger, and Herrmann, Douglas. 1987. A Taxonomy of Part-Whole Relations. *Cognitive Science*, **11**, 417-444.

Woodger, J.H. 1937. *The Axiomatic Method in Biology*. Cambridge University Press, Cambridge.

Zadeh, Lotfi. 1965. Fuzzy Sets. *Information and Control*, **8**, 338-353.

13
The nature of semantic relations: a comparison of two approaches

ROGER CHAFFIN
DEPARTMENT OF PSYCHOLOGY
TRENTON STATE COLLEGE
TRENTON, NJ 08650

DOUGLAS J. HERRMANN
DEPARTMENT OF PSYCHOLOGY
HAMILTON COLLEGE
CLINTON, NY 13323

Abstract

The widespread use of relations between ideas as explanatory constructs in psychology has led theorists to overlook the need to provide a theoretical account of relations themselves. Among the phenomena that a psychological theory of semantic relations should account for are the ability of people (1) to judge some relations as more similar than others, (2) to distinguish one relation from another, (3) to identify instances of common relations, (4) to express relations using everyday words and expressions, (5) to recognize instances of relation ambiguity, and (6) to perceive and create novel relations. These abilities are not readily explained by theories which treat relations as unitary, unanalyzed constructs. A theory of relation elements is described which accounts for the nature of relations between ideas in terms of more primitive relational elements which are supported by the concepts involved in a particular relation.

Introduction

Relations between ideas have long been viewed as basic to thought, language, comprehension, and memory. Aristotle explained the sequence of ideas in recall in terms of the relations of contiguity, similarity, and contrast. John Locke used relations between ideas to account for the formation of complex from simple ideas and for the ability to reason [Rapaport 1974, pp. 66-85].

The current use of relations as a theoretical construct in psychological and linguistic theories continues this tradition. Relations are used by linguists as the basis for semantic theories, by lexicographers to account for the structure of the lexicon, and by psychologists as the building blocks of semantic memory. In psychology, for example, network models of semantic memory represent concepts as nodes connected by marked pointers which are the theoretical primitives in the theories [e.g., Anderson 1976; Norman and Rumelhart 1975; for reviews see Chang 1986; Johnson-Laird et al 1984]. The relations themselves are treated as unproblematic; it is assumed that each relation can be unambiguously identified by the theory builder and by the people whose abilities the theories are designed to explain. The only theoretical issue that is recognized with respect to relations is the question of which relations to include. Network theories account for phenomena like recall and inference; relations themselves are not explained. Relations are unitary, unanalyzed theoretical primitives. For this reason we will speak of this as the *unitary* approach to semantic relations.

There is another way of viewing semantic relations. Relations can be seen as phenomena that themselves require description and explanation. For example, Hume [1739/1965, pp. 82-86] analyzed the cause-effect relation into the elements of contiguity in space, contiguity in time, succession and constant conjunction. The work of Geoffrey Leech [1974], John Lyons [1968, 1977], and D.A. Cruse [1979, 1986] follows Hume's model, analyzing semantic relations to account for their nature and properties. These linguists have provided careful descriptions of the standard semantic relations, antonymy, synonymity, class inclusion, the part-whole relation. In their analyses, relations are themselves the subject of explanation. We will refer to this as the *analytic* approach to semantic relations.

The analytic approach leads us to ask questions about the nature of semantic relations, not as theoretical constructs, but as a psychological and linguistic phenomenon. In this chapter we will examine three abilities that should be explained by any theory of relations. People are able to compare relations, to identify relations, and to create novel relations. We will examine two phenomena involving each ability. These are listed in Table 1.

Table 1. Six relation phenomena that an adequate theory of semantic relations should explain.

Phenomenon	Description	Example
	People frequently...	

Relation Comparison

Phenomenon	Description	Example
1.Relation Similarity	judge some relations as more similar than others	Which relation is more similar to bird-robin, *auto-car* or *night-day*?
2.Relation Discrimination	distinguish one relation from another	Which relation is the same as tree-leaf, *garden-flower* or *face-nose*?

Relation Identification

Phenomenon	Description	Example
3.Relation Verification	verify instances of common relations	Which is a type of bird, a *lion* or a *flamingo*?
4.Relation Expressions	express relations with common words and phrases	Is a piston a *component* or a *fragment* of an engine?

Relation Flexibility

Phenomenon	Description	Example
5.Relation Ambiguity	identify the relation of a word pair in more than one way	A display can be *part of* an exhibit and a display can be *the same thing as* an exhibit.
6.Relation Creativity	perceive and create novel relations	*Agenda* is to *meeting* as *menu* is to ... ?

People can compare relations. First, they can judge some relations as more similar to each other than others. For example, people see the relation of *car-engine* as more similar to the relation of *Vatican-Italy* than to that of *baker-bread*. The latter does not involve the element of spatial inclusion present in the first two. Second, the complement of the ability to judge similarity is the ability to recognize difference. This is done in solving analogy problems. For example, the relation of *flock-lamb* is seen as the same as that of *family-child* and different from that of *bird-fledgling*.

People can identify relations. The third phenomenon is that, when presented with pairs of words, people are able to decide whether each pair is an example of a specific target relation, e.g., whether *finger-hand* and *diamond-jewel* are examples of the part-whole relation. Fourth, people can also use common words and phrases to express relations. For example, people know that an engine is a *component* of a car and that a drummer is a *member* of a band.

Relations are not fixed, immutable entries. The fifth phenomenon that we will describe is the fact that the relation of a word pair can be ambiguous. For example, *display-exhibit* might be viewed as synonyms (*A display is the same as an exhibit*), as class inclusion (*A display is a kind of exhibit*), or in a part-whole relation (*A display is part of an exhibit*). Sixth, the production and recognition of relations is a creative ability, e.g., the relation of *frigate-blueprint* can be readily identified although the reader may never have considered the relation of these particular terms before.

These diverse phenomena must be explained by theories of relations. We will outline a unitary and an analytic theory of relations. Then, after we have described the six phenomena, we will compare the ability of the two theories to account for them. We will argue that the unitary approach does not provide a satisfactory account because, although relations figure prominently in unitary theories, and these theories are intended to account for semantic phenomena, they were never intended to *explain* relations. It was assumed that relations did not require explanation, or possibly were explained by some other theory. We will find that in order to explain relations it is necessary to assume that relations are normally composed of more primitive elements that account for their characteristics and for people's abilities to make judgments about them.

Two theories of semantic relations

Network theory

There are a number of memory and linguistic processing theories that have used a network approach to semantics [e.g., Anderson 1976; Collins and Loftus 1975; Glass and Holyoak 1975; Norman and Rumelhart 1975]. The following are the common assumptions of these theories about the nature and processing of relations [Chang 1986; Johnson-Laird et al. 1984].

Representational assumptions

1. A relation between two concepts is represented by a marked link between two nodes that represent the concepts, e.g.,

$$\text{ROBIN} \xrightarrow{\text{ISA}} \text{BIRD}$$

2. For any pair of concepts there is only one link; each link has one marker; and each marker is unitary.

3. There is a limited number of different types of markers. The exact number is open, but a commitment to parsimony in the introduction of theoretical primitives has led most theorists to posit fewer than 20.

Processing assumptions

1. Relations between concepts are identified by searching the network from one or both nodes representing the two concepts to find a path joining the two nodes.

2. The pathway identified can be evaluated to determine whether it is of the nature required by the task at hand. The evaluation is straightforward since each link is clearly and unambiguously marked. (As a result little attention has been paid to this process by network theorists.)

3. Processing times for relation judgments are determined by the length of the path between the two concepts, the number of branches that must be checked, and the level of activation of the links. The contribution of the evaluation process is frequently assumed to be constant.

Relation element theory

Analytic approaches to relations have not been widely pursued in psychology. Relation element theory represents a preliminary account of some of the more obvious properties of relations and relation judgments [Chaffin and Herrmann 1986; Herrmann and Chaffin 1986].

Representational assumptions

1. A relation R between two concepts x and y is composed of one or more dyadic relation elements $(E_a, \ldots, E_n)$ that are supported by the representation of the concepts.

$$_xR_y \longrightarrow (E_a, \ldots, E_n)$$

2. Relation elements may be hierarchically organized so that the presence of one element depends on the presence of another, or elements may be independent of one another. In the following representation independent elements are separated by commas and dependent elements appear in parentheses following the element that they depend on,

$$_xR_y \longrightarrow (E_1(E_2(E_3)), E_4, \ldots, E_n).$$

3. Relations may share one or more elements. The greater the proportion of elements two relations have in common the more similar they are. Thus $_xR_y$ is more similar to $_iR'_j$ than to $_mR''_n$.

$$_xR_y \longrightarrow (E_1, E_2, E_3)$$
$$_iR'_j \longrightarrow (E_1, E_2, E_4)$$
$$_mR''_n \longrightarrow (E_1, E_4, E_5)$$

Processing assumptions

1. Relations between concepts are constructed by comparing representations of the two concepts to identify common and complementary structures which provide the elements of the relation.

2. Relation judgments involve the comparison of elements of a stimulus relation against a criterial set of elements dictated by the specific task the person has to perform.

3. The thoroughness of the evaluation of each element of a stimulus relation depends on how clearly that element is or is not present in the stimulus relation being evaluated.

4. The order in which elements are evaluated is determined by their hierarchical organization. Dependent elements are processed after the elements on which they depend. The order of processing of independent elements is not constrained.

Six relation phenomena

1. Relation similarity

People can make reliable judgments about the similarity of relations. To judge that two things are more similar to each other than they are to a third it is necessary to identify ways in which the things compared are the same and ways in which they are different. The perception of similarities and differences requires that the things compared be decomposed into aspects in terms of which the comparisons can be made [Tversky 1977]. This is recognized in the aphorism, "You can't compare apples and oranges." This is true if apples and oranges are considered as unanalyzable wholes. But if the wholes are decomposed into aspects in which they are the same – size, shape, nutritional value – and different – texture, taste, color – the comparison is easily made. In the same way, similarity judgments about semantic relations require the decomposition of the relations into more basic relational elements in terms of which they are the same and in terms of which they differ.

Judgments about the similarity of relations were studied in an experiment in which undergraduates were asked to sort relations into groups, putting examples of the same or similar relations into the same group and examples of different relations into different groups [Chaffin and Herrmann 1984]. Thirty-one different semantic relations were each represented by five word pairs that exemplified the relation. The five word pairs for each relation were listed on a card. The cards were given to subjects to sort. A hierarchical clustering analysis of the sorting frequencies produced the clustering of relations shown in Figure 1. Relations joined at a higher proximity level (lower in the figure) were sorted together by more subjects. Two examples of each relation are given in Table 2 which lists the relations in the same order as in Figure 1. An a priori classification of the relations is indicated by the Roman numerals in Figure 1.

There were five major clusters or families of·relations. From the left of the figure these are: contrasts (I, e.g., *alive-dead*), class inclusion (II, e.g., *animal-horse*), similars (II, e.g., *car-auto*), case relations (IV, e.g., *artist-paint*), part-whole (V, e.g., *engine-car*). The families are organized in terms of their similarity to one another. The most fundamental division is between the family of contrast relations and the other four families of non-contrast relations. The non-contrast relations are divided into logical relations – class inclusion and similarity – which involve comparison of properties, and pragmatic relations – case and part-whole relations – that are based on a pragmatic association through a common event rather than on similarity of meaning [Klix 1980]. The relations within each family are also organized in terms of similarity. For example, the part-whole relations are divided into relations with discrete parts, e.g., *car-wheel*, and relations for which the parts are not readily distinguishable one from another, e.g., *mile-yard*.

Each family can be examined in more detail and a finer clustering of relations discovered. A second study used the same procedure to study the part-whole family together with other similar relations [Chaffin, Herrmann, and Winston 1988]. Again 31 relations were included; they were sorted by 35 subjects. The results are summarized in the clustering solution in Figure 2. Examples of the 31 relations are listed in Table 3. An a priori classification is indicated by Roman numerals.

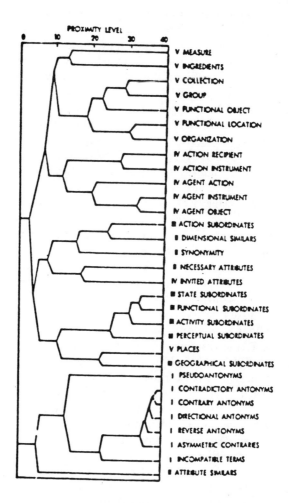

Figure 1. An empirical taxonomy of semantic relations
(A hierarchical clustering solution for 31 word-pair relations
from Chaffin and Herrmann (1984). Relations joined at lower
levels in the figure, i.e., with higher proximity levels,
were sorted together more frequently. Classification in the
a priori taxonomy is indicated by Roman numerals.)

Table 2. Examples of thirty-one semantic relations.

(from five families listed in the order shown
in Figure 1 from Chaffin and Hermann, 1984)

I. CONTRASTS	Contrary	old-young, happy-sad
	Contradictory	alive-dead, male-female
	Reverse	attack-defend, buy-sell
	Directional	front-back, left-right
	Incompatible	happy-morbid, frank-hypocritical
	Asymmetric contrary	hot-cool, dry-moist
	Pseudoantonym	popular-shy, believe-deny
	Attribute similar	rake-fork, painting-movie
II. SIMILARS	Synonymity	car-auto, buy-purchase
	Dimensional similar	smile-laugh, annoy-torment
	Necessary attribute	bachelor-unmarried, tower-high
	Invited attribute	food-tasty, cut-knife
	Action subordinate	talk-lecture, cook-fry
III. CLASS INCLUSION	Perceptual subord.	animal-horse, flower-rose
	Functional subord.	furniture-chair, tool-hammer
	State subord.	disease-polio, emotion-fear
	Activity subord.	game-chess, crime-theft
	Geographic subord.	state-New Jersey, country-Russia
	Place	Germany-Hamburg, Asia-China
IV. CASE RELATIONS	Agent-action	artist-paint, dog-bark
	Agent-instrument	farmer-tractor, soldier-gun
	Agent-object	baker-bread, sculptor-clay
	Action-recipient	sit-chair, hunt-prey
	Action-instrument	cut-knife, drink-cup
V. PART-WHOLE	Functional object	engine-car, tree-leaf
	Collection	forest-tree, fleet-ship
	Group	choir-singer, faculty-professor
	Ingredient	table-wood, pizza-cheese
	Functional location	kitchen-stove, house-dining room
	Organization	college-admissions, army-corps
	Measure	mile-yard, hour-minute

There are seven major branches in the clustering solution in Figure 2, which again agree substantially with the a priori taxonomy. Most of the part-whole relations (I, *car-engine*) are clustered in the right-hand two

Table 3. Examples of word pairs used in sorting task to represent thirty-one part-whole and similar relations

(from Chaffin et al. 1988 – relations are listed in the order shown in Figure 2. Roman numerals indicate a priori classification.)

I. PART-WHOLE

<u>Integral Object-Component</u>

Dramatic event-section	Book-chapter, symphony-movement, opera-act
Dramatic event-content	Joke-punchline, story-plot, film-climax
Functional location-component	Kitchen-refrigerator, classroom-desk, store-cash register
Living thing-component	Ivy-leaf, tulip-petal, lion-mane
Complex artifact-component	Telephone-dial, typewriter-key, camera-lens
Simple artifact-component	Cup-handle, pencil-eraser, fork-prong

<u>Event-Feature</u>

Event-actor	Rodeo-cowboy, wedding-bride, trial-defendant
Event-prop	Banquet-food, birthday-present, Halloween-candy

<u>Object-Topological Part</u>

Object-relational location	Room-corner, box-side, mountain-foot

<u>Collection-Member</u>

Organization-unit	UN-delegation, army-battalion, college-registry
Collection-member	Forest-tree, fleet-ship, library-book
Group-member	Fraternity-brother, herd-cow, mafia-don

<u>Area-Place/Time</u>

Natural area-place	Desert-oasis, continent-mountain range, earth-ocean
Named area-place	Florida-Everglades, Wyoming-Yellowstone, Caribbean-St.Thomas
Named time-occasion	February-Valentine Day, summer-July 4th, Easter-Good Friday

<u>Mass-Portion</u>

Measure-unit	Mile-yard, gallon-pint, pound-ounce
Mass-natural tiny piece	Salt-grain, snow-flake, wood-sliver
Mass-measured portion	Pie-slice, loot-cut, land-parcel

Table 3 (continued)

II. STUFF	
Mass-stuff	Trash-paper, compost-grass, salad-lettuce
Object-stuff	Bike-aluminum, lens-glass, box-cardboard

III. CLASS INCLUSION

Kind of artifact	Vehicle-car, utensil-spoon, tool-hammer
Kind of state	Disease-polio, emotion-fear, marital status-divorced
Kind of natural object	Animal-horse, flower-rose, metal-copper
Kind of activity	Sport-football, crime-theft, art-ballet

IV. REPRESENTATION

Activity-plan	Banquet-menu, meeting-agenda, course-outline
Object-representation	Person-portrait, wiring-diagram, event-report

V. STAGES

Process-phase	Launch-liftoff, moon-full, growing up-adolescence
Continuous activity-phase	Driving-steering, cycling-pedaling, swimming-kicking
Discrete activity-phase	Shopping-buying, traveling-arriving, gardening-digging

VI. ATTRIBUTES

Object-attribute	Tower-height, food-taste, bed-comfort
Disposition-stuff	Burn-coal, curdle-milk, evaporate-water

thirds of the figure. To the left of the part-whole relations are the stuff relations (II, *bike-aluminum*). These two merological relations concerned with constituency are separated from the other main clusters. To the left of the stuff relations is class inclusion (III, *bird-robin*), followed by representation (IV, *wiring-diagram*). Next is a type of part-whole relation, the activity-stage relation (I-iv, e.g., *cycling-pedaling*) which the subjects saw as distinct from other part-whole relations. The two attribute relations (V, *tower-height*) are on the left of the figure, distinguished from all the other relations and from each other.

The part-whole relations are divided into eight clusters, three of which include a single relation. The most general distinction was between the

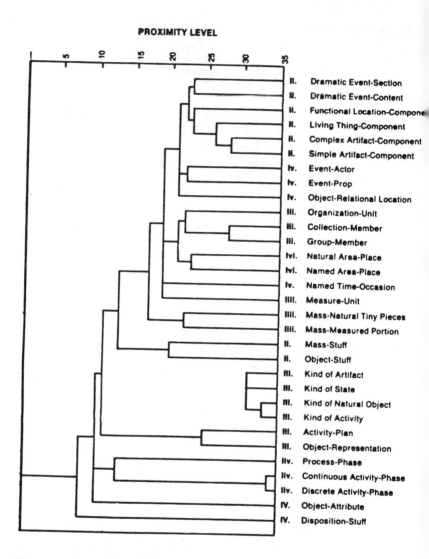

Figure 2. An empirical taxonomy of part-whole relations and relations with similarities to the part-whole relation.
Hierarchical clustering solution for 31 word-pair relations
from Chaffin et al. [1988]

two mass-portion relations (I-iii, *pie-slice*, *salt-grain*) and other part-whole relations. Mass-portion relations are homeomerous, i.e., each part has the same nature as the whole, e.g., each grain of salt is "salt" and each slice of pie is "pie," while other part-whole relations are non-homeomerous, i.e., the parts are not similar to the wholes, e.g., each tree is not the forest. The nonhomeomerous relations, in turn, fall into two groups distinguished by whether the parts play a functional role or not. In the left hand cluster are relations in which the location of the parts is not constrained by function, e.g., to be part of a forest a *tree* does not have to be in any particular location in the *forest*. These include the area-place (I-vi, *Washington-White House*) and collection-member (I-ii, *forest-tree*) relations. In the right hand cluster the location of the parts is constrained by their function (e.g., the *handle* of a *cup* must be in the right place to serve its function). These include two separate clusters containing the event-feature (I-v, *banquet-food*) and the integral object-component relations (I-i, *cup-handle*).

The subjects in these two experiments were able to perceive similarities between the relations and thus were able to identify elements that the relations had in common and elements that distinguished the relations from each other. The elements of the relations that subjects relied on most heavily to distinguish the relations are apparent in the major divisions of the taxonomies. In Figure 1 the main distinctions were between contrast and non-contrast relations and between relations based on a comparison of properties (class inclusion and similarity) and relations based on a pragmatic association (event and part-whole). In Figure 2 the main distinctions were between merological and non-merological relations, between parts that are similar to their wholes and those that are not, and between parts that are functionally related and those that are not. These distinctions are relational elements that distinguish relations in a family from one another.

The ability of relation elements to provide a detailed account of the similarities between relations was tested by Theresa Stasio who derived relation elements from the linguistic and psychological literature for the 31 relations in the Chaffin and Herrmann [1984] sorting study [Stasio, Herrmann, and Chaffin 1985; also see Chaffin and Herrmann 1986]. The elements are listed in the second column of Table 4 and briefly described in Table 5. The elements were assigned on the basis of linguistic considerations rather than on the basis of the sorting data.

Table 4. Thirty-one semantic relations and their relation elements listed in the order shown in Figure 1.

(Based on Stasio et al., 1985. Family elements common to all members of a family are listed in caps; specific elements that distinguish relations within a family are in lower case. Dependent elements are listed in parentheses after the elements they depend on; independent elements are separated by commas.)

Relation Families	Relation Elements
I. <u>CONTRASTS</u>	
Contrary	DIMENSION(BIPOLAR(Symmetrical), Continuous)
Contradictory	DIMENSION(BIPOLAR(Symmetrical), Dichotomous)
Reverse	DIMENSION(BIPOLAR,Dichotomous, Vector)
Directional	DIMENSION(BIPOLAR,Dichotomous,Spatial)
Incompatible	DIMENSION(BIPOLAR)
Asymmetric contrary	DIMENSION(BIPOLAR,Continuous)
Pseudoantonym	DIMENSION(BIPOLAR,Connotative)
Attribute similar	INTERSECTION(Overlap(Attribute, Discrete))
II. <u>SIMILARS</u>	
Synonymity	INTERSECTION(Inclusion(Bilateral))
Dimensional similar	INTERSECTION(Overlap),Dim(Unip)
Necessary attribute	INTERSECTION(Overlap),(Attribute, Possession))
Invited attribute	INTERSECTION(Inclusion(Attribute (Possession,Connotative)))
Action subordinates	INTERSECTION(INCLUSION(UNILATERAL))
III. <u>CLASS INCLUSION</u>	
Perceptual subord.	INTERSECTION(INCLUSION(UNILATERAL))
Functional subord.	INTERSECTION(INCLUSION(UNILATERAL))
State subord.	INTERSECTION(INCLUSION(UNILATERAL))
Activity subord.	INTERSECTION(INCLUSION(UNILATERAL))
Geographic subord.	INTERSECTION(INCLUSION(UNILATERAL))
Place	INCLUSION(PARTIVE(Possession),Locative)

Table 4.(Continued)

Relation Families	Relation Elements
IV. CASE RELATIONS	
Agent-action	EVENT(Agent,Act)
Agent-instrument	EVENT(Agent,Instrument)
Agent-object	EVENT(Agent,Object)
Action-recipient	EVENT(Act,Object)
Action-instrument	EVENT(Act,Instrument)
V. PART-WHOLE	
Functional object	INCLUSION(PARTIVE(Attached,Component, Property,Possession))
Collection	INCLUSION(PARTIVE(Homogeneous, Property,Possession))
Group	INCLUSION(PARTIVE(Homogeneous,Property, Possession,Social))
Ingredient	INCLUSION(PARTIVE(Component,Property, Possession, Locative))
Functional Location	INCLUSION(PARTIVE(Attached, Component,Property,Possession))
Organization	INCLUSION(PARTIVE(Attached,Component, Property, Possession,Social))
Measure	INCLUSION(PARTIVE(Homogeneous))

The similarity of the 31 relations to each other was computed as the proportion of shared elements and correlated with the sorting frequencies from Chaffin and Herrmann [1984] to determine how well element similarity accounted for the sorting data. The correlation was substantial, $r(463) = .71$, $p < .001$. The relation elements accounted not only for the clustering of relations into families but also for the similarity of families to one another. This was indicated by the significant correlation of element similarity and sorting frequency for relations from different families, $r(378) = .40, p < .01$. Relation elements also accounted for similarities within families. This was indicated by correlating element similarity and sorting frequency for relations in the same a priori family. The relation elements for contrast relations were the most successful, $r(28) = .75$, $p < .05$, followed by class inclusion, $r(15) = .52$, $p < .05$. Correlations for the other families approached significance suggesting a need for further refinement of the elements for these families.

Table 5. Relation elements and their definitions
(based on Stasio et al., 1985; definitions and ordering
have been changed to facilitate exposition)

Relation Elements	Description
I. Elements of Intensional Force	
Denotative	Wi and Wj share denotative meaning
Connotative	Wi connotes Wj
II. Dimensional Elements	
Dimension	Wi and Wj share a single dimension
Unipolar Position	Wi and Wj are on same side of midpoint
Bipolar Position	Wi and Wj are on opposite sides of midpoint
Symmetrical Position	Wi and Wj are equidistant from midpoint
Continuous	Wi and Wj can be qualified; dimension is gradable
Discrete	Wi and Wj cannot be qualified; dimension is non-gradable
Dichotomous	If Wi then not Wj; Wi and Wj are mutually exclusive
Spatial	Wi is spatially opposite Wj
Vector	Wi is directionally opposed to Wj
III. Elements of Agreement	
Inclusion	Wi is included in Wj semantically or physically
Overlap	Meanings of Wi and Wj overlap; Wi and Wj are semantically similar
Intersection	Wi is semantically included in Wj
Unilateral Inclusion	Wj includes all of Wi but Wi does not include Wj
Bilateral Inclusion	Wi and Wj include each other; Wi=Wj
Attribute	Wj is an attribute of Wi; Wi "is" Wj
IV. Propositional Elements	
Event	Wi and Wj related by an event
Action	Wi and Wj related by an action
Agent	Wi is the agent of an action
Object	Wj is the object of an action
Instrument	Wj is the instrument used for an action
V. Elements of Part-whole Inclusion	
Partive Inclusion	Wj is physically included in Wi
Locative Inclusion	Wj is "in" Wi
Social	Wj is part of Wi by agreement
Attachment	Wj is attached to Wi
Homogeneous	Wj's are interchangeable
Property	Wj is a property of Wi
Component	Wj is a "component" of Wi
Possession	Wi "possesses" a property or attribute

Relation elements give a good account of similarities between relations. However, in a sorting task subjects are explicitly required to make comparisons between relations. It may be argued that people's ability to decompose relations into elements under these conditions does not provide assurance that relations are normally decomposed into elements. The subjects were obliged to find some basis for their sorting. The elements they used, the argument runs, may have been merely the result of a process of deliberate reflection and analysis that bears no relation to the normal processing of relations. In the next two sections we will describe evidence that the decomposition of relations into elements occurs in a variety of tasks including those in which comparison of relations is not explicitly called for.

2. Relation discrimination

The ability to discriminate between relations is the complement of the ability to recognize similarities between relations. One task which requires discrimination between relations is the solution of analogy problems in which the goal is to select the key pair whose relation matches that of a stem pair from among several distractor pairs. The identification of the key requires decomposition of the relations into elements, just as in the case of a similarity judgment. The key is the relation which shares the most elements with the standard.

The elements that make up a relation can be divided into two components, a family component and a specific component. The family component consists of the elements that are common to all the relations in the same family (the capitalized elements in Table 4). For example, all contrast relations share the elements of common dimension and bipolar opposition. The specific component consists of the elements that distinguish one relation in a family from another. For example, contraries (*hot-cold*) are opposed on a continuous dimension, while contradictories (*alive-dead*) are opposed on a dichotomous dimension.

The Semantic Relations Test (SRT) was constructed by Julie Ross [Ross, Herrmann, Vaughan, and Chaffin 1987] to test subjects' knowledge of these two components for the five relation families identified by Chaffin and Herrmann [1984]. The SRT contains three types of items that test subjects' knowledge of the family and specific components of relation knowledge. The three types are illustrated in Table 6 and the differences between them are summarized in Table 7. In *heterogeneous-same* items, the key is distinguished from the distractors by both the family component and the specific component. For example, in item 1 in Tables 6 and 7 the stem (*inside-outside*) matches the key (*purchase-sale*) on both the family component (contrast) and the specific component (directional). In *heterogeneous-different* items, the key is distinguished by the family component

Table 6. Examples of three types of analogy problem from the Semantic Relations Test.

The subjects' task is to select the choice pair whose relation matches most closely the relation of the target pair.

Stem Pair		Choice Pairs	
1. inside	hammer	upstairs	wheel
outside	nail	downstairs	bicycle
2. top	office	vegetable	life
bottom	desk	apple	death
3. front	entrance	absence	poverty
back	exit	presence	wealth

alone. For example, in item 2 in Tables 6 and 7 the stem pair (*top-bottom*) matches the key (*life-death*) on the family component (antonym) but not on the specific component (directional and contradictory, respectively). For homogeneous items, all of the comparison pairs were from the same relation family. The key was distinguished only by the specific component. For example, in item 3 in Tables 6 and 7, all of the pairs have the same family component (contrast) but only the key (*entrance-exit*) matches the stem (*front-back*) on the specific component (directional).

The three types of questions were constructed for each of the five main relation families. Each question type required the use of different components of relation knowledge. In order to answer a heterogeneous-same item correctly subjects could draw on knowledge of either the family or the specific component, or both. To give a correct answer to a heterogeneous-different item subjects could rely only on knowledge of the family component. To give a correct answer to a homogeneous item, subjects could rely only on knowledge of the specific components.

A typical set of data for the SRT is shown in Figure 3 which gives the percent correct responses for the three item types for each family. The data comes from 120 subjects in a study by Searleman, Herrmann, Chaffin, Parsons and Vaughan [1986]. The ability to answer each item type was different for each family. Knowledge of the family and specific components thus differed from family to family. For the contrast family accuracy was high for the two kinds of heterogeneous item and at chance level for the homogeneous items. Heterogeneous items involve the family component; homogeneous items only the specific component. Thus the family component was accurately distinguished, i.e., contrasts are easily distinguished

Table 7. Family and specific components of relations for the three types of items on the Semantic Relations Test (From Ross et al. [1987]. "+" indicates key. "*" indicates component(s) on which stem and key match and which distinguish the key from the distractors.)

	Components of Relation Knowledge		
		Family	Specific
Item #1: (Heterogeneous-same. Family and specific components match)			
Stem	Inside Outside	*Contrast	*Directional
Choices	Hammer Nail	Case	Instrument-Object
	+Upstairs Downstairs	*Contrast	*Directional
	Wheel Bicycle	Part-whole	Functional
Item # 2: (Heterogeneous-different. Family components match)			
Stem	Top Bottom	*Contrast	Directional
Choices	Office Desk	Part-whole	Locational
	Vegetable Apple	Class Inclusion	Collateral
	+Life Death	*Contrast	Contradictory
Item # 3: (Homogeneous. Specific components match)			
Stem	Front Back	Contrast	*Directional
Choices	+Entrance Exit	Contrast	*Directional
	Absence Presence	Contrast	Contradictory
	Poverty Wealth	Contrast	Contrary

from other relation families, but subjects could not distinguish the specific component, i.e., subjects could not distinguish one contrast relation from another. This result is not surprising. Contrast was the most distinctive of the relation families in the sorting study [Chaffin and Herrmann 1984], but the different types of contrast relation, e.g., contrary and contradictory, are not familiar to most people.

For the part-whole family accuracy was again higher for heterogeneous than for homogeneous items. Unlike the contrast relations, however, accuracy for the homogeneous items was well above chance. This pattern of results indicates that the family component was more readily distinguished than the specific component, but that subjects had some knowledge of both. Unlike the contrast relations, the specific component of part-whole relations is reflected in numerous common terms for various part-whole relations, e.g., *section, member, portion, piece*, etc. Familiarity with these relational concepts may account for subjects' accuracy on the homogeneous part-whole items.

The SRT results demonstrate that analogy problems are solved by decomposing relations into more basic components [Chaffin and Herrmann 1986]. The correct choice is the word pair whose components match those of the standard pair most closely. The SRT data thus extend to another task the evidence that relation judgments involve decomposition of relations. The SRT provides evidence of the decomposition of relations into only two components of relation knowledge, the family and specific components. This is sufficient, however, to establish that the discrimination of relations requires their decomposition into more basic constituents, and makes it reasonable to suppose that these components are further decomposed into relation elements.

In the sorting and analogy tasks that we have considered so far subjects are explicitly required to compare relations. The next section provides evidence that relations are decomposed into elements in tasks in which there is no explicit requirement to compare relations.

3. Relation identification

People can identify the relation of word pairs. Relation identification has been intensively studied by psychologists in the past two decades. In a typical relation identification or verification task subjects must determine whether the relation between the two stimulus words is an example of a target relation that the subjects are asked to identify. For example, the task might be to answer the question, "Is A part of B?" for a number of stimulus word-pairs. To make these decisions a person must have a representation of the target relation, e.g., *part of*, against which the stimulus relation can be compared.

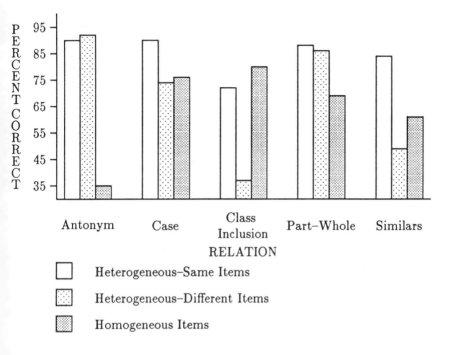

PERCENT CORRECT

Antonym   Case   Class Inclusion   Part–Whole   Similars
RELATION

☐ Heterogeneous–Same Items

▨ Heterogeneous–Different Items

▨ Homogeneous Items

Figure 3. Percent correct responses for analogy items on the Semantic Relations Test as a function of relation family and type of analogy item (Ross et al., 1987).

Evidence of such a comparison process is provided by the most robust finding of the relation verification literature; the latency of semantic decision is affected by the similarity of the relation between the two stimulus words to the target relation that the subject has been asked to identify. [Smith 1977; Herrmann, Chaffin, Conti, Peters, and Robbins 1979; Herrmann and Chaffin 1986; Kintsch 1980]. "Yes" responses are faster to good examples of the target relation and "no" responses are slower to pairs whose relation has some elements in common with the target relation. An example of the relation similarity effect for "yes" responses is provided by a study in which subjects were asked to make part-whole decisions [Chaffin and Herrmann 1988]. Word pairs were selected that were very good examples of the part-whole relation (e.g., *car-engine*), moderately good examples (e.g., *bike-tire*), or poor examples (e.g., *bed-pillow*). An equal number of non-part-whole pairs were also selected. The pairs were randomly ordered and

presented to subjects one pair at a time, on a screen. Subjects decided, for
each pair, whether it was an example of a part-whole relation or not, and
pressed one of two buttons marked "yes" and "no" to indicate their decision. Decision time was measured. The results are summarized in Table 8.
"Yes" responses were faster and more accurate for better examples of the
part-whole relation.

**Table 8. Mean latencies of correct responses (in secs)
and percent errors (in parentheses) for part-whole judgments**
(Chaffin and Herrmann 1988. "Yes" Responses were required
for part-whole and "no" responses for non-part-whole pairs.)

	PART Relation Similarity			NON-PART Relation Type		
	Hi	Medium	Low	Pseudo-parts	Coord-inates	Unre-lated
Example	CAR ENGINE	KITCHEN CUPBOARD	BED PILLOW	AIRPLANE FENDER	ARM LEG	TREE GAS
Latency	1.217 (3.5)	1.263 (6.8)	1.576 (21.0)	1.623 (22.7)	1.581 (10.2)	1.364 (6.4)

For "no" responses relation similarity has the opposite effect. We will
use a study of antonym and synonym decisions as an illustration [Herr-
mann et al. 1979, Expt 3]. One group of subjects made antonym decisions while another made synonym decisions. All subjects were presented
with the same five types of relation. Among the relations presented were
pseudo-antonyms (e.g., *popular-shy*), pairs having some of the elements of
antonymy (see Table 4), and pseudo-synonyms (e.g., *slow-late*), pairs having some of the elements of synonymity. Examples of the five relations used
are shown in Table 9 together with the results. For the antonym decision
group, "no" responses were slowest to pseudo-antonym pairs, while for the
synonym group "no" decisions were slowest to pseudo-synonym pairs. Thus
responses were slower for relations that shared some of the elements of the
target relation, i.e., the pseudo-relations. But it was not the pseudo-relation
pairs themselves that caused the slow responses. Responses to the pseudo-
synonyms by the antonym group were relatively fast, as were responses to
the pseudo-antonym by the synonym group. The slow responses were due
to the similarity of the pseudo-relation to the target relation.

Table 9. Mean latencies of correct responses (in secs) and percent errors (in parentheses) for antonym/synonym judgments (Herrmann et al., 1979, Expt 3.) "Yes" responses were required for antonyms in the antonym task and for synonyms in the synonym task; all other relation types required a "no" response.

	Relation Type				
	Antonyms	Synonyms	Pseudo-antonyms	Pseudo-synonyms	Unrelated words
Example	HOT COLD	FINE EXCELLENT	POPULAR SHY	SLOW LATE	SALTY BRIGHT
Judgment Task					
Antonymy	1.274 (9.2)	1.248 (6.2)	1.655 (22.3)	1.343 (1.9)	1.257 (0.8)
Synonymity	1.206 (0.4)	1.540 (14.2)	1.340 (0.8)	1.743 (26.2)	1.385 (0.4)

Similar effects have been found for decisions about other relations. The effects for class inclusion decisions are the most studied effects in the semantic decision literature. When subjects are asked to decide if concepts are members of a target category, "yes" decisions are faster for more typical members, e.g., *robin-bird*, than for less typical members, e.g., *duck-bird* and "no" decisions are faster for nonmembers that are similar to the target category, e.g., *salmon-bird*, than for nonmembers that are dissimilar, e.g., *rock-bird* [Chang 1986; Kintsch 1980; Rosch and Mervis 1975; Smith 1977].

Relation similarity effects indicate the operation of a process of evaluating the stimulus relation against a criterion that represents the target relation. The evaluation process is fastest when the stimulus relation clearly matches or does not match the target relation, and takes longer when the match is less clear [Chaffin and Herrmann 1988; Herrmann and Chaffin 1986].

A study of synonym decisions examined in detail the nature of the criterion used in a synonym identification task [Herrmann, Chaffin, Daniel, and Wool 1986, Expt 2]. Synonymity provides an interesting case because there are two different definitions of the relation which subjects might use to identify synonyms. According to the informal definition, found in the psychological literature and in everyday use, synonymity requires simply that the meaning of two words overlap to a considerable extent [Herrmann

1978]. According to this definition, synonymity is simply a high degree of similarity and so synonym and similarity judgments should be affected by the same variables. In particular, both should be affected by overlap of both connotative and denotative meaning. According to the more formal definition, dominant in the linguistic and philosophical literatures, synonymity requires that the denotative meaning of one term completely overlap the denotative meaning of the other term [e.g., *Webster's New Dictionary of Synonyms* 1973]. According to this definition, overlap of connotative meaning is not an element of synonymity and would not affect synonym judgments.

Synonym decisions were evaluated by comparing three groups of subjects. One group made "yes"/"no" decisions about whether pairs of words were synonyms or not, a second group rated each pair for their degree of synonymity, and a third group rated the pairs for similarity. If the subjects rating synonymity use the informal definition in which synonymity is equivalent to similarity, then the synonymity and similarity ratings would be affected both by denotative overlap and by connotative overlap. If synonym judgments are based on the formal definition, then synonymity judgments would be affected by denotative but not by connotative overlap while similarity ratings would be affected by both denotative and connotative overlap. The measures of denotative and connotative similarity were provided by two additional groups of subjects. Denotative similarity was directly rated. Connotative similarity was obtained from semantic differential ratings [Osgood, Suci, and Tannenbaum 1957].

The results showed that subjects used the formal definition of synonymity, a definition that was different from that for general similarity. Synonym judgments (both ratings and "yes"/"no" decisions) were predicated by denotative similarity, but not by connotative similarity. General similarity, in contrast, was predicted by both denotative and connotative similarity. Thus the criterion that was used for judging synonymity was different from the criterion used to judge general similarity. The study also showed that similar decision processes were used in the speeded "yes"/"no" decision task and in the unspeeded rating task; the same results were obtained in both tasks.

The criterion that is used to evaluate the relation of each stimulus pair represents the subject's concept of the target relation. This concept consists of elements of the target relation. The idea that the criterion is decomposable into more basic elements is strongly suggested by the effect of relation similarity on decision times. As argued above, similarity must be computed by decomposing the things compared into more basic elements in which they are similar and in which they differ [Chaffin and Herrmann 1984; Tversky 1977]. Direct evidence that relation elements are evaluated in relation judgments comes from a study of antonym judgments.

To be antonyms two words must be symmetrically positioned about the midpoint of a dimension that involves the denotative meaning of both words (see Table 4). Three elements of the antonym relation were directly assessed for 100 antonym and pseudoantonym word pairs. The three elements affected both speeded "yes"/"no" judgments and unspeeded relation similarity ratings [Herrmann et al. 1986, Expt 1]. Clarity of the dimension of opposition was measured as agreement between subjects who were asked to label the dimension of each of the pairs. The nature of the opposition was varied by selecting 50 antonym pairs, opposed on a denotative dimension of meaning, e.g., *hot-cold*, and creating 50 pseudo-antonym pairs, opposed on a connotative dimension e.g., *popular-shy*. Symmetry of opposition was assessed by subjects who indicated the position of the members of each pair on a line representing the dimension of opposition and bisected by a vertical mark representing the midpoint of the dimension. Symmetry was quantified as the ratio of the distances of each term from the midpoint.

The results provided evidence of an effect of each of the three elements of antonymy on antonym judgments. The probability of an antonym response and degree of antonymy ratings were higher for pairs that were denotatively rather than connotatively opposed, higher for more symmetrically opposed pairs, and higher when the dimension of opposition was clearer, for connotatively opposed pairs. As in the study of synonym decisions, the same results were obtained in the speeded "yes"/"no" decision task and in the unspeeded rating task.

In the studies we have described so far the target relation was a widely known relation and remained the same throughout the experiment. Other studies indicate, however, that the criterion may change from trial to trial and can involve very specific requirements that are unique to a particular context. In a study by Roth and Shoben [1983, Expt. 3] subjects were shown a context sentence, e.g., *Stacy volunteered to milk the "animal" whenever she visited the farm*. The context sentence was followed almost immediately by a stimulus word, e.g., *cow*. The task was to decide whether the stimulus word could possibly be a referent of the category term (indicated by quotes) in the context sentence. The standard effects were obtained. "Yes" responses were faster to typical members of the target category (e.g., faster to *cow* than to *goat*) and "no" responses were slowed by similarity to the target category (e.g., slower for *bull* than for *bear*). The important point about the procedure is that the target category was an ad hoc one created by the context sentence and changed on each trial. The study thus demonstrates that the criteria that are used to evaluate relations may be unique to a particular context and may change from trial to trial.

Decisions in relation verification tasks are not always made by directly evaluating the stimulus relation against a criterion representing the target relation. When subjects are asked to make class inclusion decisions, "no" responses may be based on a successful search for a counter-example. For example, people may decide that "All birds are chickens" is false by thinking of a robin and deciding that it is not a chicken. Use of such a counter-example strategy was demonstrated in a study of class inclusion decisions by Lorch [1978, Expts 3 and 4; also Holyoak and Glass 1975]. Subjects responded "yes" to sentences like "All cedars are trees" and "no" to sentences like "All birds are chickens." Category association norms were used to select some categories for which examples are highly accessible, e.g., *fish* and other categories for which examples are less accessible, e.g., *music*. "No" responses were faster for more accessible categories. This suggested that subjects had made their decision by finding counter-examples, using pre-existing relations stored in memory.

In summary, studies of relation verification tell us five important things about relations. First, the effect of relation similarity suggests that similarity is evaluated and this, as we have seen in previous sections, implies that relation elements are evaluated. Second, relation identification requires the use of relation knowledge as a criterion against which to evaluate stimulus relations. Third, examples of relations (word pairs in the studies we have reviewed) vary in how typical they are of standard relations, like the part-whole relation, and typicality affects decision time. In this respect relations are like other concepts [Rosch and Mervis 1975]. Fourth, relations are not fixed, immutable concepts, but can be subject to fine modifications on a trial to trial basis. Fifth, some relations are directly stored in memory and do not have to be computed from knowledge of the two concepts that form the arguments of the relation.

4. Relation expressions

In the previous section we saw that students can identify examples of several semantic relations. The knowledge of relations required for this is, in part, the result of schooling. School children are taught to identify the most common relations including antonymy, synonymity, and the class inclusion and part-whole relations. The number of "standard" relations that are explicitly learned in this way is small.

Of the standard relations only antonymy and synonymity have commonly accepted names and these names find little use outside of academic discourse. Lyons [1977] discusses the inadequacies of the various names for the class inclusion relation and recommends the term "hyponymy." For the part-whole relation the names "partonymy" [Miller and Johnson-Laird 1976, p.242] and "meronymy" [Winston, Chaffin, and Herrmann 1987] have been suggested. Even the term "antonymy" is of recent vintage, coined in 1870 [*The Shorter Oxford Dictionary, 3rd Ed.*, 1965], and there is disagreement about the range of relations to which the term should be applied [*Webster's New Dictionary of Synonyms* 1973].

While *names* of relations are few and little used, there are ways of *expressing* relations that are part of the average speaker's everyday vocabulary. The relation of antonymy is expressed by the sentence frame, "A is the opposite of B." Class inclusion is expressed by sentences of the form "A is a kind of B," "A's are a type of B," "A's are B's" and related expressions. Synonymity is likewise expressed by "A's are B's" and "An A is the same as a B," and also by the metalinguistic expression, "'*A*' means '*B*'." Meronymy is expressed by "A is part of B," "A is partly B," and related expressions. There are a large number of such relation expressions. There are, for example, at least 40 fairly general words for different kinds of parts, e.g., *component, member, portion, feature*, and a much larger number of more specialized terms, e.g., *shard, rasher*. How do these part-terms correspond to the part-whole relations listed in Figure 2?

This question was addressed by a study conducted in our laboratory by Donna Transue [1982]. Thirty-one part terms, i.e., terms that can occur in the frame "A is a (*part-term*) of B," were selected to sample the variety of relations represented by the 400 or so synonyms for "part-of" listed in *Roget's Thesaurus* [1962]. A sentence illustrative of the most frequent type of use of each part-term was created, based on the performance of 15 subjects who were asked to use each term in a sentence. The illustrative sentences were typed on separate cards with the part-term capitalized and underlined. The cards were given to 45 students who were instructed to sort them into piles containing part-terms that were similar in meaning. The instructions emphasized that sorting was to be based on the meaning of the part-term and not of the whole sentence.

A hierarchical clustering solution for the sorting frequencies is shown in Figure 4. There were five major clusters of part-terms, representing parts of processes, events, places, masses, and objects. The left-most cluster in Figure 4 contains two part-terms that express stages of processes (*phase, stage*). Next to this is a single term (*role*) that refers to part of an event. Events can be described in terms of scripts [Schank and Abelson 1977] of which roles are one part. The third cluster contains five terms that refer to parts of places (*area, region, zone, section, division*). The fourth cluster is a large one containing terms that refer to portions of masses. These parts have in common that they are homeomerous, i.e., similar in nature to the whole. The homeomerous cluster itself has two main subdivisions: relations in which the part is based on measurement (*share, percentage, portion*), and those in which the part is determined by the nature of the material or object (*slice, piece, bit, sliver, drop, grain, lump, scrap, chip, fragment, fraction*). The fifth major cluster, on the right of Figure 4, consists of terms referring to non-homeomerous parts and includes three kinds of part-whole relation: object-component (*component, feature, part*), collection-member (*item, member*) and state-cause (*factor, element*).

The grouping of part-terms in Figure 4 corresponds fairly closely to the empirical taxonomy of part-whole relations described earlier which was obtained by asking subjects to sort word pairs exemplifying part-whole relations [shown in Figure 2; Chaffin et al. 1988]. Four of the clusters correspond directly: activity-stage (*shopping-buying*), event-feature (*rodeo-cowboy*), area-place (*Florida-Everglades*), and mass-portion (*salt-grain, pie-slice*). The cluster of part-terms referring to nonhomeomerous parts of objects corresponds to three types of part-whole relation: integral object-component (*car-wheel*) and collection-member (*herd-cow*), and a third relation not included in the word-pair sorting task, state-cause (*test-taking-anxiety*).

The agreement between the clusters obtained in the two sorting tasks indicates that there is a correspondence between elements of the meanings of part-terms and elements of the part-whole relations that are perceived between pairs of words. The ability of subjects to sort part-terms indicates that the meanings of part-terms, like the relations to which they refer, can be decomposed into more basic elements. The elements on which subjects sorted the part-terms can be readily identified. For example, *share, percentage* and *portion* were clustered together on the basis of referring to part-whole relations in which the whole is a mass object and the parts are homeomerous and are the result of a division based on measurement. The agreement of the two sorting studies suggests a correspondence of part-terms and part-whole relations, that part-terms are the names of relational concepts. If so, the study of relation terms may be a high-road to the understanding of the variety and nature of semantic relations. Unfortunately the high-road is not without its obstructions. One of these is the polysemy of relation expressions, which is illustrated in Figure 5.

"Is" can be used to express class inclusion, synonymity, attribution, and the stuff relation. The organization of these expressions is straightforwardly hierarchical. This is not the case for "has." "Has" can be used to express the belonging relation and some part-whole relations. The hierarchical organization of these expressions is, however, tangled. The process-stage relation is expressed by "part of," but not by "has" (indicated by the dotted line in Figure 5), while collection-member relations can be expressed by both "belongs to" and "part of."

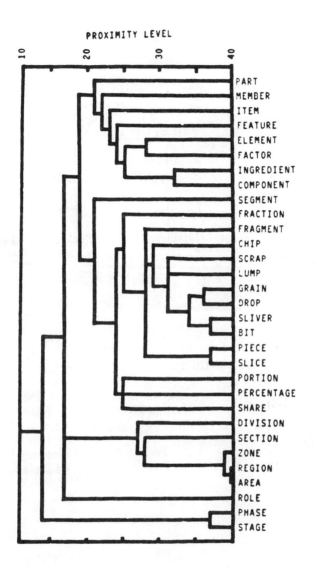

Figure 4. An empirical taxonomy of part-terms: hierarchical clustering solution for 31 part-terms [Transue, 1982]
Part-terms joined at lower levels in the Figure, i.e., with higher proximity levels, were sorted together more frequently.

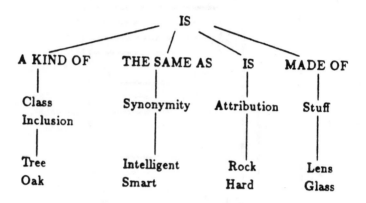

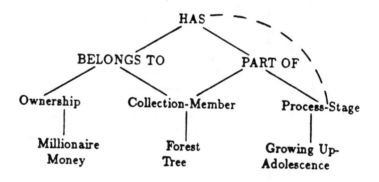

Figure 5. Two examples of the quasi-hierarchical organization
of relation expressions

A second source of difficulty in mapping relation expressions onto word-pair relations is that the relation of a pair of words is not an immutable entity but may change with the context, being viewed one way in one context, and another way in a different context. Relation ambiguity is discussed in the next section.

5. Relation ambiguity

The relation of a word-pair can be ambiguous for two different reasons. The less interesting case is due to the polysemy of one or both of the words. For example, *bathroom-lavatory* may be synonyms or in a part-whole relation because *lavatory* has two different senses. We will not discuss this type of relation ambiguity. More interesting are cases of relation ambiguity which depend not on an ambiguity of the words, but on an ambiguity of the relation. For example, *display-exhibit* may be viewed as a part-whole relation, "A *display* is part of an *exhibit*," or as synonyms, "A *display* is an *exhibit*," or class inclusion, "A *display* is a kind of *exhibit*." *Display* and *exhibit* do not change their meanings when their relation is viewed differently; only the situation used to instantiate them changes. One can think of a book exhibit that contains a display of cognitive science texts, or of the same display of cognitive science texts alone in another context where it might be called an "exhibit" or a "display." The meanings of the terms have not changed, merely the particular instantiation. The terms "exhibit" and "display" are vague as to the particular physical setup and the ambiguity of their relation depends on this vagueness.

Relation ambiguity is a common phenomenon that occurs between a wide variety of different relations. Some examples are given in Table 10. The word pairs listed on the left may be seen as examples of either of the relations named and illustrated under the headings "Relation 1" and "Relation 2." The list is not exhaustive but is intended only to suggest that the possibilities for relation ambiguity are very numerous.

As with other kinds of ambiguity, we often do not see the possibility for ambiguity in word-pair relations until they are drawn to our attention. What determines which of the possible relations between two words will be perceived? One factor is the relation that is expected. We examined the role of the expected relation in a recent experiment. Subjects saw pairs whose relation was either unambiguously part-whole (*sentence-paragraph*), unambiguously synonym (*autumn-fall*), or ambiguous. The ambiguous pairs included pairs like *display-exhibit*, and *cellar-basement* that might be viewed as synonym or part-whole pairs. Twelve pairs of each type were randomly ordered and presented to two separate groups of 22 students. One group was asked to identify examples of the part-whole relation, the other to identify synonyms.

Table 10. Examples of the ambiguity of word-pair relations

Word pair	Relation 1		Relation 2	
	Relation Name	Example	Relation Name	Example
Exhibit	Part-whole	Kitchen	Synonym	Lawyer
Display		Cupboard		Attorney
Friendship	Part-whole	Shopping	Class	Disease
Love		Buying	Inclusion	Polio
Blanket	Class	Chair	Synonymy	Car
Rug	Inclusion	Rocker		Auto
Mile	Part-whole	Pie	Similar	Laugh
Yard		Slice		Smile
Pepper	Coordinates	Deer	Contrasts	Night
Salt		Bear		Day
Judge	Contrast	Life	Agent-	Carpenter
Defendant		Death	Object	Nail
Laureate	Object-	Tower	Ownership	Heir
Honor	attribute	Height		Bequest

The relation identified in the ambiguous pairs tended to be the relation
that the subjects were looking for. The results for the two tasks are shown
in Table 11. The part-whole and synonym pairs were correctly identified
in both tasks, i.e., part-whole pairs were overwhelmingly identified in the
part-whole but not in the synonym identification task, and the synonym
pairs were overwhelmingly identified in the synonym but not in the part-
whole identification task. The results for the ambiguous pairs were quite
different. These were identified equally often in the two tasks, in the part-
whole task as part-whole relations, and in the synonym task as synonym
relations. (Each ambiguous pair received some identifications as a part-
whole and as a synonym relation.) Thus, the way that the subjects saw
the ambiguous relations was determined, in part, by the relation they were
looking for. Subjects looking for synonyms saw pairs like *exhibit-display*
as synonyms; subjects looking for part-whole pairs saw the same pairs as
part-whole.

**Table 11. Percentage of word pairs identified as examples
of the target relation in the part-whole and synonym
identification tasks**

Relation type	Example	Identification Task (P-W)	(S)
Part-Whole (P-W)	Sentence Paragraph	89.9	0.1
Synonym (S)	Fall Autumn	10.6	93.6
Ambiguous (A)	Exhibit Display	53.8	51.9

The subjects' expectation was directly manipulated in our experiment
by instructions to look for a particular relation. What factors determine
expectations about relations in more natural settings? In some cases expectations may be controlled by very general cognitive strategies. Markman
and Hutchinson [1984] found that children normally attend to thematic or
case relations (e.g., *dog-bone*), but that when one of the words is unknown
the children attend instead to class inclusion relations (e.g., *dog-cat*). The
strategy has an obvious utility in constraining the possible meanings of
novel words. Relation expectations may play similar roles in other situations.

In other cases the relation that is perceived will depend simply on those
aspects of the two concepts that are of interest. For example, the relation
of *kitchen-refrigerator* can be viewed in a variety of ways. For most people
the most salient aspect of a refrigerator is its function; these people might
describe their refrigerator as a *component* of their kitchen, a relation like
that of *car-wheel*. On the other hand, a person with a small kitchen and a
large refrigerator may find size to be a more salient attribute and describe
their refrigerator as a *portion* of the kitchen, a relation like that of *pie-
slice*. People with expensive new refrigerators may think of the appliance
as a *feature* of the kitchen. A person planning a new kitchen may view the
refrigerator as an *ingredient*. The relation of *kitchen-refrigerator* can thus
support a variety of interpretations, each highlighting different aspects of
the situation.

The phenomenon of relation ambiguity makes the point that relations
are constructed from knowledge of the two concepts related and that a
particular relation may make use of some aspects of the two concepts and
ignore others. If a relation encompassed all aspects of the meaning of two

words, then there could only be a single relation between the two words. If two words have more than one relation, then each relation must be based on somewhat different aspects of the two concepts. This point about relation ambiguity may be clarified by comparison with ambiguity in other domains. The closest parallel is with the categorization of concepts. A piano, for example, can be seen as a musical instrument or as an article of furniture. The object is the same in either case, but different attributes are made salient by each classification. A word pair, more strictly a pair of word senses, may likewise support more than one relation. A relation need not give equal weight to all aspects of the meaning of the two words. Relations typically emphasize some aspects and ignore others.

6. Relation creativity

The identification of relations is a productive ability. People can identify the relation of novel pairs, learn new relational concepts, and produce new relations by elaborating familiar relations or by concatenating familiar relations in a propositional framework. We will consider each case in turn. First, people are usually able to identify the relation of novel pairings of words even if they have never been exposed to a particular pair before and so have never had an opportunity to consider its relation. For example, the reader may never have considered the relation of *frigate* and *blueprint*, but can easily recognize the relation as a familiar one, similar to more familiar examples like *meeting-agenda*. Alternatively, knowledge of which relations are salient for a concept may be a source of hypotheses about the meaning of an unfamiliar word, e.g., *turtle-carapace*. The absence of a relation between two words, e.g., *justice-ketchup*, can also be identified and this too is a productive ability.

Second, people are able to learn new relational concepts when given examples and instruction. For example, many people do not distinguish contraries, e.g., *hot-cold*, and contradictories, e.g., *alive-dead*, as different relations. When examples of the two relations are presented and the difference between a continuous and a dichotomous dimension is described the distinction between the two relations is rapidly learned [Conti 1978].

Third, people can elaborate a relation to produce a more complex novel relation [Chaffin and Peirce in press]. This can be done in two ways, by adding specifications to a relation or by concatenating relations. The addition of specifications to a relation is illustrated in Table 12, which shows word pairs from a Graduate Record Exam (GRE) analogy item. The choice pairs all share some relation with the stem pair, *clapper-bell*, but differ in the level of detail at which they match the stem. The distractor *tongue-mouth* shares the relation of spatial inclusion with the stem pair. This is not, however, as close a match as the distractor *horn-automobile*, which shares the part-whole relation with *clapper-bell*; the part-whole relation involves the element of spatial inclusion as well as other elements, such as attachment and functional connection. The following pairs in the table each represent relations that match the stem at increasing levels of detail, as indicated by the relation expressions in the righthand column in Table 12. The correct answer to the analogy problem is the final pair, *hammer-piano*, whose relation matches that of the stem in the most detail: A is a component that produces sound by striking B.

Table 12. Word pairs from graduate record exam analogy items.
Each of the choices has the same relation as the stem. The choice pairs are listed in order of the complexity of relation shared with the stem, with the least complex first and the most complex (the correct answer) last.

Stem Pair	Choice Pair	Relation Expression
Clapper-bell	Tongue-mouth	A is in B
Clapper-bell	Horn-automobile	A is part of B
Clapper-bell	Speaker-radio	A is a component of B that produces sound
Clapper-bell	Needle-phonograph	A is a component of B that produces sound by contact with B
Clapper-bell	Hammer-piano	A is a component of B that produces sound by striking B

Each relation in Table 12 depends on the one above it, in that the more specific relations include the more general relations and add additional specifications or elements. The elements of each relation are thus hierarchically organized, with the elements of the more complex relations dependent on the elements of the simpler relations. For this reason each word pair can be described by the relation expressions for all the pairs above it in the table, e.g., a hammer is in a piano, is part of a piano, etc.

Elements are not always hierarchically dependent on each other in this fashion. The elements of a relation can also be independent of another. Part-whole relations like *car-wheel* appear to involve a conjunction of independent elements including spatial inclusion, proximity, attachment, and functional connection, each of which can occur independently of the others.

A second way in which novel relations can be created is by concatenating independent relations within a propositional frame. An example, also drawn from a GRE analogy item, is shown in Table 13. The relation of the stem pair, *irrevocable-repeal,* can be expressed by, "Something which can be *B*'d cannot be *A*." The relation is composed of three simpler relations: action-object (*repeal-law*), object-necessary attribute (*law-revocable*), and contradiction (*revocable-irrevocable*). The three relations are concatenated and the intermediate arguments (*law* and *revocable*) omitted. This is represented in Table 13 as a network of labelled links connecting nodes representing the arguments. The number of word pairs that share such a complex relation is limited, but it is clear that other examples can be found. The reader may like to try. One is, of course, the key for the analogy, *ineluctable-avoid,* which has the same representation as the stem in Table 13 [Bejar, Chaffin, and Embretson 1988].

The relation similarity of concatenated relations can be reliably judged and, like all similarity judgments, requires decomposition of the relations. Similarity is determined both by the number of concatenated relations shared and by the similarity of those relations. Thus, *uncharted-survey* is similar to *irrevocable-repeal* because it shares two of the three concatenated relations, lacking only the contrast relation. *Immovable-anchor* is more similar, having three concatenated relations, but in place of an action-object relation it has an action-instrument relation. The closest to the stem is *unwieldy-lift* which differs from the stem only in using a pseudo-contradictory instead of a contradictory relation. Explanation of the similarity of this pair requires not only an account of the concatenated relations, but also of the elements of which contrast relations are composed.

Relations of the complexity of *irrevocable-repeal* and *hammer-piano* tax our ability to identify relations accurately, when presented out of context as they are in analogy problems. Their difficulty, however, makes the point that relation identification is a creative ability. The time and effort required to understand these complex relations make it very apparent that the relations are not directly stored in memory.

A comparison of the unitary and analytic approaches

The major difference between the unitary and analytic approaches to semantic relations is the issue of whether relations are analyzable into more primitive components. A second difference concerns the question of whether most relations are directly prestored in memory, as network theories assume, or computed from the representation of the concepts, as relation element theory assumes. A third difference is the importance assigned to evaluation processes in making judgments involving relations. For network theories, this process, although necessary, assumes little importance because all relations are clearly and unambiguously represented by relation

Table 13. Word pairs from a graduate record exam analogy item involving concatenated relations. (* indicates the key-pair.)
Relations are represented by a network of labelled links. The choice pairs are concatenations of similar relations. The correct choice has exactly the same relation as the stem. Other choices vary in similarity to the stem.

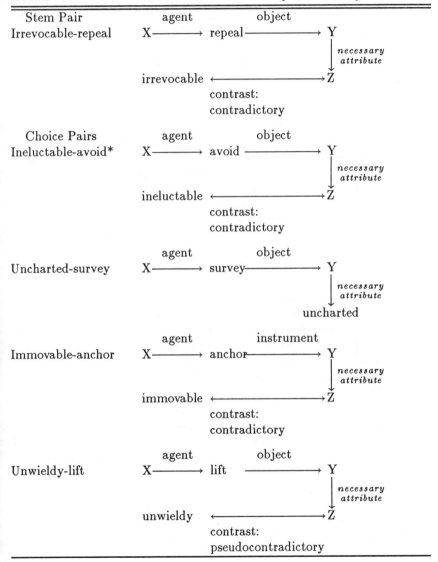

markers; the explanatory focus is on retrieval processes. For relation element theory the evaluation process is central, since it is responsible for the initial identification of a relation and for all judgments about the relation. These three points of comparison are addressed by different phenomena.

1. *Relation similarity.* Similarity judgments require that the things compared be decomposed into aspects in which they are the same and different. The evidence that subjects can reliably sort relations in principled ways thus supports the assumption of relation element theory that relations are composed of elements. Network theories cannot directly account for graded similarity judgments about relations since markers are unitary. Two markers are either the same or different, like apples and oranges.

Two defenses of the network position are possible. First, a network might contain markers for each of the major families of relations in Figures 1 and 2. This *family marker* position accounts for the major feature of the sorting data, the families of relations. Relations that have the same marker would be sorted together and each type of marker would appear as a separate family in a clustering solution. Family markers do not, however, account for the similarity between families or for the similarity of relations within families. These similarities were accounted for by relation elements [Stasio et al. 1985; Chaffin and Herrmann 1987].

2. *Relation discrimination.* The ability to distinguish relations within a family is required to solve analogy problems in which all of the choices come from the same family, i.e., homogeneous items on the SRT (Semantic Relations Test) of Ross et al. [1987]. This ability is not, therefore, explained by the family marker position. According to this position all of the choice pairs for homogeneous analogy items have the same relation marker and so all are equally good answers. Responding to these items should therefore be at chance level. Responding to homogeneous items on the SRT was, however, well above chance for three of the five relation families studied. The family marker position does not, therefore, provide an adequate account of the ability to evaluate the similarity of relations.

According to relation element theory, analogy items are solved by comparing the elements of the stem relation with the elements of each of the choice relations. The choice that matches most closely is the key. The SRT provides evidence for this account by showing that degree of knowledge of the family and of specific components differs by relation family. Thus, in solving analogy items people decompose relations into at least a family and a specific component.

The ability to sort semantic relations and the ability to solve analogies both require the decomposition of relations into more basic constituents. These abilities thus provide support for relation element theory, which identifies the more basic constituents as relation elements, and are inconsistent with network and other unitary approaches which assume that relations are unanalyzable semantic primitives.

3. *Relation identification.* We have discussed and rejected one defense of network theories against the criticism that they do not account for relation similarity judgments. A second defense is that the similarity judgments made in relation sorting and analogy tasks do not reflect the way that relations are normally processed. People can decompose relations into elements when given time for prolonged reflection, the argument runs, but do not do so in the ordinary course of relation comprehension.

Evidence relevant to this claim comes from studies of relation verification in which subjects make relation judgments under time pressure, typically responding in less than two seconds. Performance in the relation verification task can be assumed to reflect the rapid processes of relation identification involved in the comprehension of relations in everyday situations. The relation similarity effect, the most robust effect in the relation verification literature, strongly suggests that relation verification involves the processing of relation elements. The most direct evidence for an evaluation of relation elements comes from evidence that three elements of antonymy affect antonym judgments in a speeded relation verification task and in an unspeeded rating task.

Relation element theory explains relation verification as a process of comparing elements of the stimulus relation against elements of the target relation that the subject is asked to look for. The effects of relation similarity on the latency of relation verification are attributed to this comparison process. The effect for "yes" responses is due to the fact that good examples of a target relation have the criterial relation elements more clearly than poorer examples and so require less prolonged evaluation. The effect for "no" responses is attributed to the fact that pairs whose relation resembles the target relation have some of the elements of the target relation, both independent and dependent, and these must be evaluated. For pairs whose relation has no resemblance to the target relation, only the independent elements need be processed; the processing of dependent elements is made unnecessary by the absence of the higher order elements on which they depend.

Network theories provide a plausible account of relation similarity effects for "yes" responses in terms of distance of the pathway between the two concepts, or the level of activation of the link; good examples of a relation are more closely or more strongly linked. The relation similarity effect for "no" responses is, however, problematic for network theories [Smith 1977]. One suggestion is that pairs whose relation is more similar to the target relation may also have more possible pathways to be searched [Collins and Loftus 1975]. Another course is to attribute the effect, not to retrieval processes, but to the evaluation process, as relation element theory does [Collins and Loftus 1975]. The difficulty in this case is to account for the nature of the criterion which, to be the source of a similarity effect, cannot be a unitary marker but must be made up of simpler elements.

Context effects of the sort demonstrated by Roth and Shoben [1983] present a similar kind of difficulty for a network theory. The effect must be attributed to changes in the criterion due to the context. This is readily explained by relation element theory as the addition or alteration of an element in the criterion. Such small adjustments to a criterion are not possible for network models because the criterion is a unitary marker.

One effect for which network theories do provide a good account is the effect of counterexample frequency on the latency of "no" responses [Lorch 1978; Holyoak and Glass 1975]. This effect appears to be due to the retrieval of prestored relational knowledge of the kind that network theories assume forms the basis of all relational knowledge. In order to account for this type of effect relation element theory must also allow that some relational knowledge is directly stored in memory. Unlike network theories, however, relation element theory does not assume that this is the case for all relational knowledge, but only for relational knowledge that is directly learned. For example, children learn examples of antonymy in school; relations may be directly stored for these pairs.

4. *Relation expressions.* Network theories provide a ready account of relation expressions, e.g., *component, portion,* by treating them as lexical entries for relation markers. However, this account assumes that the meanings of relation terms are unitary like the relation markers. The ability of subjects to sort part-terms into meaningful groups thus provides the same kind of difficulty for a network theory as the ability to sort word pair relations discussed above. The view that the meanings of relation expressions are represented by relation markers also makes the strong assumption that there is a one-to-one correspondence of relation terms and relation markers. This is a questionable assumption given the phenomenon of relation ambiguity.

The ability to sort relation expressions is readily explained by relation element theory: the meanings of relation expressions are decomposable into constituents that correspond to relation elements. Expressions are sorted on the basis of the number or proportion of elements that they share. The relation element account would allow a one-to-one correspondence of relation expressions and word pair relations; it would also be possible that the mapping is less close. The phenomenon of relation ambiguity makes the latter position the more plausible alternative.

5. *Relation ambiguity.* The fact that word pair relations can be ambiguous means that there cannot be a one-to-one relation between word pair

relations and relation expressions, as network theories assume, unless relation expressions share the same ambiguities. This does not appear to be the case; "A display is part of an exhibit" does not mean the same thing as "A display is the same as an exhibit." Rather each relation expression appears to refer to some aspects of a word pair relation and not to others. Thus a refrigerator may be a *component, portion,* or *feature* of a *kitchen* depending on the aspect of a relation that is most salient at the time.

The phenomenon of relation ambiguity indicates that the relation that is perceived between two concepts does not necessarily exhaust all of the aspects of the representation of the two concepts. There may be other aspects that did not enter into the first relation, but which contribute to the elements that make up the second relation. Relation ambiguity thus requires an account of relations that recognizes that they are constructed from concepts that are themselves decomposable.

This type of an account can be provided by relation element theory. When the relation of two concepts is identified, the most salient of the relation elements that can be supported by the two concepts will be extracted. The nature of the relation can then be identified by matching these elements to a criterial set of elements which may be drawn from a relational concept stored in memory, or constructed on the basis of information present in the context, or some combination of the two. The relation identified in this way may not encompass all of the relation elements that the two concepts are capable of supporting. In this case there is the possibility that another package of relation elements may be derived from the same concepts and matched to another relational concept. In this case the relation of the two concepts is ambiguous, like that of *exhibit-display.*

Relation ambiguity is not readily accounted for by network theories. An assumption of the network approach is that each pair of concepts is connected by a single pointer with a single marker. The phenomenon of relation ambiguity contradicts this assumption. What would a network theory look like if this assumption were abandoned? The theory would look like a relation element theory. The fundamental assumption of the relation element approach is that relations are decomposable into more primitive elements. Multiple pointers or multiple markers between nodes would embody this assumption of relation element theory.

6. *Relation productivity.* The ability to view the relations of a single word pair at more than one level of complexity is explained by relation element theory in the same way as relation ambiguity is explained. The relation identified at a particular time need not make use of all of the elements that a pair of concepts can support. As more elements are added, the complexity and specificity of the relation identified increases. As with relation ambiguity, this phenomenon is not readily explained by network

theories as it appears to require that nodes representing concepts may be connected by multiple pointers or markers.

The productive nature of the ability to perceive relations supports the assumption of relation element theory that relations are constructed from concepts as required, rather than being prestored, as assumed by network theories. The identification of a novel word pair, e.g., *frigate-blueprint*, with a familiar relational concept is explained as the result of constructing elements on the basis of knowledge of the two concepts and matching them with elements of a relation concept stored in memory. A network theory, in contrast, must make the implausible assumption that every relation between two concepts that can be recognized is directly represented in memory.

The ability to concatenate relations is, in contrast, readily explained by a network model. Network theories would account for the identification of a concatenated relation, e.g., *irrevocable-repeal*, as the result of a process of tracing a path in a network. Network theories can also account for the similarity of concatenated relations which is due to variations in the number of relations linked. For example, the relation of *uncharted-survey* is a concatenation of two of the three relations involved in *irrevocable-repeal* and the two relations are therefore similar. Network theories do not, however, account for the similarity of concatenated relations when that similarity depends on the similarity of two individual links. For example, the relation of *unwieldy-lift* differs from that of *irrevocable-repeal* in having a pseudo-contradictory instead of a contradictory relation for one link. Explanation of the similarity of contradictory and pseudo-contrary relations, we have argued above, requires relation elements.

Relation element theory accounts for concatenated relations in a similar fashion to network theory with the important difference that the relations that are concatenated are represented by elements rather than by unitary markers. This allows relation element theory to account for the similarity of pairs like *irrevocable-repeal* and *unwieldy-lift* in terms of the similarity of the relations that are concatenated. The pseudo-contradictory relation that is concatenated to produce *unwieldy-lift* involves opposition in connotative meaning while the contradictory relation in *irrevocable-repeal* involves opposition in denotative meaning.

Conclusion

Relations are abstract concepts. The phenomena that we have examined reveal five characteristics that relational concepts share with concrete concepts of the kind that have been studied in some detail by psychologists [e.g., Smith and Medin 1981]. First, relations are analyzable into more basic elements. The same has been widely assumed of other concepts [e.g.,

Miller and Johnson-Laird 1976; Tversky 1977]. Second, individual instances of relations, represented in our discussion by word pairs, vary in the degree to which they are typical of particular relations. Differences in typicality are also characteristic of instances of concepts of concrete objects and of colors [Rosch and Mervis 1975]. Third, relations vary in the ease with which they can be expressed. Some relations require only a short phrase, e.g., *part of*, others require more elaborate expression, e.g., *a component that produces sound by striking*. Descriptions of examples of other concepts are similarly characterized by a range of codability [Brown and Lenneberg 1954]. Fourth, individual instances of relations may be seen as examples of more than one relational concept, e.g., *exhibit-display*. Similarly, concepts of physical objects may be identified in terms of two more general concepts, e.g., a *piano* is both a *musical instrument* and a *piece of furniture*. Fifth, a new relation may be recognized as an elaboration or concatenation of other, familiar relations. Similar flexibility is characteristic of other types of concepts; e.g., in addition to the familiar concept of a *strawberry*, we can recognize overripe strawberries, or a cross between a strawberry and a raspberry.

The assumption that network and other unitary theories explain semantic relations is mistaken. The unitary approach takes the view that relations are represented in memory by unitary markers. This does not, of course, constitute an explanation of the nature of the relational concepts; it simply asserts that they are represented. What then is the function of the relation markers that appear in network theories and other unitary accounts of memory and meaning? Relation markers are theoretical constructs; their value must be assessed in terms of the adequacy of the theories in which they appear. The domain of these theories is wide, but to the extent that the theories claim to give an account of semantic relations and the phenomena that characterize them, unitary markers must be inadequate [Johnson-Laird et al. 1984; but see Chang 1986].

An explanation of relational concepts must account for their nature in terms of their composition. Such an account is given by relation element theory. The theory provides an account of the phenomena described here that is superior to the unitary account. Relation element theory also directs attention to important phenomena and raises questions that are obscured by a unitary approach. For example, relation element theory raises the question of how relation elements are derived from the representation of concepts; whether totally new relation elements can be readily created; and whether some or all elements are cognitive universals. These questions merit further inquiry. It is only through careful examination of the phenomena that characterize semantic relations that such questions can be approached. We have given a preliminary characterization of six of these phenomena.

Acknowledgments

We thank our colleagues Alan Searleman, Jon Vaughan, and Mort Winston for numerous discussions about semantic relations. We thank our students who contributed to the research we have described: Gina Conti, Margaret P. Daniel, Donald Peters, Julie Ross, Theresa Stasio, Peter Robbins, Valerie Tatro of Hamilton College and Ann Adam, Keith Andrews, Donna Transue, Alyce Russo, and Phillips Williams, of Trenton State College.

The writing of this chapter was supported by a post-doctoral fellowship from the Educational Testing Service to the first author and by a fellowship from the University of Manchester to the second author.

References

Anderson, J. R. 1976. *Language, Memory, and Thought.* Hillsdale, NJ: Erlbaum.

Bejar, I., Chaffin, R., and Embretson, S. 1988. Applying cognitive research results to GRE test development: Analogies. Manuscript in preparation.

Brown, R., and Lenneberg, E. H. 1954. A study in language and cognition. *Journal of Abnormal and Social Psychology,* 49, 454-462.

Chaffin, R. and Herrmann, D. J. 1984. The similarity and diversity of semantic relations. *Memory and Cognition,* 12, 134-141.

Chaffin, R. and Herrmann, D. J. 1986. Relation element theory: A new account of the representation and processing of semantic relations. In D. Gorfein and R. Hoffman, eds. *Learning and Memory: The Ebbinghaus Centennial Conference.* Hillsdale, NJ: Erlbaum.

Chaffin, R. and Herrmann, D. J. 1988. Effects of relation similarity on part-whole decisions. *Journal of General Psychology,* 115, 131-139.

Chaffin, R., Herrmann, D. J., and Winston, M. 1988. A taxonomy of part-whole relations: Effects of part-whole relation type on relation naming and relation identification. *Cognition and Language,* 3, 1-32.

Chaffin, R., and Peirce, L. in press. *A taxonomy of semantic relations for the classification of GRE analogy items.* Educational Testing Service, Technical Report.

Chang, T. M. 1986. Semantic memory: Facts and models. *Psychological Bulletin,* 99, 199-220.

Collins, A. M., and Loftus, E. F. 1975. A spreading activation theory of semantic processing. *Psychological Review,* 82, 407-428.

Conti, G. 1978. *Quine, Meaning, and Opposition.* Unpublished honors thesis. Hamilton College, Clinton, NY.

Cruse, D. A. 1979. On the transitivity of the part-whole relation. *Journal of Linguistics*, **15**, 29-38.

Cruse, D. A. 1986. *Lexical Semantics*. Cambridge: Cambridge University Press.

Glass, A. L., and Holyoak, K. J. 1975. Alternative conceptions of semantic memory. *Cognition*, **3**, 313-339.

Herrmann, D. J. 1978. An old problem for the new psychosemantics: Synonymity. *Psychological Bulletin*, **85**, 490-512.

Herrmann, D. J., and Chaffin, R. 1986. Comprehension of semantic relations as a function of definitions of relations. To appear in F. Klix, ed., *Learning and Memory*. Berlin: North-Holland.

Herrman, D. J., Chaffin, R., Conti, G., Peters, D., and Robbins, P. 1979. Comprehension of antonymy and the generality of categorization models. *Journal of Experimental Psychology: Human Learning and Memory*, **5**, 585-597.

Herrmann, D. J., Chaffin, R., Daniel, M. P., and Wool, R. S. 1986. The role of elements of relation definitions in antonym and synonym comprehension. *Zeitschrift für Psychologie*, **194**, 134-153.

Holyoak, K. J., and Glass, A. L. 1975. The role of contradictions and counterexamples in the rejection of false sentences. *Journal of Verbal Learning and Verbal Behavior*, **14**, 215-239.

Hume, D. 1739/1965. *A Treatise of Human Nature*. L.A. Selby Bigge, ed., Oxford: Clarendon Press.

Johnson-Laird, P. N., Herrmann, D. J., and Chaffin, R. 1984. Only connections: A critique of semantic networks. *Psychological Bulletin*, **96** 292-315.

Kintsch, J. 1980. Semantic memory: A tutorial. In R. S. Nickerson, ed., *Attention and Performance*, **8**. Hillsdale, NJ: Erlbaum.

Klix, F. 1980. On the structure and function of semantic memory. In F. Klix and J. Hoffman, eds., *Cognition and Memory*. Amsterdam: North Holland.

Leech, G. 1974. *Semantics*. Baltimore: Penguin Books.

Lorch, R. F., Jr. 1978. The role of two types of semantic information in the processing of false sentences. *Journal of Verbal Learning and Verbal Behavior*, **17**, 523-537.

Lyons, J. 1968. *Introduction to Theoretical Linguistics*. London: Cambridge University Press.

Lyons, J. 1977. *Semantics*, **1**. London: Cambridge University Press.

Markman, E. M. and Hutchinson, J. E. 1984. Children's sensitivity to constraints on word meaning: Taxonomic versus thematic relations. *Cognitive Psychology*, **16**, 1- 27.

Miller, G. A., and Johnson-Laird, P. N. 1976. *Language and Perception*. Cambridge, MA: Harvard University Press.

Norman, D. A., and Rumelhart, D. E. 1975. *Explorations in Cognition*. San Francisco: Freeman.

Osgood, C. E., Suci, G. J., and Tannenbaum, P. H. 1957. *The Measurement of Meaning*. Urbana, University of Illinois Press.

Rapaport, D. 1974. *The History of the Concept of Association of Ideas*. New York: International Universities Press.

Roget's International Thesaurus of English Words and Phrases (3rd ed.). 1962. NY: Crowell.

Rosch, E. C., and Mervis, C. B. 1975. Family resemblances: Studies in the internal structure of categories. *Cognitive Psychology*, **7**, 192-233.

Ross, J. L., Herrmann, D. J., Vaughan, J., and Chaffin, R. 1987. Semantic relation comprehension: Components and correlates. ERIC Document ED 274-683.

Roth, E. M. and Shoben, E. J. 1983. The effect of context on the structure of categories. *Cognitive Psychology*, **15**, 346-378.

Schank, R. C., and Abelson, R. P. 1977. *Scripts, Plans, Goals and Understanding*. Hillsdale, NJ: Erlbaum.

Searleman, A., Herrmann, D. J., Chaffin, R., Parsons, S., and Vaughan, J. 1986. Ability to identify semantic relations as a function of handedness, strength of handedness, handwriting posture, sex, and familial sinistrality. Unpublished manuscript.

Smith, E. E. 1977. Theories of semantic memory. In W. K. Estes, ed., *Handbook of Learning and Cognitive Processes*, **5**. Hillsdale, NJ: Erlbaum.

Smith, E. E., and Medin, D. L. 1981. *Categories and Concepts*. Cambridge, MA: Harvard University Press.

Stasio, T., Herrmann, D. J., and Chaffin, R. 1985. Predictions of relation similarity according to relation definition theory. *Bulletin of the Psychonomic Society*, **23**, 5-8.

The Shorter Oxford English Dictionary (3rd Ed.). 1965. C. T. Onions, ed. Oxford: Oxford University Press.

Transue, D. 1982. *Looking at partonymy*. Unpublished honors thesis, Trenton State College.

Tversky, A. 1977. Features of similarity. *Psychological Review*, **84**, 214-241.

Webster's New Dictionary of Synonyms. 1973. P. B. Gove, ed. Springfield, MA: Merriam.

Winston, M., Chaffin, R., and Hermann, D. J. 1987. A taxonomy of part-whole relations. *Cognitive Science*, **11**, 417-444.

14
Relational models and metascience*

WILLIAM FRAWLEY
DEPARTMENT OF LINGUISTICS
UNIVERSITY OF DELAWARE
NEWARK, DELAWARE 19716

Abstract

Metascience is based on an understanding of the language that scientists use. Each branch of science has its own scientific sublanguage – and the changes in that sublanguage reveal the changes in the focus of the science itself. Scientific revolutions are mirrored by revolutions in the language. Relational models, particularly the one designed by Mel'čuk, provide powerful tools for understanding the semantic structure of scientific language and studying the ways the structure changes.

Introduction

The paper that follows is designed to illustrate how the relational models of computational lexicography can be used in the service of a particular kind of descriptive metascience. This project requires several disclaimers.

First, what follows is neither wholly computational lexicography nor wholly metascience. Since the paper concerns the connection between the

---

* I wish to express my thanks to Igor Mel'čuk, and to an anonymous referee, who made helpful suggestions for revision.

two, I often gloss over certain details of metascience, apparently glibly, not because the issues are unimportant but because I approach the topic as a linguist first and foremost.

Second, I sometimes avoid discussion of certain issues in computational lexicography, again because I have a split purpose. If computational linguists and philosophers choose to take me to task for my arguments, I ask that they do so only for my sins of commission, not those of omission; I plead no contest to the latter, given my purposes.

Third, I am not here to judge kinds of metascience since I have no intention to add to the already numerous schools of metascientific thought. I prefer, instead, to try to work within one school, using the tools of computational lexicography, in order to document how a type of metascience can be done consistently and reasonably clearly.

Finally, the project which follows does not require that one reject all schools of metascience other than the one discussed, only accept the premises of one kind of metascience, textual metascience. No doubt, this exercise raises more questions than answers, probably because the claims are, at least, specific and, therefore, unlike mystical theories, can be understood by people other than their proponents.

The varieties and goals of metascience

Several years ago, the linguist James McCawley, with typical McCawley humor, published a book titled *Thirty Million Theories of Grammar*. The irony in his title is meant to call attention to the fact that in linguistics there are as many theories of grammar as there are practitioners of the discipline. If one changes "grammar" to "metascience," McCawley's title becomes an accurate description of the current scene in the study of the nature and progress of scientific knowledge.

Even a cursory survey of the varieties of metascience bears out the claim that schools of metascience have been proliferating, not quite at the rate of one per person, but at the rate of one per principle. A shopping list of schools of metascience includes the following: logical empirical metascience [Carnap 1967]; general cognitive metascience [Kuhn 1970, 1977]; empirical cognitive metascience [Mitroff 1974]; descriptive, evolutionary, cognitive metascience [Campbell 1977]; naive cognitive metascience [McCloskey 1983]; falsificationist metascience [Popper 1975]; methodological metascience [Lakatos 1970]; sociological metascience [Bloor 1976]; ethnomethodological metascience [Gilbert and Mulkay 1984]; semiotic metascience [Gopnik 1977]; dialectical hermeneutic metascience [Habermas 1970]; documentational metascience [Garfield 1979]; and even anarchistic metascience [Feyerabend 1972]. If one also includes the human sciences as the object of inquiry of metascience, then there are also such schools as deconstructionist metascience [Derrida 1977] and discursive metascience [Foucault 1972].

There is unity in the apparent diversity, however; that unity lies in the goals of the pursuit itself. Metascience is a species of epistemology, and all versions of metascience adhere to the principles of epistemological analysis, which itself follows two lines of inquiry (see, e.g., Hamlyn 1970, whose discussion remains one of the most succinct and lucid of all the expositions of epistemology; see also White 1982).[1]

The first line of inquiry may be called "essentialist" because it concerns the *nature of the object* under scrutiny. Essentialism focuses on the following major questions, a list meant to be illustrative, not exhaustive, of typical concerns: What is knowledge? Is knowledge an object, an activity, or a process? What kinds of knowledge are there? Is belief a form of knowledge? Is there such a thing as scientific knowledge as distinct from, say, mere social knowledge? Is there true knowledge to be distinguished from pseudo-knowledge? Are some forms of knowledge more reliable than others? What is the scope of knowledge distinguished as such? Is there general knowledge that exceeds all particular lines of inquiry? Is knowledge composite or unitary? Is knowledge built up out of epistemological atoms, or is it ready-made?

The second line of inquiry may be termed "proceduralist" since it concerns the *means of knowledge*, not the thing itself. Proceduralism does not address the existence and forms of knowledge, but the ways that knowledge is gotten, maintained, and advanced. Typical proceduralist questions are: How is knowledge possible? Does knowledge develop, and if so, how? What is the relation between a knowing subject and the object of knowledge? Can knowledge be said to exist outside of a knowing subject, and if so, how is that known? How is knowledge justified? How are claims to knowledge discarded or maintained? How does knowledge progress? How is knowledge transferred from one knower to another? How does an innovation occur?

Typical epistemological concerns do not always necessarily fall neatly under either essentialist or proceduralist domains. For instance, truth can be either an essentialist problem – e.g., self-evident truth or truth inhering in the object of knowledge – or a proceduralist problem – e.g., argued truth, theory-bound truth, or statistical truth. Entire schools of epistemology do not fall neatly into essentialist or proceduralist camps either, since different sorts of epistemology can privilege certain questions and answers and assign them to different, perhaps contrary, domains.

---

[1] In the discussion that follows, I am indebted to Ferreira 1988.

When we look specifically at metascience, insofar as it is a branch of epistemology, it follows the same variable route as all epistemologies. By taking scientific knowledge as a special object of inquiry, metascience seeks to essentialize it in certain ways. Is scientific knowledge self-evident, for example? Is scientific knowledge a thing or an activity? Are there forms of scientific knowledge? Is there a priori scientific knowledge? Similarly, metascience proceduralizes scientific knowledge. How does a scientist differ from a naive person in acquiring scientific knowledge, for example? Is scientific knowledge justified in a consistent, inconsistent, or ad hoc manner? How does schooling contribute to scientific knowledge? These lines of inquiry may privilege certain essentialist questions over proceduralist ones, or vice versa, but the same questions have to be asked by any school of metascience, even if the school deems the answers absurd.

A few examples may clarify matters at this point. Logical empiricist metascience, once the received view in metascience but now seriously out of vogue, put the answers to essentialist questions in the external world: knowledge was fact, and the groundwork of any science lay in observational statements, which clearly reflected objects in the world. Scientific knowledge was something that was discovered, not something determined, and thus proceduralist questions were reduced to a minimum. All proceduralist questions were answered by logic, and logical justification preceded understanding.

On the other hand, cognitive metascience, of the sort engendered by Kuhn's work, answers the essentialist and proceduralist queries differently. Cognitivism assumes naive realism, but sees scientific knowledge as a cognitive construct: the essence of scientific knowledge is concepts. What kinds of knowledge are there? There are prototypical concepts, "exemplars," and constellations of concepts, "disciplinary matrices." What is the difference between scientific knowledge and non-scientific knowledge? The differences lie in their conceptualization. Cognitive metascience shifts the focus of essentialism to intension and puts the rest of the baggage of metascience in proceduralist inquiry. How do we get scientific knowledge? We form a social group. Who gets scientific knowledge? Only those who are privileged to join the social group are legitimate "scientists."

We can generate more peculiar schools of metascience by giving more peculiar answers to essentialist and proceduralist questions. Feyerabend's metascientific anarchism answers essentialist questions rather simply: scientific knowledge is power, and power is traded and dealt. The rest of anarchistic metascience is devoted to proceduralist issues. Who deals in scientific knowledge? Who has made great power deals in the past? Which groups have been crushed out of existence in the trading of scientific knowledge?

Naive cognitive metascience, to give another example, answers the essentialist questions very much as Kuhn does, but offers different proceduralist answers. How is conceptual scientific knowledge obtained? It is gotten through inference procedures that are quite unlike formal inference, through what might be called "naive induction." Who gets scientific knowledge? Only those who are schooled in science learn science as concepts.

The upshot of this long preamble is that while the scene of metascience is diverse, epistemology deals out a limited number of principles to metascience, and the diversity is accountable for the privileging of certain epistemological concerns. This is not to say that metascience is thereby simplified; it is to say, instead, that metascience is understandable.

From text-based science to computational lexicography

Over the past decade or so, it has become increasingly clear that several forms of metascience share some fundamental ideas about how science operates. Work in cognitive metascience, ethnomethodological metascience, semiotic metascience, and rhetorical metascience suggests that the scientific enterprise is largely constituted by language, and a particular kind of language at that: text. The arguments for this position are long and detailed, and I treat them more thoroughly elsewhere [see Frawley 1981; Frawley 1986; Frawley 1987]. This convergence can be seen in the consensus that science, like all forms of advanced knowledge in industrialized countries, is the activity of *specialized language users* who have spent a considerable period of apprenticeship in a *language institution* – otherwise known as a *school*. Those who have learned the linguistic practices of their superiors pass these (literate) practices on to other specialized language users, with this entire process circularly defining scientists as both the sources and judges of the linguistic practice. [See, especially, the citations and arguments in Frawley 1986 and Frawley 1987; see also Bourdieu and Passeron 1977.]

A simpler and more apposite way to see all this is to examine the answers which these schools give to some of the essentialist and proceduralist questions outlined above.

What is scientific knowledge? Scientific knowledge is conceptual information gotten from texts instructed in science classes at school. Scientific knowledge is therefore something that is comprehended and is thus a semantic object primarily [see, e.g., Olson 1977].

What kinds of scientific knowledge are there? There are as many kinds of scientific knowledge as there are particular textual practices or domains. A priori knowledge is historically textual a priori knowledge. Kinds of scientific knowledge correlate with the sublanguages involved in the textual practices that constitute school [see, e.g., Foucault 1972, who calls the sublanguages "discursive spaces"].

What is true scientific knowledge, as compared to pseudo-scientific knowledge? True scientific knowledge is that information which is *cited* most often in scientific texts [see, e.g., Derrida 1977].

What is the scope of scientific knowledge? There is no general scientific knowledge because there are no general scientific texts. General texts only trivialize scientific knowledge, in much the same way as popular books trivialize scientific texts. There are only specialized texts with a limited domain and readership; scientific knowledge is thus limited to specialized texts [see, e.g., Frawley 1987].

Is scientific knowledge composite? It is, because texts themselves are composite. Scientific texts are built out of semantic and rhetorical atoms, as are all texts. Syntax takes a secondary role here because the focus of textual study is the text units themselves [see Gopnik 1972]. In short, scientific knowledge is only textually articulated knowledge, and that knowledge is clearly constructed from basic units.

How is scientific knowledge possible? Scientific knowledge is possible only through schooling and reading because these are the two activities that are the basis of the institution that creates and certifies scientists. All other scientific activities, such as laboratory work, fieldwork, etc., are subordinate to reading and writing because the latter activities identify the very problems, and the typical solutions, of a science to begin with. Thus, scientific knowledge is possible only insofar as the reading and writing of specialized texts are possible [see Frawley 1987].

How are the participants of scientific knowledge involved in science? Scientific participants are selected not only by the school system to succeed [see, e.g., Bourdieu and Passeron 1977], but also by their very reading habits and the nature of reading itself. With science as the interaction of readers/writers with scientific text, scientific investigation first becomes a question of how texts are read and written, and, in that activity, it is known that the structure of the text itself is crucial.

How is scientific knowledge justified? Truth is a matter of propositional coherence and "intertextuality," to use a term in vogue in more humanistic textual study. This means that scientific truth is a matter of how texts refer to other texts: truth is a claim in discourse.

How does scientific knowledge progress? This question has perhaps the simplest answer of them all: through publishing. Scientific progress is not a cumulative enterprise, but a fragmentary one. Scientific knowledge is not accumulated, in the Kuhnian sense, but is distributed, with some of the texts selected in schools and institutes and some abandoned and lost in the maze of scientific publication. In all cases, the growth of scientific knowledge is a measure of the growth of its literature [see, e.g., Anthony, East, and Slater 1969].

The essentialist questions focus on the scientific text. The procedural-ist questions focus on the activity of reading (and writing), with the text given priority. If metascience is correctly argued to be a version of text study, then metascience (or its descriptive part, at least) is converted to a knowledge representation system sufficiently rich and specific to model the semantic structures underlying the sublanguages which constitute the texts of scientific disciplines.

For the past seven years or so, I have been working on developing such a system, deriving it almost totally from the meaning-text model of I.A. Mel'čuk [1981]. That model is itself based on Mel'čuk's Explanatory Com-binatorial Dictionary [hereafter ECD – see Mel'čuk et al. 1984, among many other citations]. My own model amounts to a computational-semantic system that explicitly represents the sublanguages of the sciences.

There are currently dozens of knowledge representation systems for tex-tual information, so why this sort of system? The answer is that the best scheme is one which relies on lexical relations, as does the ECD, for reasons outlined below. Thus, the system below does not have to be exactly as it is to be the best system for the representation of sublanguage texts, but whatever the system, it must be lexical-relational.

There are several types of knowledge representation systems for the se-mantic information underlying texts in general: the propositional system, the rhetorical system, and the conceptual system. We will look at each briefly and judge it against the requirements for texts in sublanguages.

The propositional system is one of the earliest developed knowledge rep-resentation systems for text [see, e.g., Kintsch and van Dijk 1978]. The assumption behind the propositional system is that any text can be ana-lyzed into its constituent propositions, and it is the organization of these propositions which forms the knowledge base for the text. The proposi-tional system is a semantic version of the (now untenable) assumption that a discourse is a set of sentences strung together by conjunctions.

The propositional system poses several problems for the analysis of texts in scientific sublanguages. For one thing, propositional systems typically have superficial systems of connectives so that the semantic parsing of the text links the propositions in simple precedence and dominance relations. The interesting linkages across propositions in the text are thereby lost or incorrectly collapsed into a small set (e.g., class membership, implication, etc.). The gist of the text remains, but its structure does not, apart from the hierarchical organization of propositions from main to peripheral "ideas."

For another thing, propositional systems do not show how the propositions themselves are put together. This is critical because much of the empirical work on scientific sublanguages reveals that the best approach to the sublanguage is a lexical one: i.e., the approach should begin with propositional constituents, not with propositions. This is evident in the work of Gopnik [1972] and especially in the recent, detailed work of Phillips [1985], who argues that network representations of the structure of scientific texts must be organized around "nuclear nodes" which represent the lexicon of science: "in most instances nuclear nodes represent the foundations of cognitive structures critical to the construction of subject matter" [Phillips 1985, p. 143]. Furthermore, even approaches to scientific sublanguage that claim to be propositional are actually lexical, or require elaborate lexical structures to derive the propositions. A good instance of this is the work by Hobbs [1986], whose model relies on first-order calculus but must be augmented with selectional restrictions.

Finally, the propositional system has, in fact, been used in the past as a model of metascience, and not very successfully. Propositional systems were the basis of logical positivist metascience, and while some types of scientific knowledge were amenable to propositional representation, it has become apparent that not all, or even very much, of such knowledge should be reduced to propositional formalisms. This is one of the central findings of ethnomethodological metascience, where it is shown that the everyday discourse that constitutes scientific knowledge is very different from a formal system.

In contrast, the rhetorical system operates from the assumption that textual organization derives from abstract discourse predicates (rhetorical predicates) that link propositions into typical discourse forms. Rhetorical systems are the backbone of "schema approaches" to text. This system has developed, to a great extent, from work like Grimes' [1975], which has postulated a set of categories such as EXEMPLIFICATION, EQUIVALENCE, ATTRIBUTION, and so on, to link the propositions of any text: different text structures and text types result from differential choice of rhetorical predicates and differential organization of those predicates.

Rhetorical systems have been very useful in discourse analysis, psycholinguistics, and even in some forms of computational-semantic text processing [see, e.g., McKeown 1985]. However, they remain problematic for the analysis of texts in scientific sublanguage. A primary reason for their limited usefulness is that rhetorical systems do not provide for the *necessary* structure of texts, but only for heuristics in text production and comprehension. As McKeown [1985, p. 53] says, they "are not grammars of text," but "common patterns of description that are used to effectively achieve the discourse purposes considered." In short, rhetorical systems provide *variable plans*, not *necessary* information.

Another problem with rhetorical systems is that they are well-suited for narrative text, but not for much else. In spite of the fact that texts in scientific sublanguage are sometimes viewed theoretically as narratives [MacIntyre 1980; Kuhn 1977, ix-xiii], and in spite of the fact that scientific texts often contain narrative sections [Friedman 1986; Pettinari 1982], scientific text is something quite different from narrative, as is evident from its cohesive structure [Smith and Frawley 1983] and its rhetorical structure [Blanton 1982].

Problems with the narrative view of scientific text are actually the result of a larger problem with the rhetorical system and its applicability to science. Rhetorical systems place great emphasis on the macrostructure of the text since, after all, the rhetorical system defines the macrostructure, which is constituted by the rhetorical predicates. Scientific text, whatever the macrostructure, places very little emphasis on the macrostructure itself. The textual organization is highly predictable, and its description needs no rich catalogue of rhetorical relations. This is not to say that the macrostructure is unimportant, since the macrostructure is related to the communicative purpose of the text and thus to such problems as anaphora resolution and deixis [see, e.g., Lehrberger 1986]. It is just to say that the range of forms of scientific text is limited. The functional load in science is carried by the *vocabulary*, not the structure.

The third system, the conceptual system, relies on the reduction of all textual information to a small set of conceptual/semantic primes, with these primes then organized into hierarchies by another small set of logical links or inferences. The classic system of this sort is Schank's Conceptual Dependency [see Schank and Abelson 1977], which relies on the hierarchical arrangement of primes through a small set of connectives to produce an abstract of input text or discourse.

Conceptual systems have their successes. They work very well within restricted domains of knowledge, where the subtleties of information can be lost with no appreciable affect on the representation or the text. This is because conceptual dependencies must abstract away from the input. Marsh's [1986] study of Navy Casualty Reports relies on this procedure, and does so effectively, by reducing input to a restricted set of semantic types, irrespective of the tokens as input. Hobbs' [1986] system does likewise, by constructing atomic propositions from abstract primes for medical reports. But it is worth noting that Hobbs' system still requires an intermediate knowledge base, derived from lexical information, between the abstract, conceptual level and the surface text.

The problems which conceptual systems pose for the analysis of texts in scientific sublanguage are clear. First, conceptual systems lose track of the lexicon entirely because they are decompositional systems and therefore rely on entailed primitives, not on the lexicon itself. This effectively eliminates the specificity required for scientific sublanguage (see below). Second, the set of linkages across primitives is not sufficiently large to capture all, or even an interesting part, of the semantic information that underlies the text. This is not to say that the conceptual systems cannot be augmented with a richer set of relations and made more robust. The situation is quite the opposite, in fact, since one of the advantages of the conceptual system is its arbitrariness, and relations can be added whenever and wherever needed. However, what is lacking, or, at least, vague, is whether or not the conceptual relations are even appropriate for scientific sublanguage and text since it appears that scientific text relies on elaborate lexical cohesion, not logical or rhetorical cohesion, for unity [see Smith and Frawley 1983]. This means that a set of *surface-sensitive* relations is required, and, thus, the abstractness of conceptual systems turns out to be a deficit in the case of scientific sublanguage.

When one looks at what the practical analysis of texts in scientific sublanguage has brought to the fore [e.g., Grishman and Kittredge 1986; Kittredge and Lehrberger 1982], it seems that successful analysis of scientific text must proceed from a lexical base. There are two reasons for this: (1) a lexical model of scientific sublanguage focuses on content; (2) a lexical model is surface-collocational.

Let us first consider content. There are all sorts of arguments that content supersedes form in texts in scientific sublanguage and, further, that content is roughly equatable to lexicon. The initial arguments in this matter have been presented above: that rhetorical form in scientific texts is of minor importance and that cohesion in scientific texts is effected lexically.

It turns out that the form of scientific texts, as represented by rhetorical predicates in rhetorical systems and by connectives in both propositional systems and conceptual systems, determines little else but the distinguishing stylistic features of science. For example, problems of textual form in the sublanguage of science concern anaphora resolution [see Lehrberger 1986], which is not a problem of scientific knowledge at all, but a question of editing.[2] This does not mean that anaphora resolution is not impor-

---

[2] To put it another way, anaphora resolution in scientific text is no different from anaphora resolution in any other kind of text; at least, that is what seems to be the case thus far in the study of scientific text. If anaphora resolution turns out to be different for scientific text, then this is all the better for both rhetorical models and for scientific sublanguage in general.

tant – it is significant for such things as automatic processing of texts in a sublanguage. Rather, it means that the heart of the matter lies elsewhere especially because analyses of texts in scientific sublanguage can get along without these formal questions, or, at least, the descriptions can be sufficiently amended to include formal features, once the work on content is done [see Walker and Amsler 1986]. Phillips puts the matter a bit more technically when he says that discourse form is to be downplayed in the analysis of scientific texts because the "items which operate on the interactive plane [discourse form, WF] to guide the reader through the complexities of the conceptual relations ... appear only relatively infrequently as nuclear" [1985, 143].

This leaves us with the problem of what content is, and that directly impinges on the question of surface-collocation. As a sublanguage, the language of science appears not to be a proper subset of English or any other natural language since the rules that operate in scientific language often are not in the standard form of the language of which the sublanguage appears to be a part.[3] This means that the language of science is relatively autonomous. As a consequence, both the syntax and semantics of the sublanguage of science – i.e., the content of scientific texts – must be described in their own terms. One indication of this relative autonomy is that the sublanguage of science is characterized by a peculiar phraseology. Sager [1986] and Hirschman [1986] both argue this point: what distinguishes scientific sublanguage is its *surface-distributional* features. Sager, for instance, says that the "distinguishing feature of sublanguage is that over certain subsets of the language the phenomenon of selection, for which rules cannot be stated for the language as a whole, is brought under the rubric of grammar" [1986, 4], which means that lexical selection appears to be "syntactified" in scientific sublanguages, giving surface collocation a high functional load. Similar claims can be found in all the collocational studies of scientific sublanguage, Finin [1986] and Friedman [1986], for example. And Phillips is perhaps the most forthright on the matter: "... on the basis of the regular co-occurrence of items separated from each other by relatively small numbers of intervening words, groupings of lexical items could be discerned which clearly articulate the principal cognitive content of the texts [of the science under investigation, WF]" [1985, p. 140].

That the content of texts in scientific sublanguage is determined by the surface-collocational features of the language is more clearly supported by the fact that some computational systems for the analysis of scientific

---

[3] The autonomy of sublanguages is by no means the received view: see, e.g., Harris 1976; below I argue more fully for the view that sublanguages are not proper subsets of the natural language of which they seem to be a part.

sublanguage fail because they are not sufficiently rich to capture all the surface-collocational distinctions which the sublanguage presents. Thus, Hirschman [1986, p. 221] has to "discard certain 'noisy' operators," such as prepositions and part-whole predicates, in her analysis because they have "too wide a distribution, which causes some 'noise' or blurring of the patterns" in the sublanguage [1986, p. 216]. While prepositions no doubt pose problems because of their high frequency, they are crucial to sublanguage analysis because they show specific semantic dependencies, or the "very stuff" of collocation! Discarding them may be immediately practical, but a sufficiently rich, surface-collocational model is called for here: the model presented below, I will argue, is one such system. Similarly, Marsh [1986, 108, fn. 1] eliminates lexical relations from her analysis because they "relate the semantic patterns to each other" [1986, 108], and do not provide intra-pattern cohesion. This is just not true: semantic relations of the sort she identifies do, in fact, relate propositional constituents – CAUSE, for example. Again, this problem in sublanguage analysis lies in the absence of a sufficient representational apparatus for all surface collocations.

In a nutshell, the question of a metascience based on the representation of the sublanguage in scientific texts comes down to an elaborate dictionary, but one which delineates not only the lexical structure of the sublanguage, but the surface-collocational features of the sublanguage as well. What is needed is a lexicographic representation that meets both Sager's [1986] observation of lexical selection syntactified and Phillips' [1985] claim that the lexicon underlies text. To my knowledge, there is only one such dictionary, Mel'čuk's ECD. We now turn to an examination of the ECD and its applicability to the problems at hand.

Some lexicographic formalisms for metascience

The Explanatory Combinatorial Dictionary has been developed principally by I.A. Mel'čuk [see, e.g., Apresyan, Mel'čuk, and Žolkovsky 1970; Mel'čuk 1981; Mel'čuk et al. 1984]. It has evolved out of a representational scheme for the information underlying texts for an automatic paraphrase project and thus it is both a dictionary and a lexically-based text processing system. Prima facie, the ECD meets the needs discussed above.

The assumptions and organization of the ECD are straightforward. A dictionary must represent all the lexico-syntactic information of an entry in succinct form and do so through a system which captures the deep and surface regularities of the lexicon. Every entry consists of the lexical item (which may be a phrase, if the phrase functions as a single item) with its syntactic, semantic, and lexical domain.

As for the syntactic domain, every lexical item is considered to be the name of a situation, whether that item is a verb, preposition, action nominal, stative nominal, or whatever, and all situations have a specified number of participants. The relations of the participants to the event are syntactically specified, as are the grammatical categories of the participants, prepositions, and morphology. The lexical item "theft," for example, obviously not a predicate, still has participants: namely, the thief (the first participant), the object stolen (the second participant), and the victim (the third participant). "Thief" is the "subject" of "theft," the "object stolen" is the "object" of "theft," and so on.

The semantic domain is more complicated. Every entry first receives an analytical definition, unlike a standard defining formula, which incorporates the syntactic specifications. This gives a core meaning of the entry and specifies how the participants are involved in the logical predicates underlying the entry. The semantic domain of an entry is ultimately an entailed, atomic proposition about the entry.

Finally, there is the lexical domain. This is represented through a system of lexical functions, or abstract semantic operators, which relate *actual lexical items* to *each other*. The currently developed list of lexical functions is in the Appendix, and the reader is enjoined to study them prior to considering the material below. Several things should be borne in mind, however.

First, the lexical functions express both paradigmatic and syntagmatic co-occurrence (substitutional and parametric, in the terminology of the ECD). Therefore, while both types of functions are in the metalanguage, the former are semantically empty, and the latter are not. This has the effect of producing not only the underlying lexical structure, in oppositional form, but also the surface co-occurrence. As argued above, both features are needed for a sublanguage model.

Second, the items that are related by lexical functions are those that actually occur in the language. The only abstraction that occurs in the model is in the metalanguage, unlike other models of the semantic/lexical structure of texts, for example. The advantage of this is that deep and surface lexical structure can be directly represented in the same system.

Third, all lexical functions can be combined to produce more specific relations across lexical items. For instance, Incep + Oper can give the beginning of an action, and Fin + Oper can yield the end of an action. Such combinations increase the number of possible co-occurrences substantially, but it is worth mentioning here that, in practice, no entry seems to instantiate more than one-tenth of the possible lexical functions (Mel'čuk personal communication).

The upshot of this entire process is that the full range of meaning of any entry can be specified explicitly. This is quite unlike either current models of text structure or current dictionaries.

Let us consider a brief example from ordinary language before we turn to the sublanguages of science. The word "give" has the following syntactic domain (the syntactic and semantic domains below are slightly simplified for ease of exposition):

GIVE: verb 1=X 2=Y 3=Z

  N N TO N
      N (3 < 2)

(This indicates that "give" has three participants: X, the first or subject, is a bare noun (it might be noted that "give" can take subject complements, as in "that you are here gives me a headache," but this is a different sense of "give" and therefore a separate entry word, or "give" #2; the reason for this is that in the latter sense, nothing is transferred – the arrival does not transfer the headache – and "give" in this sense is more like "cause"); Y, the second or object, is a bare noun; Z, the third or indirect object, is a noun which takes the preposition "to" or a bare noun which, if a bare noun, must precede Y: this captures the difference between "X gives Y to Z" and "X gives Z Y.")

The semantic domain looks as follows:

X transfers Y to Z such that Z now possesses Y and X does not possess Y.

(This atomic proposition indicates the semantic relations among the participants; it should be noted that no mention is made of the apparent need for X and Z to be human or animate, because this is a question of co-occurrence with "transfer" and "possess," not with "give.")

LEXICAL FUNCTIONS:

$Conv_{321}$(give) = take (from 1)
S_1(give) = giver
S_2(give) = gift, etc.

Now, this sort of representation can easily be given for any lexical item in the sublanguage of science, with the result being a full relational specification of the lexical information surrounding the item and its collocations in short, its textual combinatorics. We can do this in two ways. The first is to reduce to ECD form the definitions of entries in existing lexicons of scientific sublanguages; the second is to write new entries from "lexicographic fieldwork" in science. We will look at examples of each.

First, let us construct some relational formalisms for the lexicons of science by working with existing lexicons and converting them to ECD form. We will look at two entries, one from zoology [Leftwich 1963] and one from geology [American Geological Institute 1962, hereafter AGI]. Similar studies of entries from biology can be found in Frawley [1986].

The geological term is "winze." Its definition is as follows: "A vertical or inclined opening, or excavation, connecting two levels in a mine, differing from a raise only in construction" [AGI 1962, p. 540]. From this definition, we can derive a fair amount of useful lexicographic information, though not nearly all that is required for a full ECD entry; these deficiencies will be discussed below.

First, it appears that "winze" has two participants, the two levels. That is, the things that are directly connected by the situation labeled "winze" are the things connected by the digging; the mine itself is not a participant because the mine is not connected to the levels by means of "winze"; rather, the mine is the locus of "winze" and thus bears a different, non-participant relation. The syntactic domain of "winze," therefore, is as follows:

WINZE: noun $\qquad$ X=1 $\qquad$ Y=2

$\qquad\qquad\qquad\qquad$ N $\qquad\qquad$ N

The entry in the existing lexicon indicates that the participants must be bare nouns.

The semantic domain is as follows:

$\qquad$ vertical connection of X and Y

The lexical domain is roughly as follows (illustrative propositions follow each functional formula):

$Func_1$(winze) = connect (A winze connects a level with something else.)
$Func_2$(winze) = connect (same as above, because 1 = 2)
$Gener$(winze) = excavation (A winze is a kind of excavation.)
$Qual_0$(winze) = vertical, inclined (A winze is vertical or inclined.)
S_{loc} (winze) = mine (A winze typically appears in a mine.)
S_1(winze) = level (A winze is involved with levels.)
S_2(winze) = level (same as above)
Syn(winze) = raise (A winze is also a raise.)

While the above gives some of the lexical information about "winze," it gives only a small part. One way to expand the entry is to check the entries for terms mentioned in the definition. In the lexicon of geology under consideration, only "raise" appears as another entry, and in all the definitions of "raise," only the fourth is relevant: "A mine shaft driven from below upward; also called upraise, rise, and riser" [AGI 1962, p. 411]. This definition allows us to amend the above lexical domain with Gener(winze) = shaft.

However, further investigation of the additionally related terms produced by the entry for "raise" reveals that "drive" and "upraise" are not defined elsewhere in the lexicon and therefore are of no further help; "rise" and "riser" are defined, but there is nothing relevant to "winze." "Shaft" is defined, but the only relevant information is as follows: "Often specifically applied to approximately vertical shafts, as distinguished from an incline or inclined shaft" [AGI 1962, p. 447]. This suggests that the formula Gener(winze) = shaft is not to be included because a winze can be inclined while a shaft cannot. In fact, it may very well be that a shaft is a kind of winze, but this information will have to be discovered through interviews with geologists.

A brief ECD entry for "winze," then, reveals that some of its paradigmatic and syntagmatic structure can be specified, but not very much. Some of the most interesting questions remain unanswered. In particular, much of the phraseology surrounding "winze" is not represented. This is a problem with most lexicons of the sciences, which provide synonyms and something of an atomic proposition for a term, but nothing about how it actually selects co-occurrence. For instance, we need to know what kinds of verbs can go with "winze," if any, and what kinds of prepositions it can take. We also need to know more about the paradigmatic structure, such as whether or not the term has any opposites or contrasts.

The above brief entry for "winze" is thus a start, but only a start; a fuller and more useful entry would have to be derived from lexicographic interviews with geologists, at which point one could ask questions such as the following. Is there a name for a group of winzes (Mult)? Is there some way of talking about the closing off of a winze (Liqu)? Can there be more or less of a winze (Minus, Plus)? Can "winze" ever be used attributively, as in "winze X" (A_0)? Some of these questions, if not all, may be absurd to geologists. If so, that is all the better since the absence of related items shows the specific lexical structure of "winze." But, clearly, the questions have to be asked.

Now, let us consider a term from zoology, "endostyle," defined as follows:

> A glandular ciliated groove running along the floor of the pharynx in Amphioxus, in some Tunicates, and in the larvae of lampreys (Cyclostomata). It produces threads of mucus to which food particles adhere and which are passed dorsalwards round the pharynx and backwards into the gullet by ciliary action. From observations of the development of the lamprey it can be shown that the thyroid gland has evolved from the endostyle [Leftwich 1963, p. 82].

The above mini-text about "endostyle" suggests that the term has two participants: namely, the haver of the endostyle and what the endostyle produces. The syntactic domain is thus:

$$\text{ENDOSTYLE: noun} \qquad X=1 \qquad Y=2$$
$$N \qquad\qquad N$$

The semantic domain is as follows:

X's gland for Y

The lexical domain is as follows:

$Func_0(endostyle) = $ run
$Func_2(endostyle) = $ produce
$Gener(endostyle) = $ groove
$S_{loc}(endostyle) = $ pharynx
$S_1(endostyle) = $ lamprey, Amphioxus, Tunicate
$S_2(endostyle) = $ mucus
$Qual_0(endostyle) = $ ciliated, glandular

This lexical entry shows some interesting things. First, while there are connections to other purely zoological terms, such as "Amphioxus," the information for the latter entries does not tell us much about "endostyle." The lexical information here represented is about as full a picture as is available from an existing lexicon.

Second, whereas the geological entry lacked a great deal of supporting information, information which had to be garnered elsewhere, "endostyle" has a rich informational environment. Unfortunately, much of it is not lexical, or not specifically related to the lexical item at hand. For instance, the information in the second clause of the definition is more appropriately collocated with "mucus" than with "endostyle"; the fact that food adheres to mucus is, in terms of lexical functions, $S_2(mucus) = $ food and

$Oper_2(mucus)$ = adhere (to). This tells us less about the endostyle than it does about what mucus does, and perhaps such things ought to be under the entry "mucus." The lesson here is that sheer increase of information in a dictionary entry does not ensure completeness or utility, just as brevity does not ensure succinctness. What is critical is that the *correct* lexical information be given.

Third, there appears to be some information in this definition that is appropriate to defining the entry but which the ECD cannot handle, and that is the fact that the thyroid gland *derives from* the endostyle. There is no clear way of indicating in the ECD provenience relations: i.e., that "endostyle" is the source of "thyroid gland." Other relational models have a relation for this notion [see Evens et al. 1983], and it is unclear whether the ECD needs to, or can, accommodate this notion, along the lines of the following: Prov(thyroid) = endostyle. This is important for sublanguages which are developmental and evolutionary, but the representational apparatus remains an open question.

Finally, it is again evident that some lexicographic fieldwork must be done among zoologists to answer such questions as the following. Does "endostyle" have any opposites (Anti)? Are there any verbs for the operation of the endostyle, other than "produce" (Func)? What are the prepositions for "endostyle": "to endostyle," "at endostyle," etc. (Loc)? Again, these questions may sound ridiculous to zoologists, but only these kinds of questions reveal the full co-occurrence of the item.

Since each of the above entries has required lexicographic fieldwork, let us now turn to information gathered from such work. The term to be defined is from physics: "mass." Interviews with physicists [see Frawley 1984] reveal that the entry has the following syntactic, semantic, and lexical domains.

MASS: noun	X=1	Y=2	Z=3
	N	N	N

X's ratio of Y to Z

LEXICAL FUNCTIONS:

> Anti A_0(mass) = massless
> Anti(mass) = zero mass
> Centr(mass) = center of mass
> Cont $Oper_0$(mass) = conserve
> Cont S_0(mass) = equation of continuity
> Culm(mass) = point mass

Excess(mass) = mass excess (only in subatomic physics)
$Fact_0$ S_{med}(mass) = pair creation
Fin S_0(mass) = annihilation, conversion (into energy)
$Func_0$(mass) = circulate
$Func_2$(mass) = react to, determine
$Labor_{12}$(mass) = determine
$Labor_{21}$(mass) = change (motion of), accelerate
$Labor_{23}$(mass) = produce
Magn(mass) = dense
Minus $Func_0$(mass) = decrease
Mult(mass) = crystal
$Oper_1$(mass) = have, be characterized by, possess
Plus $Func_0$(mass) = increase
Pred(mass) = be
Propt(mass) = because of, out of, from
S_1(mass) = body, particle
S_2(mass) = force
S_3(mass) = acceleration
S_{res}(mass) = weight
Sympt(mass) = manifestations of
Syn(mass) = energy
Ver(mass) = rest mass, proper mass

Such an entry as the above, while necessitating painstaking questioning of physicists and detailed notetaking during interviews (as in any linguistic fieldwork), is superior to the previous two in depth and accuracy. Both paradigmatic and syntagmatic co-occurrences are captured in this representation, and such collocations reveal some interesting and useful things not only about "mass," but also about the sublanguage of physics.

Perhaps the most interesting paradigmatic finding is that while there are specific types of mass in physics – point mass, excess mass, rest mass, proper mass, etc. – mass is not a type of anything itself! Also, "mass" has an opposite and a synonym, quite atypical in technical sublanguage: what is the opposite of "syntax" in linguistics, or of "debug" in computer science, for example? Thus, the lexical structure of "mass" in the sublanguage of physics is fairly richly developed.

Much of the actual phraseology of "mass" is also represented. "Mass" selects certain verbs: mass circulates, bodies have mass, force produces acceleration through mass, acceleration changes a body through mass, mass increases, mass decreases, mass is conserved, etc. Such findings give a particularly nice indication of the kind of talk that constitutes physics and that differentiates physics texts from texts in ordinary language, where, for example, "mass" is highly unlikely to "do" anything.

Two advantages fall directly out of the example of "mass." First, lexicographic fieldwork in the sciences (perhaps complemented by detailed study of existing lexicons of sublanguages) is the most productive means of discovering the full meaning and the semantic structure of a term. Second, a relational representation scheme for lexical information, such as the ECD, captures succinctly the co-occurrences of any item. The lexical functions for "mass," in fact, form the basis for generating a mini-text about "mass." After all, dictionary definitions are actually very peculiar types of texts about entry words. It just so happens that traditional dictionaries provide very limited texts about the entry words and thereby eliminate much of the actual phraseology surrounding the entry. The ECD, since it has also been the basis of text-generation systems, and since scientific text relies heavily on lexical structure, is a lexical schema for a prototypical or summarial text about an entry. The informal discussion of the phraseology of "mass," above, could be made more rigorous and more text-like so that a mini-text about "mass" will result.

This property of ECD entries, that they also form a schema for text, can be seen readily in the reduction of text to lexical-functional form. Below is an excerpt from a neuroscience text; each sentence is numbered for subsequent reference:

(1) "We know that cortisol, norepinephrine, dopamine and serontin are found in the brains of humans. (2) Cortisol has been found in higher concentrations in brain tissue than in blood (400ug/100 mg. brain and 15 ug/100 ml. of blood: Touchstone, 1966). (3) In rats isotypically labeled cortisol, when injected intravenously, enters brain tissue" [McClure and Cleghorn 1969, 533].

To reduce this to lexical-functional form – that is, to the necessary lexical relationships – we must first eliminate all markers of discourse and syntax so that the purely lexical information can be identified. This is a fairly simple task since texts in scientific sublanguages often have general discourse markers [see Lehrberger 1986]; it is also clear that some forms, such as conjunctions and auxiliaries, are restricted to syntax. Much of the material remaining after the elimination of discourse and syntax is lexical anyway, as can be seen below.

In the three excerpted sentences, the following forms are markers of syntax and discourse (D = Discourse, S = Syntax):

Sentence (1):
    We know that: D – rhetorical marker of external evidence
    and: S – conjunction of NP's
    are: S – syntax of passive
    the: D – definiteness marker

Sentence (2)
    has been: S – syntax of perfect passive
    than: S – syntax of comparative
    (400 ug/ ... Touchstone, 1966): D – specific information
        rhetorically marked by parentheses: note that
        this information is not necessary to
        the meaning of any lexical item, but is simply a
        further specification of existing lexical structure

Sentence (3)
    when: D – temporal discourse marker

The elimination of the above leaves us with the lexical dependencies listed below. The terms to be linked are to the left, and the reduction of each dependency is to the right. Where the terms are repeated, they are abbreviated (c = cortisol, etc.).

Sentence(1)

cortisol – find (= found)
norepinephrine – find (=found)
dopamine – find (= found)
serontin – find (=found)
$$\left.\right\} \text{Oper}_0(c, n, d, s) = \text{find}$$

cortisol – in brain
norepinephrine – in brain
dopamine – in brain
serontin – in brain
$$\left.\right\} \text{Loc}_{in} + \text{S}_{loc}(c, n, d, s) = \text{in brain}$$

brain – human $\text{S}_1(\text{brain}) = \text{human}$

Sentence (2)

cortisol – find (= found)	$\text{Oper}_0(c) = \text{find}$
cortisol – in higher concentrations	$\text{Manif} + \text{Plus} + \text{Mult}(c) = \text{in}$ higher concentrations
concentrations – in brain tissue	$\text{Loc}_{in} + \text{S}_{loc}(\text{con.}) = \text{in}$ brain tissue
concentrations – in blood	$\text{Loc}_{in} + \text{S}_{loc}(\text{con.}) = \text{in blood}$

Sentence (3)

cortisol – enters	$Func_2(c)$ = enter
cortisol – injected	$Oper_1(c)$ = inject
injected– intravenously	$Adv_1(inject)$ = intravenously
cortisol – labeled	$Oper_1(c)$ = label
labeled – isotypically	$Adv_1(label)$ = isotypically
injected– in rats	$Loc_{in} + S_{loc}(inject)$ = in rats

From a lexical standpoint, the excerpt concerns cortisol, what it can do and what can be done to it. Most of the excerpt is reducible to an elaborate ECD entry for "cortisol": what the first participant does to cortisol, where cortisol is found, etc. But the implication of the above exercise is straightforward. Insofar as text in scientific sublanguage is lexically organized, a relational representation scheme such as the ECD explicitly shows the semantic organization of such text.

It appears then that the formalisms of a certain kind of computational lexicography are useful in representing the sort of information which a descriptive textual metascience requires. That is not to say that the descriptive project is thereby completed. Nor is it to indicate that the above representations are exhaustive and that all that remains to be done is a simple cataloguing of lexical dependencies. Rather, it is to argue that a relational representational scheme provides the necessary apparatus for a sublanguage metascience. We now turn to some answers to metascience questions that these formalisms suggest.

Sublanguage answers to some metascience questions

ECD descriptions of lexical items in scientific sublanguage provide answers to some of the epistemological questions raised above, but not to all the questions. For instance, it is unknown how the formalisms above provide answers to such essentialist problems as kinds of knowledge, the status of belief, and true vs. pseudo scientific knowledge. Given the arguments made in the previous sections, answers to these questions necessitate such things as a lexicalist theory of belief and a lexicalist theory of truth. The first seems a mysterious object indeed, but not unimaginable; the second requires truth to shift from propositions to the constituents of propositions, again a mysterious, but not unimaginable, enterprise.

In spite of the problems, the ECD does shed some light on the nature of scientific knowledge. Obviously, according to the arguments above, scientific knowledge is a lexical structure. More importantly, because scientific knowledge is said to lie in an encyclopedic dictionary of the sublanguage, scientific knowledge takes on the properties of all lexical knowledge and is therefore always subject to change. This is not to say that the sublanguage lexicon is not stable or not representable. Rather, it is to say that there is no scientific knowledge which cannot be modified, as is true of all lexical knowledge. ECD entries for the lexicons of sublanguages capture the dynamism of lexical (and hence scientific) knowledge because meaning, in an ECD, is not a list which is looked up, but a *computation*. Meaning is not so much indicated in an ECD as much as it is *derived* by the mechanisms of the ECD. This sort of relational model is, therefore, as much a dictionary of potential words as it is of present and past words (see below for more on this). Because the ECD computes meaning, the meaning that constitutes scientific sublanguages can always be modified. By this argument, scientific knowledge is something to be updated constantly, not a body of timeless principles.

Perhaps the best answers which the ECD provides are to the essentialist questions about the scope of scientific knowledge. A fundamental concern of metascience is the range of scientific knowledge. In particular, is scientific knowledge distinct from ordinary knowledge, and if so, how? Or is scientific knowledge subsumed by ordinary, general knowledge?

In terms of the arguments of this paper, these questions convert to the following: are scientific sublanguages subsets of a particular natural language (e.g., English), or do they just intersect with natural languages? Do ECD entries for lexicons of science show a markedly different semantic structure for the sublanguages of science as compared to the semantic structure of ordinary language?

Questions such as the above have been a recent focus of attention of researchers in the theory of sublanguage. Three answers have been provided: (1) scientific sublanguages are proper subsets of some variety of a language (usually the standard language), (2) scientific sublanguages are subsets of the "whole" natural language (in all its varieties), and (3) scientific sublanguages intersect with natural languages [see Lehrberger 1986; Harris 1976].

The first answer is wrong, for the simple reason that there are rules of the standard variety of a language which are not in the scientific sublanguage and vice versa.[4] For example, the sublanguage of medical diagnosis has a productive rule which allows postnominal adjectives [see Dunham 1986, 179], but this is not a productive rule of standard English. Similarly, the

---

[4] I leave aside the important question of whether or not there even is such a thing as the standard variety of the language since answer #1 assumes that there is. But if there is not, and there is good reason to suppose that there is not, then #1 falls through automatically.

sublanguage of aircraft repair manuals appears to contain no determiners [see Lehrberger 1986], but standard English obviously contains determiners.

The second answer may be correct, but trivial. To say that a scientific sublanguage, for instance, is part of the "whole" of English is only to say that it is a variety of English. But that misses the point. Some English creoles are also part of the "whole" of English, but they are unlike any other variety of English. The creole analogy is even more relevant here. To say that scientific sublanguages are part of the "whole" of, say, English is to say that the language of science is a *relexification* of English, a process well known among creolists by which a language maintains its syntax but changes its lexicon entirely (for political, economic, and social reasons). Science is lexically different from other varieties of language, but it is not simply a relexified version since the syntax and even morphology of scientific sublanguages differ markedly from any other variety of the language. Scientific sublanguage is more like a pidgin or creole *based on*, say, English: all of the language, not just the lexicon, changes. The grammar, morphology, and lexicon of scientific sublanguages diverge from those of the "whole" language, and certainly a fruitful line of inquiry into sublanguages would be into their status as pidgins and creoles.

To put the whole matter another way, a sublanguage is not necessarily a subset. For example, one subset of English is the set of sentence adverb/determiner pairs, gotten by taking the first two words of every English sentence that begins with a sentence adverb and a noun preceded by a determiner. In no way does this subset form a sublanguage. To bring this point directly to the argument of this paper, insofar as scientific knowledge equals scientific language, scientific knowledge cannot form a proper subset of general knowledge since scientific language does not form a proper subset of general language, a point made less linguistically by an entire book of papers on the differences between scientific and commonsense representations of the world [Hobbs and Moore 1985].

The third answer, that sublanguage and ordinary language intersect, seems the most tenable. Scientific sublanguage does share features of some varieties of a language whose lexicon it has appropriated (just as a creole does), but there are marked differences (again, just as in a creole). For example, Fitzpatrick, Bachenko, and Hindle [1986, p. 45] argue that in the telegraphic sublanguage of military communication, there is "no way to distinguish between ... passives and past tense intransitives." In English, there are mechanisms to distinguish the two forms, but this merely shows that English and the English-like sublanguage of military communication intersect; the former does not contain the latter. More interestingly, it is well known that many languages do not make any distinction between passives and intransitives anyway, as a standard practice in the grammar [see, e.g., Keenan 1985], so military sublanguage, though not a sublanguage of English in this regard, is a *language of some sort* since it conforms to universal principles of natural language [just as creoles do: see Bickerton 1981]. Lehrberger's [1986, p. 37] concern over whether sublanguages are learnable because they may violate universal principles of language is thus put to rest. Sublanguages are learnable because they are languages, but not proper subsets of a particular language.[5]

If scientific sublanguage has a certain autonomy, then scientific knowledge likewise has a certain autonomy. Scientific knowledge is not a subset of general knowledge since scientific sublanguage and ordinary language are not really translatable [see Frawley 1987], though perhaps paraphrasable [see Lehrberger 1986]. This divergence in scope between ordinary knowledge and scientific knowledge can be seen in the meaning of the word "water" in medical sublanguage and in ordinary language. Hobbs [1986, p. 58] argues that, in medical sublanguage, "the only relevant fact about 'water' is that it may be a medium for the transmission of a disease." On the other hand, the Random House Dictionary of the ordinary language defines water as "a transparent, tasteless, odorless, colorless liquid...," as do other dictionaries. Thus, the lexical functions for an ECD entry for "water" in ordinary language are as follows:

$$Qual_0(water) = transparent$$
$$Qual_0(water) = tasteless$$
$$Qual_0(water) = odorless$$
$$Qual_0(water) = colorless$$

In medical sublanguage, however, an ECD entry for "water," in terms of lexical functions, must specify the following:

$$Func_2(water) = transmit$$
$$S_2(water) = disease$$

And the entry for "disease" must contain the following:

$$S_{med}(disease) = water$$

---

[5] This problem is worth pursuing further. For instance, the absence of determiners in some scientific sublanguages is clearly in accord with universal principles, as is the absence of copulas. My guess is that sublanguages are very much like pidgins and therefore transparently reflect universal grammar, as Bickerton 1981 argues. It might be interesting to study the kinds of word orders that sublanguages allow or whether aspectual distinctions in sublanguage verbs outnumber or develop into tense distinctions.

Thus, the semantic structures of medical and ordinary language differ radically for the word "water." In the former, "water" is distinctly related to particular nouns and verbs, while in the latter, "water" has a more attributive structure. Hobbs [1986] gives other lexical differences between the semantic structure of ordinary language and that of medical sublanguage. He argues that the words "laboratory," "manage," "history," and "vertical" have a semantic structure in medical language (and hence in medical knowledge) that is incommensurable with that of ordinary language. A similar point is made by Wiser and Carey [1983] regarding the incommensurability of the current language of thermal experiments and seventeenth century descriptions of the same phenomena. It appears that such differences are not restricted to "technical terms" since even the most "ordinary" lexical item in a sublanguage is "technical." Put a different way, this means that many more terms than ordinarily thought are "technical," and one might even go so far as to argue that function words take on a technical status in a sublanguage.

The point, of course, is that, insofar as knowledge structures equal semantic structures in the sciences, the scope of scientific knowledge and the scope of ordinary knowledge are incommensurable, and such facts are not only represented by a relational model like the ECD, but they are also understandable from the view that a sublanguage intersects with other languages and is not a subset of any language or language variety.

Now, just as one essentialist question can be addressed by a relational model such as the ECD, so can one proceduralist question. As with essentialist questions, many proceduralist issues are not readily answered by the study of sublanguage. For instance, it is not immediately evident how scientific knowledge is justified or acquired since solutions to these problems necessitate a lexical theory of justification and a theory of the acquisition of lexical information from specialized text. The latter is more easily developed than the former, given the state of affairs in psycholinguistic studies of lexical processing [see Johnson and Hwang 1983].

However, the question of progress in scientific knowledge can be addressed directly by a relational model of lexical structure. This can be done through the study of lexical gaps, which are literally *holes in the lexicon.* Because any lexicon instantiates only a portion of the total possible semantic structure, there always exist potential new words. For instance, English has no word for "cause to make a telephone call," and we would say that English has a lexical gap in this regard. Needless to say, if the semantic structure of a language is viewed as a totality, then the language has many more gaps than actual lexical items.

One should recall here that Mel'čuk has himself argued (see above) that any lexicon instantiates only about one-tenth of all possible lexical functions. Thus, the ECD, or any similar relational model, captures not only the current lexical status of the language, but also its potential expansion (the other nine-tenths). The ECD is, for that matter, as much a dictionary of the future as it is of the present because it contains the possibility of computing possible words in a systematic way by combining lexical functions and computing new relations across existing lexical items. In short, the full range of lexical gaps can be predicted by the ECD. [6]

A good example of how the ECD captures lexical gaps, and thereby characterizes progress in scientific knowledge, appears in a recent paper [Veltman 1986] on the Higgs boson, a hypothetical subatomic particle predicted by the prevailing theory of elementary physical processes, and the Higgs field, the region of the Higgs boson. It should be understood that neither the boson nor the field is known to exist – "no evidence of its (the Higgs boson's) existence has been found" [Veltman 1986, 76]; nonetheless, both can be spoken of with reasonable accuracy and confidence.

Veltman's paper is in fact devoted wholly to writing the lexical structure of "Higgs boson" and "Higgs field" into the sublanguage of subatomic physics by computing new relations across old terms in the sublanguage. Below are statements extracted from the paper which are fillings of lexical gaps, or structuring of the lexicon around the terms in question. They are reduced to comparable ECD lexical functions to illustrate how the ECD represents this new lexical information.

1. "... the Higgs boson is the mediating particle of the proposed Higgs field" [p. 76]: Gener(Higgs boson) = mediating particle, S_{loc}(Higgs boson) = Higgs field
2. "The Higgs field is thought to generate mass by coupling to particles" [p. 76]: $Func_2$(Higgs field) = generate (mass), $Func_1$(Higgs field) = couple to (particles), S_1(Higgs field) = particle, S_2(Higgs field) = mass
3. "In order to endow particles with mass, the Higgs field, if it exists, would have to assume a uniform, nonzero value even in the vacuum" [p. 76]: $LabReal_{12}$(mass) = endow (where 1 = Higgs field and 2 = particle: this means that 1 realizes in 2 the entry word), $Func_3$(Higgs field) = assume, S_3(Higgs field) = value, $Qual_0$ (value) = uniform, non-zero
4. "... the Higgs field would be a scalar field ..." [pp.76-77]: Gener(Higgs field) =scalar field
5. "... the Higgs field is spinless, the Higgs boson must also be spinless" [p. 77]: $Qual_0$(Higgs field) = spinless, $Qual_0$(Higgs boson) = spinless

---

[6] This does not mean that the actual instantiations can be predicted since this is a matter of sociolinguistics; nonetheless, one can predict what might be instantiated.

Evidently, what Veltman is doing in the paper is specifying as much of the lexical structure of the new terms as possible, and this is done by computing new functions across the terms. The startling fact here is that this is done without regard for the extensions of the terms. It is admitted that the existence of the particle is unknown, but this does not affect progress in the intensional structure of subatomic physics. More to our purposes, the ECD provides a useful metascientific tool here by representing explicitly all the new computations in the filling of the lexical gaps. For all intents and purposes, Veltman is writing several new entries in the lexicon of subatomic physics, and the ECD shows the network of these new entries.

One might ask at this point whether or not anything is gained in meta-science by the above. After all, the ECD provides only a descriptive answer to the proceduralist question of scientific progress, not a predictive answer. If one could predict lexical/epistemological progress, then one would be in much better metascientific stead.

A first answer to this problem is to say that a lot is gained by an explicit description to begin with. Without a clear picture of just what sort of relationships are being computed, one can make few interesting statements about the sublanguage at all.

A second answer is that a clear description lets us see what sorts of lexical functions a particular sublanguage privileges; from that, we may make some predictions about where and how a sublanguage lexicon will expand and progress. For example, we know that the sublanguages of the science are heavily nominal [Frawley 1987], and we also know what sorts of relations are typically used to define nouns [Smith 1985]. From a comparative analysis of nominal definition of a sublanguage, we might predict where expansion of the lexicon will occur and which relations will be preferred by that sublanguage. For instance, subatomic physics appears to place great emphasis on the verbal linkages of terms ("mass circulates," "Higgs field endows, couples, assumes"), but not much on the development of antonyms or synonyms; some terms in biology are directed more toward aspectual processes, such as termination [see Frawley 1986]. We might also suppose that taxonomic sciences, such as zoology or botany, will focus on generic relations.

Moreover, the investigation of which relations a particular science privileges is motivated by the fact that sciences differentiate both from ordinary knowledge and earlier versions of themselves by shifting their focus from properties to relations. Wiser and Carey [1983] point this out in their discussion of the historical differentiation of heat and temperature. They further show that a careful study of the lexicons of sciences at different historical periods reveals different scientific views of the world and is a use-ful tool for the analysis of scientific progress [see Wiser and Carey 1983,

p. 292]. Similarly, a principal difference between naive physics and scientific physics is that in the former, "mass" and "weight" are viewed as properties of bodies, whereas in the latter, "mass" is a relation and "weight" is a result.

Thus, while it must be admitted that a relational model of scientific progress is primarily descriptive, it does provide the basis for a more predictive metascience. The ECD gives a picture of the total number of directions that lexical advance in a sublanguage can take. A comparative study of sublanguages can tell us which directions tend to be chosen.

Conclusion

The gist of this paper is fairly easily rendered. The work of one kind of metascience, textual, lexically-based metascience, is facilitated by a relational model of semantic structure such as the ECD offers. The project turns on explicit and detailed descriptions of the semantic structure of sublanguages; such descriptions yield specific answers to some traditional problems in metascience, those problems themselves derived from larger epistemological issues.

It might be argued that such descriptions reduce metascience to a rather homely exercise, a kind of semantic accountancy done in disregard of the interesting ways that scientists cut Nature at its joints or even discover Nature's joints. Again, as in the introduction, I plead no contest, but for specific reasons.

First, the sort of metascience derived from the above demonstrations is predicated upon the fact that science is largely *intensional* and that the purpose of metascience is to describe the intensional structure. Work in semantics and philosophical linguistics, AI, and cognitive science has shown that extensional structure is no more complicated than intensional structure [see the papers in Gentner and Stevens 1983, for example]. Carnap's extensionalist accountancy is no more inherently privileged than any intensionalist program. Cutting Nature at its joints is no more complicated or meritorious than the schemas used to cut Nature. This leads to the second point.

It looks as if extensionalist science needs intensionalist science to find Nature to begin with. As Boyd [1979] has argued, scientific practice consists of largely verbal instrumentation. If metascience is to tell us how and why scientists look where they look and what they look at, then we need a description of the instruments deployed. To put it all another way, intensionalist metascience is concerned with the "frame problem" of science, or the question of what kind of information selectively defines a domain. For instance, we know that the leap from naive physics to scientific physics requires a sense of the localization of entities and inferences within a rigid domain and the restriction of meaning wholly to the sublanguage of physics [Larkin 1983]. Insofar as the ECD gives different representations for different domains of knowledge in the sciences, it is the beginning of a systematic approach to the frame problem of science.

Appendix: Lexical Functions from the ECD

Below is each function with its meaning in the metalanguage and an example from ordinary English. Each formula should be read from left to right: $f(x) = y$; it should also be clear that each formula can be easily put into more clearly relational notation, by having the entry word and output as nodes and the function as the label on a relational arc, for example: $x(f)y$. This material is adapted from Mel'čuk et al. [1984, 49-51].

1. A_0 adjective derived from entry word
$A_0(\text{dog}) = \text{doggy}$

2. A_1, A_2 typical adjective for numbered participant
$A_1(\text{suspicion}) = \text{full of}$

3. $\text{Able}_1, \text{Able}_2$ ability of numbered participant
$\text{Able}_1(\text{fear}) = \text{fearful}$
$\text{Able}_2(\text{fear}) = \text{fearsome}$

4. Adv_0 adverb from entry word
$\text{Adv}_0(\text{happy}) = \text{happily}$

5. $\text{Adv}_1, \text{Adv}_2$ adverb from numbered participant
$\text{Adv}_1(\text{fear}) = \text{fearfully}$

6. Anti   antonym (exact or near)
$\text{Ant}(\text{happy}) = \text{sad}$

7. Bon   standard praise for entry
$\text{Bon}(\text{advice}) = \text{sound}$

8. Caus   cause
$Caus(sit) = set$

9. Centr   center of
$Centr(city) = heart$

10. Cont   continue
$Cont(go) = keep, keep on$

11. Contr   non-antonymic contrast
$Contr(chair) = table$

12. $Conv_{ijk}$ conversive (opposite where participants switch roles)
$Conv_{321}(buy) = sell$

13. Culm   culmination of
$Culm(ability) = peak$

14. Degrad   degradation of (dimension can be specified: e.g., color, movement, etc.)
$Degrad(marriage) = fall apart$

15. Epit   standard epithet (representing a part of entry)
$Epit(body) = physique$

16. Excess   excessive functioning of (dimension can be specified, as in Degrad)
$Excess(eyelid) = flutter$

17. $Fact_{0,1,2}$ verb meaning "the realization of," with the entry as grammatical subject and the participants as objects
$Fact_0(suspicion) = confirm$

18. Figur   metaphor of the entry
$Figur(love) = fire$

19. Fin   stopping of
$Fin(fly) = land$

20. $Func_{0,1,2}$ verb which takes the entry as subject of first participant, second participant, etc.
$Func_1(idea) = come to$

21. Gener   generic word
    Gener(blue) = color

22. Germ   the core of
    Germ(problem) = crux

23. Imper   the command associated with
    Imper(care) = Watch out!

24. Involv   verb meaning non-participant involvement
    Involv(scent) = fill

25. Incep   the beginning of
    Incep(fly) = take off

26. Labor_{ij} verb which takes the participants ij as subject
    and object and the entry as secondary object
    Labor_{12}(esteem) = hold (i.e., x holds y in esteem)

27. LabReal_{ij} verb meaning "the realization of,"
    with the first two participants as subject and
    object and the entry as secondary object
    (a combination of Labor and Real)
    LabReal_{12}(mind) = bring to (x brings y to mind)

28. Liqu   the elimination of
    Liqu(group) = disband

29. Loc_{in} preposition for "in"
    Loc_{ab} preposition for "from"
    Loc_{ad} preposition for "to"
    Loc_{in}(house) = in

30. Magn   intensity (can specify dimension of quantity
    or duration)
    Magn(hatred) = deep

31. Manif   is manifest in, with the entry as subject
$$\text{Manif(tear)} = \text{well up}$$

32. Minus   less of
$$\text{Minus(wind)} = \text{slacken}$$

33. Mult   a regular aggregate of
$$\text{Mult(paper)} = \text{ream}$$

34. Nocer   to harm, injure, or impair
$$\text{Nocer(access)} = \text{cut off}$$

35. Obstr   to function with difficulty
$$\text{Obstr(justice)} = \text{obstruct}$$

36. $\text{Oper}_{1,2,3}$ verb which takes numbered participant
as subject and entry as object
$$\text{Oper}_1(\text{party}) = \text{throw}$$

37. Perm   permit or allow
$$\text{Perm(go)} = \text{let}$$

38. Plus   more of
$$\text{Plus(joy)} = \text{grow}$$

39. $\text{Pos}_{1,2,3}$ positive attributes of numbered participants
$$\text{Pos}_1(\text{game}) = \text{skilled}$$

40. Pred   copula for nouns and adjectives
$$\text{Pred(prey)} = \text{fall, be}$$

41. Propt   preposition for "because of"
$$\text{Propt(greed)} = \text{out of}$$

42. Prox   to be on the verge of
$$\text{Prox(disaster)} = \text{on the brink of}$$

43. $\text{Qual}_{1,2,3}$ highly probable qualities of numbered participants
$$\text{Qual}_1(\text{theft}) = \text{sneaky}$$

44. $Real_{1,2,3}$ verb meaning to realize with entry
as object and numbered participants as subject
$Real_1$(ambition) = realize

45. S_0 noun for entry
S_0(hate) = hatred

46. $S_{1,2,3}$ typical noun for numbered participant
S_2(crime) = victim

47. S_{inst} typical instrument
S_{loc} typical location
S_{med} typical means
S_{mod} typical mode
S_{res} typical result
S_{loc}(house) = yard

48. Sing   one instance of
Sing(paper) = sheet

49. Son   to emit a typical sound
Son(frog) = croak

50. Sympt   to be a physical symptom of
Sympt(fire) = smoke

51. Syn   synonym and near synonym
Syn(happy) = glad

52. V_0 verb for entry
V_0(song) = sing

53. Ver   true, correct, or proper
Ver(ruling) = fair

It should be noted that some of the above examples are more properly represented with multiple functions in combination, as is possible in the ECD. Thus, for Liqu above, the formula should actually be $LiquFunc_0$(group) = disband: i.e., the elimination of the group's functioning is "disband." $Incep$(fly)= take off should be $IncepOper_1$(fly) = take off: i.e., the inception of the pilot flying is "take off"; Minus (wind) = slacken should actually be Minus $Func_0$(wind) = slacken: i.e., the action of the wind's lessening is "slacken."

References

American Geological Institute. 1962. *Dictionary of geological terms.* Garden City, NY: Doubleday.

Anthony, L.J., H. East, and M. Slater. 1969. The growth of literature in physics. *Reports on Progress in Physics* **32**, 709-767.

Apresyan, Y., I.A. Mel'čuk, and A.K. Žolkovsky. 1970. Semantics and lexicography: Towards a new type of unilingual dictionary. *Studies in syntax and semantics*, ed. by F. Kiefer, Dordrecht: Reidel, 1-33.

Bickerton, Derek. 1981. *Roots of language.* Ann Arbor: Karoma.

Blanton, Mackie J-V. 1982. The pragmatic structure of rhetorical maturity in the sciences. *Linguistics and literacy*, ed. by W. Frawley, NY: Plenum, 125-144.

Bloor, David. 1976. *Knowledge and social imagery.* London: Routledge and Kegan Paul.

Bourdieu, Pierre and Jean-Claude Passeron. 1977. *Reproduction in education, society, and culture.* London: Sage.

Boyd, Richard. 1979. Metaphor and theory change: What is 'metaphor' a metaphor for? *Metaphor and thought*, ed. by A. Ortony, Cambridge: Cambridge University Press, 356-408.

Campbell, Donald T. 1977. Descriptive epistemology: psychological, sociological, evolutionary. William James Lectures, Harvard University.

Carnap, R. 1967. *The logical structure of the world and pseudoproblems in philosophy.* Berkeley and Los Angeles: University of California Press.

Derrida, Jacques. 1977. Signature event context. *Glyph* **1**, 172-197.

Dunham, George. 1986. The role of syntax in the sublanguage of medical diagnostic statements. *Analyzing language in restricted domains*, ed. by R. Grishman and R. Kittredge, Hillsdale, NJ: LEA, 175-194.

Evens, Martha, Bonnie Litowitz, Judith Markowitz, Raoul Smith, and Oswald Werner. 1983. *Lexical-semantic relations: A comparative survey.* Edmonton, Alberta: Linguistic Research, Inc.

Ferreira, Elrod. 1988. A critical inquiry into three epistemologies of language acquisition. Ph.D. Dissertation, University of Delaware.

Feyerabend, Paul. 1972. *Against method: Outline of an anarchistic theory of knowledge.* London: New Left Books.

Finin, Timothy. 1986. Constraining the interpretation of nominal compounds in a limited context. *Analyzing language in restricted domains*, ed. by R. Grishman and R. Kittredge, Hillsdale, NJ: LEA, 163-174.

Fitzpatrick, Eileen, Joan Bachenko, and Don Hindle. 1986. The status of telegraphic sublanguages. *Analyzing language in restricted domains*, ed. by R. Grishman and R. Kittredge, Hillsdale, NJ: LEA, 39-52.

Foucault, Michel. 1972. *The archaeology of knowledge*. NY: Random House.

Frawley, William. 1981. Lexicography and the philosophy of science. *Dictionaries* **3**, 18-27.

Frawley, William. 1984. New forms of specialized dictionaries. Paper presented at the Modern Language Association, Washington, DC.

Frawley, William. 1986. Science, discourse and knowledge representation: Toward a computational model of science and scientific innovation. *The languages of creativity: Models, problem-solving, discourse*, ed. by M. Amsler, Newark, DE: University of Delaware Press, 68-91.

Frawley, William. 1987. *Text and epistemology*. Norwood, NJ: Ablex.

Friedman, Carol. 1986. Automatic structuring of sublanguage information: Application to medical narrative. *Analyzing language in restricted domains*, ed. by R. Grishman and R. Kittredge, Hillsdale, NJ: LEA, 85-102.

Garfield, Eugene. 1979. *Citation indexing: Its theory and application in science, technology, and the humanities*. NY: John Wiley.

Gentner, Dedre and Albert Stevens, eds. 1983. *Mental models*. Hillsdale, NJ: LEA.

Gilbert, G. Nigel and Michael Mulkay. 1984. *Opening Pandora's box*. Cambridge: Cambridge University Press.

Gopnik, Myrna. 1972. *Linguistic structures in scientific text*. The Hague: Mouton.

Gopnik, Myrna. 1977. Scientific theories as meta-semiotic systems. *Semiotica* **21**, 211-225.

Grimes, Joseph. 1975. *The thread of discourse*. The Hague: Mouton.

Grishman, Ralph and Richard Kittredge, eds. 1986. *Analyzing language in restricted domains*. Hillsdale, NJ: LEA.

Habermas, J. 1970. *Knowledge and human interest*. Boston: Beacon Press.

Hamlyn, D.W. 1970. *The theory of knowledge*. Garden City, NY: Doubleday.

Harris, Zellig. 1976. On a theory of language. *Journal of Philosophy* **73**, 253-276.

Hirschman, Lynette. 1986. Discovering sublanguage structures. *Analyzing language in restricted domains*, ed. by R. Grishman and R. Kittredge, Hillsdale, NJ: LEA, 211-234.

Hobbs, Jerry. 1986. Sublanguage and knowledge. *Analyzing language in restricted domains*, ed. by R. Grishman and R. Kittredge, Hillsdale, NJ: LEA, 53-68.

Hobbs, Jerry and Robert Moore, eds. 1985. *Formal theories of the commonsense world.* Norwood, NJ: Ablex.

Johnson, C. and R. Hwang. 1983. Learnability of technical vocabulary depends upon familiarity, comprehensibility, and imagery. *Psychological Reports* **53**, 767-770.

Keenan, E. 1985. Passive in the world's languages. *Language typology and syntactic description, I: Clause Structure*, ed. by T. Shopen, Cambridge: Cambridge University Press, 241-281.

Kintsch, Walter and Teun van Dijk. 1978. Toward a model of text comprehension and production. *Psychological Review*, **85**, 363-394.

Kittredge, Richard and John Lehrberger, eds. 1982. *Sublanguage*. Berlin: de Gruyter.

Kuhn, T. S. 1970. *The structure of scientific revolutions*. Chicago: University of Chicago Press.

Kuhn, T. S. 1977. *The essential tension.* Chicago: University of Chicago Press.

Lakatos, Imre. 1970. Falsification and the methodology of scientific research programs. *Criticism and the growth of knowledge*, ed. by I. Lakatos and A. Musgrave, Cambridge: Cambridge University Press, 91-196.

Larkin, Jill H. 1983. The role of problem representation in physics. *Mental models*, ed. by D. Gentner and A. Stevens, Hillsdale, NJ: LEA, 75-98.

Leftwich, A.W. 1963. *A dictionary of zoology.* Princeton, NJ: van Nostrand.

Lehrberger, John. 1986. Sublanguage analysis. *Analyzing language in restricted domains*, ed. by R.Grishman and R. Kittredge, Hillsdale, NJ: LEA, 19-38.

MacIntyre, Alisdair. 1980. Epistemological crises, dramatic narrative, and the philosophy of science. *Paradigms and revolutions*, ed. by G. Gutting, Notre Dame, IN: University of Notre Dame Press, 54-77.

Marsh, Elaine. 1986. General semantic patterns in different sublanguages. *Analyzing language in restricted domains*, ed. by R.Grishman and R. Kittredge, Hillsdale, NJ: LEA, 103-120.

McCloskey, Michael. 1983. Naive theories of motion. *Mental models*, ed. by D. Gentner and A. Stevens, Hillsdale, NJ: LEA, 299-324.

McClure, David and Robert Cleghorn. 1969. Hormone imbalance in depressive states. *The future of the brain sciences*, ed. by S. Bogoch, NY: Plenum, 525-553.

McKeown, Kathleen. 1985. *Text generation.* Cambridge: Cambridge University Press.

Mel'čuk, I.A. 1981. Meaning-text models: A recent trend in Soviet linguistics. *Annual Review of Anthropology* 10, 27-62.

Mel'čuk, I. A., Arbatchewsky-Jumarie, N., Elnitsky, L., Iordanskaja, L., Lessard, A. 1984. *Dictionnaire explicatif et combinatoire du français contemporain. Recherches lexico-sémantiques. I.* Montreal: University of Montreal Press.

Mitroff, Ian. 1974. *The subjective side of science.* Amsterdam: Elsevier.

Olson, David. 1977. The languages of instruction: On the literate bias of schooling. *Schooling and the acquisition of knowledge,* ed. by R. Anderson et al., Hillsdale, NJ: LEA, 65-89.

Pettinari, C. 1982. The function of a grammatical alternation in fourteen surgical reports. *Linguistics and literacy,* ed. by W. Frawley, NY: Plenum, 145-185.

Phillips, Martin. 1985. *Aspects of text structure: An investigation of the lexical organization of text.* Amsterdam: Elsevier.

Popper, Karl. 1975. *Objective knowledge.* Oxford: Oxford University Press.

Sager, Naomi. 1986. Sublanguage: Linguistic phenomenon, computational tool. *Analyzing language in restricted domains,* ed. by R. Grishman and R. Kittredge, Hillsdale, NJ: LEA, 1-18.

Schank, Roger and Robert Abelson. 1977. *Scripts, plans, goals, and understanding.* Hillsdale, NJ: LEA.

Smith, Raoul N. 1985. Conceptual primitives in the English lexicon. *Papers in Linguistics,* 18, 99-137.

Smith, Raoul N. and William Frawley. 1983. Conjunctive cohesion in four English genres. *Text* 3-4, 347-373.

Veltman, Martinus. 1986. The Higgs boson. *Scientific American,* 255, 5, 76-84.

Walker, Donald and Robert Amsler. 1986. The use of machine-readable dictionaries in sublanguage analysis. *Analyzing language in restricted domains,* ed. by R. Grishman and R. Kittredge, Hillsdale, NJ: LEA, 69-84.

White, Alan. 1982. *The nature of knowledge.* Totowa, NJ: Rowman and Littlefield.

Wiser, Marianne and Susan Carey. 1983. When heat and temperature were one. *Mental models,* ed. by D. Gentner and A. Stevens, Hillsdale, NJ: LEA, 267-297.

Index